Forged in War

Forged in War

The Naval-Industrial Complex and American Submarine Construction, 1940–1961

Gary E. Weir

Naval Historical Center
Department of the Navy
Washington
1993

Library of Congress Cataloging-in-Publication Data

Weir, Gary E.
  Forged in war : the naval-industrial complex and American
submarine construction, 1940–1861 / Gary E. Weir.
        p.   cm.
  Includes bibliographical references and index.
  ISBN 0–045274–15–7
  1. Submarines—United States.   2. Shipbuilding industry—United
States.   3. Military-industrial complex—United States.   I. Naval
Historical Center (U.S.)   II. Title.
V858.W46   1992
338.497623825790973—dc20   92–40998

For sale by the U.S. Government Printing Office
Superintendent of Documents, Mail Stop: SSOP, Washington, DC 20402–9328
ISBN 0-16-038258-0

The Author

Gary E. Weir, a native of New York City, graduated from Manhattan College in 1973 with a B.A. in history. He studied German history and naval-industrial relations under Professor John H. Morrow at the University of Tennessee, Knoxville, receiving his Ph.D. in history in 1982. After a year on the faculty of the U.S. Naval Academy, Dr. Weir joined the Contemporary History Branch of the Naval Historical Center, where he wrote the present volume as well as its predecessor, *Building American Submarines, 1914–1940* (Naval Historical Center, 1991). He is preparing an official history of naval oceanography for the Center. His other publications include *Building the Kaiser's Navy: The Imperial Naval Office and German Industry in the Tirpitz Era, 1890–1919* (Naval Institute Press, 1992) and articles in *Military Affairs, Naval War College Review, International History Review, Mariner's Mirror, Naval History,* and the *Naval Engineers Journal.*

He is an Associate Professor of History for the University of Maryland University College and the recipient of fellowships from the McClure Foundation, the Office of Naval Research, and the DAAD (German Academic Exchange Service).

For my parents
Mary Ellen Weir
and
Edward Thomas Weir
who always made coming home a special delight.

Contents

Illustrations

Foreword

Forged in War discusses the naval, industrial, and scientific network that designed and built American submarines from 1940 to 1961. The author, Dr. Gary E. Weir, argues that this triangular complex emerged from World War II. That conflict not only integrated the Navy and the submarine industry, but also promoted the involvement of many scientists who had the expert knowledge to develop submarine designs, systems, and instrumentation. The intimate professional relationships forged by global war, and the sense of purpose and urgency during the later Cold War, led to a period of remarkable innovation and productivity in the sixteen years after 1945. We hope that Dr. Weir's assessment of this major accomplishment will be of interest to the naval, industrial, and scientific personnel who are involved in developing today's submarines, and will contribute to the knowledge of all others concerned with the naval profession.

I wish to thank those who assisted Dr. Weir in preparing this history. Dr. Edward J. Marolda, Head of the Naval Historical Center's Contemporary History Branch, managed the project from the outset and deserves special credit. Our dedicated senior editor, Sandra J. Doyle, guided the manuscript through the editorial and publication process. In addition, several scholars noted for their work on the history of submarines and naval technology offered their valuable comments and advice on the manuscript. They include Commander Fred Byus of the Office of the Assistant Chief of Naval Operations for Undersea Warfare; Dr. Francis Duncan, formerly a historian with the Department of Energy and a well-known authority on Admiral Rickover and the nuclear submarine program; Norman Polmar, the noted naval analyst; and Professor Clark G. Reynolds, Chair of the Department of History, University of Charleston, and a member of the Secretary of the Navy's Advisory Committee on Naval History.

Special thanks also go to reviewers from within the Naval Historical Center: Dr. William S. Dudley, Senior Historian; Charles R. Haberlein of the Curator Branch; Dr. James Reckner, who held the Secretary of the Navy's Research Chair in Naval History during 1991–1992; and Dr. Robert J. Schneller, a member of the Contemporary History Branch.

As is true for all of the histories published by the Naval Historical Center, the opinions and conclusions expressed in this history are solely those of the author. They do not reflect the views of the Department of the Navy or any other agency of the U.S. Government.

Dean C. Allard
Director of Naval History

Preface

What does the future hold for American submariners and the powerful, elegant ships they drive far beneath the surface of the world ocean? With the end of the Cold War and a crushing American national debt placing the future of the American submarine force in question, critical decisions are in the offing. Thus it is unfortunate that no historian has yet analyzed the partnership between the Navy, industry, and science responsible for producing submarines in the United States. The present study addresses this shortcoming by examining, for the period from 1940 through 1961, the nature of the naval-industrial complex for submarines forged by World War II.

From the outset, it was important for the range and purpose of this study to be precisely defined. Otherwise the subject at hand might perish in an ocean of general information and interesting, but tangential, subjects related to undersea warfare. As a result, the interaction between the Navy Department, the submarine industry, and the scientific community in the process of submarine design and construction takes center stage. Other facets of submarine warfare, such as torpedoes or submarine-launched, ballistic missiles, deserve historical studies unto themselves. At present we lack insightful histories of American torpedo development and submarine sonar as well as a truly historical analysis of the Polaris project. Given the prime focus of this book, however, these subjects are treated here only as important influences on design and construction. Only those companies involved with building the boat and its main components, and those scientists directly concerned with hydrodynamics, underwater sound, and other aspects of undersea warfare directly affecting design and construction play a role in this analysis.

As used in the following pages, the term "naval-industrial complex" depends in part upon Samuel Huntington's definition of the military-industrial complex as stated in "The Defense Establishment: Vested Interests and the Public Interest." He characterized this elusive and often misunderstood component of Western society and economy as "a large permanent military establishment supported by and linked to a variety of related industrial, labor, and geographical interests." With this well-crafted definition, Huntington fashioned a flexible analytical framework from a contemporary, hackneyed phrase. His perspective provides a firm foundation for the discussion and analysis in the following pages.

Rather than a single historical event or political-economic entity, the naval-industrial complex has many unique and distinct components. Each component reflects the development, significance, and construction of a particular vessel or weapons system within its peculiar historical context. These parts emerged from World War II as a network of distinct relationships, all developing simultaneously but linked by the common motives of national defense, mutual growth, and profit.

As one aspect of this much larger picture, the naval-industrial complex for submarines grew naturally between 1940 and 1961, responding to the political environment, the strategic circumstances, and a perceived national need. This association did not conform to the views of an individual or confirm the value of a particular system of management. Neither was it planned or predetermined by one of the major players in this drama. Instead its character was defined gradually by the demands of international conflict and scores of talented people who addressed the problems and possibilities of submarine warfare.

Although my abiding interest in submarines brought me to this subject, the patience and assistance of a great many people sustained my effort and helped me bring the project to a successful conclusion. For most of my supporters this is the end of a two-volume effort inaugurated in 1987 when I began working on *Building American Submarines, 1914–1940*, published by the Naval Historical Center in 1991. For their help with difficult concepts and their continued confidence I thank Captain Harry A. Jackson, USN (Ret.), Rear Admiral Albert G. Mumma, USN (Ret.), Rear Admiral Robert L. Moore USN (Ret.), Captain William Roseborough, USN (Ret.), Captain Henry Arnold, USN (Ret.), Captain Donald Kern, USN (Ret.), Captain Ralph Smith, USN (Ret.), and Captain James Bethea, USN (Ret.). I am particularly grateful to Vice Admiral Kenneth C. Malley who permitted me to review significant Polaris project documentation during his tenure at the Strategic Systems Program Office.

On the civilian side many active and retired scientists and corporate officers kindly took the time to further my work. Jack Leonard and Frank Horan, both retired officials of the Electric Boat Division, General Dynamics Corporation, as well as Henry Nardone, the company's current director of the Trident program, kindly made time to answer my questions on engineering matters and industry's relationship with the Navy. I also thank Neil Runzel and Graham Gavert, public affairs officers for the Electric Boat Division, and Charles Giles of the company's technical library, for their cooperation and assistance.

Essential information on the role of the scientific community and clarification of important concepts came from Allyn Vine, William Schevill, J. Lamar Worzel, and Mary Sears of the Woods Hole Oceanographic Institution. This book benefited significantly from their friendship, patience, and insight. Dr. John Brackett Hersey, formerly of the Woods Hole Oceanographic Institution and founding director of the Navy's Maury Center at the Naval Research Laboratory, sat for three interviews shortly after open-heart surgery. I am grateful for his generosity and forbearance.

At the Naval Historical Center, Dr. Ronald Spector, then Director of Naval History, initially approved this project, and the current Director of Naval History, Dr. Dean C. Allard, supported and nurtured the study with insight and advice for which I am grateful. Dr. Edward Marolda, Head of the Contemporary History Branch, offered guidance, support, and editorial expertise. Our senior editor, Sandra Doyle, as always, deftly guided the manuscript through final editing and the publication process. The manuscript also benefited from the comments of my colleagues Dr. Jeffrey Barlow, Dr. Michael Palmer, Dr. Robert Schneller, and Robert Cressman. Charles Haberlein of the center's Photographic Section provided excellent technical and historical advice. Shirley Rosenberg and her crew at SSR, Incorporated, skillfully handled the range of editorial tasks and editorial perceptions that a manuscript of this scope demands.

I am also indebted to many superb archivists who deciphered finding aids, located collections, and momentarily put aside what they were doing to further my work. They include the archives staff of the Hagley Museum; Barry Zerby, Dr. Cary Conn, Richard von Doehnhoff, and Richard Boylan of the National Archives; Kathleen Lloyd, Michael Walker, Regina Akers, John Hodges, and Bernard Cavalcante of the U.S. Navy's Operational Archives; William Galvani and Theresa Cass of the Submarine Force Library and Museum; June Gable of the Strategic Systems Program Office; Lee Hunt and Dixie Gordon of the Naval Studies Board of the National Academy of Sciences; Janice Goldblum and Karla Bowen of the National Academy of Sciences; Dr. Joseph Marchese and Wes Pryce of the David Taylor Research Center; and last, but certainly not least, William Dunkle and Susan Putnam of the Woods Hole Oceanographic Institution.

The support of the Navy Department Library was also essential, and for their consistent enthusiastic support I thank John Vajda, Dale Sharrick, and Glen Helm.

At home my wife and colleague, Catherine Tuggle, constantly offered love and support as well as hours of marvelous discussion about those aspects of the past that we both enjoy immensely. My eight-year-old daughter, Lili, gave me welcome opportunities to play, go for a walk, or tell stories just when I needed them most. Finally I hope the dedication speaks the volumes of gratitude for which I shall never find adequate words.

Introduction:
Themes and Interpretations

World War II truly transformed the traditional association between the Navy, industry, and science. The historian William H. McNeill first described this relationship in its often turbulent early stages as a "command technology." At the turn of the century, industry built larger, faster, and more powerful ships in direct response to the special demands of naval leaders such as Admiral Sir John Fisher, Great Britain's First Sea Lord; Admiral Alfred von Tirpitz, Chief of the German Imperial Naval Office; and Admiral George Dewey, Chairman of the U.S. Navy's General Board.[1] Instead of allowing the private sector to develop more effective engines of war in response to international market forces, these naval leaders ordered specific weapons and technologies to support preferred naval strategies and policies. In developing these command technologies, the armaments industries and the navies of the major Western powers inaugurated a relationship that represented the first stage in the evolution of the naval-industrial complex.[2]

Although a well-established and mutually profitable relationship between the Navy and industry had prevailed in surface ship construction as early as the 1880s, nothing comparable existed for submarines before World War I. In 1916 and 1917, however, the compelling circumstances of American mobilization changed the situation significantly. Preparing for the conflict brought the Navy and its submarine contractors close together in spite of dissimilar perspectives on their tasks and responsibilities.

The Navy's mission to develop and build warships and industry's desire for profit and growth, although certainly legitimate ambitions, were completely incompatible. To obtain a better product, the Navy naively expected industry to commit its talent and resources beyond the provisions of the contract that defined the responsibilities of both sides. This same kind of myopia led contractors, like Electric Boat Company, or EB,

---

[1] Von Tirpitz held this position from 1898 through 1916. Fisher was First Sea Lord from 1904 to 1910. The General Board advised successive U.S. Secretaries of the Navy on the general characteristics for vessels required by the Navy. For a recent analysis of the Royal Navy's response to technical innovation and its effect on fiscal policy and strategy, see Jon Sumida, *In Defense of Naval Supremacy, Finance, Technology, and British Naval Policy, 1889–1914* (Boston: Unwin Hyman, 1989).

[2] William H. McNeill, *The Pursuit of Power* (Chicago: University of Chicago Press, 1982), chap. 8.

to believe that the Navy could settle for submarines with poorly designed engines, terrible habitability, and numerous other flaws.[3]

During and after the World War I legal and technical disputes seemed to affirm for the Bureau of Construction and Repair and the Bureau of Engineering the purely mercenary nature of the private sector.[4] The Nelseco controversy of 1920–21, involving the New London Ship and Engine Company, an Electric Boat subsidiary, provided a classic example. This heated debate between the U.S. Navy and Electric Boat over the poor performance of diesels produced by Nelseco seemed to affirm for each party its worst expectations of the other. Construction on the 800-ton S-class submarines, designed during the war, stopped briefly in 1921 until both parties understood the problem and sought a mutually acceptable solution. The Navy Department feared that if it did not take the initiative and provide industry with greater incentive and expert technical guidance, American submariners might have to settle for a product off the shelf.

If naval authorities perceived contractors such as Electric Boat and Lake Torpedo Boat Company of Bridgeport, Connecticut, as mercenary, the private sector submarine builders naturally had a different image of themselves and thus drew different lessons from disputes like the Nelseco controversy. They were businessmen with a product to sell, determined to maintain their technological edge. These private companies intended to pursue research and development on their own terms, at their own pace, and profit by selling the results to the Navy. Thus, in the first few years after World War I, the interdependence that would oblige EB to anticipate the Navy's needs was not yet a vital part of that company's policy. This was still a decade away.

After World War I, the hardships imposed by the political and budgetary climate in the United States denied private industry any new submarine construction between 1925 and 1931. The virtual absence of new construction demonstrated the dependence of the private sector upon naval contracts. Electric Boat managed to survive this long dry spell by building everything from machinery to pleasure boats. But Lake Tor-

---

[3] In 1914, only two firms in the United States, both located in Connecticut, were capable of producing submarines: Lake Torpedo Boat Company of Bridgeport, founded by inventor Simon Lake, and Electric Boat Company of Groton, which built (usually at subcontracting shipyard facilities) the designs pioneered by the inventor of the submarine and one of the company's founders, John Holland. Before World War I the Navy's best facilities—at Portsmouth, New Hampshire, and Mare Island, California—served the submarine fleet only as repair and overhaul centers.

Although it ostensibly shared the submarine market with Lake, Electric Boat actually dominated the industry. In the lean years before America began to anticipate involvement in the Great War, the company lobbied hard on Capitol Hill. By 1914, it had either built or contracted to build the overwhelming majority of the Navy's submarines.

[4] The Bureau of Steam Engineering (BUSENG) became the Bureau of Engineering (BUENG) in 1920.

pedo Boat Company, the Navy's only other private prime contractor for submarines, closed its doors for the last time in 1924.

The Bureau of Construction and Repair and the Bureau of Engineering required the technical cooperation of private industry to supplement their own efforts at both naval research facilities and the Navy's submarine shipyards, Portsmouth and Mare Island. But mutual dependence did not automatically provide the incentive and direction necessary for building submarines and advancing the technology. This situation led the Navy to take the initiative in a number of areas during the interwar period. Dissatisfied with industry's early control over the technology and the market, the Navy's technical bureaus permitted Lake's demise and utilized all available assets to develop the Portsmouth Naval Shipyard into a first class submarine design and construction facility. Naval authorities also played the role of coordinator or catalyst for certain essential technologies, supporting and supplementing work by firms like Kollmorgen Optical Corporation on periscopes and naval, industrial, and university teams on radio transmission and underwater sound. This interaction during a period of severely limited financial resources made the bureaus more sensitive to the trials of the private sector, while providing naval and civilian personnel with valuable experience.

Experience was the key. The Navy and industry needed to probe the strategic potential of the submarine and address its technical challenges. Inexperience with submarines and their particularly demanding engineering problems quickly sparked controversy and intense debate over design, technology, and strategy.

Indeed, after the Great War, uncertainty prevailed within the Navy Department and the submarine force over issues as basic as strategy and mission. Clarity and consensus in these matters were essential for the development of a successful submarine design. In a letter to Josephus Daniels, Secretary of the Navy, penned as the Nelseco controversy came to a head, Captain Yates Stirling, Jr., then commandant of the Philadelphia Navy Yard, forcefully pointed out the primitive and near-useless state of the submarines then in service, especially the new 800 ton S-class. His comments sparked a tumultuous strategy, mission, and design debate that lasted for another decade, coming to a climax between 1928 and 1930.

During these years Commander Thomas Withers, commanding officer of Submarine Division Four, repeatedly called for an offensive strategy and solo tactics similar to those employed by the Imperial German Navy during the war. When the Naval War College and the Submarine Officers Conference endorsed the commander's views, naval authorities finally began to give serious consideration to aggressive, independent, blue water operations as the submarine's primary mission, rather than to coastal defense or intelligence gathering.[5] Naval architects and engineers immediately realized that this new strategic perspective demanded a larger, more reliable, and habitable submarine designed for long-range offensive missions.[6]

These ideas on mission, strategy, and design did not immediately capture the entire Navy the way they did the submarine community. It took another decade for them to take root, and even then it was often difficult for the submariners to make themselves heard. In a letter written to his friend Commander Francis S. Low, Admiral Charles A. Lockwood, commander of the Pacific submarine force during World War II, lamented the scattering of his submarines along a 30- to 40-mile scouting line during Fleet Problem 21 in 1940. He believed that submarines restrained in this fashion did not serve the fleet as well as the tactical freedom of offensive patrols. Lockwood concluded by saying, "We learn the same lessons each year and I hope to live to see the day when we will be allowed to profit from them."[7]

Due to the initiative of Withers, the Submarine Officers Conference, and the staff at the Naval War College, operating independently against enemy forces and inflicting casualties eventually became the primary task of American submarines. Coastal defense virtually disappeared as a submarine assignment, while gathering intelligence for the fleet remained an important, but secondary, mission.

The American fleet submarine, which so effectively executed an offensive strategy against the Japanese during World War II, represented a new synthesis formed by Stirling's assault on the technical reliability of the S-class submarine and Withers's strategic challenge. After these first steps, the support and sensitivity of Admirals Henry A. Wiley, Harry E. Yarnell, and Samuel M. Robinson proved critical. Wiley, as Commander in Chief,

<hr/>

[5] The Naval War College is located at Newport, Rhode Island. The Submarine Officers Conference, founded in 1926, was composed of a group of active submarine officers who served in an advisory capacity to the General Board and the CNO on all submarine matters.

[6] By 1934 a design of approximately 1,475 tons assumed the primary place within the submarine community as the best size and configuration for satisfying the Navy's desire for reliability, range, and habitability. In March 1936 the General Board's final recommendations to the Secretary for the 1937 construction program gave 1,450 tons as the "minimum compatible with a proper balance of the required military characteristics to meet the intended employment of the submarine." BUENG and BUC&R could more easily accommodate the characteristics desired by the Submarine Officers Conference and the General Board in a 1,500-ton boat than the 1,100–1,200-ton type suggested earlier. The success and popularity of the *Salmon* (SS 182)–*Sargo* (SS 188) design in the fleet testified to a final consensus achieved within the Navy by 1936. Gary E. Weir, *Building American Submarines, 1914–1940* (Washington: Naval Historical Center, 1991).

[7] Charles Lockwood to Francis Low, 17 May 1940, series 4, file 8, box 14, Submarines/Undersea Warfare Division (Subs/UWD), Operational Archives (OA), Naval Historical Center (NHC).

U.S. Fleet and former chairman of the General Board, along with the staff at the Naval War College, permitted Withers's ideas to prosper in a potentially inhospitable environment. Yarnell and Robinson, as successive chiefs of the Bureau of Engineering from 1928 to 1942, utilized German technology from Maschinenfabrik Augsburg-Nürnberg at a time when America could not afford the extensive diesel research and development program that the submarine force desperately needed.[8]

For these naval leaders practical experience suggested that the Navy clearly define its goals and take the initiative in its relationship with industry. In this way, they believed, the construction program could produce the best possible submarines for the Navy and ensure growth and profit for the private sector. These assumptions began to take hold of naval policy toward industry with the advent of the Withers-Naval War College strategic formula, the resumption of regular construction in 1931, and early New Deal support for fleet expansion in the form of the Vinson-Trammel Act of 1934 and the Second Vinson Act of 1938.

When the unwelcome prospect of global conflict presented itself, the Navy and private industry initiated and financed a massive expansion program within the shipbuilding industry. This ambitious effort inaugurated an era of unprecedented integration and cooperation between the Navy and its contractors, supported by a national commitment to naval expansion absent during the 1920s.

The entry of the Manitowoc Shipbuilding Company of Manitowoc, Wisconsin, into the submarine market in 1940 illustrated the Navy's success in establishing its authority over industry before Pearl Harbor. Assistant Secretary of the Navy Charles Edison approved the proposal made by the Bureau of Construction and Repair that Electric Boat should provide the technical and administrative assistance necessary for Manitowoc to produce clones of *Growler*. Twenty years earlier, the Navy's inferior technical knowledge and junior position in the naval-industrial relationship would have made this type of action impossible. But now the situation was so substantially changed that the Navy could determine how and to what degree it wanted EB to support the Wisconsin company. Considerable naval investment in expanded EB facilities at Groton and Bayonne, New Jersey, during 1940 provided added incentive for the company to comply with the Navy's wishes.

In the final analysis, both parties had to overcome the ancient ambivalence between buyer and seller. Although this ambivalence would never entirely disappear, the Navy and industry gradually managed to identify and reconcile their contending motives, goals, and expectations in the

___
[8] Robinson was chief of BUENG when the merger with BUC&R that took place in 1940 created BUSHIPS. He became the first chief of the new bureau.

process of composing solutions to their occasionally paralyzing confrontations. In this way, by 1940, early incompatibility gave way to a greater degree of cooperation and a mature command technology for submarines.

As the Navy and industry prepared for war, the Roosevelt administration asked the scientific community to take similar measures. In June 1940 the President authorized the creation of the National Defense Research Committee to sponsor and coordinate defense-related scientific research and development, much of which applied directly to undersea warfare. One year later, the Office for Scientific Research and Development, under the direction of Vannevar Bush of Washington's Carnegie Institution, assumed the role of parent organization to the committee.

The wartime blend of naval, industrial, and scientific resources gave birth to the naval-industrial complex for submarines. This triple alliance rested less upon the cooperation of agencies and companies than upon the personal relationships of naval and civilian leaders. Although funds and suitable working conditions certainly depended on various institutions and government agencies, the success of the naval-industrial complex depended on people. They worked together effectively in an environment characterized by professional respect, strongly held common motives, both public-spirited and mercenary, and a degree of mutual trust regardless of affiliation that their counterparts of the 1990s would find remarkable. Motivated by occupation, interest, and necessity, they sustained this wartime alliance into the Cold War era.

After the fall of Japan, the U.S. Navy found itself in competition with the Soviet Union. The beginning of the Cold War allowed the U.S. Armed Forces, and the Navy in particular, little time to reevaluate their mission. Soon both sides in the new, ideological struggle started to exploit the advanced submarine technologies developed by the Germans and demonstrated by the Walter propulsion system and the Type XXI, XXIII, and XXVI U-boats. The submarine became one of the most important postwar weapons systems, and navies on both sides of the Iron Curtain worked to design and build vessels that would go faster, dive deeper, and remain underwater longer.

The coming of the Cold War, combined with the revolution in submarine technology initiated by the Germans, induced the postwar U.S. Navy to intensify its commitment to the submarine. The Navy Department sponsored programs that perfected the schnorchel, made nuclear propulsion a reality, generated new shipbuilding materials, adapted missile technology to submarines, and dramatically increased submerged speed. American submarines set the standard after World War II, supported by both the naval-industrial complex created during the war and a sustained congressional commitment to the submarine as an integral part of national defense.

Chapter 1

Coming Up To Speed, 1940–1943

In the decade before Pearl Harbor the aggressive and threatening behavior of Imperial Japan and Nazi Germany made another major world
conflict a disturbing possibility. Although Americans strongly desired to
avoid war, an increasing number of the nation's leaders realized the need
for a stronger defense and more modern weapons. Japanese expansion in
the Far East, German rearmament, the remilitarization of the Rhineland in
violation of the Versailles Treaty, Hitler's annexation of Austria, and the
Japanese air attack on the American gunboat *Panay* combined with President Franklin D. Roosevelt's domestic popularity to provide him with the
congressional support necessary to improve the national defense.

Both the U.S. Army and Navy appreciated the need to make up for
the consequences of isolationism and lean budgets of the interwar years.
The Navy's special priorities included modern aircraft, aircraft carriers,
escort vessels, submarines, and underwater sound gear. Thus during
Roosevelt's first two terms in office, heightened motivation and slowly
increasing congressional appropriations allowed the Navy to build submarines already authorized and to plan for future construction.

The outbreak of war in Europe on 1 September 1939 added a sense of
urgency. It became essential for the Navy's technical bureaus to build more
submarines and to launch a program to help finance the expansion of contractor facilities in preparation for full-scale mobilization. Suddenly the
growing fear of American participation in the war created a demand for
factory space and skilled labor absent just a few years earlier. To make up
for the reduction in the Armed Forces and the corresponding contraction
in the armaments industry after the Great War, the Army and Navy designed support programs for their most important contractors. The naval-
industrial complex for submarines emerged from this intense effort by the
Navy Department and the private sector to prepare for an uncertain future.

Congressional Consent

The authorization for fleet expansion came from Congress in three
stages. First, the Vinson-Trammel Act of 1934 gave the Navy authority to

bring the fleet up to the full complement allowed by the London Naval Treaty of 1930, which permitted a submarine force of only 52,700 tons of front line vessels. Signatories to the treaty could replace or overhaul any overage units as long as the basic tonnage limit was observed. As an authorization, the act did not provide the necessary funds to build additional vessels but, given past experience, naval supporters felt confident that Congress would not fail to appropriate the necessary funds over the next few years.

The act also addressed public concern over excess profits in the armaments industry. The Vinson-Trammel Act was passed less than one year before the Nye Commission congressional hearings in 1935 and 1936. The hearings seemed to confirm public suspicions that defense contractors had accumulated extraordinary profits from government business during the Great War. Two important features of the legislation addressed this concern: The act limited private profits on government armaments contracts to 10 percent, and it required the President to build every other ship at a naval shipyard.[1]

The second stage in the process of authorizing naval expansion came with the legislation popularly known as the Second Vinson Act, named after Representative Carl Vinson, the chairman of the House Committee on Naval Affairs. This measure passed Congress on 17 May 1938 and authorized the President to exceed the construction limits of the Vinson-Trammel Act by 20 percent. This authorization would allow the Navy to build nine submarines more than the forty-six permitted by the 1934 legislation.[2]

Once war began in Europe, Congress passed two more bills in successive months in the summer of 1940 authorizing the final stage of the American naval expansion program before Pearl Harbor. The Act of 14

[1] Aircraft industry profits were limited to 12 percent. Dating back to its experience in World War I, the Navy Department used two basic types of contracts to regulate industry profits. A fixed-price contract determined the cost of the construction project at the outset and the amount of profit the contractor would realize. Used before and during World War I, this instrument emerged as the contract preferred by the Navy during the interwar period. The cost-plus-percentage-of-cost type of contract allowed the purveyor to realize as profit a percentage of the total cost incurred for production. The Navy Department discontinued this form after the war because it encouraged profiteering. The contractor had no incentive to keep costs down, because the contractor's profits rose at the same rate as costs.

Cost-plus-percentage-of-cost contracts are often confused with the cost-plus-fixed-fee type. The latter specifies profits in dollar amounts regardless of cost, and the Navy continued to use it after 1918.

[2] For general information on the 1934 and 1938 legislation, tonnage allowed, and numbers of vessels authorized, see George T. Davis, *A Navy Second to None: The Development of Modern American Naval Policy* (New York: Harcourt, Brace, and Co., 1940), chap. 14. For additional information on the Vinson acts, see Michael A. West, "Laying the Legislative Foundation: The House Naval Affairs Committee and the Construction of the Treaty Navy, 1926–1934" (Ph.D. diss., Ohio State University, 1980). For the requirement that every other submarine be built at a navy yard, see Lewis Compton to Mayor T. S. Burgin of Quincy, MA, 9 Aug 1937, box 7, Assistant SECNAV Alpha Files, RG 80, National Archives and Records Administration (hereafter NA), Washington, DC.

June 1940 permitted an increase of 21,000 tons, or fourteen submarines. Then on 19 July Congress passed the most ambitious of the prewar American naval bills. This measure, often called the Seventy Percent Expansion Act, permitted the Navy to add 70,000 tons of submarines to the fleet. It represented an additional forty-seven boats.[3]

Existing Forces

The Navy Department prepared its submarine forces for the possibility of conflict by first taking stock of its commissioned vessels and seeking to reinforce them with submarines decommissioned during the interwar years. In June 1940 Acting Secretary of the Navy Charles Edison authorized a program to augment the Navy's sixty-four commissioned submarines with three reserve divisions drawn from retired O-, R-, V-, and S-class boats.[4] Edison, an MIT graduate and son of the famous inventor Thomas A. Edison, had served in both state and national governments since 1934, managing various New Deal recovery programs. An earlier form of this plan two years before had projected recommissioning only twenty-one vessels. Before that program was discontinued in the spring of 1939, *S 21*, *S 24*, *S 26*, and *S 30* appeared on the reserve list. Edison's initiative restored this program and added four new reserve submarine divisions to the fleet before the end of 1940.

Submarine Division Nine consisted of the reactivated *Barracuda* (V 1), *Bass* (V 2), and *Bonita* (V 3). Division Forty-Four included the four S-class boats activated in 1938–1939 as well as *S 1*, *S 31*, *S 32*, and *S 33*. The *R 1*, *R 3*, *R 5*, *R 6*, *R 12*, and *R 16* comprised Division Forty-Two. Eight O-class submarines and *S 11* combined to form Division Forty-Three in the final months of 1940.[5]

---

[3] The numbers of submarines have been calculated at an average displacement per boat of 1,475 tons. For pertinent sections of the legislation, see *Dictionary of American Naval Fighting Ships* (Washington: Naval History Division, 1964), 1:244.

[4] *Annual Report of the Secretary of the Navy* (Washington: GPO, 1940).

[5] The O-class vessels were *O 2*, *O 3*, *O 4*, and *O 6–10*. Memo for RADM Ingersoll, 17 Oct 1940; Commander Submarine Squadron (COMSUBRON) Two to CNO, 10 Dec 1940; W. A. Saunders (former Officer in Charge of Submarines in Commission in Reserve at New London, CT), 29 Nov 1940; CNO to Commander Submarine Division (COMSUBDIV) Nine et al., 5 Oct 1940, box 1116, Office of the Secretary of the Navy (including CNO and JAG) General Correspondence 1940–42 (hereafter SECNAV GENCORR 1940–42), RG 80, NA.

Combining the influence of the French diesel propulsion—which first appeared in Leubeuf's *Aigrette* in 1900—with the American designs of John Holland and Simon Lake, the U.S. Navy's submarines took on a familiar configuration from 1909 through American entry into World War I. Submarines of the E, H, K, L, M, N, O, and R classes ranged in displacement from 287 to 510 tons, with the fastest boats capable of a top surface speed of barely 14 knots on diesel power. For details on each vessel, see *Dictionary of American Naval Fighting Ships*, vol. 1.

This early effort to augment the submarine force gave the Secretary and the technical bureaus a taste of the problems they would soon encounter on a much larger scale.[6] As many decommissioned submarines were returned to reserve status, the need for new parts and facilities quickly grew out of proportion to the private sector's ability to respond. The Navy acted promptly to deal with the problem. The technical bureaus bypassed the normal bidding and approval system with their major vendors to speed up the process of returning the retired submarines to reserve status. The Secretary authorized firms like Electric Boat Company (EB) of Groton, Connecticut, to acquire new equipment, purchase spares, or manufacture necessary parts before concluding a formal agreement. In each case both parties agreed to postpone legal details and formalities, with the Secretary providing the basis for a later contract by communicating the particulars of a preliminary arrangement by letter or telegram.[7]

In some cases the Bureau of Ships (BUSHIPS) and the Bureau of Supplies and Accounts eliminated the need for new contracts with many important vendors by supplementing existing arrangements. In such cases, both partners simply agreed to the expansion of an already approved agreement. As expressed in a BUSHIPS communication to the Secretary of the Navy, using supplementary contracts,

> will eliminate time required for preparation of a requisition, advertising for bids, and award of a new contract. It will also eliminate preparation and approval of plans and design work in connection with same, reduce inspection and other administrative costs thus making possible deliveries to the best interests of the Government.[8]

Similar situations occurred throughout the submarine industry. Most of the boats returning to reserve service, for example, required new storage batteries. In this case BUSHIPS's primary vendor, the Electric Storage Battery Company, had a difficult time keeping pace with the recommissioning program. The sudden flood of naval orders exceeded the

---

[6] The term "technical bureaus" refers to the Navy's Bureau of Engineering, Bureau of Construction and Repair, and Bureau of Ordnance. In 1940, the first two combined to form the Bureau of Ships, or BUSHIPS. There are a few instances in the book when it would be more accurate to use the Bureau of Engineering, the Bureau of Construction and Repair, or the joint bureau created in 1939 that used both names. To avoid confusion, BUSHIPS is used in the text throughout to provide uniformity.

[7] L. Y. Spear (Vice President of Electric Boat) to SECNAV, 18 Jul 1941; James Forrestal to EB, 2 Apr 1941; BUSHIPS to Commandant New York Navy Yard, 25 Nov 1940; SECNAV to Supervisor of Shipbuilding (SUPSHIPS), Groton, CT (telegram), 6 Sep 1940, box 1116, SECNAV GENCORR 1940–42, RG 80, NA.

[8] BUSHIPS to SECNAV, 4 Nov 1941, box 1116, SECNAV GENCORR 1940–42.

company's production capability. Indeed, a memorandum for the assistant to the Chief of Naval Operations (CNO), Rear Admiral Royal Ingersoll, indicated that "due to pressure 'to hurry,' Electric Storage Battery Co. had the misfortune to turn out considerable 'bad active' battery material and this has resulted in a corresponding slow down."[9]

Thus, finding the $500,000 the Navy Department spent restoring each vessel represented only part of the difficulties that emerged during the recommissioning program.[10] The technical bureaus and the private sector quickly realized that both the Navy and industry needed to upgrade their capabilities, create new facilities, and find or train hundreds of skilled workers. Private companies like EB and Electric Storage Battery would now have to cope with a surge in demand for new products and overhauls. The Navy Department in turn could no longer depend solely upon the naval shipyards at Portsmouth and Mare Island. It needed new support facilities both to complete the recommissioning program and to sustain the ongoing effort to keep the frontline submarines in fighting trim.

To address these needs, BUSHIPS, under the command of Rear Admiral Samuel Robinson, called upon the navy yards at Pearl Harbor and Philadelphia, as well as the San Diego destroyer base, to act as support facilities for EB, Portsmouth Naval Shipyard, and Mare Island Naval Shipyard. The basic facilities were certainly available at these locations, but the problems of acquiring skilled personnel, sufficient tools, and adequate time made the task much more complicated than the bureau expected.

On 10 April 1941 BUSHIPS noted that Pearl Harbor was having difficulty performing some overhauls and alterations, and suggested steps to remedy the situation. In his response the commandant of the Pearl Harbor Navy Yard noted that a concerted effort had already begun to procure additional draftsmen, planners, and estimators to direct the expansion of the yard's facilities and skilled work force. Bringing the yard up to the standard necessary to do repair and recommissioning work would take a considerable amount of time and effort.[11]

In the autumn of 1941 the CNO and BUSHIPS reassigned four regular submarine divisions, along with responsibility for their overhaul and upkeep, to the Philadelphia Navy Yard. This yard was one of those originally selected to help restore the old submarines to the reserves, but it

---

[9] Memo for RADM Ingersoll, 17 Oct 1940, box 1116, SECNAV GENCORR 1940–42.

[10] For an example of the type of repairs and the money spent, see the account of *R 20* in Sep 1941: Commandant U.S. Navy Yard, Philadelphia, to CNO, 20 Sep 1941, box 1118, SECNAV GENCORR 1940–42. There were exceptions to this average cost. The largest of the commissioned submarines that the Navy decided to modernize were *Argonaut* (V 4), *Narwhal* (V 5), and *Nautilus* (V 6).

[11] Commandant Pearl Harbor Navy Yard to BUSHIPS, 16 Apr 1941; BUSHIPS to Commandant Pearl Harbor Navy Yard, 10 Apr 1941, box 1117, SECNAV GENCORR 1940–42.

lacked the necessary skills and experience to overhaul the boats on schedule. Indeed, the Navy's operational submarines found the capacity for regular support and overhaul at Philadelphia only after the Navy Department transferred experienced personnel there to supervise improvement of the facilities and procurement of additional skilled labor. A memorandum from the Office of the Chief of Naval Operations noted the need for this action as early as October 1940 because "Navy Yard, Philadelphia has not overhauled a submarine since 1918."[12]

At the destroyer base at San Diego, the third installation selected for submarine refurbishment and overhaul, BUSHIPS built new facilities adjacent to the base in an area called the Blackman Estate. An expenditure of $1,725,000 was required for dredging and for constructing three finger piers, a quay wall, and, among other necessities, housing for both officers and enlisted men.[13]

In addition to arranging for expanded naval facilities and more convenient contract arrangements, the new Secretary of the Navy, William Franklin Knox, a colonel in the Army Reserve and general manager of the Hearst newspapers, authorized BUSHIPS in 1941 to curtail the number and duration of acceptance trials for both new and recommissioned submarines.[14] His plan, formulated in conjunction with BUSHIPS, provided for a carefully composed but shorter trial schedule, thus reducing the time it took to transfer completed or overhauled submarines from the yards to the operational forces.[15] Twenty-five years before, the Bureau of Construction and Repair had used this same technique to increase the size of the submarine force as America entered the Great War.

In taking this action, BUSHIPS carefully avoided abdicating its joint responsibility with the CNO for acceptance trials.[16] Electric Boat had encouraged BUSHIPS to go beyond simply abbreviating the trial schedule

---

[12] Memo for RADM Ingersoll, 17 Oct 1940, box 1116; BUSHIPS to CNO, 9 Oct 1941, box 1117; BUSHIPS to COMSUBRON 2, 18 Sep 1940, box 1117, SECNAV GENCORR 1940–42.

[13] BUSHIPS to Commanding Officer, Destroyer Base, San Diego, 9 Dec 1940; Commandant Eleventh Naval District, San Diego, to CNO, 11 Apr 1941, box 1117, SECNAV GENCORR 1940–42.

[14] Secretary Claude Swanson died on 7 July 1939. Charles Edison served as Acting Secretary until he assumed the office in his own right on 2 January 1940, serving until 24 June. Lewis Compton then served as Acting Secretary until Knox took over on 11 July.

[15] "Recommended Tests for Recommissioned Submarines," [1941]; CNO to SECNAV, 3 Feb 1941; CNO to SECNAV, 18 Sep 1941, box 1117, SECNAV GENCORR 1940–42.

[16] Although BUSHIPS was responsible for the construction of the submarines and the character of the trial schedule, the CNO's office provided the Board of Inspection and Survey (BdI/S) to conduct the preliminary and final trials of every submarine destined for service with the Navy. The Board of Inspection and Survey was under the supervision of the Deputy Chief of Naval Operations for Logistics.

for its submarines. But the bureau refused to reduce the number of these tests to the extent suggested by EB. In a communication to the company on 23 October 1941, Secretary Knox indicated the importance of striking a balance between the need to add submarines to the fleet and the desire for quality and dependability:

> The Bureau of Ships states that it is, in general, in sympathy with the contractor's proposals but not to the extent that the trials be curtailed as much as recommended. Under present conditions, preliminary acceptance trials assume greater importance than normally, as it is necessary to insure that the vessels are ready for unlimited service when delivered. To this end, it is considered advisable to conduct sufficient trials to demonstrate the quality of the vessels and those trials necessary to obtain essential tactical and other operating data.[17]

The command technology that evolved during the interwar period could not, as yet, cope with the rapid growth demanded by the threatening international situation. The Navy Department knew what it wanted to build, but its experienced industrial partners and those individuals skilled in submarine design and construction were still too few.

New Submarine Construction

A few months before the passage of the Second Vinson Bill in May 1938, the former congressman, senator, and governor of Virginia, Secretary of the Navy Claude A. Swanson, had asked Charles Edison, his Assistant Secretary, to manage the accelerated construction program. In response to Swanson's request Edison commissioned a long-term naval analysis of the program authorized by Congress and, taking into account future Navy plans, tried to define difficulties and suggest solutions.

Edison advanced a general scheme designed both to reduce the complexity of the program authorized by the Vinson-Trammel Act and to interest old and new vendors in doing business with the Navy. To raise quality, Edison suggested that Portsmouth and Mare Island compete with the private sector for contracts on the basis of construction cost and time. He also suggested that BUSHIPS decentralize design and procurement and adopt longer production runs. Initiating major design changes every other year rather than annually, he reasoned, would per-

---

[17] CNO to SECNAV, 18 Sep 1941; EB to BUSHIPS, 10 Jun 1941; SUPSHIPS Groton to BUSHIPS, 30 Jul 1941; BUSHIPS to SECNAV, 8 Sep 1941; SECNAV (Forrestal as Acting) to EB, 23 Oct 1941, box 1117, SECNAV GENCORR 1940–42.

mit the Navy and the private sector to produce more submarines with the tools, machinery, and experienced workers already in place.

Edison also recommended that the Secretary of the Navy persuade Congress to authorize partial exemptions to both the Walsh-Healy Act governing the labor hours spent per week on government contracts and the profit restrictions imposed by the Vinson-Trammel Act.[18] The Navy Department would need some exceptions to these measures if it expected industry to find submarine construction attractive and profitable. He also pursued the possibility of extending the work week up to twelve hours beyond the federally imposed limit of thirty-six hours on government shipbuilding contracts.

Finally, Edison believed that the General Board of the Navy should clearly define the approved characteristics of any vessel by 1 January of each year. This precise determination of the Navy's desires, coupled with keeping design changes to an absolute minimum during construction, would give every contractor a far better grasp of what BUSHIPS expected.[19]

Edison began to implement these ideas after Congress passed the Second Vinson Act. He issued orders to limit the number of design changes authorized by the technical bureaus during construction. Historically, these midstream modifications to the contract design precipitated numerous and frustrating slowdowns and delays in the construction process. The memory of diesel engine performance in the S-class submarines during the interwar period, as well as similar predicaments with surface vessels, was still fresh.[20] Edison ruled that the yards could not implement any change requiring more than $10,000 in cost or two weeks' work time without direct approval from the Secretary of the Navy.[21]

He then approached Rear Admiral Joseph R. DeFrees, former Commander Submarine Force, U.S. Fleet, on the best ways to expedite construction. Admiral DeFrees had wide experience in procurement and management. He had served in the Bureau of Engineering (BUENG) after the Great War, later accumulated extensive experience with torpe-

---

[18] "Madame Perkins and the Submarines," 20 Feb 1937; "Government Steel," 21 Feb 1937, box 8, Assistant SECNAV Alpha File, RG 80, NA. These sources illustrate the effect of the Walsh-Healy Act on the willingness of industry to sign government contracts: "The act provides that no government contract exceeding $10,000 shall be valid unless the contractor institutes a forty hour week, pays wage scales approved by the Secretary of Labor, eliminates workers under 18 years of age from his force, and meets the secretary's pleasure as to other working conditions." (*Chicago Tribune*)

[19] G. J. Rowcliff (JAG Office), Memo for the Assistant SECNAV, [March?] 1937; Assistant SECNAV to all Bureaus, 15 Mar 1937, box 7, Assistant SECNAV Alpha File.

[20] Weir, *Building American Submarines*, chap. 6; G. E. Weir, "The Navy, Industry, and Diesel Propulsion for American Submarines, 1914–1940," *Naval Engineers Journal* 101 (May 1989): 207–19.

[21] Assistant SECNAV Charles Edison, Memo on the Construction Program, 9 May 1938, box 7, Assistant SECNAV Alpha File.

does as inspector of ordnance at the Naval Torpedo Station at Newport, Rhode Island, and attended the Army Industrial College in 1925.

The admiral suggested improvements in three areas. First, given the experience of the 1920s, an uninterrupted construction program was absolutely necessary to develop the skills, facilities, tools, and workmanship necessary to sustain a submarine fleet. Second, the United States ran a risk with its lack of uniformity; the submarine community needed standard types to conduct independent patrols and offensive operations, free of the frequent design changes and lesser modifications.[22] Last, DeFrees complained of a lack of skilled labor and adequate facilities. He lamented, as did the Navy Department when restoring old submarines to reserve status, the critical shortage of men in the shipbuilding trades and occupations. The admiral concluded his report by insisting that shipbuilding projects needed more hours and fewer strikes. He also encouraged more efficient utilization of those skilled workers who could not operate in shifts, such as draftsmen and engineers.[23]

In spite of the critical weaknesses defined by DeFrees, which not even the demands of war would solve completely, the pace of expansion increased. In July 1938, on the heels of the Second Vinson Bill, the technical bureaus submitted a ten-year shipbuilding plan to the Secretary of the Navy that called for building forty-six submarines between 1939 and 1948. These vessels would displace approximately 1,475 tons each, and their construction would span the ten-year period.[24] Secretary Swanson approved this plan as a basis for future budget proposals and planning by Edison and the technical bureaus.[25]

In addition Swanson ordered an increase in the pace of construction. Issued by letter on 30 December 1938, the Secretary's instruction emphasized the critical shortage of skilled labor as the major obstacle to the success of the expansion program. As chief of the Navy's prime submarine yard, the commandant at the Portsmouth Naval Shipyard responded to the Secretary's concerns by employing shifts, permitting overtime, and hiring as many skilled workers as possible. In this way he hoped to complete five of his submarines one to two months ahead of schedule. The boats included *Searaven* (SS 196), *Seawolf* (SS 197), *Triton* (SS 201), *Trout* (SS 202), and *Squalus* (SS 192).[26]

---

[22] Weir, *Building American Submarines*, chap. 3.

[23] RADM J. R. DeFrees to Edison, 6 Dec 1938, box 7, Assistant SECNAV Alpha File, RG 80, NA.

[24] 1939 = 6, 1940 = 8, 1941 = 6, 1942 = 6, 1943 = 4, 1944 = 1, 1945 = 0, 1946 = 4, 1947 = 5, 1948 = 6.

[25] Joint Letter, BUC&R, BUENG, and BUORD to SECNAV, 14 Jul 1938, box 8, Assistant SECNAV Alpha File.

[26] Commandant Portsmouth Naval Shipyard to SECNAV, 6 Mar 1939, box 4020, SECNAV GEN-CORR 1926–40, RG 80, NA.

Electric Boat also responded quickly to the call for accelerated construction. The company kept all of its new submarines either on or ahead of its construction schedule. By the first quarter of 1940 EB had saved as much as six and one-half months of the time it usually took to build three *Sargo*-class boats.[27]

The two-year construction program implemented in fiscal 1941 severely tested the ability of EB, Portsmouth, and Mare Island to sustain this level of performance. The plan funded twenty-eight submarines distributed among the three yards. Electric Boat received sixteen; Portsmouth, eight; and Mare Island, four. Every submarine, regardless of construction yard, had to undergo a four-week shakedown cruise and a review by the Navy's Board of Inspection and Survey before joining the fleet.[28]

The EB submarines were *Gato*-class boats (SS 212–227), the first of the "fleet submarines" that would distinguish themselves in World War II.[29] The navy yards built twelve of the *Drum* class (SS 228–239).[30] Each vessel took about twenty months to complete. The Navy commissioned those boats built at Portsmouth and Mare Island almost two months before completion to allow the yard to prepare the living quarters and conduct the builder's trials. EB delivered its submarines already complete.

Between the Vinson-Trammel Act of 1934 and the second Vinson Act of 1938, Congress had authorized fifty-six submarines, a total of 81,956 tons. Since these figures reflected the imminent demise of the London

[27] BUC&R/ENG Joint Report on Construction Progress, 10 Mar 1940, box 8, Assistant SECNAV Alpha File, RG 80, NA. *Sargo*-class characteristics: displacement = 1,450 tons (surface); speed = 20 knots (surface), 8.75 knots (submerged); propulsion = HOR and GM diesels with GE electric motors for submerged running.

For a complete set of technical statistics, see *Dictionary of American Naval Fighting Ships* 1:246.

[28] BUC&R/ENG Joint Memo on the Approved Two-Year Building Program, 27 May 1940, box 8, Assistant SECNAV Alpha File. Construction Assignment Memorandum, 9 Jul 1940, series 1, file 5, box 2, Subs/UWD, OA.

Gato- and *Drum*-class characteristics: displacement = 1,526 tons (surface); speed = 20.25 knots (surface), 8.75 knots (submerged); propulsion = *Gato*: GM diesels with GE electric motors for submerged running; *Drum*: Fairbanks-Morse diesels with Ellsworth electric motors.

For a complete set of technical statistics, see *Dictionary of American Naval Fighting Ships* 1:247–49.

[29] The roots of the fleet-submarine concept went back to World War I. When the primary arm of the Navy was the surface fleet and the submarine played the role of newcomer, the latter was seen as a novel type of submersible destroyer. As such it was supposed to serve as an escort, picket, and screen, providing protection and intelligence. Unfortunately the submarine technology of the time could not provide a boat capable of running at 20 knots on the surface to keep pace with the battleships. Thus American submarines from the T class through the V class and, later, those following the designs of *Salmon*, *Sargo*, and *Gato* were often called fleet submarines, but no American submarine ever fulfilled the requirements for the role. Instead, by the time the submarines were capable of the necessary speed, the strategy had changed and their primary mission no longer asked them to operate on close coordination with a surface force.

[30] Although the three principal classes of fleet submarines during World War II were *Gato*, *Balao*, and *Tench*, technical variations within each class often prompted submariners and BUSHIPS to refer to particular groups of submarines by more specific class names, like *Gunnel* or *Drum*.

Treaty limits set in 1930, the Navy Department took measures to increase industrial capability by initiating apprenticeship and training programs to improve skills and allocating greater resources for tools and replacement parts. Under the direction of Secretary Charles Edison and his successor, Frank Knox, BUSHIPS increased the number of engineers and draftsmen in its service. In cooperation with the Civil Service Commission, it borrowed people from other agencies and trained them to suit the Navy's needs. Continuing to tap both public and private expertise, Edison permitted a variety of yards and companies to compete in the design of lead vessels. Once a particular design proved successful, he chose a single facility to accomplish the refinements and perform the drafting work needed to build the follow-ships of the same class.[31] This procedure would avoid costly duplication.

Under Edison's direction the Navy Department also encouraged facility expansion by providing financial assistance to naval contractors. On 28 June 1940 the Secretary of the Navy received authority from Congress to assist the shipbuilding industry by providing structures and facilities, on government land or at other locations, for use by the private sector. Congress also authorized the Secretary to provide funds from naval appropriations either to upgrade these properties or, when necessary, to purchase additional structures and resources. If the expense proved too great, private industry was to assume part of the cost with the guarantee of reimbursement. Shipyard and subcontractor facilities financed in this way were called emergency plant facilities.[32]

As the Seventy Percent Expansion Act passed the Congress in the summer of 1940, the Navy simplified the facility acquisition process. With the outbreak of war in Europe, President Roosevelt had proclaimed a limited national emergency and created the Council for National Defense, composed of members from labor, industry, and agriculture, to help coordinate American war resources. The council's Advisory Commission now helped the Navy create what became known as the defense-type contract. This arrangement vested the individual companies with the complete ownership of new facilities until the Navy repaid the private investment.[33]

[31] A. T. Church, Memo on New Construction, 4 Apr 1939, box 7, Assistant SECNAV Alpha File, RG 80, NA; Davis, *A Navy Second to None*, 380.

[32] R. H. Connery, *The Navy and the Industrial Mobilization in World War II* (Princeton, NJ: Princeton University Press, 1951), 89–90; E. P. Allen, *Policies Governing Private Financing of Emergency Facilities, May 1940 to June 1942*, Special Study Number 12 (Washington: U.S. Civilian Production Administration, 1946).

[33] Connery, *The Navy and the Industrial Mobilization*, 90; Allen, "Policies Governing Private Financing of Emergency Facilities," 20 Sep 1944.

When the resources available to the Navy fell short, the Congress authorized the Navy Department to cooperate with other government agencies to secure the construction of the required facilities. The Act of 25 June 1940 allowed the Reconstruction Finance Corporation (RFC) to assist the Navy. As historian Robert H. Connery observed, "the RFC created a subsidiary agency, the Defense Plant Corporation, on August 22, 1940, to carry out the purposes of the Act. Under Defense Plant Contracts the government paid the cost of the new facilities and leased them to the manufacturer." [34]

As the international situation worsened, the Advisory Commission urged Congress to allow amortization of private investment in these new facilities via income tax returns over five years rather than the initially planned twenty-five. This action would provide an incentive for greater participation by private industry in the rearmament program. Without these assurances many contractors refused to commit their resources over the long term because the market for the products provided by these emergency facilities might disappear after a short war. This feeling pervaded the submarine industry. Corporate leaders remembered well the demise of Lake Torpedo Boat Company of Bridgeport, Connecticut, in 1924 and the hardship caused by the complete absence of new construction from 1925 to 1931.

After much debate Congress passed the legislation requested by the Advisory Commission on 8 October 1940. Companies investing their own capital had to obtain certificates of necessity, non-reimbursement, and government protection to take advantage of the accelerated amortization. The first certificate justified the investment as part of the emergency measures authorized by the President. The others guaranteed that the company was selected for defense work by a government agency and had not yet received compensation for the services rendered.[35]

BUSHIPS instituted rigorous procedures for managing the facility expansion program. The bureau relied on each supervisor of shipbuilding (SUPSHIPS) at the various shipyards to determine the need for additional facilities. The individual supervisor had to satisfy himself that neither the existing plant nor any nearby could produce the needed vessel or system in the desired quantity and quality. If it proved necessary to ac-

[34] Connery, *The Navy and the Industrial Mobilization*, 90.

[35] Ibid., 90–91. Companies engaged in special work on defense contracts for the Navy were permitted to apply for tax exemptions on specific tool or machine purchases required to complete the Navy contracts. Authorization for these exemptions were called Certificates of Necessity. The following documents show the process by which the certification was procure.d by General Motors on various specific purchases in 1941: BUSHIPS to SECNAV via Certification Supervisory Unit, 22 Jan 1941 and 25 Nov 1941, General Correspondence of the Bureau of Ships, 1940–45 (hereafter BUSHIPS GENCORR 1940–45), RG 19, National Archives, Washington National Records Center (NA/WNRC), Suitland, MD.

quire new facilities to meet BUSHIPS's demand, the SUPSHIPS had to find at least two "reputable firms who are in a position to provide the facility at a reasonable cost and in the time required and to make the contract with that firm which quotes the minimum price under satisfactory conditions." [36] As the BUSHIPS representative, SUPSHIPS had to attend all negotiating sessions with the contractors and he alone had the authority to sign an agreement for the bureau.

To provide SUPSHIPS with sufficient negotiating flexibility, the bureau gave him authority to employ any one of four contract forms for these agreements.[37] The first was a firm-price document that limited profit to 8 percent of any contract exceeding $25,000. The second, the fixed-fee type of contract, restricted the fee, or the amount of profit, to 7 percent of the total estimated project cost. The last two contract forms offered variations on these types. The fixed-fee-with-bonus contract provided a special bonus along with a fixed fee, the total not to exceed 7 percent of the estimated cost. The last type provided a variation on the firm-price type by permitting adjustment clauses for labor and materials. In all four types, BUSHIPS warned the supervisors that each "of the facilities should be the minimum which could be reasonably expected to accomplish the intended purpose, due consideration being given to time and cost." [38]

The bureau then expected SUPSHIPS to provide monthly progress reports on each project, complete with essential contract data, plans, and photographs. He was also responsible for acquisition of the required machinery and tools. BUSHIPS would assist the supervisor in setting priorities affecting materials and delivery, as well as the establishment of any new facilities required by subcontractors.

Electric Boat and Manitowoc

Armed with these incentives, in the summer of 1940 the Navy Department began building an elaborate network of reliable submarine con-

---

[36] BUSHIPS to SUPSHIPS, Bath, Quincy, et al., 2 Aug 1940, box 8, Assistant SECNAV Alpha File, RG 80, NA.

[37] Once a contract agreement went into effect, BUSHIPS applied the same system of on-site supervision at the shipyards and factories for submarines as it did for surface ships. A SUPSHIPS and his staff of inspectors and engineers took up residence at each shipyard. They reported to BUSHIPS on the progress of construction as well as on weight and cost changes at variance with the contract design. As the on-site representative of BUSHIPS, the SUPSHIPS's office also approved or rejected any design changes suggested by the vendor. In addition BUSHIPS provided a corps of resident and itinerant purchasing inspectors of both naval machinery and naval materials who supervised the production of related parts and systems at a host of subcontractor plants all over the country. In this way the bureau tried to ensure that the shipyards built sound vessels and the subcontractors delivered systems to the yards that met naval specifications and standards.

[38] BUSHIPS to SUPSHIPS, Bath, Quincy, et al., 2 Aug 1940, box 8, Assistant SECNAV Alpha File.

tractors upon the foundation of vast experience available at Electric Boat and at Portsmouth Naval Shipyard in New Hampshire. To amplify the Navy's effort at Portsmouth, BUSHIPS expanded the services at Mare Island Naval Shipyard, Mare Island, California, and reintroduced the Cramp Shipbuilding Company of Philadelphia to submarine construction. Both of these yards would take technical direction from Portsmouth. In the private sector Secretary Edison reached an agreement with EB to enlarge dramatically the company's facilities in Groton, Connecticut, and Bayonne, New Jersey. The Navy Department also drew Manitowoc Shipbuilding Company (MSC) of Manitowoc, Wisconsin, into the submarine business as a follow-yard for EB. To this core of five prime contractors the Navy Department gradually added a network of subcontractors from all over the country, supplying everything from diesel engines to periscope optical sets.

The plan to expand Electric Boat's facilities at Groton and Bayonne marked the first step in the creation of this network and the Navy Department's first use of its emergency powers in the submarine industry. Negotiations began in the early summer of 1940. In a communication to BUSHIPS on 25 June 1940, Electric Boat's vice president, Lawrence Y. Spear, estimated that the company would need about $ 1.5 million to accomplish the necessary plant extensions. Spear believed that if "a negotiated contract is placed with us for thirteen submarines in addition to the three recently awarded us, additional plant facilities will be necessary to enable us to make the deliveries required by the Department." [39]

As the negotiations for plant expansion continued in the summer of 1940, the estimate of the company's needs grew with the increased naval construction authorizations of June and July. At a meeting held on 10 June 1940, the Navy Department and EB agreed that the latter would receive $1,422,000 under contract Nod–1541 to improve its physical plant and purchase new tools to expedite delivery of the sixteen submarines currently on order. EB's main plant at Groton received $1,261,000, and the remaining $161,000 went toward improving the company's Electro-Dynamic motor plant in Bayonne, New Jersey. [40] EB's cost estimate for

[39] L. Y. Spear to BUSHIPS, 25 Jun 1940, box 403, BUSHIPS GENCORR 1940–45, RG 19, NA/WNRC.

[40] BUC&R–BUENG Joint Memo, "Electric Boat Company, Groton, Conn." 10 Jun 1940, box 403, BUSHIPS GENCORR 1940–45. By 1942, the total expenditure on the Electro-Dynamic Works at Bayonne amounted to $476,000. Electro-Dynamic Works, Bayonne to BUSHIPS, 27 Jan 1942, box 404, BUSHIPS GENCORR 1940–45.

The initial arrangement gave EB title to those construction facilities and tools for which it paid 50.5 percent of the cost. The government was vested with those facilities for which it paid the whole price. For an example of the 100-percent Navy ownership contract, see BUSHIPS to Allis-Chalmers, 1 Jan 1942; and BUSHIPS to Director of Purchases, OPM, 30 Apr 1941, box 113, BUSHIPS GENCORR 1940–45.

The old yard on the north side of Electric Boat Company, one of the Navy's prime submarine contractors, July 1945.

the project rose to $2,633,100 when the Navy Department funded twenty-five of the additional submarines authorized by the Seventy Percent Expansion Act of 19 July.[41] In each case, upon receiving the Navy Department's assistance, EB agreed that "throughout the useful life of this facility, the Government will be given priority in the use thereof, and the facility will be preserved for National Defense purposes."[42]

After the United States entered the war, both submarine orders and naval investment in EB increased. By the summer of 1942 BUSHIPS reestimated the cost of expanding the company's facilities at $4,650,000.[43] In addition, during the year preceding the attack on Pearl Harbor, Electric Boat committed $1 million of its own funds for capital improvements. As a

[41] SUPSHIPS to BUSHIPS, 6 Aug 1940; EB to SUPSHIPS, 5 Aug 1940, box 403, BUSHIPS GENCORR 1940–45.

[42] EB to SUPSHIPS, Groton, 14 Aug 1940 and 24 Jul 1940; Lewis Compton (Acting SECNAV) to EB, 23 Sep 1940, box 1986, BUSHIPS GENCORR 1940–45.

[43] When the work was completed in 1943, the total amount invested in Nod-1541 came to $4,991,250. EB to BUSHIPS, 3 Feb 1943, box 407, BUSHIPS GENCORR 1940–45.

To accommodate the Navy's need for new submarines, Electric Boat built the new Victory Yard, south of company headquarters in Groton, July 1945.

result, the rate of construction rose from 9.15 submarines per year before the summer of 1940 to approximately 15 submarines per year two years later.[44]

In January 1942 the Navy Department authorized a further expansion of the company's facilities at a site formerly occupied by the old Groton Iron Works.[45] The government quickly acquired this site, just one-half mile down Eastern Point Road from the main EB plant, after the local press reported that a Norwegian firm had expressed interest in the property.[46] Under BUSHIPS contract Nobs–380, the bureau built a government-owned shipyard at this location, which became known as the

[44] CAPT N. L. Rawlings (Liaison Officer for the Price Adjustment Board and Head of Shipbuilding for BUSHIPS) to Price Adjustment Board, 12 Jun 1942, box 405, BUSHIPS GENCORR 1940–45.

[45] EB to SUPSHIPS, Groton, 14 Aug 1940 and 24 Jul 1940; Compton to EB, 23 Sep 1940, box 1986; Rawlings to Price Adjustment Board, 12 Jun 1942, box 405, BUSHIPS GENCORR 1940–45.

[46] Forrestal (Acting SECNAV) to FDR, 2 Jan 1942; "Minutes of Conference," 31 Dec 1941; BUSHIPS to SECNAV, 2 Jan 1941, box 403, BUSHIPS GENCORR 1940–45.

Victory Yard. In this case an investment of $9,410,757 enabled EB to further increase its output by nine submarines each year.[47]

The Navy Department soon discovered that its investment in EB contributed to lower submarines costs. According to a BUSHIPS's note to the national Price Adjustment Board, the contract price for EB submarines dropped $150,000 between 12 June 1940 and 9 September of the same year. Twenty-four months later BUSHIPS and EB completed the facilities expansion initiated under Nod–1541 and Nobs–380.[48] With new plant space, tools, and scores of boats on order, the Navy Department paid $345,000 less than the June 1940 price levels for each of the twenty-five submarines awarded to EB in 1942 under contract Nod–1513.[49]

Manitowoc Shipbuilding Company

In 1940 BUSHIPS drew another private contractor into the submarine business as a support facility for EB. The Manitowoc Shipbuilding Company entered into an agreement with the Navy in September to build EB submarines under license. The bureau decided to pursue a long production run with the *Gato*-class submarines; Manitowoc would provide the Navy with duplicates of its *Growler* (SS 215) design, first produced by EB at Groton. MSC would employ this submarine as a prototype for the SS 265–274 series, using EB patents, supervision, training, and special systems installation.[50]

---

[47] Rawlings to Price Adjustment Board, 12 Jun 1942, box 405, BUSHIPS GENCORR 1940–45.

[48] LT R. B. Carothers, Officer in Charge of Construction, to BUSHIPS, 24 Jul 1943, box 407, BUSHIPS GENCORR 1940–45.

[49] Rawlings to Price Adjustment Board, 12 Jun 1942, box 405; EB to BUSHIPS, 18 Aug 1943, box 1988, BUSHIPS GENCORR 1940–43.

Some naval officers viewed some of the price reductions made by EB with skepticism. Given the limits on profit written into all Navy contracts, it occasionally appeared as if the company was reducing its prices and liabilities in its own way rather than waiting for the Navy Department to do so via renegotiation. What a company executive might view as good business sense drew a different reaction from "AMM" (Captain Armand M. Morgan, head of BUSHIPS Submarine Section). The route slip attached to the 18 August source, cited above, reads: ". . . it does not look like any great gift to me. A contract price of $2,612,800 per submarine is *not* low & the charges canceled are to the contractor's favor. Also, is this not preempting the renegotiation system? However, the proposal, if legal, would reduce the paperwork in the Supervisor's office and thus advance the war effort and has merit on this basis."

The savings at EB were more substantial than BUSHIPS had managed to get with Portsmouth and Mare Island. On the *Gato* class, the Navy's first generation of fleet submarines, EB's total cost amounted to approximately $4,674,000. Portsmouth exceeded this amount by nearly $1 million, and Mare Island topped that by another $140,000. The Navy Department expected this disparity and realized the difficulty of making a valid comparison. See below for the McShane Report and a further discussion of this matter.

[50] EB–Manitowoc Agreement, 14 Sep 1940; Manitowoc to SUPSHIPS, Manitowoc, 2 and 22 Nov 1940, box 1986, BUSHIPS GENCORR 1940–45. By autumn 1941 MSC had decided to set aside private and Maritime Commission construction in order to concentrate on building the Navy's submarines. The reason given was the Navy Department's investment in MSC since 1940, especially in terms of plant expansion and retooling. MSC to BUSHIPS (CDR N. L. Rawlings), 5 Nov 1941; SUPSHIPS, MSC (CDR G. C. Weaver), 29 Oct 1941, box 704, BUSHIPS GENCORR 1940–45.

Building submarines on the western shore of Lake Michigan inspired some interesting innovations in construction and delivery. To permit year-round work, MSC built its submarines in segments inside heated construction sheds. The sections then traveled to the ways by mechanical doodlebug, or tractor-mover. Here the yard force installed the machinery and welded the hull sections together. The company then slid the vessels sideways into the Manitowoc River, a waterway too narrow to permit the traditional stern-first launch. After each submarine passed acceptance trials in Lake Michigan, MSC turned the vessel over to the Inland Waterways Corporation, which brought each boat down the Mississippi River to New Orleans on a barge from Lockport, Illinois.[51]

This arrangement initially placed a considerable burden on Electric Boat. The company agreed to "license Manitowoc under all patents owned or controlled by it which may be used in the construction of the said ten submarines." In addition to providing experts to supervise and assist in the construction at Manitowoc, EB negotiated with its *Gato*-class subcontractors for the purchase of materials required by MSC. The Groton firm even carried the insurance that protected the vessels after they reached New Orleans and began the final stage of their trip to Groton. Once the submarines arrived, EB had to install the periscopes and masts. All of these services were rendered for a sum equal to their cost, plus a fixed fee of $126,560.[52]

The advantage of this arrangement to the Navy was the speed and simplicity in acquiring a large number of submarines in the most cost-effective manner. Secretary Edison and his successor, Frank Knox, believed this plan would save design and construction time and the expense of new tools and equipment, spare parts, planning, and testing.[53]

The Manitowoc agreement proved successful in spite of some initial difficulty. Although Electric Boat cooperated with BUSHIPS as the plan unfolded, the company exhibited a degree of reluctance to extend to

---

[51] SUPSHIPS, MSC, to Commandants, Mare Island and Portsmouth, 16 Oct 1941, box 703; Memo of a Conference in Captain Jones' Office at the Bureau of Ships, 9:30 a.m., 17 Sep 1940, box 701; MSC to BUC&R/BUENG, 22 May 1940, box 701; Weaver to BUSHIPS, 1 Dec 1943, box 1986, BUSHIPS GENCORR 1940–45. William T. Nelson. *Fresh Water Submarines: The Manitowoc Story* (Manitowoc, WI: Hoeffner Printing, 1986), chaps. 2 and 3.

In 1943 the Germans employed similar techniques in a much more ambitious effort to employ factories all over the country to mass-produce the Type XXI high-speed U-boat. The Ministry of War Production under Albert Speer commissioned General-Director Otto Merker of the Magirus-Works (automobiles) in Ulm to undertake this kind of sectional construction and assembly. E. Rössler, *Geschichte des Deutschen Ubootbaus* (Munich: J. F. Lehmanns Verlag, 1975), 297ff.

[52] EB–Manitowoc Agreement, 14 Sep 1940, box 1986, BUSHIPS GENCORR 1940–45, RG 19, NA/WNRC.

[53] For a discussion of these motives, see BUSHIPS to Bureau of Supplies and Accounts, 23 May 1941, box 1987, BUSHIPS GENCORR.

A hull section of *Growler* (SS 215), an Electric Boat submarine, March 1941. Using EB's designs, patents, and supervision, Manitowoc Shipbuilding Company in Wisconsin built clones of the *Growler* on the Great Lakes during World War II, March 1941.

the new contractor all of the supervisory and technical assistance the agreement required.[54] Although its directors negotiated for Manitowoc, Groton refused to place orders or guarantee that its private subcontractors would offer Manitowoc the same prices EB paid on long-term projects. Electric Boat expected few of its suppliers to sign a long-term agreement without some provision for rising costs and prices.

These circumstances caused a certain degree of tension between the staff at MSC, led by Charles C. West, MSC's president, and the visiting experts sent by EB, under its agreement with Manitowoc, to give advice on submarine construction. According to observations made by Comman-

---

[54] Sun Shipbuilding and Drydock of Chester, Pennsylvania, tried to enter the submarine market in 1933 but was forced out by EB. According to communications between Sun, the Navy JAG, BUC&R, and BUENG, the company had to raise its price beyond the acceptable range to the Navy in order to cover the costs of royalties on EB submarine patents. The bureaus were not in the position at the time to grant Sun a waiver of patent liability, given the importance of EB to the Navy's new plans for construction in the early 1930s. Sun Shipbuilding Co. to JAG, #SS/L4–2 (350703–1), 18 Jul 1935; BUC&R and BUENG to JAG, #SS/L4–2 (350703–1), 30 Jul 1935, box 4020, SECNAV GENCORR 1926–40, RG 80, NA.

Hull section of *Pogy* (SS 266), a *Gato*-class submarine, built at Manitowoc Ship-building Company, September 1941.

der Armand M. Morgan, wartime director of the Submarine Section of BUSHIPS, West and his staff did not like the attitude of the EB advisors. At the time Commander Morgan noted that "neither Supship, Mani-towoc (Comdr Weaver) nor Mr. West want EB Co supervision. Mr. West has privately told me that he resents EB Co attitude of ownership." This kind of friction was to be expected in an unusual relationship of this sort. Electric Boat took exception to the idea of aiding a possible postwar com-petitor, but in the end it reluctantly fulfilled its contract obligations.[55]

Considerable administrative costs represented an important reason for EB's lack of enthusiasm for its role in the Navy Department's plans for Manitowoc. On the strength of naval investment in the company's facili-ties and the promise of new contract awards, EB became a conduit for much of the material and many of the systems needed to build the com-pany's *Gato*-class designs. BUSHIPS permitted Manitowoc to make local purchases of those items not peculiar to EB designs. But the Groton firm

---

[55] It should be mentioned here that Commander Morgan tended to be highly critical of EB's busi-ness practices. BUSHIPS to EB (route slip for the Morgan comment), 29 Mar 1943, box 406, BUSHIPS GENCORR 1940–45, RG 19, NA/WNRC. See also the route slip on the following docu-ment related to price reductions initiated by EB in 1943: EB to BUSHIPS, 18 Aug 1943, box 1988, BUSHIPS GENCORR 1940–43.

had to negotiate the procurement of unique materials and systems for all of the yards using EB *Gato* plans, billing the Navy Department at cost and absorbing most of the labor and administrative charges.[56]

Portsmouth, Mare Island, and Cramp

EB had its design, engineering, and construction capabilities expanded with the addition of MSC as a follow-yard. In a like manner, the Navy extended the considerable material and human resources at Portsmouth by duplicating the yard's designs at both Mare Island and Cramp Shipbuilding.

Between 1940 and 1943 the Navy Department commissioned an expansion of the facilities and work force at Portsmouth to ensure that it could sustain the yard's productive capacity as well as its role as the country's leading submarine builder.[57] Employing 11,000 workers in 1941, Portsmouth increased this number to 20,000 in two years. It operated around the clock on a three-shift system, seven days per week, for the duration of the war. Under the command of Rear Admiral Thomas Withers, the yard added a building basin and a new dry dock. In 1942 the Navy Department authorized a new steel-covered shiphouse containing five building ways, and allowed Portsmouth to build an electrical manufacturing shop for the production of electrical boxes and switches.[58]

---

[56] SUPSHIPS, Manitowoc, to BUSHIPS, 10 Apr 1941; F. B. Bently (EB Purchasing Agent) to Eric H. Ewertz (EB Representative at Manitowoc), 25 Feb 1941; EB to SUPSHIPS, Groton, 9 Feb 1942, box 1987, BUSHIPS GENCORR 1940–45.

The *Gato*-class fleet submarine design was derived directly from the design of the *Tambor* class, for which BUC&R served as the design agent, and Portsmouth drew the contract designs. But, as the two primary construction yards, EB and Portsmouth revised the plans in particular ways. Thus while the boats were generally identical, they often differed in particulars—as in the shape of the conning tower or the use of hydraulic rather than electrical power in some cases. John D. Alden, *The Fleet Submarine in the U.S. Navy: A Design and Construction History* (Annapolis: Naval Institute Press, 1979), 54–57; 74–75; 78–79.

When EB charged the Navy for drawing up a new set of SS 215 working plans for MSC, Captain Armand Morgan, drew the attention of his colleagues at the bureau to the fact that EB was already required, as part of its contract with the Navy, to provide the bureau with a set of these drawings on request. To him, the company was paid twice for the same service in this case. Forrestal to MSC, 26 Dec 1940, box 701, BUSHIPS GENCORR 1940–45.

On 13 January 1945 the agreement between EB and MSC was changed—due to the favorable war conditions and the cancellation of many submarine contracts—from a cost-plus-fixed-fee contract to a single fixed-price arrangement set at $570,000. BUSHIPS to SUPSHIPS, MSC, 13 Jan 1945, box 1988, BUSHIPS GENCORR 1940–45.

[57] From 1941 to August 1945 Portsmouth delivered seventy-nine submarines to the Navy. This exceeded EB's total by one. R. E. Winslow III, *Portsmouth-Built: Submarines of the Portsmouth Naval Shipyard* (Portsmouth, NH: Portsmouth Marine Society, 1985), 79. For the pre–World War II role of Portsmouth, see also Weir, *Building American Submarines*.

[58] This facility was located in Somersworth, New Hampshire, some eighteen miles to the northwest of the yard.

These measures, combined with the prewar design and construction capability of the yard, dramatically improved productivity at Portsmouth. As historian Richard Winslow observed, "From four subs in 1941, the Yard produced twelve in 1942, nineteen in 1943, thirty-two in 1944, and twelve through August 1945." [59]

Mare Island Naval Shipyard in California, a follow-yard for Portsmouth during the interwar years, also experienced considerable growth. During the first year of the war in Europe, the yard's work force grew to over 14,000. Before the end of the war, Mare Island built a wide variety of vessels, among them eighteen Portsmouth-designed submarines.

The Navy Department began the first submarines built at Mare Island under the emergency conditions of 1940 by extending existing contracts. *Tinosa* (SS 283) and *Tullibee* (SS 284) benefited from this time- and labor-saving device. To build these copies of the Portsmouth-designed SS 236–239 and the SS 281 and 282, the submarine planning force at Mare Island merely broadened the supply contracts for the two new vessels. According to BUSHIPS the "subject vessels are being constructed at the Navy Yard, Mare Island, and in order to obtain full advantage of the duplication in design, it is essential that identical equipment be furnished." This practice continued into 1942 when Portsmouth supplied procurement services for Mare Island on the contract for the SS 285–291 according to an arrangement then in effect for the SS 228–239 and SS 275–284. In certain cases, to ensure quick production and exact duplication, the Navy Department even negotiated with EB to procure equipment for Mare Island, as well as for Portsmouth and Cramp Shipbuilding.[60]

Under the command of Rear Admiral Wilhelm L. Friedell, Mare Island instituted some creative planning and production practices before and during the war. In 1940 the yard administration divided its unified planning and production departments into specialized offices according to ship type. Thus the yard had a type-superintendent for submarines, supported by engineering specialists and experienced workers.

In 1941, when the increased demand for ships strained the talents and capabilities of the yard's enlarged work force to its limits, BUSHIPS and Mare Island embarked on a farm-out program. The yard employed hundreds of small contractors in California and six other western states. Under this program independent private foundries and factories supplied the yard with thousands of spare parts. The program became even more ambitious after an agreement signed on 2 December 1941 sent most of the work on Mare Island's destroyer escorts and landing craft to Denver.

[59] Winslow, *Portsmouth-Built*, 79–91.

[60] BUSHIPS to Bureau of Supplies and Accounts (BUSANDA), 23 May 1941, box 1987; BUSHIPS to Portsmouth et al., 6 Jan 1942, box 2105, BUSHIPS GENCORR 1940–45.

Naval Historical Center

To meet the demands of war, the Portsmouth Naval Shipyard in New Hampshire added an electrical shop, a dry dock, and a new shiphouse with five building ways, March 1945.

NH 46551

This wartime rally at Portsmouth Naval Shipyard took place on 15 December 1941, eight days after the Pearl Harbor attack.

Private contractors in Colorado shipped the completed vessels, in sections, over the mountains to the yard for finishing and launching. This plan permitted Mare Island to keep the construction of its submarines and larger warships on schedule, while responding to other naval needs.[61]

The Navy Department also sponsored the resurrection of the Cramp Shipbuilding Company. Although Cramp had a long-standing international reputation as a surface-ship producer, it also had limited experience with submarines. Between 1910 and 1914 it built G 4 to Italian designs under contract to the American Laurenti Company. After World War I, the production of American warships declined dramatically, and the results of the Washington Naval Conference of 1921–1922 ensured that this trend would continue. In 1927 Cramp reluctantly withdrew from the shipbuilding business. At the insistence of the Navy Department, the New York firm of Harriman Ripley and Company agreed in 1940 to convert the old Cramp facilities, unused for thirteen years, into a modern shipyard capable of building surface ships and submarines.[62]

Cramp's performance as one of BUSHIPS's five prime submarine contractors during World War II illustrates some of the problems inherent in rapid expansion of firms relatively new to the submarine industry. The successful construction of fourteen submarines at Cramp during World War II also demonstrated the facility with which the Navy Department and BUSHIPS integrated the new firm into a command technology quickly becoming a part of the naval-industrial complex.

Bringing Cramp back to the shipbuilding business immediately placed the company in competition with other yards for factors of production scarce during wartime. The yard found it particularly difficult to recruit skilled labor. According to Captain James S. Bethea, who as a lieutenant commander served as one of the two senior inspection officers for the supervisor of shipbuilding at Cramp,

> The place was opened under the most adverse of conditions that you can think of. All of the competent labor had been hired by the Philadelphia Navy Yard, by New York Ship[building Corporation] across in Camden, and by Sun Ship[building Company] down the river a short way. It became very difficult to hire competent labor. The management in the yard was very, very lacking in know how, in discipline, and in knowledge of how to run an industrial establishment. . . . The Navy further complicated the

[61] Arnold S. Lott, *A Long Line of Ships: Mare Island's Century of Naval Activity in California* (Annapolis: Naval Institute Press, 1954), 207–216.

[62] Henry E. Rossell, President, Cramp Shipbuilding Company, Philadelphia, "Address to the Technology Club of Philadelphia," 15 May 1945, box 133, Records of SECNAV James Forrestal, 1940–47 (hereafter Forrestal Records 1940–47), RG 80, NA. This is the source used for the background information on Cramp.

The Mare Island Naval Shipyard Yard, a follow-yard for Portsmouth, was able to accelerate submarine production by using subcontractors who kept the yard well supplied with spare parts, December 1943.

situation by putting in one of the most complex programs you can think of: building cruisers, submarines, and handling ship conversions. . . . I was exposed daily to how not to do so many things, it could not have been better experience for my career anywhere I wanted to go.[63]

Thus it was not surprising that procuring materials and scheduling emerged as a major problem for Cramp in building the SS 292–303 and the SS 425 and 426. Directed by BUSHIPS to rely on Portsmouth for specifications and procurement assistance, Cramp's submarine builders quickly discovered that Portsmouth had its limits. By the spring of 1942 BUSHIPS decided that Cramp would need additional assistance. The volume of work at Portsmouth increased, making it exceedingly difficult for that facility to provide all of the assistance Cramp required. The company could not turn to EB or Manitowoc because the boats designed at Groton employed different test pressures and a distinctive arrangement of auxiliary systems.[64]

---

[63] CAPT James Bethea, interview with author, 4 Mar 1991, NHC Oral Histories, OA.

[64] SUPSHIPS, Groton, to SUPSHIPS, Cramp, 27 Jan 1942, box 1995, BUSHIPS GENCORR 1940–45, RG 19, NA/WNRC.

Naval Historical Center

The William Cramp Shipbuilding Company faced recruitment and procurement problems when it re-entered the naval-industrial complex for wartime submarine construction. The Philadelphia-based company quickly overcame obstacles and built twelve *Balao*-class submarines during World War II.

In one prominent case Cramp desperately needed a contractor to supplement its supply of torpedo tubes from Portsmouth and Mare Island. By April 1942 the supervisor of shipbuilding at Cramp was urging BUSHIPS to allow the company to develop a private source for these components. Portsmouth could barely supply its own submarines, and Mare Island could furnish Cramp with only eighty tubes. Since each of the SS 292–303 series of *Balao*-class boats under construction at Cramp required six tubes forward and two aft, the consignment from Mare Island would equip only eight of the twelve vessels in question.

Cramp entered into negotiations for torpedo tube fabrication with the E. I. du Pont de Nemours & Company of Wilmington, Delaware, and the Kohler Company of Kohler, Wisconsin. On 15 June 1942 Kohler signed a letter of intent to supply Cramp with torpedo tubes for its submarines. The initial agreement placed an order for forty tubes with Kohler, on a cost-plus-fixed-fee arrangement, to allow the company to "tool up and get into production." Thereafter Kohler would supply another 180 tubes at a firm price.[65]

Even after Cramp secured Kohler as a supplier, the shipyard ran the risk of not completing its submarines on schedule. In support of the Cramp-Kohler agreement the Navy Department signed a facilities expansion contract with Kohler that included vital machine tools. When the firm failed to receive this equipment on time, Kohler and Cramp once again felt the anxiety of falling behind schedule.

The importance of schedules and the pressure placed on the yards to deliver on time led many firms to overcompensate by demanding early delivery on all of the materials, systems, and tools needed to complete the vessels. Cramp reacted in this way during the Kohler episode. Naval authorities responded by agreeing to the company's request for a conference to resolve problems of timely delivery and production schedules, while rejecting Kohler's appeal for early consignment on all of the contract items. The latter request had caused Commander Morgan of BUSHIPS Submarine Section to comment that long-term delivery of material to Cramp should not cause delay.

> This material as promised, . . . should *not* cause a delay in the completion of the vessels. Cramp's demands are unreasonable and unnecessary. Ports[mouth] builds a submarine from keel laying up to completion in less than nine months. Cramp wants the steel for the C. T. (conning tower) almost last thing put on, about 1 year before completion. I cannot recommend diverting material needed at *producing* yards to fulfill such a request." [66]

Of course Cramp did not have the experience with submarines found at Portsmouth. But with the training of the interwar period behind them, the Navy Department and BUSHIPS had sufficient background in working with submarine contractors to satisfy Cramp's needs while effectively integrating the new company into the complex technical and business relationships that produced fleet submarines.[67]

---

[65] SUPSHIPS, Philadelphia, to BUSHIPS, 15 Apr 1942; Cramp to SUPSHIPS, Philadelphia, 9 Apr 1942; Cramp to SUPSHIPS, Philadelphia, 10 Aug 1942; Letter of Intent, Kohler to Cramp, 15 Jun 1942 (source of quote); SUPSHIPS, Philadelphia, to Cramp, 6 Jun 1942, box 2122, BUSHIPS GENCORR 1940–45.

[66] Route Slip (signed AMM [515] 8/10/42), SUPSHIPS, Philadelphia, to Inspector of Naval Material, Pittsburgh, 8 Aug 1942, box 2108, BUSHIPS GENCORR 1940–45.

[67] SUPSHIPS, Philadelphia, to BUSHIPS, 15 Apr 1942; Cramp to SUPSHIPS, Philadelphia, 9 Apr 1942; Cramp to SUPSHIPS, Philadelphia, 10 Aug 1942; Letter of Intent, Kohler to Cramp, 15 Jun 1942 (source of quote); SUPSHIPS, Philadelphia, to Cramp, 6 Jun 1942, box 2122; Cramp to BUSHIPS, 30 Oct 1942; Cramp to SUPSHIPS, Philadelphia, 4 Aug 1942, box 2108; Subcontract between Cramp Shipbuilding Co. and Kohler Co., 15 Jun 1942, box 2106, BUSHIPS GENCORR 1940–45.

The initial failure of BUSHIPS to supply a sufficient number of torpedo tubes as "government furnished items" from Portsmouth, EB, or Mare Island reflected the strain placed on industrial resources by naval requirements in the early months of the war.[68] Cramp's agreement with Kohler for the *Balao*-class torpedo tubes illustrates that both BUSHIPS and the Navy Department's prime contractors made the most of available resources and, when required, extended the network of competent subcontractors serving the building yards.

Construction Costs

Of the five building yards producing the Navy's submarines during the war, EB did the job more cheaply than any of the others. On its contract for the SS 222–227 and SS 240–264, EB recorded a unit cost of $2,765,000. It was $284,500 less than Manitowoc's and $846,250 less than Cramp's costs. Since Cramp and Manitowoc were relative newcomers to submarine construction, EB's considerable experience would account for some of these differences. But EB was also less expensive than highly experienced Portsmouth. When these two yards were compared by the Price Adjustment Board in the spring of 1942, EB's unit cost on the SS 222 fell below those recorded at Portsmouth and Mare Island by about $1 million.[69]

This difference did not surprise the Navy Department. In 1938 the department had Lieutenant Commander Ralph E. McShane compare the cost of building ships at private yards and naval facilities. In his report McShane concluded that the private yards would produce ships more cheaply. Without underestimating the capital risks borne by the private sector in doing business with the Navy, McShane cited higher government pay rates and liberal leave policies, as well as the burden of soliciting and administering the bidding for all submarine contracts as some of the primary reasons for higher costs at the naval shipyards.[70]

Portsmouth compensated for its more expensive unit costs by building its vessels faster than any other facility in the early months of the war. In the

---

[68] "Government furnished items" was contract jargon for materials and systems that, according to the contract, the Navy Department agreed to procure for the company or shipyard in question.

[69] Price Adjustment Board to Rawlings, and reply, 18 May and 12 Jun 1942, box 405, BUSHIPS GENCORR 1940–45.

[70] Rawlings to Price Adjustment Board, 12 Jun 1942, box 405, EB to BUSHIPS, 18 Aug 1943, box 1988, BUSHIPS GENCORR 1940–43. "The Problem of Comparing the Costs of Ships Built at Navy Yards With Ships Built at Private Yards," 1940 (written 1938), box 8, Assistant SECNAV Alpha Files, RG 80, NA. McShane did not underestimate the problem of comparing the two types of shipyards and the different determining factors affecting each in its own environment. A comparison could be made only in the most general terms, citing the most outstanding factors involved.

spring of 1942 it took EB an average of fourteen months to complete a submarine. Portsmouth did the job in nine and one-half months; it took Mare Island twelve, and Cramp, seventeen. Throughout the war Portsmouth compared well with EB in this aspect of submarine construction, actually building one more vessel than its Groton competitor by war's end.[71]

Observations

Between 1940 and 1943 the Navy Department, armed with congressional support, successfully directed a dramatic increase in both the submarine force and the industrial base for submarine construction. This process demonstrated a renewed commitment to submarines and marked the birth of the naval-industrial complex for submarines.

These events were the product of a forty-year evolution. In the crucible of the interwar period naval authorities, plagued by fiscal and technical trials, defined the type of vessel and the strategy they wished to employ as well as the character of the naval-industrial relationship. Then between 1940 and 1943 the Navy Department used its dominant position in the command technology for submarines to fashion a central core of building yards according to its preferred strategy and production planning. With American preparation for war, the old command technology gave way to a thoroughly integrated naval-industrial complex for submarines. From now on, working closely with the submarine force and anticipating their needs became an integral part of the private sector's recipe for prosperity.

In the process of enlarging American submarine construction capability, the Navy Department naturally encountered some fundamental difficulties. Cramp's anxiety over construction and delivery schedules, the resentment at MSC over Electric Boat's ownership attitude, and the technical challenges of building submarines on the Great Lakes were just a few. But overcoming these complications demonstrated the flexibility of the naval-industrial relationship and the excellent management skills exhibited by the significant players in this drama, such as Charles West of MSC, Secretary Charles Edison, Rear Admiral Samuel Robinson of BU-SHIPS, and Lawrence Spear of EB. Because of their efforts, the United States entered the war with five shipyards building the standardized *Gato*-class fleet submarine, rather than just two.

---

[71] Price Adjustment Board to Rawlings, and reply, 18 May and 12 Jun 1942, box 405, BUSHIPS GENCORR 1940–45, RG 19, NA/WNRC.

The new Allis Chalmers electric control shop, April 1942.

Chapter 2

Subcontractors and Scientists, 1940–1943

Mobilization involved much more than congressional funding and the interaction between the Navy and its prime contractors. Building and operating submarines depended heavily upon both the people who possessed an unrivaled knowledge of the ocean environment and those able to supply essential systems and components. As submarine warfare and antisubmarine warfare (ASW) became more significant and sophisticated in the critical years between 1940 and 1943, the scientists and industrialists, working outside the shipyard gates and the Navy Department buildings, took their place in the front rank of those essential to the development and operation of the emerging naval-industrial complex. They included the dizzying array of specialized companies meeting every need of the shipyards, as well as hundreds of scientists working for the Navy and the National Defense Research Committee (NDRC). Together with the shipyards and the Navy, these two sources provided the final ingredient for the naval-industrial complex fashioned by World War II.

The success of the submarine construction program from 1940 through 1943 depended not only on the five yards that formed the core of American construction capability, but also on the network of subcontractors that supported them. Like the building yards, the Navy's major subcontractors also participated in the facility expansion program. In this way the experiences of yards and subcontractors were similar. Yet their individual capabilities and the highly specialized nature of their products posed different challenges for the developing naval-industrial complex for submarines.

Although mobilization drew scores of contractors into the submarine business, a careful examination of naval interaction with a few leading companies demonstrates some of the essential characteristics of the naval-industrial complex in this period. The Navy Department's relationships with Kollmorgen Optical Corporation of Brooklyn, New York, General Motors Corporation (GM) of Detroit, Michigan, and Hooven, Owens, Rentschler (HOR) of Hamilton, Ohio, afford an excellent opportunity to draw a more complete picture of the naval-industrial complex as it emerged in the early years of World War II.

Subcontractor Expansion and Mobilization

The Kollmorgen Optical Corporation was one of the more important small subcontractors and an essential high-tech firm. It had a long history of working with the Navy and held a monopoly on submarine periscopes before and during World War II. Working on a much larger scale, General Motors became a major supplier of the diesel engines that powered the fleet submarines during the war. With the Navy Department's help, GM embarked on a massive expansion program and used a complex network of small private subcontractors to respond to increased demand from the Navy. As a result the company produced engines quickly, forcing BUSHIPS and the building yards to address delivery and scheduling problems. The last of the three firms, HOR, became embroiled with BUSHIPS and the Board of Inspection and Survey in a technical debate over the quality of its submarine diesel engines. The interaction on this issue provides interesting insights into technical problem-solving during this period.

Kollmorgen Optical Corporation

In 1940 Kollmorgen was the only American firm producing periscopes and the sole source of research and development services in the field of submarine optics. This ability made the firm vital to the war effort both for reliable standard periscopes and for the development of a high-altitude periscope for spotting aircraft. The latter occupied a particularly important place on BUSHIPS's list of wartime priorities.[1]

Just as BUSHIPS and the Submarine Officers Conference (SOC) set about examining the first experimental Kollmorgen high-altitude periscopes at the Washington Navy Yard in December 1940, the bidding concluded on contract Nod–1551 for the expansion of the company's facilities in Brooklyn.[2] This defense plant contract included lathes, machine tools, and a new four-story facility at the southwest corner of Franklin Avenue and Wallabout Street in New York City. The new plant would enable Kollmorgen to develop the high-altitude periscope and build the eighty-six conventional scopes ordered in the fall of 1940 by the Navy Department through contract Nos–

---

[1] The effectiveness of aircraft in ASW operations made the high altitude periscope particularly necessary to spot approaching aircraft.

[2] JAG to Kollmorgen, 26 Nov 1940 (copy of Nod–1551), box 656, BUSHIPS GENCORR 1940–45, RG 19, NA/WNRC. SOC was an advisory board comprised of operational submariners and engineers who advised the Chief of Naval Operations and the Secretary of the Navy on submarine matters. It was created in 1926.

National Archives, RG 19

Two interior views of Kollmorgen's periscope shop, June 1943.

77942. The contract also included a commitment to provide twenty sets of repair shop spare parts and tool sets. Kollmorgen and BUSHIPS desperately needed the new facility for which the government paid $145,300 including the usual tax waiver because of its importance to the war effort.[3]

Every branch of the Armed Forces relied on Kollmorgen for optical equipment. For example, the firm formed an essential part of the team that fabricated the Norden bomb sight, delivering twenty-five sets of optics a day at peak production late in the war. Kollmorgen also manufactured the spyglass-type telescopes for all branches of the military. Naval authorities regularly expressed concern about this company's ability to fulfill its naval contracts in a timely fashion. In early 1941 SOC did not feel secure that BUSHIPS could rely on Kollmorgen to keep pace with the projected construction plans for new submarines. The minutes of the SOC meeting on 26 January 1941 noted the new Kollmorgen facilities under construction, but nonetheless "remarked that in view of other demands of the defense program on the optical industry, it is not now by any means a certainty that periscope production will meet the need of the new ships."[4]

This concern stemmed particularly from the desire for a well-designed and durable high-altitude periscope. In January 1941, the Navy Department's Committee on the Test of a High Angle Periscope examined three Kollmorgen instruments at the Washington Navy Yard. Type 1 (88–KA–40/1.414) and Type 3 (88–KA–40/1.99) had the same elevation capabilities, 61 degrees above the horizon on low power and 49 on high power. Type 2 (89–KA–40/1.414 H.A.), the new design, provided a dramatic improvement in both categories: 90 and 78 degrees, respectively. At that time, the committee recommended against adopting the newer instrument because of a flaw in the prism tilt mechanism and reduced light transmission.[5]

It took nearly six months of intensive work to correct this problem. Although the complexity of the new Type 2 made it difficult to service while on patrol, the committee nonetheless adopted the instrument for standard use. The submarine force desperately needed its reliable prism tilt device and improved wake, or "feathering," characteristics. These characteristics would improve the range of observation while reducing the visibility of the raised periscope as it cut through the water.[6]

[3] SUPSHIPS, New York, to Kollmorgen, 31 Dec 1940; SUPSHIPS Memo, 27 Dec 1940; Walter Kidde Constructors to Frank S. Parker, Architect and Engineer, 21 Dec 1940, box 656, BUSHIPS GENCORR 1940–45. SOC Memo, 28 Jan 1941, series 2, files 6 and 7, box 5, Subs/UWD, OA.

[4] BUSHIPS to OPNAV, subj: Submarine Officers Conference Report of 26 January 1941, 21 Apr 1941, series 2, file 7, box 5, Subs/UWD. B. H. Walker, *Periscopes, People, and Progress* (North Adams, MA: Excelsior Printing Company, 1984), 11–13.

[5] Report of the Submarine Officers Conference of 28 Jan 1941, 20 Feb 1941, box 214, SECNAV–CNO Correspondence, 1940–41 declassified, RG 80, NA.

[6] CNO to BUSHIPS, 22 Jul 1941, box 1117, SECNAV (including CNO and JAG) GENCORR 1940–42, RG 80, NA.

Only Kollmorgen could provide these vital services. As a result, the Navy Department willingly sponsored the company's further expansion. In spite of a mid-summer strike in 1941 by the International Brotherhood of Electrical Workers, the new Kollmorgen facility was 97 percent complete by October. The company successfully filled its early Navy contracts thanks to the new assets, but still struggled to keep up with orders from the submarine force. As a result, in the spring of 1942, the Navy Department approved the construction of another new facility for Kollmorgen in Long Island City under contract Nobs–176 and at a cost of $264,000.[7]

In the Kollmorgen case, an essential subcontractor found it difficult to keep pace with the submarine construction program. But if the Navy Department discovered a means of rapidly expanding the capacity of the building yards, thereby increasing the number of boats under construction, it could not accomplish the same with periscopes. Even with its expanded facilities Kollmorgen struggled to meet the Navy demand for periscopes, averaging one per day at the height of production in 1944. This work required painstaking research and development as well as the precision crafting of lenses, tubes, and mechanisms.

Expansion in response to a national emergency was much more difficult for highly specialized firms on the cutting edge of important technologies than for the shipyards. Wartime support from the Navy Department transformed Kollmorgen into a much larger firm better able to provide periscopes and research and development services. But the company could neither manufacture these important capabilities overnight nor sustain them without a long-term commitment to submarines both from Congress and the Navy Department.

General Motors Corporation

General Motors experienced different circumstances from Kollmorgen, both in the complexity of the technology and the scale of expansion. This company supplied BUSHIPS with submarine diesel engines from its Cleveland Diesel Engine Division and heat transfer equipment for those engines from another plant in LaGrange, Illinois. GM began producing diesels for the Navy's submarines after 1930, when it acquired the Winton Company of Cleveland, Ohio. It entered a competition to produce the best submarine diesel sponsored by the Bureau of Engineering in 1932 and thereafter became a regular naval vendor for submarine propulsion components.

---

[7] SUPSHIPS, New York, to Assistant SECNAV, 30 Jul 1941; BUSHIPS Memo for the SECNAV and the War Production Board, 11 Apr 1942; Kollmorgen to BUSHIPS, 14 Oct 1941, box 656, BUSHIPS GENCORR 1940–45.

GM's size and resources made it an important contractor for the Navy from the beginning of the war emergency. In October 1941 the company received a letter of appreciation from BUSHIPS for its contribution to the acceleration of diesel production since 1939. The Navy did not fund all of this new construction. Beginning in September 1940, GM committed $1,125,000 of its own funds to increase output.[8]

Soon after the attack on Pearl Harbor, BUSHIPS entered into negotiations with GM to expand the company's facilities to meet the needs of mobilization. The anticipated mass production of submarines and other vessels now made the $75 million in business done by the company in 1941 look modest. With GM already backlogged for $200 million in diesel orders, BUSHIPS placed $307 million in additional engine orders with the company on 15 January 1942.

The naval authorities at BUSHIPS knew how the company would react. J. B. Jackson, assistant general manager at GM's Cleveland Diesel Division, responded with a request for plant expansion assistance "because," as Jackson commented in a conference with BUSHIPS officers, "we feel the capacity is well beyond the use of our ordinary commercial work and that the company would not be warranted in putting its capital into short-time expansion."[9] The surge in production would last only for the duration of the war. GM officials echoed the sentiments of the directors at EB when faced with similar requests from the Navy. GM wanted to support the war effort, but the company could not make commitments that might turn into extraordinary postwar burdens.

The Secretary of the Navy approved the expansion scheme as outlined in BUSHIPS contract Nobs–427. The agreement authorized and funded the acquisition of seventy-six acres of land in Brooklyn Village, Ohio, about 2.5 miles from the main offices of GM-Cleveland, for the purpose of erecting a facility for the production of marine diesel engines. The project would cost the Navy Department $9,960,000.[10]

GM would have little trouble meeting the Navy's diesel requirements. The new facility guaranteed that GM's prewar diesel production would triple, and the engine in question posed no technical problems. In conjunction with the Navy's submariners, the company had mastered the design and manufacture of submarine diesel technology well before the war began. In addition, GM worked with an extensive network of sub-

---

[8] BUSHIPS to C. E. Wilson, 10 Oct 1941; Preliminary negotiations between representatives of BUSHIPS and GM/Cleveland Diesel Engine Division for the expansion of plant facilities, 16 Jan 1942, box 515, BUSHIPS GENCORR 1940–45.

[9] Ibid.

[10] BUSHIPS Memo for SECNAV and Director of Purchases, OPM, 23 Jan 1942; BUSHIPS to JAG, 1 Feb 1942, box 515, BUSHIPS GENCORR 1940–45. The estimated value of the property was $100,000.

contractors who responded quickly to the new demand. According to R. S. Huxtable of the GM-Cleveland administrative department, the company was able to draw immediately upon the resources of 254 subcontractors, with 46 specializing in machine work.[11]

To sustain these activities and keep pace with demand, the Navy Department continued to finance expansion at GM in 1942 and 1943. It invested $7 million in the Electro-Motive Division at LaGrange, Illinois, and another $456,000 in the Harrison Radiator Division at Lockport, New York. In 1942 the company also used government funds to enlarge its engineering department space at the Cleveland Diesel Engine Division.[12]

GM continued as one of BUSHIPS's largest and most important submarine propulsion suppliers until submarine production slowdowns began in late 1943. The company not only worked on standard submarine engines, but also produced an experimental 2,000 horsepower diesel for the bureau in 1942.

During this period rapid expansion and vastly increased production precipitated delivery problems and questions about priorities and schedules. The President did not commission the Army-Navy Munitions Board to set priorities for raw materials, manufacturing, and construction projects until 6 May 1942. It finally ended an open conflict between the Munitions Board and the Office of Procurement and Materials (OPM) over the authority to set standards governing the allocation of war resources.[13]

But some companies, like GM, could not wait for the resolution of this conflict to begin expanding their facilities and increasing their output. As a result the Navy Department frequently had to obtain a priority rating from the board for construction projects already underway or ask for the reconsideration of a low rating to keep an important undertaking well supplied.

The irregular pace of production and delivery also created difficulties in the timely supply of parts and materials. Some contractors needed time to come up to expected production levels. Early in the war the Submarine Supply Center at the Philadelphia Navy Yard suffered from a

[11] BUSHIPS to Wilson, 10 Oct 1941; Preliminary negotiations between representatives of BUSHIPS and GM/Cleveland Diesel Engine Division for the expansion of plant facilities, 16 Jan 1942, box 515, BUSHIPS GENCORR 1940–45.

[12] BUSHIPS to Facilities Section (Production Branch), Office of Procurement and Material, 17 Dec 1942, box 518; Negotiations for the Expansion of Plant Facilities, 18 Feb 1942; BUSHIPS Memo for Assistant Chief of OPM and Director of Purchases, War Production Board, 27 Feb 1942; Short Contract for Nobs–594 (LaGrange), 4 Mar 1942; Memo for Assistant Chief of OPM and Director of Purchases, War Production Board, 25 Feb 1942, box 515; BUSHIPS to H. M. Beshers, War Production Board, Instruction Branch, 9 Jun 1942; Copy of Nobs–594, 20 Feb 1943, box 517; Inspector of Machinery, Cleveland, to BUSHIPS, 4 Feb 1942, box 2021, BUSHIPS GENCORR 1940–45.

[13] Connery, *The Navy and the Industrial Mobilization*, 170ff.

shortage of spare parts and frequently directed the yards and subcontractors to make independent arrangements for material and parts supply.[14] Private industry found this situation disconcerting because the Navy Compensation Board would decide after these transactions just how much recompense a vendor would receive.[15]

For the submarine industry the most important of these delivery and scheduling problems emerged with the early arrival of parts and systems at the building yards. The shipyards could not assemble the boats fast enough and lacked sufficient space to store all of the engines, parts, and materials delivered too early for immediate installation. The growing supply even exhausted the storage space at the U.S. Navy's Diesel Supply Depot in Harrisburg, Pennsylvania.[16]

BUSHIPS addressed the problem by finding additional storage facilities for engines and parts manufactured by GM and other contractors. In one case the submarine base at New London provided an alternative to the Diesel Supply Depot for early engine deliveries to EB. While these conditions persisted, the Navy Department compensated yards, companies, and storage facilities for the costs incurred in the care and preservation of stored submarine components.[17]

In the end the standardized American fleet submarine and its interchangeable components provided the best and most comprehensive solution. BUSHIPS simply began diverting completed engines to submarines ready for diesel installation, whether or not the engine in question was earmarked for that boat or yard.[18] In many cases this practice presented naval and industrial managers with difficulty in keeping track of propulsion systems and their proper destination. But this practice did permit the submarine construction program to stay on schedule.

---

[14] The Pacific coast supply center was located at the Mare Island Naval Shipyard.

[15] BUSHIPS to Commandant, Philadelphia Navy Yard, 19 Jul 1943, box 2010; BUSHIPS to Fairbanks-Morse, 3 Jan 1942, box 432, BUSHIPS GENCORR 1940–45.

[16] Officer in Charge, U.S. Naval Diesel Supply Depot, to BUSHIPS, 20 Jun 1942 (see attached route slip), box 2022, BUSHIPS GENCORR 1940–45.

[17] This problem afflicted other yards as well. The SUPSHIPS at Manitowoc authorized, with BUSHIPS's approval, the construction of an $8,000 prefabricated facility for engine and motor storage. This construction eliminated the costly practice of sending to warehouses all over the city of Manitowoc machinery that had arrived early. For further discussion of this and other examples of delivery problems, see box 2020, BUSHIPS GENCORR 1940–45.

[18] MSC to SUPSHIPS, Manitowoc, 15 Dec 1941; SUPSHIPS, Manitowoc, to BUSHIPS, 15 Dec 1941, BUSHIPS to SECNAV, 19 Dec 1941, Acting SECNAV Forrestal to EB, 27 Dec 1941, box 2020; SUPSHIPS, Groton, to BUSHIPS, 17 Apr 1942, box 2022; Navy Department to HOR, 24 Sep 1941; SUPSHIPS, Groton, to BUSHIPS, 19 Sep 1941; EB to SUPSHIPS, Groton, 17 Sep 1941, box 2019, BUSHIPS GENCORR 1940–45.

Hooven, Owens, Rentschler Company

Like GM, HOR manufactured diesel engines for the Navy's submarines. Unlike the GM product, HOR engines developed a history of technical problems that both the Navy and the company struggled to resolve.[19]

In the mid-1930s HOR participated in a submarine diesel competition sponsored by the Bureau of Engineering that initiated GM and another major engine producer, Fairbanks-Morse and Company of Beloit, Wisconsin, into the corps of naval propulsion contractors. Producing diesels in America under license to Maschinenfabrik Augsburg-Nürnburg (MAN), HOR entered the submarine market in 1934 by introducing the U.S. Navy to a 700-rpm German U-boat power plant capable of 1,300 brake horsepower (bhp).[20]

In the decade before World War II many American diesel producers were plagued by technical problems. Some encountered poor materials, and others found welding technique and quality a recurring problem. With the HOR submarine diesels, brittle steel construction caused parts to break or wear out long before their time.

At first the experts at BUENG, including the innovative and feisty bureau chief, Rear Admiral Harold G. Bowen, attributed the difficulties to departure from the original German designs and expressed confidence in HOR's ability to correct the problem. Admiral Bowen had shipbuilding experience as production manager of the Puget Sound Navy Yard before going to BUENG in 1931 as assistant chief. He assumed command of BUENG in the spring of 1935. Three years into his tenure the inspection of *Salmon* (SS 182) conducted by the Board of Inspection and Survey cited excessive cylinder-head wear, as well as broken piston rods and cross-head nuts, as major flaws in the vessel's performance record. In spite of Bowen's verdict, the board recommended rejection of the HOR engines because they did not meet the dependability requirements of the contract.[21]

Later that month, the board again suggested rejecting HOR diesels, this time after inspecting *Seal* (SS 183). The board found excessive engine block wear and a history of piston rod and nut breakage, in addition to consistently premature wearing of the cylinder heads. Combined with the performance of other HOR engines in the submarine fleet, the

---

[19] HOR was a division of the General Machinery Corporation, incorporated in Delaware.

[20] Weir, "The Navy, Industry, and Diesel Propulsion for American Submarines," 216–17. Brake horsepower is the horsepower measured by the force applied to a friction brake or by an absorption dynamometer attached to a shaft or flywheel. Put simply, it is the horsepower reading obtained when certain standard instruments, like a friction brake, are used to measure the power output of an engine.

[21] Report of Material Inspection of *Salmon* (SS 182) by the Board of Inspection and Survey (Bd I/S), 2 Aug 1938, box 4111–A, SECNAV GENCORR 1926–40, RG 80, NA.

board concluded that "the main engines of the SEAL are in poor condition, are not strong and well built, are evidently still in the experimental stage and do not meet requirements of Article 18 of Contract Nod–728 and recommends that they be not accepted." [22]

The board's evaluation of the HOR diesels touched a nerve in BUENG. Less than two years after taking over as bureau chief, Bowen had decided to introduce the Navy to turbines driven by high-temperature, high-pressure steam and initiated this program with the destroyer *Somers* (DD 381), commissioned in 1937. Made during a time when conventional boiler systems easily met the criteria for propulsion as set down by the Navy's General Board, this decision drew sharp criticism from the operational officers and the Board of Inspection and Survey. Bowen argued that the new system would provide greater economy, while ensuring a safer, cooler, and quieter fire room. Rear Admiral Joseph DeFrees, Director of Shore Establishments at the Navy Department and former Commander Submarine Force, U.S. Fleet, expressed the opposition viewpoint when he commented that the "Chief of the Bureau of Engineering has not sold the high temperature design to operating Naval personnel. *They question the advisability of gambling with National defense by installing experimental and unproven engine designs which are not required to meet the military characteristics laid down by the General Board.*" [23]

It was in the midst of this turbine debate that Bowen had to address the HOR problem. The admiral felt that the engineering prerogatives of his bureau had come into question, and he defended BUENG as the Navy's authority on engineering and "engineering progress." When the Board of Inspection and Survey took the lead in rejecting the HOR engines as it had the high-temperature, high-pressure turbines, Bowen took up the challenge.[24] He reminded the board that its duty lay primarily in seeing that "the terms of the contract and the guarantees are met with respect to new vessels," not in attempting to arrogate to itself functions that properly belonged to the head of BUENG in his capacity as engineer-in-chief of the Navy.[25]

For Bowen the performance of the HOR diesels took second place to a concerted effort to preserve the authority and prerogatives of BUENG. In December 1938 Bowen's frequent adversary on these technical issues, Admiral DeFrees, wrote to Charles Edison, Assistant Secretary of the Navy and director of the naval construction program, condemning the

---

[22] Report of Material Inspection of *Seal* (SS 183) by Bd I/S, 29 Aug 1938, box 4115, SECNAV GENCORR 1926–1940.

[23] Harold G. Bowen, *Ships, Machinery, and Mossbacks* (Princeton, NJ: Princeton University Press, 1954), 64–126 (see especially 97–99). Italics in the original.

[24] BUENG to CNO, 22 Nov 1938, box 7, Assistant SECNAV Alpha File, RG 80, NA.

[25] Bowen, *Ships, Machinery, and Mossbacks*, 99–100.

HOR engines. He presented Edison with a litany of grievances against the HOR products that propelled *Pompano* (SS 181), *Salmon, Seal, Skip-jack* (SS 184), *Sargo* (SS 188), *Saury* (SS 189), *Spearfish* (SS 190), *Sead-ragon* (SS 194), and *Sealion* (SS 195). According to the admiral, "the principal engine defects are excessive cylinder block, cylinder head, and piston rod wear; excessive carbon deposits; piston rod breaks and seizures; broken cross head nuts, and piston ring troubles."

Other major figures within the Navy shared DeFrees's concern. In January 1939, the Chief of Naval Operations, Admiral William D. Leahy, questioned the reliability of the HOR diesels and decided against their installation in *Sealion* and *Seadragon*. The following month, in a letter to Captain Claude A. Jones, the Navy's supervisor of shipbuilding at the Electric Boat Company in Groton, Assistant Secretary Edison argued forcefully against the continued use of HOR engines. In this letter Edison used the argument and supporting evidence supplied by DeFrees in his memorandum submitted two months earlier.

In responding, Captain Jones desperately argued in support of Admiral Bowen's position. To change the engines now or discontinue using the HOR type, he asserted, would deprive the Navy of an important submarine propulsion contractor and jeopardize the timeliness of the entire construction program.[26] In his own letter to Edison, D. R. Battles, the assistant to the vice president of EB, strongly supported Jones, primarily because of the extra costs involved if the production schedule were allowed to slip.[27]

By the spring of 1939 Bowen had prevailed. He argued strongly that remedial measures could successfully address the problems plaguing the HOR diesels. In May he reported that the company had adopted a plan to improve the reliability of the engines by flame-hardening the cylinders and engine blocks, improving the quality of the cylinder heads, and replacing the brittle piston and rod connections with ball and socket joints. BUENG would conditionally accept the engines and allow payment for contract services only after successful completion of the remedial work and demonstrated improvement over a six-month trial period.[28]

---

[26] Minutes of the SOC of 20 December 1938, 6 Jan 1939, box 113, General Board Subject Files 1900–1947, RG 45. Charles Edison to CAPT C. A. Jones, 2 Feb 1939, box 7, Assistant SECNAV Alpha File; Navy Department Memo for Charles Edison penned by RADM J. R. DeFrees, 9 Dec 1938, box 4025, SECNAV GENCORR 1926–40, RG 80, NA.

[27] EB to BUENG, 13 Feb 1939, box 112, General Board Subject Files 1900–47, RG 45, NA.

[28] Bowen to SECNAV via Bd I/S, 23 Mar 1939, box 7, Assistant SECNAV Alpha File; Bd I/S to CNO, 10 Jul 1939; BUENG to JAG, 24 May 1939; BUENG to Files, 6 May 1939, box 4112, SECNAV GENCORR 1926–40, RG 80, NA.

For example, $50,000 was withheld pending the final acceptance of *Sealion*'s main engines. BU-SHIPS to SECNAV, 22 Oct 1940, box 1124, SECNAV GENCORR (including JAG and CNO) 1940–42, RG 80, NA.

Improving these engines consumed valuable time, and progress came slowly. The diesels from *Pompano,* removed from the vessel and sent back to HOR in Hamilton, Ohio, for tests, remained there for a full year while the submarine lay inactive. A report, filed in September 1939 by the Board of Inspection and Survey on *Sealion,* commented on the prohibitive noise in the vessel's engine room. But in October the board gave the improved engines installed in *Salmon* a positive evaluation based upon the alterations done by HOR. Events began to confirm the view at BUENG that the engines could become a reliable submarine propulsion system.[29]

This intense debate over the quality of the HOR diesels did not prevent the company from participating in the plant expansion program in 1940. To sustain the firm as a third source of submarine diesels and a supplier of propulsion systems for small surface craft, Under Secretary of the Navy James V. Forrestal approved a new facility for HOR at a cost of $1,508,500. The company was also drafted into a research and development project funded under defense contract Nod–1428 to increase the power output of the standard submarine diesel to 2,000 hp. It would represent a 25 percent improvement over the engines then available from GM, HOR, and Fairbanks-Morse.

Unfortunately the restored reputation of HOR and its diesels was short lived. In 1939 the Bureaus of Engineering and Construction and Repair were combined as part of the process that created the Bureau of Ships. Admiral Bowen was transferred to the post of director at the Naval Research Laboratory (NRL). When the HOR engines in the *Gunnel* class began to experience gear breakage on a regular basis during 1941 and 1942, the entire history of the engines and the debate surrounding their performance began anew. Without Bowen to lead the fight, Admiral Ernest J. King, in his combined role as CNO and Commander in Chief, U.S. Fleet, ordered the HOR diesels removed from operational submarines and discontinued in future construction.[30]

[29] Preliminary Test—Machinery Retrials of SS–181, 7–8 Sep 1939, box 135, Office of the CNO/Bd I/S (Reports of Inspections, 1925–44), RG 38. Bd I/S Report on the Preliminary Trials of the *Sealion* (SS 195), 25 Sep 1939, box 1123, SECNAV GENCORR (including CNO and JAG) 1940–42; Report of Final Trials and Final Trials of Propelling Machinery—Bd I/S, 3 Oct 1939, SECNAV GENCORR 1926–40, RG 80, NA.

BUENG concurred with Bd I/S that HOR should provide a substantial number of replacement parts against the possibility of continued major breakdowns. On 19 January 1940 BUENG requested twenty-one replacement cylinder blocks from the company.

[30] General Machinery Corp. to SECNAV, 13 Feb 1941; BUSHIPS to JAG, 24 Jul 1941, box 1135, SECNAV GENCORR (including CNO and JAG) 1940–42, RG 80, NA. Naval Inspector of Material at HOR, Hamilton, OH, to BUSHIPS, 4 Aug 1941, box 2019; HOR to BUSHIPS, 21 Jul 1942, box 2024, BUSHIPS GENCORR 1940–45, RG 19, NA/WNRC. VCNO to BUSHIPS, 19 Feb 1943; COMINCH to BUSHIPS, 14 Feb 1943; COMSUBRON 50 to COMINCH, 30 Dec 1942; Commanding Officer, *Gunnel* (SS 253) to CNO, 26 Nov 1942; VCNO to COMINCH, n.d.; BUSHIPS to COMINCH, 27 Feb 1943, box 704, SECNAV–CNO Correspondence, Secret [declassified] Series 1943, RG 80, NA.

In contrast to the Kollmorgen and GM cases, the problems with the HOR diesels revealed a conflict within the Navy Department that resulted in the selection of troublesome submarine engines. Although time and experience proved Bowen correct in his selection of high-temperature, high-pressure steam for surface vessels, the conflict over this technology drove him to defend BUENG against DeFrees, Edison, and the Board of Inspection and Survey. Had he not felt a challenge to the competence of the bureau, Bowen might have evaluated the HOR diesels differently. As it turned out, the conflict that ensued between the Navy's operational, administrative, and engineering communities exacerbated the admiral's natural inclination to place more confidence in himself and his bureau personnel. Thus BUENG fought for the retention of the HOR diesels for reasons that had more to do with politics than engineering.

Science and Submarines

After the Navy and industry, the third vital component of the naval-industrial complex for submarines that emerged during World War II was the Navy's profitable relationship with the scientific community. In the late 1930s, with a war threatening to erupt in Europe and conflict already raging in China, both the Navy and civilian science became aware once again of the value of physics, oceanography, and other sciences to the performance of the submarine fleet. Echo-ranging research at the Naval Research Laboratory had taken the earlier work in the field by Constantin Chilowsky of Switzerland, Paul Langevin of France, and the U.S. Navy's Harvey C. Hayes to the point where the behavior and composition of the ocean medium had become a major factor limiting the range and performance of the latest sonar apparatus developed by the Navy. For the submarine community this problem laid the foundation for some of the most important interwar advances in electronics, physics, and oceanography.[31]

---

[31] Chilowsky moved to the United States before World War II, where he experimented with plastic materials to replace the Rochelle salt crystals originally used in his piezoelectric work before and during the Great War. He was in contact with Dr. John T. Tate, head of Division 6 of the National Defense Research Committee, in October of 1943 on this subject. Chilowsky to Tate, 29 Oct 1943, box 61, Office of Naval Research (ONR)–GENCORR of the Coordinator of Research and Development 1941–45, RG 298, NA. John Herrick, *Subsurface Warfare: The History of Division 6, National Defense Research Committee*, chap. 5, Naval Studies Board Archive, National Academy of Sciences (NSBA/NAS).

The piezoelectric effect, upon which Langevin's work was based, is the process of generating an electric polarization in certain crystals—Rochelle salt, for example—by applying mechanical stress. Langevin's device was a primitive transducer, designed to send out a conical beam of sound from a surface ship or submarine with sufficient power to produce a return echo. It would enable the monitoring vessel to determine the location of the object causing the echo, whether iceberg, animal, ocean bottom, or submarine.

One particularly valuable discovery resulted from a routine sonar training exercise in 1936. Working with their sonar system and an American submarine in the vicinity of Guantanamo Bay Naval Base in Cuba, the crew of the destroyer *Semmes* (DD 189) discovered that their sonar equipment worked well early in the day, but that this level of performance did not continue into the afternoon hours. With Navy approval, a team from Woods Hole Oceanographic Institution (WHOI) in Massachusetts, led by assistant director Columbus O'D. Iselin, returned to the Caribbean with *Semmes*, then under the command of Lieutenant William Pryor. Following Pryor's hypothesis that excessive oxygen bubbles produced by the resident marine life would interfere with sonar sound transmission, the oceanographers studied the water in and out of Guantanamo Bay. The team discovered that horizontal echo-ranging transmissions from the destroyer were affected by the change in surface water temperature as the day became warmer. Iselin christened this process of diurnal warming the "afternoon effect." Specialists in acoustics already knew that temperature dramatically affects the behavior of sound underwater. But this phenomenon varies according to season, time of day, and location. Since a submarine did most of its work in the uppermost layers of the ocean, where the water temperatures vary significantly, this knowledge had direct operational applications absolutely vital to the future success of American undersea warfare.

In 1937 the Submarine Signal Company of Boston and WHOI sent another party of oceanographers and sonar engineers to the Caribbean to gather data on underwater sound propagation. This expedition uncovered the presence of thermal gradients, or layers of dramatic temperature decrease, and their effect on underwater sound transmission. On this project scientists used the bathythermograph (BT), first developed in 1934 at Woods Hole by Carl-Gustav Rossby of the Massachusetts Institute of Technology (MIT) and refined over the next three years by his colleague, the South African, Athelstan Spilhaus.[32] This instrument provided the scientist with data on water temperature variation as depth increased and allowed a better analysis of the all-important course of sonar signals through the water. As historian Susan Schlee observed,

> The [sound] beam was bent either upward or downward each time it
> passed from one layer into another (as light is bent passing through a
> prism) and consequently it could fail to detect a submarine which lay di-

---

[32] Spilhaus was a meteorology student of Rossby's at MIT and worked with the U.S. Army in the Far East in World War II.

rectly in its path. The implications both for submarines and submarine hunters were not difficult to grasp.[33]

The outbreak of the European war in 1939 focused greater attention in the United States on the need both for cooperation between science and the Navy and for federal support for further ocean research. In June 1940 civilian scientists and the Roosevelt administration established the National Defense Research Committee under the direction of Dr. Vannevar Bush, to perform essentially the same task for the Armed Forces as the Naval Consulting Board and National Research Council of World War I.[34]

Responding to these first signs of scientific mobilization, Columbus Iselin, now director of WHOI, suggested on 5 August 1940 that the NDRC tap the institution's facilities and expertise to support the Navy's mission. He felt that, for the Navy, the "meaning of the words 'ocean' and 'atmosphere' seemed to be little more than 'water' and 'air'." Close cooperation with Woods Hole could change that state of affairs. The "Oceanographic" could provide teaching facilities, consultation, independent studies, meteorological services, and the skill to develop and produce precision instruments.

As a result of Iselin's effort, the Navy signed its second contract with WHOI in September 1940, committing both parties to an investigation of underwater sound. This $100,000 agreement resulted in the seminal study entitled "Sound Transmission in Seawater," written by Iselin and Maurice Ewing, the latter a Woods Hole associate and physicist from Lehigh University.[35]

In November the NDRC, at the request of Secretary of the Navy Frank Knox and Admiral Bowen, director of the Naval Research Laboratory and scientific aide to the Secretary, authorized the creation of a subcommittee to investigate the problem of submarine detection and the state of American scientific and technical knowledge in ASW. Dr. Edwin H. Colpitts, a

---

[33] Susan Schlee, *On the Edge of an Unfamiliar World* (Boston: E. P. Dutton, 1973), 285–90. Columbus O'D. Iselin, "WHOI History During the War Years, 1941–1950," [1960?], McLean Laboratory, Woods Hole Oceanographic Institution (WHOI) Data Library/Archives. Herrick, *Subsurface Warfare*, chap. 2.

[34] In 1916 the National Academy of Sciences established the National Research Council (NRC) to facilitate research with military applications through committees of scientific experts in all war-related fields. The academy kept abreast of the latest European advances in underwater sound and submarine detection by gathering scientific intelligence with the aid of its Research Information Service, established during the war by the NRC in Washington, D.C., Rome, London, and Paris.

[35] Herrick, *Subsurface Warfare*, chap. 3; Schlee, *Unfamiliar World*, 281–83; Iselin, "WHOI History During the War Years, 1941–1950," 1–2, 10ff. WHOI's first contract for the Navy, awarded in July 1940, involved a study of marine organisms that fouled the bottom of ships and the development of a paint to reduce the fouling problem. Iselin was director of Woods Hole from 1940 to 1950.

former vice president of Bell Telephone Laboratories, chaired the sub-committee. In January 1941, after two months of intense investigation at a wide variety of naval facilities, the group issued its "Report of the Subcommittee on the Submarine Problem," also known as the Colpitts Report.

The committee's evaluation of the state of America's ASW capability made it clear that the Navy desperately needed to advance its knowledge of the effect of the ocean environment on the submarine. Admiral Bowen rejected the report as something he would find difficult justifying to the Navy Department. But scientists like Frank B. Jewett, president of both Bell Telephone Laboratories and the National Academy of Sciences, and Max Mason, president of the Rockefeller Foundation, gave the report their endorsement and support. Detection methods employed state-of-the-art supersonic echo-ranging equipment that usually worked well up to several thousand yards and under favorable conditions. But in too many instances, natural conditions rendered the ASW vessel blind.

Further oceanographic research and instrument development seemed absolutely necessary. In addition to recommending better training for sound equipment operators, the Colpitts Report suggested long-range research in sound transmission and reception as well as magnetic, microwave, and radio-acoustic devices to supplement standard sound equipment. The Navy and civilian science also had to determine the complete spectrum of underwater sounds emitted from various types of ships under as many conditions as possible in order to improve silencing and detection. Most important, the Colpitts subcommittee urged the Navy to study the "sound propagating properties of oceanic waters over the entire frequency range likely to be involved in the use of detecting devices." They included studies already under way to support the Navy and Merchant Marine, as well as research into variations in temperature, salinity, convection, density, sound scattering, attenuation, and reverberation.[36]

The Colpitts committee appealed to Navy and civilian scientists for research that would provide effective oceanographic data and instruments for the ASW and prosubmarine effort if the United States entered the war in which the U-boat already played an extremely important part. Sounding a call to arms for scientists, Colpitts and his colleagues emphasized, "that a much more comprehensive and fundamental research program is needed. . . . The gravity of the emergency is such that the pre-

---

[36] Herrick, *Subsurface Warfare*, chap. 3; The Colpitts Report ("Report of the Subcommittee on the Submarine Problem"), 28 Jan 1941 (see especially 9), NSBA/NAS. Attenuation is the reduction of the intensity of sound as it moves further away from the source. Reverberation is the continuation of a sound at a given point after direct reception from the source has ceased. It is usually caused by reflection off another surface, scattering due to various kinds of matter often present in air or water, or vibration excited by the original sound. Willem Hackmann, *Seek and Strike: Sonar, Anti-Submarine Warfare, and the Royal Navy, 1914–1954* (London: HMSO, 1984), 251.

sent research facilities and personnel are wholly inadequate. We need the best talent of the country. In these days of aroused patriotism that talent is available." [37]

With the experience of the Great War to guide them, the Roosevelt administration and the scientific community created a more formal and better organized system to address the needs of the Armed Forces if America entered the war against Germany.[38] In response to the Colpitts Report, Rear Admiral Samuel Robinson, chief of BUSHIPS, asked Vannevar Bush, director of NDRC, to create a program for improving the nation's readiness to deal with the U-boat threat. The plan, approved on 18 April 1941 by Robinson, established, under the auspices of NDRC, central laboratories on both coasts that would direct the effort of those occupied with undersea warfare. This action led to the creation of the U.S. Navy Underwater Sound Laboratory (USNUSL) at Fort Trumbull in New London, Connecticut, for the East Coast, and named the U.S. Navy Radio and Sound Laboratory at Point Loma, near San Diego, California, as the central coordinating activity for the West Coast. The Columbia University Division of War Research (CUDWR) was located at USNUSL and operated with the laboratory under contract to the Navy. The University of California Division of War Research (UCDWR) cooperated in the same way with the Radio and Sound Laboratory at Point Loma.[39]

When Executive Order 8807 established the Office of Scientific Research and Development (OSRD) on 28 June 1941, it became the parent organization for the scientific war effort. NDRC became a part of OSRD, which provided the labor and skills required to carry the products of NDRC research through the engineering phase and into war production. Iselin became the director of Oceanographic Studies (section C–4a) for NDRC's Division C (later Division 6), and the physicist Philip

---

[37] The Colpitts Report ("Report of the Subcommittee on the Submarine Problem"), 28 Jan 1941 (see especially 10–11), NSBA/NAS.

[38] The literature on applied science and the U.S. Navy in World War I is limited but growing. The best of the most recent works is Willem Hackmann, *Seek and Strike: Sonar, Anti-Submarine Warfare and the Royal Navy, 1914–1954*. Although Hackmann concentrates on the Royal Navy, his book follows closely the developments in the United States for the entire period covered by the volume. See also, Gary E. Weir, "The Submarine and the Ocean Environment, 1914–1945," in *The Undersea Dimension of Maritime Strategy: A Conference Report*, eds. Dan W. Middlemiss, Fred W. Crickard, and Susan J. Rolston (Halifax, Nova Scotia, Canada: Centre for Foreign Policy Studies, Dalhousie University, 1991), 1–3. The best primary sources are held at the National Archives (RG 80, Secretary of the Navy Correspondence and the Naval Consulting Board), the archives of the National Academy of Sciences, and the Archives of the Hagley Museum (especially the Sperry Papers, as Elmer Sperry was a member of the Naval Consulting Board chaired by Thomas A. Edison).

[39] V. Bush to Members of the NDRC (General NDRC program as approved by RADM Robinson), 21 Apr 1941; S. M. Robinson to Navy Dept. Member of the NDRC (creation and funding of USNUSL), 10 Jun 1941, box 30, ONR–GENCORR of the Coordinator of Research and Development, RG 298, NA.

M. Morse of MIT led the Division on Sound Control (section C–9).[40]
The Navy's Coordinator of Research and Development, an office created
in July 1941 under Rear Admiral Julius A. Furer, served as liaison with
the civilian directors of the nation's scientific war effort.[41]

Under OSRD direction, NDRC negotiated hundreds of contracts with
private companies and research institutions designed to expand the
Navy's knowledge of the oceans. The most outstanding private contractors for oceanographic problems during the war were WHOI, Scripps Institution of Oceanography, La Jolla, California, and the UCDWR. All
three institutions engaged in research designed to solve operational
problems for the submarine fleet, and produced instruments and in-
structional materials to facilitate the quick application of scientific discoveries of value to the war effort.

Woods Hole took the first steps in cooperation with the Navy in the area
of wartime research into undersea warfare. In the process it demonstrated
clearly the various major consequences of a working relationship with the
military. The research entailed a practical problem-solving approach affected by pressures of time and operational demand. As in World War I,
many scientists found themselves violating the careful, painstaking scientific methodology characteristic of their discipline and training. At the
same time the work offered new and interesting subjects for research and
unlimited funds and opportunity to expand oceanographic knowledge.

Woods Hole's work with the BT offered a classic example of research
and development that had both important practical naval applications
and a broad scientific benefit. Given its awkward construction and toler-
ance for only slow surface speeds, the Rossby-Spilhaus version of the BT
required further refinements before the Navy could place it in service.
In October 1940 Maurice Ewing and his assistants, Allyn C. Vine and J.
Lamar Worzel, began working on a more refined and durable version of
the BT for use in both ASW surface ships and submarines. Their goal
was to give the Navy a way of determining sound velocity through seawater. Since water temperature was the most important factor in this calculation, the BT proved to be the perfect instrument. Allyn Vine recalled
that "our problem was not to make it necessarily more accurate but to
make it so that it was ten times more usable." [42]

---

[40] Irvin Stewart, *Organizing Scientific Research for War: The Administrative History of the Office for Scientific Research and Development* (Boston: Little, Brown and Co., 1948), chap. 4; Herrick, *Subsurface Warfare*, chap. 3. Stewart worked for Dr. Bush as the secretary of NDRC in Washington D.C. during World War II.

[41] Harvey M. Sapolsky, *Science and the Navy: The History of the Office of Naval Research* (Princeton, NJ: Princeton University Press, 1990), 20.

[42] Allyn Vine, Scientist Emeritus, WHOI, interview with author, 27 Apr 1989, McLean Laboratory, WHOI, NHC Oral Histories, OA.

During 1941 the WHOI team developed a BT model that could endure depths of over 400 feet and provide accurate data at speeds of between 15 and 20 knots. By 1942 most research vessels and convoy escorts carried BTs, and by spring of that year Ewing and Vine developed a submarine BT (SBT) designed to work from a location on the conning tower.[43] Under Vine's supervision, Woods Hole manufactured two hundred BTs before the Bristol Company of Waterbury, Connecticut, signed a contract to take on this burden in cooperation with WHOI. Bristol was later joined by the Submarine Signal Company, a pioneer in undersea warfare instruments and technology. In estimating the BT's wartime value, Iselin commented that in "the first four years of its use, over 60,000 records were accumulated and processed. From data collected by these, and later by the submarine bathythermographs, new fields of sound transmission phenomena were opened."[44]

As a result of the success of the BT project the Navy sponsored a wide variety of related research projects at Woods Hole. From the BT records and a slide rule developed to calculate the refraction of sound waves, the staff at WHOI proceeded to evaluate more accurately the operational range of the Navy's sonar equipment. In addition, Iselin and A. H. Woodcock explored further the naval implications of the "afternoon effect" and the institute organized many cruises to study underwater sound reverberation.

With the development of the SBT in 1942, Ewing and Vine also created isoballast lines for the standard 3-inch by 5-inch graph on which the SBTs recorded their temperature data. This graph allowed the submarine diving officer to quickly determine the location of density layers caused by dramatic temperature change. This information would provide the probable location of "shadow zones" in which a vessel could escape detection because of the effect of radical temperature change on the speed and direction of the active ASW sonar signal. The isoballast lines provided further insurance by actually giving the diving officer the number of tons of ballast water he would have to take in or pump out in order to maneuver the submarine quietly into the shadow zone and maintain trim without further machinery noise.[45]

In one typical example the submarine *Herring* (SS 233) recorded in its submarine patrol report for the period 11 to 17 June 1943 that the SBT

---

[43] The testing on the WHOI design for the SBT actually began with the deployment of the first of seven models on *S 20* on 12 November 1941. C. Iselin to R. Bennett, 12 Feb 1942, box 62, ONR–GENCORR of the Coordinator of Research and Development, 1941–1945, RG 298, NA.

[44] Iselin, "WHOI History During the War Years, 1941–1950," 10ff; Vine interview, 27 Apr 1989.

[45] Iselin, 11–13; Vine interview, 27 Apr 1989; "Use of Submarine Bathythermograph Observations as an Aid in Diving Operations" (joint publication of WHOI, BUSHIPS, and NDRC), Mar 1944, courtesy of Allyn Vine.

allowed the diving officer to determine increasing water density as the temperature decreased with depth near Palau.[46] This information "enabled him to adjust his trim so that during the search following each attack while we were deep he never had to pump, blow or increase speed to maintain depth." [47]

In addition to their research and instrument development, the WHOI faculty instructed naval officers both at Woods Hole and in the field in the operational application of naval oceanography. The faculty wrote manuals, held classes, rode the submarines giving lessons on the use of instruments, and acted as advisors to the commanders of American submarine forces in the Atlantic and Pacific. Woods Hole, in conjunction with the Naval Hydrographic Office in Washington, D.C., and Scripps, also participated in the creation of the series of booklets called "Submarine Supplements to Sailing Directions," which provided submarine officers with additional information regarding the most critical characteristics of the ocean in various war zones.[48]

The Navy's Pacific Coast work in wartime oceanography also illustrated the influence of the war on science and independent research institutions. Woods Hole managed to retain its independence and identity as a center for oceanographic research through the war years while working for the Navy. It did not fall under the shadow of other OSRD and Navy facilities on the East Coast, like the Navy's underwater sound lab and the Division of War Research at Columbia University. But neither could it carry the burden of satisfying all of the Navy's needs, especially in underwater sound. As a result, OSRD contracted with the University of California on 26 April 1941 to create the university's Division of War Research at Point Loma. As indicated in its charter, the "original primary objective of the Laboratory was the prosecution of fundamental sonar studies." Its major divisions covered sonar research, the development of sonar systems, and the training of naval personnel in the maintenance and use of sonar equipment.[49]

---

[46] Palau is an island in the south Pacific, roughly midway between the Philippines and the Caroline Islands.

[47] *Herring* (SS 233), 11–17 Jun 1943, book 2, Submarine Patrol Reports, Hawkbill to Whale, 1942–1944, McLean Laboratory, WHOI Data Library/Archives.

[48] Iselin, "WHOI History During the War Years, 1941–1950; "Compilations of Reports etc. for Sss in WW II"; R. J. McCurdy, "Report on Discussions With Captain Baker and Commander Todd Concerning Some Oceanographic Aspects of Anti-Submarine Warfare, August 1, 1942," McLean Laboratory, WHOI Data Library/Archives. The American scientific community also tapped the British experience in wartime oceanographic research when a member of the Woods Hole faculty, William Schevill, journeyed to Great Britain in 1943.

[49] Herrick, *Subsurface Warfare*, chap. 4; "Completion Report Made to the Chief of the Bureau of Ships Covering the Operations of the University of California Division of War Research at the U.S. Navy Electronics Laboratory, San Diego CA," 1–33, Naval Ocean Systems Center Library, San Diego. The author would like to acknowledge the assistance of his colleague, Dr. Mark Jacobson, in procuring this volume from the NOSC Library in San Diego.

The founding of UCDWR placed Scripps in an awkward position. Cooperation between the Navy's Radio and Sound Laboratory and the new Division of War Research, both at Point Loma, drew many scientists away from Scripps and into government service after 1941.[50] By July, eight of Scripps's best faculty members, including Richard H. Fleming and Eugene C. LaFond, left the institution to work on sonar problems with UCDWR. Fleming became head of the Oceanographic Section of UCDWR's Sonar Data Division, and LaFond worked directly on underwater sound research in that same division. Dr. Roger R. Revelle, a Scripps oceanographer and future director of the institution, went into the Naval Reserve as a lieutenant and served as head of the Oceanographic Division of the Navy Hydrographic Office in Washington, D.C. As the war effort expanded and the importance and size of UCDWR increased, Scripps declined in significance and suffered from personnel shortages and financial difficulties.[51]

As first director of UCDWR, UCLA's Vern O. Knudson did not have to work under similar handicaps. He had priority, personnel, and virtually unlimited financial support. His Sonar Data Division conducted research into underwater sound propagation augmented by an oceanography program for the proper interpretation and understanding of acoustic data. Under the auspices of OSRD/NDRC the data collected by this division was interpreted in conjunction with that of Scripps, WHOI, and the Sonar Analysis Group of NDRC.

UCDWR also conducted research parallel to that pursued by Woods Hole into the complex composition of seawater, the character of the ocean's surface and bottom, and the factors affecting the transmission of sound in water. The last required a knowledge of the effect of temperature, density, and depth, as well as sources of ambient noise, self-noise, circuit noise, airborne noise, and sound reverberation.

Practical applications of the Sonar Data Division's work took various forms. UCDWR's contribution to the "Submarine Supplements to Sailing Directions" came from this division's work. It also produced bottom sediment charts, sonar range charts, and the pioneering volume entitled, *Principles and Applications of Underwater Sound.*[52]

Further interesting work included the effect of marine life on submarine operations. As part of their research into ambient noise for NDRC, Knudson, R. S. Alford, and J. W. Emling studied sounds made by marine life in an effort to complement the discovery of the effect, first discov-

[50] "Special Research in the Navy," *Journal of Applied Physics* 15 (March 1944): 241–42ff.

[51] Helen Raitt and Beatrice Moulton, *Scripps Institution of Oceanography: First Fifty Years* (La Jolla: Ward Ritchie Press, 1967), 137–45. Revelle moved later to BUSHIPS to continue his oceanographic work.

[52] "Completion Report Made to the Chief of the Bureau of Ships Covering the Operations of the University of California Division of War Research at the U.S. Navy Electronics Laboratory, San Diego, CA," 78ff.

ered by marine zoologist Martin W. Johnson, that snapping shrimp had on sonar detection. In the process this University of California team not only uncovered two varieties of snapping shrimp, but also described in detail their habitat and the conditions under which submariners might encounter the creatures' constant snapping noise on sonar equipment. They also determined that shrimp noise increased at night but was only marginally affected by seasonal or daytime temperature variation. Before filing their final report, the Knudson group also identified thirty-four other types of sound-producing marine life and determined the character of their sounds to aid ASW and submarine sonar operators.[53]

The FM sonar-scanning system developed by the Sonar Devices Division in 1943 was the most important breakthrough made at UCDWR. From that point on the activities of this division were devoted entirely to perfecting the system and supervising its manufacture by the Western Electric Company. By 1945 the Navy and private industry had fabricated forty-eight complete QLA FM sonar systems, twenty-one of which saw active service on submarine war patrols.[54]

Observations

From 1940 to 1943 the demands of war brought together the three vital components required to create a naval-industrial complex for submarines: naval commitment, a capable industrial base, and scientific support.

The Vinson-Trammell Act of 1934 allowed the Navy Department to begin building in quantity the vessels that emerged from the strategy and design debates of the interwar period. The Second Vinson Act of 1938 and the Seventy-Percent Expansion Act promised a sustained commitment to design, development, and construction.

Electric Boat, along with the Navy's shipyards at Portsmouth and Mare Island, provided a core of experienced building yards to turn technical and financial commitment into submarines. When Franklin Roosevelt declared a war emergency in 1939, the Navy Department skillfully used Portsmouth and EB as a foundation for enhancing technical and design skills in the process of dramatically expanding the submarine industry to suit the country's needs.

---

[53] Ibid., 68ff; V. O. Knudson, R. S. Alford, J. W. Emling, "Survey of Underwater Sound—Report No. 3: Ambient Noise," 26 Sep 1944, NDRC (OSRD) Division 6, Section 6.1, Smith Laboratory, WHOI Records Vault.

[54] "Completion Report Made to the Chief of the Bureau of Ships Covering the Operations of the University of California Division of War Research at the U.S. Navy Electronics Laboratory, San Diego, CA," 88ff.

Examining the individual experiences of Kollmorgen, GM, and HOR offers an opportunity to appreciate the diverse problems confronting the Navy Department and industry during this period. For small high-tech firms such as Kollmorgen, naval business and financial support were required. Orders from the Army and Navy kept Kollmorgen solvent and provided resources for vital research and development in optics. Furthermore, only with the Navy Department's direct assistance could the company expand production to meet the wartime requirements of the submarine fleet.

This dependence was mutual. The Navy Department needed the scientific and technical services only Kollmorgen could provide. As long as the Navy Department continued its commitment to submarine development and construction, Kollmorgen would prosper and the submarine force would benefit from the result. One partner could not attain its goals without the other.

General Motors illustrated the power of a large American corporation to respond to wartime demand. This company had already tried and tested the diesel technology that BUSHIPS wanted for its submarines. With its network of small subcontractors and huge plant capacity, GM easily outpaced the ability of the building yards to accommodate diesel deliveries. This experience gave the bureau a foretaste of the administrative problems characteristic of mobilization and the necessity to plan for overproduction in some areas of the war economy.

In the case of HOR, the Navy defeated itself. Admiral Bowen of BUENG perceived the criticism of the HOR diesel by Admiral DeFrees and the Board of Inspection and Survey as an extension of the rancorous debate over the high-temperature, high-pressure turbine systems for surface vessels. For Bowen, solving the problems plaguing the HOR diesels became a mission to vindicate the reputation of the bureau. Naval commitment to these flawed engines demonstrated the ability of an institution to allow internal politics to interfere with important technical decisions.

The scientific community provided the final, necessary ingredient in the development of a naval-industrial complex for submarines. Research under the auspices of the Navy Department and the OSRD/NDRC gave the Navy's submariners an unprecedented degree of mastery over their vessel's natural environment. Physicists, marine biologists, oceanographers, and countless others used their knowledge of marine life, waves, underwater sound transmission, and ocean temperatures to improve the submarine and ensure the survival of its crew. Commenting on this combination, WHOI director Columbus Iselin pointed out that

> for the most part during the war period we have not been engaged in
> oceanographic research, but in the practical application of physical

oceanography. Thus, geophysicists, geologists, meteorologists, and biologists, to mention only a few of the types of investigators, all found a way to contribute to the work at hand . . . [and] the stimulation to oceanography has been very considerable.[55]

Consequently a close professional and personal relationship developed between the submarine community and scientists, such as Allyn Vine and William Schevill of Woods Hole, who instructed officers in the application of scientific developments to their craft. These scientists, and others, convinced operational officers that, when combined with instruments such as the SBT, a familiarity with the ocean environment could truly enhance their chances of survival. The value of the scientific component of the naval-industrial complex increased with the growing sophistication of undersea warfare.

---

[55] WHOI Yearly Reports for the Years 1943–1945, McLean Laboratory, WHOI Data Library/ Archives. Vine interviews, 27 Apr 1989 and 23 Sep 1989; William Schevill, interview with author, 16 Oct 1991; J. Lamar Worzel, interview with author, 22 Aug 1990; J. Brackett Hersey, interview with author, 4, 11, and 23 Oct 1991, NHC Oral Histories. Recorded Proceedings of the WHOI History Colloquy, 15–19 Jul 1991, OA.

Chapter 3

Research and Discovery, 1943–1946

In the midst of the difficult and complex reconversion to a peacetime economy, international tensions and technological innovation combined to preserve the naval-industrial complex for submarines formed during World War II. Political and ideological competition with the Soviet Union provided the incentive for sustained submarine research, development, and limited peacetime construction. Discoveries made by the Naval Technical Mission in Europe between December 1944 and November 1945, along with research in the ocean sciences sponsored by the National Defense Research Committee, the Coordinator of Research and Development, and the Office of Naval Research (ONR) in Washington, D.C., shaped the nature of postwar American submarines. Driven by national perceptions of Soviet ambition and America's role in the postwar world, the Navy and its contractors mastered demanding and revolutionary technologies and made them work far below the surface of the world's ocean.[1]

Understanding the Ocean Environment

If submerged submarines had to move faster, dive deeper, and remain below the surface longer than ever before, an intimacy with the ocean environment was a virtual prerequisite to successful design, construction, operations, and survival. From this point on, the submarines designed and built by the Navy and private industry displayed—in materials, form, and instrumentation—the increasing influence of the scientific community in the naval-industrial complex. The discoveries of the Naval Technical Mission in Europe demonstrated the important role of scientists like Dr. Hellmuth Walter in the remarkable wartime Ger-

---

[1] The National Defense Research Committee's Subsurface Warfare Division (Division 6) directed the American research effort in the ocean sciences related to submarine warfare during World War II.

man U-boat program. Civilian scientists in the United States, especially oceanographers, physicists, and marine biologists, similarly helped the U.S. Navy and private industry determine the characteristics and capabilities of the postwar submarine.

Until 1943 American scientific research in the field of undersea warfare concentrated on destroying the German U-boat fleet and reducing the threat to the coastal and transatlantic convoy system. When Allied antisubmarine warfare efforts began to pay substantial dividends in 1943 and the German submarine fleet went on the defensive, the emphasis of American research shifted. Scientists now concerned themselves more with supporting the efforts of American submariners and enhancing the performance of their vessels. Between 1943 and 1946, Woods Hole Oceanographic Institution, Naval Research Laboratory, University of California, Division of War Research, and other research groups demonstrated that, from the scientific point of view, the study of underwater sound transmission had the greatest influence on the performance of American submarines.

Early in 1943 WHOI and UCDWR, in conjunction with the Naval Hydrographic Office, issued a series of charts describing the acoustical properties of the ocean bottom in geographical areas critical to the war effort. These charts were produced as part of Navy project NS–140, "Range as a Function of Oceanographic Factors." WHOI performed the East Coast research and UCDWR, the West Coast. Edwin Colpitts coordinated the project from New York City as head of section 6.1 of NDRC's Division of Subsurface Warfare.

These maps provided submariners with a better sense of the enemy's ability to detect a submarine in certain environments. In relatively shallow sandy areas, bottom reflection made echo-ranging and listening possible at longer ranges. If the absence of ASW forces did not make evasion necessary, a sandy bottom could provide the best resting place for a submarine. Although rocky or muddy bottoms did not provide a safe place to sit, they did confound enemy sonar to a greater degree. Mud provided little bottom reflection and thus only short sonar detection ranges. In rocky areas the strong reverberation of ocean sounds both reduced reliable echo ranges and played havoc with passive listening. If submarine officers understood the character of the ocean bottom and the significance of its varied forms, their chances of avoiding detection increased.

The charts made available to submarine commanders in January and early February 1943 provided much-needed information on American and Japanese coastal waters. They covered San Diego, San Francisco, and the Columbia River area, as well as the East Coast from Massachusetts Bay to Key West and the Gulf of Mexico. By mid-February information also became available on Japanese home waters, including the middle and southern parts of Tokyo Kaiwan, the northwest coast of Kyushu, and the Tsugaru Strait between Hokkaido and the main island of Honshu.[2]

Research on underwater sound covered a wide spectrum of phenomena and the results generated numerous innovations in tactics and instrumentation. A study done in 1943 by the underwater listening section of UCDWR described some of the least understood natural phenomena of importance in submarine warfare. The study concluded that Navy and civilian scientists needed to work on sound absorption and reflection both at the surface of the ocean and on the bottom. In addition, little was known about unusual sound frequencies that occasionally penetrate the shadow zones created by dramatic changes in water temperature. These zones often mask the presence of an escaping submarine, so understanding their limits was important to the submarine community. Analysis of the temperature change data provided by the submarine bathythermograph would lead to a more complete understanding of the effect of the thermocline on the underwater transmission of sound. In closing, the authors of the report reminded the Navy that, since the adversaries in this conflict constantly moved, it was also important to study attenuation at different frequencies.[3]

The Navy and the scientific community pursued these and other avenues of essential research. During the last years of the war UCDWR took over the echo-ranging work of the U.S. Navy Underwater Sound Laboratory in New London, and studied the strength of sonar echoes, reverberation, the effect of bottom composition, and better methods of more efficiently utilizing existing sonar equipment.[4] Other research conducted by a variety of scientific groups concentrated on the submarine itself, investigating machinery noise, cavitation, and the high-pitched singing sound caused by propeller blade vibration.[5]

[2] Conference notes prepared by LT Roger Revelle, USNR, on "Charts of Bottom Sediments Prepared by NDRC," 12 Feb 1943, box 65; Colpitts to Coordinator of Navy Research and Development, 5 Feb 1943, box 62; Colpitts to CNO, 28 Jan 1943, box 62, ONR–GENCORR of the Coordinator of Research and Development, RG 298, NA.

[3] F. A. Everest and T. F. Johnston, "Outline of Proposed Program of Sound Propagation Measurements in Deep Water," 9 Nov 1943, box 65, ONR–GENCORR of the Coordinator of Research and Development 1941–45. The thermocline is a temperature gradient in a layer of seawater in which the temperature decrease with depth is greater than that of the overlying and underlying water. As chief of NDRC Division 6.1, Edwin Colpitts also wanted this type of research to include a more complete account of the differences between the Atlantic and Pacific Oceans. CDR Rawson Bennett to Colpitts, 25 Apr 1944, box 62, ONR–GENCORR of the Coordinator of Research and Development.

[4] Colpitts to G. P. Harnwell, Director of UCDWR, 3 May 1944, box 62, ONR–GENCORR of the Coordinator of Research and Development.

[5] "Survey of Underwater Sound, Report No. 2: Sounds from Submarines," 31 Dec 1943, NDRC Division 6, Section 6.1, Smith Laboratory Records Vault, WHOI. BUSHIPS Memo, "Making of Submarine Sounds," 29 Apr 1944, box 62, ONR–GENCORR of the Coordinator of Research and Development.

Some of WHOI's research led to developments of long-range significance. Dr. Maurice Ewing and J. Lamar Worzel discovered the characteristics of underwater sound channels and their possible importance for
naval warfare. In these channels, sound travels at a minimum speed. But,
as Columbus Iselin recalled, because

> of refraction effects, signals emitted in this layer can travel very long dis-
> tances without having to undergo bottom or surface reflection. Thus acousti-
> cal transmission in this layer is relatively efficient and a receiver located at
> similar depth can record signals originating several thousand miles away.[6]

In the North Atlantic this layer usually occurs at a depth of approximately 1,300 meters.

By 1943 Ewing and Worzel had developed this knowledge into the
Sound Fixing and Ranging (SOFAR) system for locating airmen forced
down in the ocean. The pilot would drop a small bomb set to explode in
the SOFAR sound channel. With the extraordinary transmission properties of this layer, the Navy could detect the submerged explosion at three
carefully situated listening stations. The time the sound took to reach
each station and a relatively simple calculation would provide a location
for rescue operations. Work on the SOFAR system laid the foundation
for the Navy's modern underwater Sound Surveillance System (SOSUS).

In 1944 Ewing and Worzel established an experimental listening station
on Eleuthera Island, about 250 miles east of the southern tip of Florida, to
test their ideas and refine SOFAR. They suggested using the system in the
Pacific, and collaborated with Dr. George P. Wollard and others on a manual entitled "A Summary of Factors Governing Sound Ranges." [7]

If the three stations broadcast a signal into the sound channel using
this same principle, but reversing the process, a submarine equipped to
receive the transmissions could easily determine its location. Developed
by Ewing and Worzel, this alternate use of the SOFAR system, called
RAFOS, formed the basis for postwar submarine navigation systems.

The discovery of the deep sea sound channel by Ewing and Worzel
had a profound effect on the future of submarine design, construction,
and capability. Their initial work on this phenomena was done during
the war at WHOI, under the auspices of NDRC section 6.1. In the final
months of the war some influential figures within the operational submarine community, such as Admiral Charles Lockwood, commander of the
Pacific submarine force, refused to support long-range pure research of

---

[6] Iselin, "WHOI History During the War Years, 1941–1950," 26–27, McLean Laboratory, WHOI
Data Library/Archives; Vine interview, 27 Apr 1989, NHC Oral Histories, OA.

[7] Ibid.

Professor Maurice Ewing of Lehigh University rests during a break on board the Woods Hole Oceanographic Institution research vessel *Atlantis*, 1938.

Woods Hole Oceanographic Institution as it appeared during World War II.

this sort because it held no promise of immediate application.[8] After the war, however, work on the transmission properties of the sound channel resumed with Allyn Vine and a team from WHOI working with the Navy's Submarine Development Group Two, based in New London, and the team of Ewing and Worzel, now affiliated with the Lamont Geological Observatory at Columbia University. The significance of this research soon went beyond the purely scientific. Everyone involved realized that the discovery of the sound channel not only provided a stimulus to science but also signaled a revolution in submarine capability that would require new tactics and perhaps a rethinking of submarine strategy.

Reflecting on his research during those years, Vine recalled the excitement of both scientists and submariners as the practical significance of the sound channels began to emerge:

> These were still real operational tests because there were real submarines at both ends, there were real skippers, and there were real oceans. And the important thing about this, we were not only learning the scientific aspect—more about underwater sound from the scientific aspect—but . . . also people around the wardroom table were conjuring up tactical usages which I found just as interesting as the science.[9]

Much of the research on underwater sound found quick application in the last months of the war. BUSHIPS authorized extensive operational testing of the submarine bathythermograph in the autumn of 1943, less than one year after the instrument was created by Ewing and Vine at WHOI. *Aspro* (SS 309) and *Dorado* (SS 248) worked for the bureau on these tests, proving the value of this instrument for finding density layers, shadow zones, and providing a means to judge the behavior of underwater sound transmissions in a given area. By June of the following year the NDRC commissioned WHOI to develop an SBT for use at depths approaching 1,000 feet.[10]

The SBT proved effective in action with the submarine fleet. In one typical example the commanding officer of *Herring* related in his patrol report for 11 to 17 June 1943 that the instrument allowed the diving officer to determine increasing water density as the temperature decreased with depth near Palau. As a consequence, the information from the SBT

---

[8] Revelle to Colpitts, 14 Sep 1944, box 63, ONR–GENCORR of the Coordinator of Research and Development 1941–1945, RG 298, NA. ADM Charles Lockwood to RADM Alan McCann and CAPT Frank T. Watkins, 2 Jun 1944; McCann to Lockwood, 5 May 1944, series 4, file 1, box 15, Subs/UWD, OA.

[9] Vine interview, 23 Sep 1989.

[10] Colpitts to Revelle, 8 Jun 1944; BUSHIPS to Commander Submarine Force, Atlantic Fleet (COMSUBLANT), 5 Oct 1943, box 62, ONR–GENCORR of the Coordinator of Research and Development 1941–1945.

allowed him to maintain depth quietly without having to pump, blow, or increase speed during a postattack search by Japanese ASW forces.[11]

NDRC and BUSHIPS also accelerated the production and installation of the QLA and JP sonar equipment. Admiral Lockwood even sent a member of his staff, Commander William B. Sieglaff, to Los Angeles in an effort to encourage quicker QLA production. These efforts were complemented by a BUSHIPS program to reduce the noise generated by the various systems and machinery on board the submarines.[12]

The effect of equipment production schedules on overhaul time and new construction concerned the shipbuilders as much as the submariners who wanted to use this equipment against the enemy. In a letter to the supervisor of shipbuilding in Groton, EB's design director, B. S. Bullard, expressed concern that the procurement and installation of the latest underwater sound equipment would delay the delivery of submarines nearing completion. The company was reluctant to accept responsibility for procuring these new systems because of the delay and the extra costs involved. EB officials preferred to introduce new equipment at an early stage of construction. This approach would permit proper installation without slowing the building schedule and seemed the best way to introduce the QLA FM sonar and other products of applied research.[13]

As the war came to a close, the scientific community, like industry, prepared to reconvert to peacetime pursuits. Created by the President and an act of Congress in late 1944, the Office of War Mobilization and Reconversion (OWMR), under the leadership of John W. Snyder, approved a schedule for the termination of OSRD and NDRC by 31 August 1945.[14] The NDRC would continue to manage any nearly completed research of continued national value through the end of 1945. The committee would also sustain long-term projects of significance until 31 October 1945, giving the armed services an opportunity to transfer these activities to other government facilities or private contractors. Less significant ventures were terminated as of 30 September.

---

[11] Gary E. Weir, "Observations on Woods Hole, Oceanography, and Submarines," *The Submarine Review* (July 1991): 51–52.

[12] Sound Test of the *Tirante* (SS 420), 11 May 1945, box 2218; BUSHIPS to COMSUBLANT et al., 20 Apr 1943, box 2052, BUSHIPS GENCORR 1940–1945, RG 19, NA/WNRC. The former is a good example of the type of testing being done on submarines by the end of the war. Lockwood to Watkins, 23 Jun 1945; Watkins to CAPT W. D. Irvin, 26 Jun 1945; Watkins to Lockwood, 9 Jun 1945; Lockwood to Watkins, 1 Jun 1945, series 4, file 1, box 15, Subs/UWD, OA.

[13] EB to SUPSHIPS, Groton, 15 Jul 1943, box 2051, BUSHIPS GENCORR 1940–1945.

[14] Stewart, *Organizing Scientific Research for War*, chap. 21 (especially 312–13). The architects of the scientific conversion were Vannevar Bush, head of OSRD, and James Conant, chairman of NDRC.

Snyder succeeded Fred M. Vinson as head of OWMR on 23 July 1945. Vinson had succeeded James F. Byrnes in April 1945. James W. Fesler, *Industrial Mobilization for War: History of the War Production Board and Predecessor Agencies* (Washington: Civilian Production Administration, 1947), 863.

The Bureau of Ships, the Bureau of Ordnance (BUORD), and the Bureau of Aeronautics (BUAER) took over the activities of NDRC Division 6, which presided over research on subsurface warfare. Select projects were assigned to Navy labs and research activities as well as private institutions. NRL, still under the direction of BUSHIPS, took over the Navy's Underwater Sound Laboratory in New London in March 1945 and, with it, much of the work in this area done by the Columbia University Division of War Research. BUSHIPS also absorbed the NDRC Sonar Analysis section directed by Dr. Lyman Spitzer of CUDWR.

When NDRC withdrew from underwater sound research at UCDWR, the Bureau of Ships entered into an agreement with the University of California on 1 March 1945 to continue some of the more promising lines of investigation. Other Division 6 projects continued at private universities and research institutions, preserving old agreements or reflecting freshly negotiated arrangements. In some cases the Navy Department used facilities built by the bureaus for private contractors during the war to house significant scientific projects.[15]

In an effort to bring some order to the Navy's postwar scattered research efforts, Secretary of the Navy James Forrestal created the Office of Research and Inventions in the spring of 1945. He appointed Admiral Harold Bowen as director and gave the new office jurisdiction over the Office of Patents and Inventions and the Office of the Coordinator of Research and Development, as well as over NRL. During the next two years Admiral Bowen presided over the transformation of his command into one of the most adaptable and productive of the Navy's research and development institutions, the Office of Naval Research.[16]

The Naval Technical Mission in Europe: Learning from German Research and Development

Much of the applied research sponsored by the Navy in the postwar era through ONR and the technical bureaus derived from submarine

[15] Stewart, *Organizing Scientific Research for War*, 307. Marvin Lasky, "Historical Review of Undersea Warfare Planning and Organization, 1945–1960, With Emphasis on the Role of the Office of Naval Research," *U.S. Navy Journal of Underwater Acoustics* XXVI (no. 2): 333. CDR Lawrence R. Daspit, BUSHIPS, to Watkins, OP–23–c, 21 Feb 1945, series 4, file 1, box 15, Subs/UWD, OA. CAPT Jennings B. Dow to Coordinator of Research and Development, 15 Feb 1945; BUSHIPS to the Office of Research and Inventions, 5 Jul 1945; WHOI–Navy Contract, 5 Jul 1945, box 63, ONR–GENCORR of the Coordinator of Research and Development 1941–45, RG 298, NA. Julius A. Furer, *Administration of the Navy Department in World War II* (Washington: GPO, 1959), 753–56.

[16] ONR was officially established when President Harry Truman signed the appropriate legislation on 3 August 1946. Sapolsky, *Science and the Navy* (Princeton: Princeton University Press, 1990), 23–29.

technology uncovered in Germany at the end of the war. In December 1944 four naval veterans of the Alsos mission to explore German scientific and technical progress suggested that the Navy Department embark upon its own comprehensive investigation of German wartime developments.[17] The Army's Combined Intelligence Priorities Committee commissioned Alsos on 11 May 1944 to investigate the progress made by the Germans in their nuclear program as well as other scientific endeavors. Alsos, the Greek word for "grove," was chosen because of the mission's importance to the head of the Manhattan Engineer District, Major General Leslie R. Groves, USA.

Heeding the advice of the Alsos naval veterans, the Navy Department in January 1945 commissioned the Naval Technical Mission in Europe to follow the advancing Allied forces for the purpose of gathering scientific and technical intelligence for the postwar American Navy. The four "founders" were Commodore Henry A. Schade, leader of the mission and later NRL director; Captain Albert G. Mumma, a future BUSHIPS chief; Captain J. P. Den Hartog, a Reserve officer and professor of mechanical engineering at Harvard University; and Captain Wendell P. Roop, who later did ground-breaking work on structural materials at the David Taylor Model Basin (DTMB) at Carderock, Maryland. They spearheaded a team composed of nearly 900 officers, civilians, and enlisted men on a year-long pursuit of the best in German research and development. Their discoveries changed the history of the American submarine.

After establishing its main headquarters in Paris during January 1945, the Naval Technical Mission initiated its field operations in late February and early March. The Ships Division of the mission's technical branch took responsibility for exploring German advances in submarine technology. Staffed by experts in materials, hull design, propulsion, and other submarine specialties, this division performed the first analysis of German wartime progress with submarines.[18]

Gathering the information entailed some risk. In describing his initial activities with the mission, Lieutenant Commander Ralph A. Smith, wartime ship superintendent at Mare Island Naval Shipyard, recalled that he went "in a Jeep, with perhaps another US EDO [engineering duty officer], a British naval 'counterpart' and an interpreter to investigate a German naval 'target' after a British 'Target Force' had secured the 'target.' (Always after the artillery and infantry had cleared the

---

[17] RADM Albert G. Mumma, USN (Ret.), first interview by Paul Stillwell, 3 Oct 1986, Annapolis, MD, tape 2, side 1, U.S. Naval Institute (USNI) Oral History Collection, OA.

[18] Office of the Chief of Naval Operations, "U.S. Naval Technical Mission to Europe," No. 25, *United States Naval Administration in World War II*, 1–26. Commodore Henry A. Schade, USN, "German Wartime Technical Developments," *Transactions of the Society of Naval Architects and Marine Engineers* LIV (1946): 83–111.

The wartime Naval Technical Mission in Europe gathered German scientific and technical information. The civilian in the center foreground is Dr. Helmuth Walter; Captain Albert G. Mumma is to his left, May 1945.

area)."[19] British forces occupied this northern area of Germany, and although initial cooperation between allies was good, the mission's leaders soon decided to operate independently. The Americans created their own target force in imitation of those instituted by the Royal Navy. The number of units in this force was determined by the quantity of jeeps the mission's leaders could find. Each vehicle accommodated one or two engineering duty officers, an interpreter, and a machine-gunner. According to Smith the mission's target forces

> proved most effective and permitted us to get much better and more complete intelligence info. We could cover more targets than the 30th [British] A[rmored].U[nit].'s [target force] and quite often arrived at the same targets at the same time. It meant going in ahead of the infantry with its inherent risks (primarily snipers) but we made it with several close calls, but no casualties.[20]

---

[19] CAPT Ralph Smith, USN (Ret), interview with author by letter, 10 Nov 1987, NHC Oral Histories. An engineering duty officer (EDO) was designated, by personal choice, for an engineering career in the Navy that would give no opportunity for a sea-going command.

[20] Ibid.

Some of the mission's activities were more elaborate and perilous. In the spring of 1945 a joint British-American task force of seventy-five men traveled approximately one hundred miles behind the German lines to Kiel. The force consisted of a detachment of British marines accompanied by five American and an equal number of British technical teams. After a British major talked the German garrison at the shipyard into surrendering, the mission explored submarines still on the ways as well as technology and designs still on the drafting tables. In the process this team captured and interrogated Hellmuth Walter, whose work on submarine closed-cycle systems promised a dramatic increase in underwater speed. Once submariners realized that at least 17 and perhaps as much as 30 knots submerged was possible, they would accept nothing else. Walter's initiative led to a revolution in modern undersea warfare.[21]

Those participating in the technical mission assembled intelligence and sent it back to the United States as quickly as possible for evaluation. In the case of submarine technology, officers like hull-specialist Commander Henry A. Arnold understood that the information taken from the Germans would shape postwar American experimentation and construction. Thirty years before the Navy had responded slowly to European submarine advances made during the Great War. In 1945 officers like Commander Arnold and Lieutenant Commander Smith expected to see practical results from their work in short order.[22]

The scores of technical reports and the products of German wartime research and development sent back by the mission to the United States—especially the mission's analysis of torpedoes, propulsion technology, the latest submarine designs, and the schnorchel—had a profound effect on the Navy's submarine force. The early wartime performance of American torpedoes was not impressive. In the first two years after Pearl Harbor the performance of the Mark 6 exploder for the Mark 14 torpedo had precipitated an intense debate between the submarine force and the Bureau of Ordnance. Repeated premature explosions and the frequency of duds with the Mark 6 caused submarine commanders to question the technology painstakingly developed for this warhead during the interwar period. Failure to immediately replace the exploder stemmed from a suspicion at the bureau that the problems could easily have many causes, including the failure of the captain and

[21] RADM Albert G. Mumma, USN (Ret.), second interview by Paul Stillwell, side 1, tape 1, USNI Oral History Collection, OA. Because of the Russian refusal to conform with the terms of the Yalta agreement for sharing the fruits of German wartime research, Admiral Harold Stark, as commander of American naval forces in Europe, approved Mumma's request to make the trip to Kiel. The project was approved by General Eisenhower before it took place.

[22] CAPT Henry Arnold, USN (Ret.), interview with author, 27 Oct 1987, NHC Oral Histories, OA.

crew to operate the weapon correctly and take responsibility for the poor results. Vested interest in Mark 6 technology at the bureau and the absence of an effective testing program for the weapon led to a heated debate over the suitability of the exploder, delaying remedial action. All the while, submarines such as *Tinosa* reported attacking targets in the summer of 1943 with as many as fifteen torpedoes and achieving only two detonations.

Neither the magnetic nor the contact exploder on the Mark 6 worked well. The inadequacy of the magnetic exploding feature became apparent early in the war, and by 1943 Admiral Chester W. Nimitz, Commander in Chief, U.S. Pacific Fleet, ordered it removed from each torpedo or inactivated. Later that year the submarine force at Pearl Harbor and BUORD also discovered that the Mark 6 firing pin was often not strong enough to withstand torpedo impact. These defects prompted changes in the firing mechanism, which were implemented at the end of 1943 and made American torpedoes far more reliable after the new year.[23] They also made the U.S. Navy eager for any useful strides in torpedo development.

Advanced German torpedo technology roughly paralleled research in the United States. In September 1944 two officers and a civilian attached to the technical mission inspected the newly captured German torpedo arsenal at Houilles on the western edge of Paris. After touring nearly 30 kilometers of underground tunnels in this expanded complex of mushroom cellars, the team collected extensive documentation on German torpedoes as well as samples of the G7a (air-driven) and the G7e (electric) torpedoes for shipment back to BUORD. Some of these weapons were fitted with the spring torpedo mechanism, or FAT, that sent the torpedo running in a pattern.[24]

By the end of September 1945 the mission had uncovered the extent and variety of German wartime developments. Torpedoes equipped with the LUT pattern running device were discovered on two railroad cars in St. Dizier and quickly returned to Paris for examination by officers attached to the mission. The Germans had derived the name for this guidance mechanism from the German phrase for "position-independent torpedo." LUT increased the possibility of success when striking back at a pursuer with a bow or stern shot. The torpedo would circle at a radius and speed adjusted according to the velocity of the pursuing ship.

---

[23] Buford Rowland and William B. Boyd, *U.S. Navy Bureau of Ordnance in World War II* (Washington: Bureau of Ordnance, 1954), 100–110.

[24] Alsos Report 39, 9 Dec 1944, series 2, box 3, Naval Technical Mission in Europe (NAVTECH-MISEU), OA.

A report written in July 1945 revealed that German research, as far back as 1942, had progressed beyond pattern-running types into acoustic homing torpedoes. This work produced the Geier system, an active acoustic homing control that nearly became operational during the war. The authors of the report observed with some relief "that none of these torpedoes was actually fired in action; they were waiting in a depot." The mission also explored the passive-homing T–4 and T–5. During the war German U-boats launched between five and six thousand T–5s, often referred to as the Zaunkönig, or Wren, with a 53 percent hit rate. Other teams discovered information on the use of hydrogen peroxide closed-cycle propulsion in torpedoes as well as an underwater rocket system for submarine defense.[25] This information helped the Navy and private sector advance work on homing torpedoes like the passive Mark 24 Fido begun in the United States during the war by the General Electric Company, Western Electric Company, and Brush Development Company.

The mission also uncovered a series of revolutionary U-boat designs developed late in the war by the German navy in direct response to the effectiveness of Allied ASW in the Atlantic. The intelligence provided by breaking the German naval codes made the efforts of the Royal Air Force Coastal Command against the U-boat ports along the French coast and the activities of the American escort carrier groups particularly effective. By May 1943 Admiral Karl Dönitz, commander in chief of the German navy, virtually abandoned his North Atlantic submarine campaign because of the terrible losses suffered by his forces. Only a submarine capable of much greater submerged speed and endurance would offer the Germans some hope of success against Allied ASW.

For the Germans the possibility of a submarine capable of high submerged speed originated with a 1933 proposal by Hellmuth Walter for a U-boat capable of 25 to 30 knots while submerged. He planned to achieve this goal by employing a closed-cycle diesel propulsion system using scrubbed diesel exhaust gases enriched with oxygen for combustion.

---

[25] The hydrogen peroxide used in the Walter system was an 80- to 85-percent concentration manufactured, for the most part, by three German firms: Electro-Chemische Werke München A.G., Otto Schickert und Co. K.G. in Bad Lauterberg, and Deutsche Gold und Silberscheideanstalt at Rheinfelden. Together they were responsible for 1,298 of the 1,565 tons per month produced during early 1944. I. G. Farben, the chemical industry giant, produced the hydrogen peroxide used by the aircraft and rocket industries. The Elektro-Chemischewerke München A.G. refined its hydrogen peroxide at Höllriegelskreuth. Letter Report 2–45, 16 Apr 1945, series 3, box 7; Technical Report 119–45, 2 Jul 1945, series 4, box 18; Technical Report 120–45, 2 Jul 1945, series 4, box 18; Technical Report 204–45, 28 Sep, series 4, box 25; Alsos Report 48, 24 Dec 1944, series 2, box 4, NAVTECHMISEU, OA. For the LUT guidance control, see Technical Report 202–45, 6 Oct 1945, series 4, box 25. For the Geier control system, see Technical Report 130–45, 28 Jul 1945, series 4, box 19, in same file.

Rather than storing the oxygen on board, the Walter system derived the gas from the chemical breakdown of concentrated hydrogen peroxide.[26]

Walter soon discovered that the chemical reaction, which separated the hydrogen peroxide into its component parts, generated considerable heat and water. Using this knowledge, Walter eventually set aside the diesel and developed a closed-cycle submarine steam turbine system. He first demonstrated this new mode of submerged propulsion in 1939 with the experimental, 80-ton, submarine *V 80*, built in great secrecy at the Krupp Germania shipyard in Kiel.

V 80 provided a foundation for a series of variations on the high submerged speed U-boat. Although small, the 28.1-knot speed achieved in its 1940 trials gave the vessel's designers a reason to feel that the Walter propulsion system and the sleek, unadorned hull form held promise for the future.

In response to the emergency conditions of 1943, the German Navy concentrated its design and engineering talent in Blankenburg, in the Harz Mountains about 70 miles northwest of Leipzig, to obtain the time, resources, and opportunity to conceive an operational, high-speed U-boat also capable of prolonged submergence. The outcome of their work was the series of submarines known as the Types XVII, XXI, and XXVI.[27]

The Type XXI U-boat, nearly ready for operations against the Allies when the war ended, represented a compromise between the diesel direct-drive submarines that formed the backbone of Germany's U-boat force and the Walter *V 80*'s promise of greater speed and endurance. The Blankenburg design team did not incorporate the submerged hydrodynamic advantages of *V 80*'s sleek teardrop hull form in the Type XXI. Instead they selected a nearly conventional hull that revealed an inverted figure-eight shape in cross-section. This hydrodynamically stable form, designed to keep the major storage battery weight low in the boat, had less in common with *V 80* than it did with the workhorse of the German U-boat fleet, the Type IXC. Learning from their experiences with *V 80* and other experimental vessels, the German designers reduced submerged resistance by streamlining the hull dramatically. In part this entailed removing the deck gun and any external fixtures that would heighten resistance, as well as reducing the size and profile of the conning tower.

This type of U-boat marked the transition between the vessels and technology commonly used during the war and the submarines of the

---

[26] The following are the sources for the discussion of the Walter closed-cycle propulsion system: Letter Report 94–45, 26 Jul 1945, series 4, box 17; Technical Report 214–45, 27 Aug 1945, series 4, box 26; Technical Report 322–45, 29 Sep 1945, series 4, box 32; Technical Report 542–45, 1 Nov 1945, series 4, box 45, NAVTECHMISEU.

[27] Letter Report Number 22–45, 5 May 1945, series 3, box 8, NAVTECHMISEU.

NH 96277

A German Type XVII submarine model undergoes aero- and hydrodynamic tests at Braunschweig during the war, 1945.

postwar world. The still experimental nature of the Walter closed-cycle turbine system and the scarcity of concentrated hydrogen peroxide forced the Blankenburg designers to adopt enhanced diesel-electric power to propel the Type XXI. The boat's 372 battery cells allowed 18 knots submerged, as opposed to the 8- or 9-knot maximum of the Types VII and IX. This kind of speed would enable the Type XXI to successfully evade any pursuing Allied ASW vessel without surfacing. If necessary, the Type XXI could escape by diving to nearly 1,000 feet (300+ meters) because of the exceptional yield strength of German ST–52 steel, which could withstand approximately 48,000 pounds of ocean pressure per square inch.[28] In addition, the Germans equipped the Type XXI with a schnorchel to provide for both battery charging and greater endurance while submerged.[29]

Of the other advanced submarines discovered by the mission, Types XVII and XXVI held the most significance for American submarine development. Three Type XVII U-boats, built at Hamburg's Blohm und Voss shipyard, united a deep, narrow fish-shaped hull with the Walter closed-cycle turbine to achieve exceptional speed. Never intended for operational service, these vessels helped the German navy test the hull and propulsion combination destined for the eventual production model, the Type XXVI. The shortage of hydrogen peroxide and the higher priority given to the rocket and jet programs of the Luftwaffe caused the cancellation of the Type XXVI before the prefabricated hull sections could be assembled into the first of the class. Nonetheless the Type XXVI U-boat displayed some unique features. Along with the capability for a continuous submerged speed of 25 knots, this submarine had ten torpedo tubes, six of them pointing aft mounted amidships at an outward angle of 10 degrees to the ship's centerline.[30]

The Naval Technical Mission discovered scores of advanced U-boats as they penetrated the northern German ports. At shipyards such as Deschimag in Bremen, the mission's target forces seized Type XXIs, some completed and others still under construction, as well as prefabricated hull sections and machinery for other advanced types. The German technique of assembling nearly complete hull sections on the ways paral-

---

[28] 3,400 kilograms per square centimeter.

[29] Rössler, *Geschichte des deutschen Ubootbaus*, 369–78. Arnold interview, 27 Oct 1987, NHC Oral Histories. Captain Arnold observed that this yield strength exceeded that of the high tensile steel (HTS) used on American fleet submarines during the war. Naval designers originally hoped for government specifications requiring a chrome-vanadium HTS with a 50,000 psi yield strength. In the end it was difficult for American steel mills to meet these requirements during mobilization so BU-SHIPS settled for a titanium-manganese alloy with a 45,000 psi yield strength. Alden, *The Fleet Submarine in the U.S. Navy*, 85.

[30] Technical Report 312–45, 13 Aug 1945, series 4, box 32, NAVTECHMISEU, OA.

NH 96270

U–3008, a Type XXI submarine, and two Type IX submarines *(left and far center)* at Wilhelmshaven, June 1945. During the postwar development of American submarines, *U–3008* was dismantled and studied at Portsmouth Naval Shipyard.

leled methods also employed during the war by the Manitowoc Shipbuilding Company and forty years later by the General Dynamics automated hull facility at Quonset Point, Rhode Island.[31]

In their research the Germans pursued prolonged submergence with as much determination as they did sustained high speed. Like their inventive submarine designs, the schnorchel was a response to Allied ASW success. The German Imperial Navy had experimented with this device during the Great War, and Hitler's navy returned to it in spring of 1943 when Admiral Dönitz's submariners needed to stay submerged for longer periods of time to avoid detection. The first installation on a U-boat came in October 1943 when a Type II received a schnorchel to provide scientists and engineers with information on the performance of the diesel en-

---

[31] For sources on Manitowoc and Quonset, see Nelson, *Fresh Water Submarines: The Manitowoc Story;* Joseph F. Yurso, "Decline of the Seventies," in *Naval Engineering and American Seapower,* ed. Randolph W. King (Baltimore: Nautical & Aviation Publishing Co. of America, 1989), 334–36.

NH 96364

A German Type XXI submarine hull section in advanced stages of interior outfitting and a bow section showing the sonar dome and torpedo tube doors, Deschimag Shipyard, Bremen.

gines under variable intake and exhaust pressures. They also needed to know the effect on the crew if the schnorchel head was momentarily covered with water. Using the schnorchel, a U-boat could make 2 to 3 knots during a battery recharge, with a recommended limit of 8 knots, and, in some cases, as much as 13 knots while cruising submerged.

The Naval Technical Mission studied every aspect of German research and development on the schnorchel. Naval officers explored German efforts to develop schnorchel heads that could better cope with the unpredictable patterns of water and wave motion on the ocean surface. They reported on a folding schnorchel design and the struggle to find room for and perfect an air-operated, telescoping schnorchel mast. Data gathered by German scientists and engineers on the performance of both 2- and 4-cycle diesel engines with the schnorchel proved particularly important as a measure of the propulsion system's compatibility with this modern expression of an ancient method of breathing underwater. As the Navy prepared to take advantage of this technology to enhance the capability of American fleet submarines, the information and equipment sent by the mission to the Navy's Engineering Experiment Station (EES) in Annapolis, Maryland, for evaluation and further development proved invaluable. Within two years the American submarine fleet had a schnorchel on an operational, high-speed submarine.[32]

For the technical experts attached to the mission, understanding the concepts underlying the German innovations meant as much as appreciating the science and engineering that generated these advances. The Germans had found themselves forced by circumstances to seriously consider new strategic and tactical concepts as well as new approaches to design, testing, and construction. The number of contractors and yards used in the German design and production effort, for example, convinced officers like Commander Henry Arnold and Lieutenant Commander Ralph Smith, as well as the leader of the mission's submarine group, Captain William R. Ignatius, that "the employment of a large number of comparatively small yards made many ship designers submarine conscious. As a result many new and varied ideas could be advanced. Some of them were bad and some only fair, but many were excellent." These officers concluded that the Germans applied creativity and diversity to a new form of submarine warfare made necessary by the course of the conflict with the allies. In the end, "the way ultimately led to the design of an intricate and interesting vessel based upon a new concept of submarine warfare, according to which submarines must remain submerged indefinitely, attain speeds heretofore considered impossible, operate at great depths, and must be highly maneuverable." With that conclusion the Naval Technical Mission uncovered the motives of the German navy and predicted the future of the American submarine.[33]

Chester Nimitz, now a fleet admiral and Chief of Naval Operations, decommissioned the Naval Technical Mission on 1 October 1945. He replaced it with the Naval Technical Unit Europe under the command of the naval advisor to the Office of the U.S. Military Government for Germany. This unit continued the work of obtaining important technical equipment from German sources and recruited German scientists who wished to work in the United States.[34]

---

[32] Technical Report 517–45, 27 Oct 1945, series 4, box 44, NAVTECHMISEU, OA. The first operational schnorchel installation came with *Irex* (SS 482) in 1947.

[33] Technical Report 312–45, 13 Aug 1945, series 4, box 32. Arnold, "Notes on German Submarine Construction," 1945 (in the possession of the author, courtesy of CAPT Arnold).

[34] CAPT Francis R. Duborg, OPNAV, to BUSHIPS, et al., 28 Aug 1947, (records center) box 17, BUSHIPS Secret Central Correspondence (CENCORR)—1947, RG 19, NA/WNRC.

National Archives, RG 19

German schnorchels undergo testing in the schnorchel tower of the Engineering Experiment Station, Annapolis, Maryland, December 1946.

Observations

Submarine production drastically decreased as World War II came to a close, but the disintegrating relations with the Soviet Union and the scientific challenge of going deeper, longer, faster, and quieter sustained the naval-industrial complex into the postwar period. High submerged speed, the schnorchel, and other advances submarine technology developed by the Germans demanded that American ship designs and construction techniques respond to a new set of assumptions.

The Navy began to respond to these challenges even before the Naval Technical Mission in Europe discovered the extent of German progress in submarine technology. The shift to pro-submarine research, as opposed to ASW, in the last two years of the war gave rise to a new appreciation of the ocean environment and a better understanding of the effects of temperature, depth, and bottom composition on tactics and detection.

Many years later at a ceremony honoring Allyn Vine for his work on the bathythermograph and the SBT, a former engineering officer on *Guitarro* (SS 363) recalled a time when his vessel barely survived a Japanese search. *Guitarro* had managed to hide under a layer of dramatic temperature change at 240 feet detected by the bathythermograph. The speaker concluded his comments by saying, "We on the 363 have always believed in the BT but this attack made salesmen for the BT out of us." As a result of such experiences, many veteran officers became great friends and apostles of oceanography.

In these circumstances the scientific community emerged as an equal partner with BUSHIPS, Portsmouth, Mare Island, and EB in charting the future of American submarines.

Chapter 4

Coping with Peace, 1943–1946

By late 1943 wartime industrial production reached its peak and the tide of the conflict had already turned in favor of America and its allies. As the day of victory and a return to peaceful pursuits approached, the naval-industrial complex encountered the inevitable challenges posed by production slowdowns and demobilization. Would the coalition of the Navy, industry, and science, forged in war, find a peacetime role? As the war came to a close, older veterans of the submarine Navy and the private sector remembered with anxiety the hard years following the Great War and the economic dislocation and uncertainty of reconversion.

Two factors guaranteed that the gradual transition to a peacetime economy would not bring with it a reprise of the halfhearted commitment and meager resources of the early interwar period. First, the submarine fleet had distinguished itself during the Second World War as one of the Navy's most effective tools. Peace might force a change in its size and composition, but the value and legitimacy of the submarine would never again come into question as it had after the Great War. Second, during the last year of the Second World War, the Naval Technical Mission in Europe discovered some revolutionary submarine designs and propulsion techniques developed by Hitler's navy. These new technologies, advances in marine science and engineering, and new approaches to submarine strategy and design sustained the naval-industrial complex for submarines through the uncertainty of the immediate postwar era.

Reconversion to a Peacetime Economy: National Policy

At the height of the Second World War the possibility of having to reconvert to a peacetime economy was hardly a major issue. In the submarine industry, as in most other sectors of the economy, the transition to a war footing was complete. The five building yards expanded their facilities with government assistance and, supported by an army of subcontractors, produced scores of submarines between 1941 and 1945.

Portsmouth and EB alone manufactured 157 vessels, with the former outproducing its Groton rival by one submarine.[1] Setting priorities for material resources and finding skilled labor, as well as coping with the pressure of production schedules, occupied the time of naval planners.

Yet as the mobilization of the nation's resources for war reached its height, Donald M. Nelson, chairman of the War Production Board (WPB), asked Ernest Kanzler in the spring of 1943 to conduct the first extensive study of the problems involved with economic demobilization and reconversion. Kanzler was the former head of WPB's Automotive Division and director general for operations. His report, submitted to Nelson in June 1943, offered the first comprehensive treatment of the reconversion problem.[2] In his conclusions Kanzler urged immediate planning and centralized control in order to avoid infighting, confusion, and duplication of authority among the various governmental agencies involved in reconversion. If the government failed to devise an effective strategy, poor management and the waste of national resources would become the hallmark of the transition to a peacetime economy.

Kanzler divided the process of reconversion into three stages. The course of the war itself would precipitate the first stage. As the conflict progressed, the needs of the Armed Forces would change according to the most important tasks at hand. As a result, industry would find itself shifting priorities to accommodate the most pressing wartime demands. This adaptability would serve the economy well when the gradual shift to peacetime production began.

Kanzler's second stage, beginning immediately after the fall of Germany, was a transition phase in which a marked increase in civilian production would begin to transform the character of the wartime economy. In the end, the third stage would witness full demobilization and a dramatic shift to the type of goods and services required by a peacetime American economy.

The search for an adequate contract cancellation clause to terminate war production contracts demonstrated the need for the timeliness and central control that Kanzler advocated. After Pearl Harbor it took the WPB's Procurement Policy Board until July 1942 to formulate a termination article for fixed-price contracts. This regulation sought to protect the government's interest and allow the firm involved to convert to civilian production as soon as possible. It provided for an equitable basis for the settlement of canceled war contracts and an early payment for work already accomplished, while inflicting a minimum of cost accounting on

---

[1] Winslow, *Portsmouth Built*, 79.

[2] J. Carlyle Sitterson, *Development of the Reconversion Policies of the War Production Board, April 1943 to January 1945* (Washington: Civilian Production Administration, 1945), 1–5.

WPB. But by the time the Procurement Policy Board produced the draft of the termination article, a wide variety of procurement agencies had already taken it upon themselves to cancel contracts.

To avoid a thoroughly chaotic situation, Kanzler nominated WPB as the perfect central agency to coordinate termination procedures for all Armed Forces procurement contracts. It could also formulate policy for the disposition of the industrial facilities and tools purchased for private industry by the Navy and other government agencies before and during the war. These decisions on disposition were to vary according to the industry in question "with individual arrangements being made with individual manufacturers."[3] In addition, Kanzler advised retaining for a time the system of wartime controls developed for the distribution of resources to industry. These measures, combined with the careful management of stockpiles, would curb unemployment and ensure stable prices.

The Kanzler Report offered three basic considerations for those responsible for planning demobilization. First, WPB, or the central agency directing demobilization and reconversion, should first determine the demand for durable goods. Then the central authority had to ascertain the best postwar disposition of government-owned facilities made available for civilian production. Finally, it was also important to carefully plan the release of materials and personnel previously controlled by the military to ensure the best use of resources and to limit dislocation in the labor market.[4]

Six months after Kanzler delivered his report to Donald Nelson, it became evident that Congress intended to address the same issues with an equal sense of urgency. At the conclusion of its deliberations in November 1943, the Senate Special Committee Investigating the National Defense Program, also known as the Truman Committee after its chairman, Harry S. Truman, urged careful planning for reconversion but did not propose any comprehensive plan. At the same time the Senate Special Committee on Post-War Economic Policy and Planning initiated a far more extensive treatment of the reconversion problem that echoed Ernest Kanzler's call for immediate centralized planning for a transition to the peacetime economy.

Encouraged by congressional attention to the problem, in September 1943 Nelson charged the Planning Division of WPB's Bureau of Planning and Statistics with the task of producing a thorough study of reconversion with an eye toward a precise definition of the problems involved. Completed in January 1944, the Planning Division report suggested that in the fifteen-month period following V–E Day, the government should expect a decline in war production of roughly 30 percent. It would translate into an unevenly distributed "decline from an annual rate of 74 billion dollars

---

[3] Ibid., 6.
[4] Ibid., 5–8.

in the third quarter of 1944, assumed as the last quarter of large scale hostilities in Europe, to a rate of 50 billion in the third quarter of 1945." [5]

Managing reconversion presented the greatest problem. The report was actually optimistic in tone regarding the ability of American business to make the transition with a minimum of disruption. Highly specialized naval contractors, such as Kollmorgen Optical Corporation, would have the greatest difficulty. The transition posed far fewer problems for more diverse companies like the General Motors Corporation. For WPB the critical issues involved both coping with the vast increase in available labor at the end of the war and efficiently directing the distribution of resources as they became available for civilian production.

As director of war mobilization, it fell to James F. Byrnes to determine the pace at which the country would reconvert to peacetime production and the agencies that would manage the effort.[6] As the WPB Planning Division prepared its report, Byrnes asked Bernard M. Baruch and John M. Hancock to develop policies and plans for postwar reconversion. Both veterans of the reconversion process after the Great War, Baruch had served as chairman of the War Industries Board, while Hancock had directed naval procurement.

At the conclusion of their three-month study in February 1944, Baruch and Hancock made their recommendations to Byrnes. They relied heavily on the reports by Ernest Kanzler and the WPB Planning Division, but resisted the suggestion that a single central agency direct the reconversion to peacetime. They advised that WPB share authority with the Armed Services, the War Manpower Commission, and the War Surplus Property Administration. The Armed Services would determine the resources needed to bring the war to a successful conclusion. Before civilian industry could resume production, the War Manpower Commission had to certify that sufficient labor was available, and then WPB would carefully monitor the release to private industry of material resources no longer needed for the prosecution of the war. At the end of the conflict the War Surplus Property Administration would determine the disposition of factories, machinery, and properties owned by the government but used by private industry between 1940 and 1945. These measures were suggested to avoid the most potent enemies of reconversion—inflation and unemployment—that could result if abundant material resources were released for civilian production too quickly while industrial layoffs and discharges from the Armed Forces swelled the labor market.[7]

---

[5] Ibid., 22–23.

[6] Byrnes became the Director of War Mobilization and Reconversion in the last quarter of 1944.

[7] Sitterson, *Reconversion Policies of the War Production Board*, 27–65; Fesler, *Industrial Mobilization for War*, 722–24; Bernard M. Baruch and John M. Hancock, *War and Postwar Adjustment Policies* (Washington: American Council on Public Affairs, 1944). This last work is the text of the official report and related documents.

In June 1944 Nelson suggested in his public statements and in testimony before Congress that the time had come to implement the reconversion policies set forth in the Baruch-Hancock Report. His comments drew an immediate reaction from some of the highest placed officers in the Navy. Nelson had to reassure Admirals William Leahy, Samuel Robinson, and Ernest King that "war production obviously must continue to be the first responsibility of the economy as long as the need for war materials persists." But he insisted that lifting certain WPB restrictions would not interfere with the war effort and would make the transition to peacetime considerably smoother. This did not reassure Admiral King and his colleagues, who feared that the relaxation of WPB controls encouraged the immediate resumption of civilian production and undermined the sense of urgency among the American people that was so important to victory. King suggested that the implementation of any reconversion orders during the summer of 1944 would certainly prolong the conflict.[8]

Lifting Wartime Controls

In spite of Navy misgivings, in September 1944 James Byrnes publicly issued a set of reconversion guidelines approved by the President. Set to take effect on V–E Day, the new regulations created a system of revised priority ratings for select prime contractors and their suppliers. Byrnes also revoked the wartime controls placed on essential materials, save for steel and copper, which would remain in force for the remainder of the quarter in which the government chose to initiate the transition. The L and M Orders, which restricted civilian production and the use of scarce materials for nonessential manufacturing, were suspended and the WPB continued to manage production and procurement. The new directives also made provision for the prompt disposition of government-owned facilities through exercise of the contractor's right to purchase or lease any properties not retained by the Navy.

Byrnes also advised returning to a 40-hour work week and lifting the wartime personnel controls. Because this action would dramatically inflate the numbers of people looking for work, he took measures to guarantee employment for the majority. He appointed a committee consisting of representatives from WPB, the War Manpower Commission, the Defense Plant Corporation, and the War Surplus Property Administra-

---

[8] Memo, Robinson to Charles Nelson, 14 Jun 1944, box 22; Memo, COMINCH to SECNAV: "Resumption of Production of Civilian Products," 7 Jul 1944; Nelson to Leahy, 10 Jul 1944; Memo, VADM S. M. Robinson to the Under Secretary, 21 Feb 1944, box 108, Forrestal Records 1940–47, RG 80, NA. Leahy was chief of staff to President Roosevelt, Robinson was the chief of BUSHIPS, and King was COMINCH/CNO.

tion to monitor unemployment and potential dislocation in the labor market after V–E Day. The committee would try to ensure that government-owned war plants continued production on a reduced scale or quickly shifted to civilian projects after the prompt sale of the facilities to the private sector. Byrnes also allowed businesses not owned by the government and not normally involved in war production to return to civilian production first. He further suggested relaxing the tax on excess profits as well as that on capital invested in postwar business ventures.[9]

On 3 October 1944 President Roosevelt formalized these policies and expanded the responsibilities of Byrnes's office, renaming it the Office of War Mobilization and Reconversion. From his enhanced position, it became Byrnes's responsibility to preserve high production levels in those areas still vital to the war effort while promoting the transition to a civilian economy.[10] The fundamental policy statements of the new authority discouraged using service in the Armed Forces and wartime resource controls to sustain a healthy economy. Rather, Byrnes favored a swift and fair transition to peacetime employment and civilian industry to avoid economic dislocation.[11]

Reconversion in the Submarine Industry: EB's Victory Yard

The sale of the Victory Yard to Charles Pfizer and Company in 1946 offers an excellent example of the difficulties involved in making the transition to a peacetime economy and the variety of forces and interests at work in the process of reconversion. The Navy built the Victory Yard during the war to help Electric Boat Company expand its capacity for building submarines. After the war the Navy Department classified the Yard as a "B" yard, intending to retain it in a form that would preserve its shipbuilding capability against the possibility of future war.

But with the drastic reduction in submarine construction in 1944 and 1945, Electric Boat had little use for the Victory Yard and had no intention of exercising its option to purchase the facility under contract Nobs–380. The future was uncertain, and retrenchment had become the order of the day.

---

[9] Report to the President from Director of War Mobilization, James F. Byrnes, on Cutbacks in the War Production program, 8 Sep 1944, box 93, Forrestal Records 1940–47.

[10] The priority of essential war production was reaffirmed to the regional WPB directors by WPB, the Navy Department, the War Department, and the War Manpower Commission in a memo issued on 1 Dec 1944. Although the message was clear, paragraphs 6, 7, and 8 cleared the way for preliminary steps toward reconversion when war production would no longer be placed in jeopardy by such measures. WPB, Navy Department, War Department, and Manpower Commission to Regional Directors, 1 Dec 1944, box 108, Forrestal Records 1940–47.

[11] Sitterson, *Reconversion Policies of the War Production Board*, 151–53.

Electric Boat Company viewed the coming of demobilization and re-conversion with considerable trepidation. The Navy's inclination to extend its profit and price limitation policies into the postwar years troubled the company's directors in particular. The highly specialized nature of the submarine business and the certain reduction in postwar construction made EB suspicious of the motives behind continued government supervision and control. These factors, combined with the memory of the harsh treatment the company had received at the hands of the Nye Commission's investigation of the armaments industry in 1935 and 1936, heightened EB's concern for the future.

In fact some wartime legislation suggested to EB that the spirit of the Nye Commission hearings had already returned. Disturbed by the possibility that rapid mobilization after 1939 contributed to inflated prices for the implements of war, Congress created the Navy's Price Adjustment Board to fulfill the mandate of the Renegotiation Act of 1942. This legislation authorized the renegotiation of select war contracts to curb those prices and profits considered excessive.[12] In November 1942 EB corporate counsel Walter S. Orr suspected the Price Adjustment Board might begin its survey of the shipbuilding industry with an investigation of six private yards. His advice to L. Y. Spear, now president of Electric Boat, indicated the anxiety caused by the prospect of an investigation and the application of stricter controls:

> I feel that we should be very cautious about renegotiations for fear that our case, perhaps the first one to be considered, might be used as a precedent and that if we can delay until some of the other people have been heard that because of the special nature of our work we may get a much better adjustment than might otherwise occur.[13]

The Vinson-Trammel Act of 1934 had already limited industrial profits on naval contracts to 10 percent. The wartime amendment to this legislation, passed by the House of Representatives on 28 March 1942, modified the 6th Supplemental Defense Appropriations Act to require "repayment of all war contract profits in excess of 6% on sales." But some federal procurement agencies argued that the amendment would not lower costs, and the Senate eventually rejected the measure. President Roosevelt then used his authority under the Second War Powers Act to authorize certain procurement agencies to audit the books of private firms to determine excessive profit.

---

[12] *The Navy and the Industrial Mobilization*, 271ff.

[13] Orr to Spear, 10 Nov 1942, box (marked) 1328, 1328–1, 1328–2, Historical Records Vault, Electric Boat (EB) Division, General Dynamics Corporation, Groton, CT.

Congressional approval of the 6 percent profit ceiling came in the form of a new amendment to the 6th Supplemental Defense Appropriations Act passed on 28 April 1942. According to an analysis by the American Enterprise Association, "this Act was based upon recommendations made by the procurement agencies that contractors be required to furnish data on actual costs and production." Firms would now have to bargain in good faith for a readjustment of the contract price to accommodate the new regulation.[14]

The Navy reclaimed excess profits from Electric Boat in the form of reduced prices on submarines then on order or under construction. In March 1943 EB returned $2,279,441.22 in profits accrued in 1941 by reducing the price on *Mackerel* (SS 204), *Gar* (SS 206), *Grampus* (SS 207), *Grayback* (SS 208), *Gato* (SS 212), *Greenling* (SS 213), and *Grouper* (SS 214). Five months later the company surrendered $9,750,000 in renegotiated submarine prices for the year ending 31 December 1942.[15]

This time of apprehension and uncertainty continued from 1943 well into the postwar period. Business was uneasy with government's role in demobilization and reconversion as envisioned by Donald Nelson and James Byrnes. All of American industry looked with trepidation on the extension of industrial controls into the postwar era. Electric Boat and other highly specialized companies divested themselves of facilities, like the Victory Yard, that they could not sustain with the reduced number of postwar government contracts. In 1943, Spear testified before the House Committee on Naval Affairs and wrote to Senator H. Styles Bridges (R–N.H.), a member of the Senate Committee on Military Affairs, arguing against the activities of the Price Adjustment Board and the possible continuation of wartime controls.[16]

Spear and other American business leaders viewed the proposed government regulation of reconversion as interference. To the president of EB the actions of the Price Adjustment Board were punitive and capricious. On 23 September 1944 Eric E. Lincoln, chief economist of the Du

[14] American Enterprise Association, "Analysis of H.R. 9246, To Provide for the Renegotiation of Contracts and for Other Purposes," 10 Aug 1950, box 003, Historical Records Vault, EB Division, General Dynamics.

[15] Spear to BUSHIPS, 17 Mar 1943; Treasury Department to EB, 11 Aug 1943; BUSANDA to Spear, 29 May 1945, box (marked) 1328, 1328–1, 1328–2; American Enterprise Association, "Analysis of H.R. 9246, To Provide for the Renegotiation of Contracts and for Other Purposes," 10 Aug 1950, box 003, Historical Records Vault, EB Division, General Dynamics. The renegotiation measure received new life as part of the Supplemental National Defense Appropriations Act of 1948, where it was covered by the amendment entitled "Renegotiation Act of 1948" that brought the ceiling down to 5 percent.

[16] L. Y. Spear (President of EB), "Statement on Renegotiation" to the House Committee on Naval Affairs, 28 Jun 1943, box (marked) 1328–2, 1328–21; Spear to Bridges, 21 Oct 1943, box (marked) 1328(9), 1328(10), 1328(11), 1000(V–1), Historical Records Vault, EB Division, General Dynamics.

Pont Company, expressed similar views. In a letter to company president Walter S. Carpenter, Jr., Lincoln argued that "the only sound position for industry to take, is to advocate a termination of all Government price and production controls as soon as possible after the end of hostilities—with at least partial relief after the German war ends."

He concluded by commenting that any

> argument in favor of a continuance of price regulation by the Government following the war, seems to me to be exactly on a par with President Roosevelt's argument in favor of a fourth term — always something uncompleted, never a "normal" condition which will leave the American economy free to sink or swim under its own efforts! [17]

The people of the Groton–New London area experienced similar anxiety. To a large degree the disposition of the Victory Yard and other expressions of government involvement in the marketplace would determine the postwar economic well-being of the region. The sale of the yard to Pfizer for the production of chemicals and antibiotics would mean industrial diversity and the promise of jobs well into the postwar era. Thus the residents of the region and their representatives in Congress exerted moral, economic, and political pressure on both the Navy and industry. If the Navy retained the yard, it might remain inactive, preserved in case of some future emergency. The local community preferred to keep the Victory Yard as an active employer, producing goods and services either under Navy control or in private hands through rental, leasing agreement, or sale.

As the war ended, the Navy and its contractors all over the country faced the same decisions. In determining how to dispose of government-owned industrial facilities, which considerations best served the welfare of the country? With the advent of peace the number of ship contracts would diminish and the submarine construction industry would experience a contraction. Could this process be quickly reversed if war came again? Did it not make sense to preserve some of the industrial capability made possible by the war as a safeguard? As of V–J Day the Navy controlled a total of 1,305 facilities valued at approximately $2,243,440,000; of 364 plants under the control of BUSHIPS, 30, including the Victory Yard, were slated for retention.[18]

---

[17] Lincoln to Carpenter, 23 Sep 1944, box 837, series II, part 2, Papers of Walter S. Carpenter, Jr., President, Records of E. I. du Pont de Nemours and Co., accession 542, Archive of the Hagley Museum and Library, Wilmington, DE.

[18] Memo, John T. Connor to Forrestal, "Navy Department: Status of Surplus Property Disposal," 23 Oct 1946, box 127, Forrestal Records 1940–47, RG 80; Forrestal to Senator Gurney, 25 Feb 1947, box 661, BUSHIPS GENCORR 1940–45, RG 19, NA.

The Navy and industry could not prevent a contraction in the submarine industry as victory approached. The Chief of Naval Operations canceled the third and final submarine construction contract at Manitowoc Shipbuilding Company in June 1944, and the last of the Great Lakes-built submarines arrived in New Orleans seventeen months later.[19] Soon afterward Cramp followed suit, and the Navy was once again down to its primary building yards of the prewar era: EB, Portsmouth, and Mare Island.[20]

Electric Boat's decision not to purchase the Victory Yard represented a further contraction. The discussion of the best alternative use for the yard first began in the fall of 1944 when the cancellation of submarine contracts began at Electric Boat. In a letter to BUSHIPS penned on 4 October, Captain Isaac Irving Yates, the supervisor of shipbuilding at Groton, announced the imminent closing of the Victory Yard machine shop because of the reduced work load. The last submarine launching at this yard was scheduled for the following May, and the Navy and EB had already begun discussing the disposition of shop tools and addressing questions about the future of the yard. In spite of planning on the national level, BUSHIPS lacked experience in this area. Thus policies for the conversion of the Victory Yard to peacetime would set a precedent within the bureau and the submarine community. A quickly scrawled note from the Shipbuilding Division on a BUSHIPS route slip said it best: "This is a good guinea pig to make pattern for plant disposal conversion etc—At present don't know wether [sic] 800, 802, 131, 760 or ? spear heads this type of action—Suggest we get together to set up a formula."[21]

As the bureau prepared to address the problem, EB Vice President O. Pomeroy Robinson suddenly announced that the company had accepted an opportunity to keep the Victory Yard machine shop open by producing 105-mm shells for the Springfield Ordnance Department of the Army. Shortly thereafter, as part of a continuing effort to keep the company solvent and the work force employed, Robinson secured a subcontract from the General Electric Company for B–29 gun turrets, which would require the machinery and staff of the Victory Yard's fabricating and welding shop (building 31). After a brief but stormy debate over the need for BUSHIPS's permission to convert a submarine yard to this kind

---

[19] Nelson, *Fresh Water Submarines*, 140–42.

[20] Although submarine construction ended with the war, Cramp did not completely vacate its government-owned facilities in Philadelphia until 31 January 1947. Thereafter the yard was under the control of the commander of the Philadelphia Navy Yard until it was leased to the U.S. Shipbuilding Corporation later that year. Like the Victory Yard in Groton, the old Cramp facility was classified as a B yard that might be needed in the event of an emergency. RADM C. D. Wheelock (Deputy Chief of BUSHIPS) to the Bureau of Yards and Docks Real Estate Division, 3 Mar 1947, BUSHIPS GENCORR 1940–45.

[21] SUPSHIPS, Groton, to BUSHIPS, 4 Oct 1944, box 407, BUSHIPS GENCORR 1940–45.

of work, the issue was settled by acknowledging the overriding national need for the ordnance and imposing a rent on EB for use of the facilities.

Robinson's reasons for making the conversion were difficult to dispute. As he pointed out to BUSHIPS on 18 January 1945:

> The submarine program has been reduced from 2.3 ships per month in June, 1944 to a requirement of .97 ships per month in December, 1944 and further to .72 ships per month in June 1945. This reduction in the submarine program results in there being no further need to use Building 31 and its facilities for this purpose. The reduction also results in a steadily increasing surplus of manpower which can be utilized on the shell production program.

Furthermore, the continuity of tasks momentarily eliminated the need for layoffs while posing no danger to the reduced submarine program. Indeed, a local New London newspaper, in reporting the news of the shell contract, emphasized that it meant the Victory Yard would not close in the spring of 1945 as previously announced by Electric Boat.[22]

As the pace of war production slowed, many of the Navy's submarine contractors made arrangements of this sort to avoid closing facilities. The bureaus carefully formulated policies concerning the disposition of government-owned facilities in each industry as the need arose. In 1945 Fairbanks-Morse and Company reduced its opposed-piston diesel production from 64 to 32 engines per month, creating a problem of what to do with the excess plant space and government-owned tools and machinery. BUSHIPS allowed some civilian commercial work after the engine production slowdown and even permitted the company to allow a chromium firm, Van der Horst, to use some of the facilities previously employed for lining diesel cylinder sleeves with that metal.

In another case the Navy's inspector of machinery stopped Fairbanks-Morse from switching a portion of its Freeport, Illinois, facility to the production of electric motors. He wanted a BUSHIPS ruling on the alternative uses of the excess plant space and tools.[23]

Electric Boat stopped using the Victory Yard on 17 August 1945, almost immediately after the fall of Japan. Shortly thereafter the debate began over the best disposition of the yard. The Navy wanted to preserve the facility's potential for building submarines, but the population of the

[22] BUSHIPS to SUPSHIPS, Groton, 27 Dec 1944; BUSHIPS to EB, 9 Jan 1945; LTCOL G. C. Smith, USA (Ordnance Department), to BUSHIPS (with route slips), 3 Jan 1945; CAPT I. I. Yates SUPSHIPS, Groton, to CAPT P. Lemler, BUSHIPS, 5 Jan 1945; M. E. Serat, Assistant to the President of EB, to BUSHIPS, 5 Jan 1945; SUPSHIPS, Groton, to BUSHIPS, 18 Jan 1945; O. P. Robinson, Vice President and General Manager of EB, to BUSHIPS, 18 Jan 1945, box 408, BUSHIPS GENCORR 1940–45.

[23] File folder 20, Spring-Summer 1945, box 437, BUSHIPS GENCORR 1940–45.

region protested through their local and congressional representatives. By early November Charles Pfizer and Company entered into negotiations with BUSHIPS for the acquisition of the yard. The company intended to produce "fine chemicals and anti-biotics such as Penicillin and Streptomycin" at the Groton location to supplement the output of its facility in Brooklyn, New York, which no longer had the space to expand.

State and local officials proved beyond a doubt that the region needed the presence of a company like Pfizer. Connecticut Governor Raymond E. Baldwin reminded BUSHIPS that Groton was essentially a one-industry town. During the height of war production Electric Boat employed approximately 12,000 men and women. Three months after the end of the Pacific war the company's work force fell to 4,000. Baldwin concluded a letter to the bureau written on 13 November by saying, "The transfer of the Victory Yard—now a part of the Electric Boat Company—to the use of an industry, employing a thousand or more persons would help effectively to stabilize the economic situation in Groton and New London, as well as thru out eastern Connecticut."[24]

Groton city officials also reminded the bureau that the Victory Yard was only one of many properties that the U.S. government had removed from the local tax rolls. Charles T. Crawhill, first selectman of the town of Groton, noted that "the town of Groton has over thirty million dollars of United States Government tax exempt property, which is over 30% more than there is taxable property in the town." Combined with growing unemployment, this situation threatened the economic survival of the Groton-New London area.[25]

Naval authorities realized the gravity of the situation and found themselves confronting a difficult decision. They had to consider the economic well-being of the workers employed at the Victory Yard. But at the same time the bureau felt strongly about preserving the yard to expedite the expansion of the submarine industry in case of an emergency. In a letter penned in July 1945 to Senator Thomas C. Hart (R–Conn.), a former admiral, Chief of BUSHIPS Vice Admiral Edward L. Cochrane explained that the bureau wanted

> to develop some use for these facilities which would permit them to be kept available against some future emergency. . . The Department now has under consideration a proposal which will permit this objective to be accomplished, and at the same time permit a productive use to be made of the facilities, thereby providing a substantial amount of gainful employment.[26]

---

[24] Baldwin to Lemler, 13 Nov 1945, box 408, BUSHIPS GENCORR 1940–45.

[25] Crawhill to Waldo E. Clark (Engineer-Secretary), Commissioners of Steamship Terminals, 12 Nov 1945, box 408, BUSHIPS GENCORR 1940–45.

[26] Cochrane to Hart, 12 Jul 1945, BUSHIPS GENCORR 1940–45.

In a memorandum for the CNO composed in early November, BU-SHIPS offered five possible alternatives for the yard's disposition. Although the bureau clearly wanted a solution that satisfied the claims of all concerned, the first two options offered in the memorandum gave priority to the Navy's plans. The Victory Yard could be sold to a well-established concern "for any peacetime use consistent with the ultimate mission of the Yard." The bureau desired a compromise that would place the facility in private hands to enhance the local economy while permitting the recovery of the yard and its reconversion to submarine production. In addition, the first alternative specifically assigned the yard's berthing facilities to the New London submarine base in response to an earlier request from Commander Submarine Force, Atlantic Fleet. The bureau approved the rest of the yard for sale to the private sector.[27]

Although BUSHIPS certainly preferred to sell the Victory Yard to a firm that would keep the facility in the shipbuilding business, the political pressure mounted to reach an agreement with Pfizer. The U.S. Shipbuilding Corporation leased the government-owned facilities operated by Cramp in Philadelphia, but no company displayed similar interest in entering the submarine business or operating a shipyard less than one mile away from Electric Boat. Charles D. Crandall, first selectman of Groton at this time, kept Senator Brien McMahon (D–Conn.) aware of the disastrous effect inactivity at the Victory Yard would have on employment, the town's tax base, and the welfare system.[28] Advisors to Secretary of the Navy James Forrestal strongly suggested that surplus plants should be advertised and disposed of quickly to protect jobs and avoid economic dislocation. In the words of Special Assistant to the Secretary Arthur Hill,

> the most important thing to bear in mind about War Plants is that we have built and operated them in secrecy. They are pigs-in-a-poke as far as most people are concerned. To get rid of them quickly and at good prices we need lots of bidding:—put the pigs on platters with apples in their mouths.[29]

The Victory Yard never attracted the kind of bidder BUSHIPS desired. But that did not diminish the importance of the facility to the local community or the Navy. Faced with only one proposal from private industry and the economic need of the local community, the Navy Department permitted BUSHIPS to declare the Victory Yard war surplus

---

[27] Memo, BUSHIPS to CNO, [1 or 2] Nov 1945, box 409, BUSHIPS GENCORR 1940–45.

[28] Crandall to McMahon, 12 Jan 1946, box 1241, BUSHIPS Confidential CENCORR 1946, RG 19, NA/WNRC.

[29] Memo, Arthur Hill to SECNAV, Obstacles to Quick Conversion, 26 Apr 1945, box 108, Forrestal Records 1940–47, RG 80, NA.

on 8 March 1946, opening the way for Pfizer to purchase the plant. Before making the declaration, the bureau took a full inventory at the yard. Then the civilian War Assets Administration stepped in to determine fair market value and ratify the sale. On 29 March 1946 this agency approved the offer of $801,000 made by Pfizer. The Navy's Material Redistribution and Disposal Office quickly cleared the property of all Navy machinery and equipment not included in the agreement. But to the dismay of the supervisor of shipbuilding in Groton, it took the War Assets Administration five months to complete its preparations. The transfer of responsibility for the Victory Yard from BUSHIPS to the War Assets Administration, legally required for completing the sale to Pfizer, did not take place until 6 August.[30]

Observations

The Victory Yard experience demonstrated the difficult adjustments involved in reconversion. EB did not want to retain the yard in an uncertain postwar environment that promised a severe reduction in the Navy's need for submarines. Furthermore the company feared the effect of extending wartime business and profit controls into the postwar era. Recalling the need for rapid industrial expansion at the beginning of the war, BUSHIPS naturally argued that the Navy Department should preserve the Victory Yard's capability to build submarines as a counterweight to contraction in the private sector submarine industry. But this policy clashed with the need to curb unemployment and preserve the economic well-being of the Groton–New London community. In the end the Navy Department bowed to the needs of the workers and the inevitable contraction in the shipbuilding business. The bureau used the Victory Yard experience to determine both the nature of the forces at work in reconversion and the proper system for disposing of government-owned facilities.

In the spring of 1945 Secretary of the Navy Forrestal had commissioned the Graduate School of Business Administration at Harvard University to study the disposition of facilities like the Victory Yard. Reflecting in their conclusions on the future of the shipbuilding industry in America and its importance to national security, the Harvard analysts repeatedly returned to the same pair of recommendations. The Navy had to preserve both the skills necessary to build essential types of warships

---

[30] BUSHIPS to War Assets Administration, 8 Mar 1946; R. G. Rhett, Chief, Operations Section Industrial Division, Office of Real Property Disposal, War Assets Administration, 29 Mar 1949, box 1240, BUSHIPS Confidential CENCORR 1946, RG 19, NA/WNRC.

and a core of reliable shipyards and contractors capable of producing the vessels. The case of EB's Victory Yard demonstrated that this would be no easy task. Market forces at work in the shipbuilding industry and regional economic needs often foiled the best-laid plans for future industrial expansion in the national defense. In postwar America, however, dramatic advances in technology and new perspectives on submarine mission and design would sustain the hard-pressed naval-industrial complex for submarines and allow it to respond to the Navy's future needs.[31]

---

[31] Harvard University School of Business Administration, "The Use and Disposition of Ships and Shipyards at the End of World War II," [Jun 1945], box 131, Forrestal Records 1940–47, RG 80, NA.

Chapter 5

Cold War Challenges, 1946–1951

With the advent of victory in the war against the Axis Powers, the operational submarine community found itself in a quandary. With its only major naval rival vanquished, the large and effective American submarine force began searching for a significant role in the postwar defense of the United States. Now, more than ever, the character of that role depended upon the nature of a new threat—the Soviet Union—and the capabilities conferred by technology.

Soon after the war a panel of naval officers under Vice Admiral Francis S. Low demonstrated that, for the Navy and the nation, the Soviet threat was in large part a function of their access to advanced German submarine technology. As Captain William Ignatius of the Naval Technical Mission correctly perceived, the postwar naval-industrial complex for submarines faced a revolution in undersea warfare sparked by the enhanced diving, speed, and endurance characteristics of advanced German designs captured by both the United States and the Soviet Union. In the process of investigating and exploiting these technologies, the Navy's technical bureaus, naval shipyards, private contractors, and the scientific community completely redefined the nature of undersea warfare while sustaining their wartime relationship in the face of a new foe.

What Next?

Anticipating a reduction in submarine construction at the end of the war, both the Navy and private industry braced themselves for lean times. The debate over the fate of the Victory Yard and its eventual sale to Charles Pfizer reflected an industrywide expectation that the demands of the postwar submarine community would be modest. Therefore, companies like Electric Boat took measures to survive the contraction in the submarine industry by reducing overhead and diversifying. The Navy for its part decided to dramatically reduce the large wartime submarine force by scrapping 20 fleet submarines, placing 106 in reserve, employing 19 as trainers, and preserving 4 as unfinished hulks for completion at some future date.[1]

Creating the reserve submarine fleet took a great deal of time and resources. The Navy did most of the work in the San Francisco area at Mare Island Naval Shipyard, Hunter's Point Navy Yard, and Bethlehem Steel Company. These facilities provided each submarine with a limited overhaul and a treatment with chemicals and paint to ensure material preservation. In addition, the ballast tanks were coated with preservative and sealed. Afterward the crews of the Navy's submarine tenders installed dehumidifying equipment, finished preserving the machinery as well as the interior and exterior of the hull, and took a complete inventory of parts and spares. Initially the process cost BUSHIPS an average of $61,888.75 per vessel placed in reserve status. But as the work force gained considerable experience, this figure fell to $41,997.80 per vessel.[2]

The U.S. Navy also needed to evaluate current Allied and captured German technology to determine the submarine's future role, appearance, and capability. Although America's most likely adversary, the Soviet Union, posed no immediate surface threat, it did have a great number of submarines designed primarily for coastal defense. Red Army success in capturing the same German submarine technology that interested the Naval Technical Mission made appreciation of the potential of German technology absolutely vital. Since the Type XXI U-boat represented a quantum leap forward in submarine development, the Navy Department had to assume that the Soviets, too, would build on this technology. During a time of American strategic redefinition and contests between the services over primary roles and missions in the national defense, the fundamental changes in the rules of undersea warfare, precipitated by high submerged speed and endurance, assumed a prominent place in formulating Navy plans for the future.

Under Allied postwar agreements the U.S. Navy acquired thirteen German U-boats of various types for testing and evaluation. This group of vessels included seven variations on the Type IX, two Type VIICs, one Type XB, and one Type XVIIB as well as two Type XXI U-boats, the *U-2513* and *U-3008*. The performance of the Type XXI vessels while in the custody of the Portsmouth Naval Shipyard confirmed the impressive reports filed by the Naval Technical Mission on the capabilities of these submarines. They

[1] Alden, *The Fleet Submarine in the U.S. Navy*, 128.

[2] Commander Mare Island Group, 19th Fleet (reserve), to BUSHIPS, 23 February 1946, box 1516, BUSHIPS Confidential CENCORR 1946, RG 19, NA/WNRC. Reduction in Force—Postwar Plans for Submarine Force and Personnel, 28 Aug 1945, series 2, file 5, box 6; Commander Submarine Force, Pacific Fleet (COMSUBPAC), to CAPT Karl G. Hensel, USN (OP–23C), 16 Aug 1945, series 2, file 6, box 6, Subs/UWD, OA.

submerged in approximately twenty seconds and on electric motors could sustain an underwater speed of 17 knots for an hour.[3]

In September 1945 both naval personnel and private contractors began conducting tests on the *U–2513* and *U–3008* for BUSHIPS at the Portsmouth Naval Shipyard. While the *U–3008* remained at the yard for a design study, the *U–2513* underwent sea trials, which included sound, standardization, turning, magnetic, torpedo, schnorchel, and other tests to display the vessel's maximum capabilities. It continued running the gamut of basic naval testing and evaluation through the early months of the new year.

Although this ship performed admirably, the team at Portsmouth discovered some interesting difficulties with its operation. The Germans had increasingly turned to hydraulic power to operate many of the systems of the Type XXI, most notably the control surfaces. This step reduced the demand on the submarine's electrical system, thereby leaving more battery power for propulsion. But the faster the submarine went, the greater the pressure on the hydraulic system to respond promptly to the rudder and diving plane controls. Designed quickly under the pressures of war, the overly elaborate hydraulic system used in the Type XXIs tended to blow gaskets and lose pressure just when power was needed to control the submarine. According to Captain Ignatius, the German engineers failed to consider "the rugged and simple construction necessary for submarine wartime service and utilized delicate and complicated mechanisms to obtain unnecessary refinements. Likewise, that they did not appreciate the leakage difficulties that could be expected is indicated by the fact that extensive piping, connections, and pistons were utilized externally." The crew could not repair any casualty outside the pressure hull, but the fragility of the system invited just such difficulties.[4]

German engineers also had trouble with submarine diesel superchargers. The *U–2513* was powered by two supercharged six-cylinder MAN diesels providing 1970 horse power at 520 rpm. When the superchargers were removed, the output of the engine dropped significantly and threw the entire propulsion system out of balance. The batteries and motors functioned well, but without the supercharger the diesels could not properly recharge the batteries after a one-hour, full-power run. Without the

---

[3] COMSUBLANT to Conference on Operational Tests to be Conducted on German Submarines, 10 Sep 1945, series 3, file 5, box 10; Commander Special Submarine Group to COMSUBLANT, 21 Feb 1946, series 3, file 5, box 11, Subs/UWD.

[4] Former German Submarine Type XXI—Report from Portsmouth Naval Shipyard, Mar 1946, series 3, file 3, box 9, Subs/UWD; Technical Report 305–45, 13 Aug 1945, box 31, NAVTECHMISEU, OA. Much of the hydraulic design that went into the Guppy conversions of American fleet submarines to high speed came from the work done on the system for Howard Hughes's giant wooden airplane, the Spruce Goose. Harry A. Jackson, letter to author, 10 Dec 1990.

services of the supercharger the U-boat's 372 battery cells required a four-hour application of 1,200 horsepower to the generators to restore them to full capacity. This lengthy recharge reduced to a certain degree the advantages offered by the ship's high submerged speed.[5]

Designed for prolonged submergence as well as increased speed, the Type XXI also forced the Germans to pay closer attention to habitability. The ship carried twenty-four oxygen bottles to help renew the air and improve the atmosphere during long submergences. This oxygen, combined with an efficient system of air conditioning, filtering, and calcium-based carbon dioxide absorbers, kept the submarine's atmosphere fresh. But at times the air conditioning system, designed to alleviate the summer heat in northern climes, proved completely inadequate for American crews conducting trials on board the *U–2513* in the tropical environment near Key West.[6]

Over the next year the Navy authorized further tests on the two vessels. The Board of Inspection and Survey conducted a routine inspection of the submarine to report its material condition. In addition, the team of William Schevill and Allyn Vine from WHOI prepared a report on the Type XXI's submerged performance. The durability of these vessels, as well as their submerged diving, surfacing, and turning characteristics at various speeds, provided important data for the Bureau of Ships in its effort to incorporate the best of this technology into American ships.[7]

The advent of the Cold War and the American analysis of these German advances in design and propulsion prompted the General Board and the Ships Characteristics Board to advise that the Navy Department pursue two avenues in the development of modern postwar attack submarines.[8] First they suggested taking some of the wartime fleet submarines and converting them to Type XXI facsimiles, called "Guppies" because of their "greater underwater propulsive power." The other recommended avenue of development, which found expression in the *Tang*-class design, sought to emulate the high speed and improved char-

---

[5] Former German Submarine Type XXI—Report from Portsmouth Naval Shipyard, Mar 1946, series 3, file 3, box 9, Subs/UWD.

[6] Ibid.

[7] Material Inspection of the U–2513 by the Board of Inspection and Survey, 3 June 1947, series 3, file 1, box 12; Submerged Performance Tests on German Type XXI Submarines, A Report by William E. Schevill and Allyn C. Vine of WHOI, 17 Mar 1947, series 3, file 3, box 12, Subs/UWD.

[8] The General Board defined the capabilities required of a new vessel or class, and the Ships Characteristics Board formulated a specific design proposal. This recommendation was debated in the General Board hearings before it was sent on to the Secretary of the Navy via the CNO. Ships Characteristics Board Procedures, 12 Sep 1947, box 18, General Board Studies 1949–1950, RG 45, NA. The Ships Characteristics Board took over the functions of the General Board when the latter was abolished in 1950. SECNAV Francis P. Matthews to CNO (ADM Forrest Sherman), 14 Apr 1950, series D/E, box 2, General Board Miscellaneous Subject Files 1919–50, RG 45, NA.

acteristics of the Type XXI from the keel up. It was up to BUSHIPS to turn these ideas into seagoing vessels.[9]

The Guppy Program

When the Chief of Naval Operations, Fleet Admiral Chester Nimitz, officially authorized the Guppy conversion program, barely a year had passed since V–J Day. Although this conversion and overhaul program never approached the scale of wartime production, Nimitz's order sent the submarine industry back to work. In June 1946 he gave his approval to convert two fleet submarines into high-speed Guppies. Portsmouth would convert *Odax* (SS 484) on the East Coast and supply Mare Island with the plans and advice that would enable it to effect the same transition on *Pomodon* (SS 486) on the West Coast. Nimitz assigned both projects the highest priority and urged BUSHIPS to strive for the earliest possible completion date.[10]

Responding to the CNO's request, BUSHIPS allowed free written communication between naval authorities and contractors on all matters related to the Guppy conversions to ensure quick and precise completion of these alterations. Bureau planners felt that sharing the expertise in various fields of science and engineering acquired over years of working with naval vessels would reduce misunderstandings as well as quickly promote and disseminate ideas. Less-restricted, written communication of design information and test results would not inhibit bureau control over the flow of classified information within a clearly defined community of naval personnel and defense contractors. Rather, it would encourage more thorough preparation from the participating contractors

---

[9] In September 1945 a submarine operations research report written for COMINCH captured the importance of increased submerged speed:

> This proposed new feature would result in increasing the efficiency of submarine approach, attack, and evasion. The submarine would be able to close to an advantageous attack position in a higher percentage of contacts than in the past. Once a contact was closed, the greater maneuverability of the submarine would allow it to attack a larger percentage of the enemy ship in the contact than in the past. The more advantageous nature of the attack position that could be gained would also result in a greater effectiveness of attack. And finally, if a counterattack developed, the submerged high speed would probably make the evasive tactics of the submarine more effective.

Submarine Operations Research Report: "Quantitative Advantage of 20–Knot Submerged Speed for U.S. Submarines," 20 Sep 1945, BUSHIPS Secret CENCORR 1945, RG 19, NA/WNRC.

[10] BUSHIPS Naval Message to Commander Portsmouth Naval Shipyard, 29 Aug 1946, box 1571; BUSHIPS Naval Message to Commanding Officer, Mare Island Naval Shipyard via COMSUBLANT and CNO, 28 Aug 1946, box 1572; CNO to BUSHIPS, 29 Jun 1946; BUSHIPS to Commander Portsmouth Naval Shipyard, 8 Aug 1946; BUSHIPS to Commander Portsmouth Naval Shipyard, 24 Jul 1946, box 1519, BUSHIPS Confidential CENCORR 1946, RG 19, NA/WNRC.

and the correct execution of assigned tasks. On particularly important issues, such as difficulties with the complex Guppy electrical systems, the bureau encouraged naval authorities and contractors to meet in conference. By encouraging this type of cooperation on the conversion project, BUSHIPS also enhanced its own position as the central clearinghouse and final authority for all matters related to the Guppy program.[11]

Less than one year after the Naval Technical Mission was decommissioned, the Portsmouth Naval Shipyard undertook the first Guppy conversion. Since the focus was on increased submerged speed, *Odax* lost its deck guns, had the outer hull streamlined, and received a "sail" to replace the conning tower. These changes increased the submarine's speed by reducing its submerged drag. After doubling the usual *Tench*-class complement of 352 battery cells, this Guppy I conversion attained a submerged speed of 18.2 knots for thirty minutes, which exceeded its surface speed by 0.4 knots. These particulars of the *Odax* conversion illustrate the action taken to increase the vessel's speed and indicate the value placed on that particular characteristic. Other changes included the removal of periscope number two and the SJ radar and relocation of the SV radar mast.[12] The bureau sacrificed a 300-kilowatt auxiliary diesel engine and associated equipment for extra internal space, installed more air conditioning equipment to improve habitability, and removed the propeller guards at the stern to lighten the load. The bureau designed new propellers for the vessel and sacrificed four torpedoes from the forward torpedo room to generate more bunk space to sustain the crew on long submergences.

Anticipating the potentially dangerous volume of hazardous gases emitted by an increased number of storage batteries, BUSHIPS commissioned a study to determine the ventilation required to keep the vessel safe. Sound emission tests revealed that the *U–2513* operated more quietly than the American fleet submarine, so BUSHIPS initiated an exten-

---

[11] BUSHIPS to Director, DTMB, 17 May 1946, box 1516; BUSHIPS to Commanders Portsmouth and Mare Island Naval Shipyards, 26 Aug 1946; CAPT H. E. Saunders (Director, DTMB) to BUSHIPS Preliminary Design Branch (Code 420), 31 Dec 1946, box 1571, BUSHIPS Confidential CENCORR 1946. BUSHIPS to Commander Portsmouth Naval Shipyard, 27 Feb 1947, box 907, BUSHIPS Unclassified CENCORR 1947, RG 19, NA/WNRC.

[12] Both the SJ and the SV radars were S-band systems developed during World War II by the Radiation Laboratory at the University of California, Berkeley, and NRL in Anacostia. Some of the research was based on information about the British multicavity magnetron obtained in a mutual exchange of wartime scientific and technical information. The SJ was primarily a surface-search radar that enabled the American submarine force to execute precise night attacks and coordinate wolfpack tactics more effectively. The SV radar, primarily a product of NRL, enhanced the submarine's ability to detect approaching aircraft as well as its surface search capability. Louis A. Gebhard, *Evolution of Radio Electronics and Contributions of the Naval Research Laboratory* (Washington: Naval Research Laboratory, 1979), 187–89.

sive program to reduce cavitation, vibration, and other manifestations of self-noise.[13]

The more advanced conversion design, called the Guppy II, added a schnorchel to the characteristics of *Odax*. BUSHIPS chose to limit the Guppy I conversions to *Odax* at Portsmouth and *Pomodon* at Mare Island, while the Navy's Engineering Experiment Station at Annapolis and the Portsmouth Naval Shipyard busied themselves perfecting an American schnorchel. After this device made its debut on *Irex* (SS 482) in 1947, the bureau transformed twenty-four fleet submarines of the *Balao-* and *Tench-*classes into Guppy IIs. This number included *Odax* and *Pomodon*, upgraded with the addition of a schnorchel.

When BUSHIPS insisted on close cooperation between the lead yards during the course of the Guppy program, the Portsmouth leadership resisted. Captain Ralph S. McDowell, commander of the Portsmouth Naval Shipyard, argued forcefully that complete cooperation between EB and Portsmouth would destroy the competitive spirit that had become a profitable tradition within the submarine community. BUSHIPS and Portsmouth had drafted the preliminary designs for the first Guppy conversions, obliging latecomer EB to master a new concept and design. To have the company educated as quickly as possible, BUSHIPS wanted Portsmouth to share its expertise. According to Rear Admiral Charles L. Brand, assistant chief of BUSHIPS for ship design and shipbuilding, the request was made for practical reasons and would not interrupt the productive competition between the two yards. In a letter sent to the Portsmouth commander on Christmas Eve 1946, he stated:

> In order to conserve time and funds, as well as to obtain maximum advantage from the alterations, it appears highly desirable to have a free interchange of design information between the Portsmouth Naval Shipyard and the Electric Boat Company. It is not considered necessary or desirable to have complete interchange of all plans in a purely routine manner. It is believed that best results can be obtained by each activity forwarding to the other results of any special tests or calculations, as well as copies of inquiries initiated to obtain particular design information.[14]

Brand knew that the quick conversion of fleet submarines to Guppies required a measure of uniformity in design to simplify procuring materials

[13] BUSHIPS to Commander Portsmouth Naval Shipyard, 24 Jul 1946, box 1571, BUSHIPS Confidential CENCORR 1946; BUSHIPS to Farrel-Birmingham, 27 Mar 1947; BUSHIPS to B. F. Goodrich, 17 Dec 1947; Farrel-Birmingham to CDR R. T. Simpson, BUSHIPS Code 641s, 25 Feb 1947; BUSHIPS to U.S. Rubber, 2 Dec 1947; The Barry Corporation to BUSHIPS, 9 Dec 1947; Firestone Tire and Rubber Company to BUSHIPS, 12 Dec 1947, BUSHIPS Confidential CENCORR 1947.

[14] RADM C. L. Brand to Commander Portsmouth Naval Shipyard and BUSHIPS Confidential CENCORR 1946, SUPSHIPS, Groton, 24 December 1946, box 1521, BUSHIPS Confidential CENCORR 1946.

and systems in a timely fashion. The supervisor of shipbuilding in Groton expressed the same concerns in a letter penned on 10 December, which discussed government-furnished materials and proper delivery times.[15]

Captain McDowell agreed with the way Admiral Brand defined the EB-Portsmouth relationship, but it did not deter him from further clarifying his position. Sharing the results of tests was not the issue, nor was the basic cooperation between the two facilities. He wanted to preserve the competition between the two yards that required them to separately address the same engineering and design problems. This process offered the Navy two distinctly different approaches to the same questions, which McDowell considered healthy.

> It is understood that this is the basis for having the two submarine design activities. It has been the practice of the Bureau to follow closely the features of the respective designs and where special merit is involved in one or the other to pass the design of that feature to the other activity and to require its adoption. . . . To freely exchange all plans would destroy the independence and competitive spirit of each establishment and eliminate in large measure the two-design system now in effect.[16]

BUSHIPS was not convinced. Captain James R. Z. Reynolds, who presided over submarine design at the bureau, characterized two distinct approaches to the problem as counterproductive. As an example he offered the battery ventilation system of the Guppy conversions. Due to fundamental design differences in layout and construction, if the Portsmouth plan proved preferable to the bureau, it would take EB seven weeks to accomplish the alterations on the vessels undergoing conversion at Groton. Reynolds offered this situation as "final proof" that only collaboration on the first design would achieve standardization and streamline the entire conversion process.[17]

In this case the bureau held its ground. During the immediate postwar period BUSHIPS directed the design, conversion, and construction of submarines through a system requiring Portsmouth and EB to collaborate more closely than ever before. In the process, the bureau upgraded the facilities at Portsmouth and arranged for Mare Island Naval Shipyard to continue its traditional role as Portsmouth's follow-yard for

[15] SUPSHIPS, Groton, to BUSHIPS, 10 December 1946, box 1519, BUSHIPS Confidential CENCORR 1946.

[16] CAPT Ralph S. McDowell, Commander Portsmouth Naval Shipyard to BUSHIPS (Code 5815), 31 Dec 1946, box 907, BUSHIPS Unclassified CENCORR 1947.

[17] BUSHIPS to SUPSHIPS, Groton (see route slip comment signed JRZR 5815), 1 Apr 1947; A. I. McKee (Design Director, EB) to SUPSHIPS, 20 Mar 1947, BUSHIPS Unclassified CENCORR 1947. RADM Andrew I. McKee, USN (Ret.), became the design director of EB upon his retirement in 1947.

submarine construction and alteration. BUSHIPS directed that Mare Island receive all pertinent information supplementary to the *Odax* alteration plans dispatched by Portsmouth in August.[18]

The bureau also courted those contractors most important to the conversion program. A concerted effort took place in late 1947 to build within the private sector a greater interest in the postwar development of submarines. The bureau permitted visits to the operating submarine fleet by select personnel from a wide variety of these contractors, including Babcock & Wilcox Company, Bendix Aviation Corporation, Allis-Chalmers Manufacturing Company, Westinghouse Electric Corporation, and Buffalo Electro-Chemical Company among others.[19]

Once the bureau resolved the initial objections against close cooperation, EB and Portsmouth worked well together with a minimum of mishaps. In April 1948 Captain McDowell complained to the supervisor of shipbuilding in Groton that EB was late with its delivery of a set of plans for a Guppy conversion. He did not want to deliver SS 343–352 after scheduled completion. But more often, effective cooperation offset most of the difficulties involved in coordination and administration. Commenting on the formulation of the designs for the *Tang* class and the first of the Navy's hunter-killer submarines (SSK), one BUSHIPS official noted that EB and Portsmouth had jointly organized the design and procurement services for these vessels even before BUSHIPS composed a contract: "I understand from Capt. Weaver [of the submarine ship branch in BUSHIPS] that arrangements between Portsmouth and EB Co have been worked out entirely between these two activities; I assume such arrangements are satisfactory to the Supply Officer at Portsmouth."[20]

During the course of the Guppy Program, the bureau continued to demand coordination between the yards to avoid disorder and delay. Confusion over the alternating current (AC) electrical power system designed for the Guppy conversions provides a case in point. EB's design director and the acknowledged dean of the Navy's submarine engineers, retired Rear

[18] Commander Portsmouth Naval Shipyard to BUSHIPS, 23 Aug 1946, box 1571; Commander Portsmouth Naval Shipyard to BUSHIPS, 12 Jul 1946, box 1520, BUSHIPS Confidential CENCORR 1946. For a good sense of the give-and-take between BUSHIPS, EB, and Portsmouth, consult boxes 905–908, BUSHIPS Unclassified CENCORR 1947.

[19] BUSHIPS to COMSUBLANT, 23 October 1947 (and many similar letters in this file for October 1947), box 905, BUSHIPS Unclassified CENCORR 1947.

[20] Commander Portsmouth Naval Shipyard to SUPSHIPS, Groton (see route slip for quote), 2 Nov 1948, box 1011; Commander Portsmouth Naval Shipyard to SUPSHIPS Groton, 19 Apr 1948, box 964, BUSHIPS Unclassified CENCORR 1948. For an example of one of these conferences at which EB and Portsmouth coordinated their efforts in design and procurement under the watchful eye of the bureau, see, "*Tang* (SS 563): Agenda—Questions and Answers for Conference at Electric Boat," 16–17 Sep 1948, box 71, BUSHIPS Confidential CENCORR 1948.

Admiral Andrew I. McKee, brought the absence of a standard plan for this system to the attention of the supervisor of shipbuilding in Groton. Mare Island had voiced the same complaint, and McKee wondered if BUSHIPS intended for each yard to produce its own scheme. Sensing from his interaction with the bureau that official policy favored close coordination, McKee suggested that EB's design could initially serve as a universal plan for the first of any class or type. This approach would allow the yards to stay on schedule while the bureau prepared an official plan. Initially each yard would receive permission to fabricate any special material not obtainable from Portsmouth in order to avoid procurement problems.[21]

McKee's plan had the additional advantage of providing valuable lead time for the purchase of materials required to meet the standards eventually set by the bureau. BUSHIPS had already addressed the problem of timely procurement in conjunction with the Submarine Supply Office (SSO) at the Philadelphia Navy Yard. A strategy for the centralized acquisition of alteration materials through Portsmouth and SSO was formulated in October and November during the conversion of *Odax*.[22]

The total cost of the Guppy conversions was considerable. Portsmouth expended $1,126,536.01 to transform *Odax* into a Guppy I.[23] Most of the Guppy I and II conversions carried out at Portsmouth and Mare Island ranged in cost from $1 million to $1.8 million, with the latter facility generating the higher costs.[24] Similar work by EB usually required more cash than Portsmouth conversions, but less than those accomplished at Mare Island. The alterations performed at EB on *Corporal* (SS 346) and *Halfbeak* (SS 352) averaged between $1.4 million and $1.6 million.[25]

Based upon Public Law 319 of 1947, which authorized President Harry Truman "to convert such vessels as he may consider best for the purposes of national defense," the Navy Department's conversion plans strained both its budget and the available construction facilities.[26] Portsmouth, Mare Island, and EB simply could not keep up with the demand. To re-

[21] EB to SUPSHIPS, Groton, 19 May 1947, box 909, BUSHIPS Unclassified CENCORR 1947.

[22] SSO to BUSHIPS, 12 Nov 1947, box 912, BUSHIPS Unclassified CENCORR 1947. There were other supply centers and control points, such as the Ships Parts Control Center at the Naval Supply Depot in Mechanicsburg, Pennsylvania. For an exact description of the duties of the SSO and the materials and systems for which it was and was not responsible see, Submarine Supply Officer, SSO, U.S. Naval Base Philadelphia, to BUSHIPS, 21 Jun 1948, box 968, BUSHIPS Unclassified CENCORR 1948.

[23] Commander Portsmouth Naval Shipyard to BUSHIPS Code 515, 30 Oct 1947, box 912, BUSHIPS Unclassified CENCORR 1947.

[24] Commander Portsmouth Naval Shipyard to BUSHIPS, Code 270, 20 Feb 1947, box 907, BUSHIPS Unclassified CENCORR 1947.

[25] Commander Mare Island Naval Shipyard to BUSHIPS, Code 5815 (see route slip for the EB conversion figures), 9 Sep 1947, box 911, BUSHIPS Unclassified CENCORR 1947.

[26] United States Statutes at Large, 80th Cong., 1st sess., 1947, vol. 61, pt. 1, box 913, BUSHIPS Unclassified CENCORR 1947.

duce the burden on the Navy's three primary submarine yards, BUSHIPS drafted the Philadelphia Naval Shipyard into the Guppy program in July 1947. At the suggestion of the yard commander, Captain Homer N. Wallin, the bureau first embarked upon a general upgrade of the facilities at Philadelphia. Portsmouth then stepped in to supply procurement assistance for the conversion of *Cutlass* (SS 478) and *Sea Leopard* (SS 483), and EB contracted to provide design advice and lead-yard services on Groton-built submarines slated for conversion at Philadelphia.[27]

Portsmouth eventually served the newcomer not only as a procurement agent, but also as a lead yard, a design consultant in conjunction with EB, and a manufacturing center. Portsmouth provided Philadelphia with the *Amberjack* (SS 522) conversion plans for application to the SS 478, SS 483, and *Sirago* (SS 485). In conjunction with the Submarine Supply Office, the veteran submarine yard procured for Philadelphia most of the systems and materials necessary for the Guppy conversions. In the only exception to this rule, BUSHIPS furnished some specialized equipment shipped directly by a private contractor to the individual naval shipyards according to a delivery schedule agreed upon by the yard, the vendor, and the bureau. Philadelphia also received from Portsmouth detailed procedures for major Guppy and schnorchel tests mandated by BUSHIPS.[28] By the end of 1947 the Philadelphia Naval Shipyard had reached the rate of productivity desired by the bureau. It could convert a fleet submarine into a Guppy every three months, and there was a possibility that the yard could cope with an accelerated pace of production if necessary.[29]

But drawing one more shipyard into the conversion program did not begin to ease the heavy workload. By 1947 BUSHIPS had ordered alterations to fleet submarines that would explore their usefulness as oilers, troop carriers, and cargo transports. Philadelphia, Portsmouth, and Mare Island accomplished many of these conversions. After 1947 the preliminary and contract designs of the *Tang* class occupied most of the Navy's design talent at Portsmouth. This yard, as well as Philadelphia, also began work on the three phases of Project Migraine that would eventually convert ten fleet submarines into radar picket boats. Add to this the Navy Department's plans for continued Guppy conversion, and the extent of the burden on naval and private construction facilities be-

---

[27] Commander Portsmouth Naval Shipyard to BUSHIPS Code 5815, 21 Aug 1947; SUPSHIPS, Groton, to BUSHIPS, 6 Aug 1947; Commandant Fourth Naval District to SECNAV, 18 Jul 1947, box 910, BUSHIPS Unclassified CENCORR 1947.

[28] Commander Portsmouth Naval Shipyard to Commander Philadelphia Naval Shipyard, 8 Oct 1947; Wallin to SUPSHIPS, Groton, 6 Nov 1947; Philadelphia Naval Shipyard Planning Department Memo #13–47, box 912, BUSHIPS Unclassified CENCORR 1947.

[29] CAPT Homer N. Wallin to CNO, 17 Dec 1947, box 1008, BUSHIPS Unclassified CENCORR 1948.

comes clear. A report composed by the planning officer at Portsmouth on the design work alone noted, "Of the three design agents mentioned it appears that Portsmouth is overloaded. Mare Island is probably at the saturation point and only the Electric Boat Company seems available to absorb additional design work." [30]

In response to these conditions, the bureau drafted the naval shipyards in Boston and Charleston into the conversion program at the end of 1947. Both yards followed the same procedure as Philadelphia had before them, with Portsmouth and EB sharing the role as lead yard. After its Philadelphia experience, Portsmouth naturally bore most of the responsibility for directing the design and procurement efforts of both new yards. Indeed, before the Guppy program concluded, Portsmouth also initiated the San Francisco Navy Yard into the conversion business. [31]

As it progressed, the Guppy program commanded more skilled workers than any other submarine project, and it eventually involved more primary submarine construction facilities than the bureau had used during World War II. Even with the facilities and labor available while converting *Odax*, the planning officer at the Portsmouth Naval Shipyard admitted that he did not expect "to do more than keep just ahead of the production schedule." BUSHIPS kept close watch over the conversion process and insisted upon weekly reports from Portsmouth describing the progress achieved and the difficulties still to overcome. [32]

Those difficulties were considerable. As the first Guppy, *Odax* set standards for the future and demonstrated the obstacles the Navy and industry still had to master in their quest for a modern, high-speed submarine. *Odax* endured a rigorous set of submerged trials in addition to the usual preliminary and final testing conducted by the Board of Inspection and Survey. Most of the problems encountered were a byproduct of the increased submerged speed. *Odax*, and later Guppies like *Amberjack* and *Trumpetfish* (SS 425), initially experienced severe stabilizer vibrations, propeller cavitation, superstructure rattling, sonar ranging prob-

---

[30] Design Work Load at the Portsmouth Naval Shipyard—Discussion in BUSHIPS, 5 and 6 Feb 1948, 13 Feb 1948, box 68, BUSHIPS Confidential CENCORR 1948.

[31] Commander Charleston Naval Shipyard to Commander Philadelphia Naval Shipyard, 24 May 1948, box 964; BUSHIPS to Commander Mare Island Naval Shipyard (see attached route slip), 1 Mar 1948, box 963, BUSHIPS Unclassified CENCORR 1948. Philadelphia assisted Portsmouth in the process of educating Charleston and Boston. Commander Portsmouth Naval Shipyard to Commander Boston Naval Shipyard, 18 Dec 1947, box 912; BUSHIPS to CNO, 17 Dec 1947, box 913, BUSHIPS Unclassified CENCORR 1947; McDowell, Portsmouth, to BUSHIPS, 28 Sep 1948, box 68, BUSHIPS Confidential CENCORR 1948.

[32] Commanding Officer *Odax* to COMSUBLANT, 30 Sep 1946; Commander Portsmouth Naval Shipyard to BUSHIPS, 4 Oct 1946; Commanding Officer *Odax* to COMSUBLANT, 28 Oct 1946 (see latter two documents for samples of progress reports), box 1571, BUSHIPS Confidential CENCORR 1946.

lems at particular angles and depths, slow responding rate-of-dive indicators, and broken radar antennae.[33]

Thus the Guppy conversions presented the bureau with a crash course on the requirements and consequences of high submerged speed. With the post-patrol reports received from the individual commanders, BU-SHIPS quickly composed a picture of Guppy performance and the most significant challenges posed by these submarines.

Procuring reliable and durable storage batteries in unprecedented numbers also posed a formidable challenge. After the streamlined hull, the extra electrical power provided by increased battery capacity allowed the Guppies to achieve remarkable submerged speeds. But the 504 battery cells required for each Guppy presented a host of difficulties to the Navy and private industry.

The first issue was one of sufficient supply. The Navy only had two vendors for submarine storage batteries, the National Battery Company of Depew, New York, and the Electric Storage Battery Company of Philadelphia. The former supplied Gould batteries for the SS 484 and the latter manufactured the Exide brand for the SS 486.

When the Navy first placed its order for Guppy-program batteries, the limited postwar production capability in this sector of the economy became apparent. Neither company could deliver its share of the 1,008 cells required for the two Guppy I conversions as promptly as the Navy required. Furthermore, both firms had trouble with their subcontractors, who were completely overwhelmed by the sudden demand. During 1946, for example, the American Hard Rubber Company had great difficulty providing hundreds of hard-rubber jars to serve as battery containers. The sudden expansion of the postwar battery market, when these companies expected just the opposite, proved one of the greatest trials of the conversion program.[34]

---

[33] Commander V. E. Schumacher, Commanding Officer *Odax*, to COMSUBLANT: "Informal Guppy Notes," 1 May 1948, box 68, BUSHIPS Confidential CENCORR 1948; Naval Speedletter—Commander Portsmouth Naval Shipyard to BUSHIPS, Code 5815, 17 Jun 1947; Commander Portsmouth Naval Shipyard, *Odax* Post-Alteration Trials—Recommendation of, 2 May 1947, box 49, BUSHIPS Confidential CENCORR 1947; Commander Portsmouth Naval Shipyard to BUSHIPS, Code 5815, 23 Jul 1947; Hyde Windlass Co. to Portsmouth Naval Shipyard, 10 Jul 1947; Report of Conference— Subj: SS484 Class Propellers. . . . 23–24 July 1947, box 910, BUSHIPS Unclassified CENCORR 1947.

[34] BUSHIPS to Commander Mare Island Naval Shipyard, 7 Nov and 10 Dec 1946, box 1572; Assistant SECNAV, Materials Division, to Inspector of Naval Material, Buffalo, NY, and Inspector of Naval Material, Philadelphia, 14 Oct 1946, BUSHIPS Contract Nobs–45000, 14 Oct 1946; BUSHIPS to Inspector of Naval Material Buffalo, NY, and Commander Portsmouth Naval Shipyard, 21 Oct 1946; Commander Portsmouth Naval Shipyard to BUSHIPS, 25 Oct 1946; Inspector of Naval Material, Newark, NJ, to BUSHIPS, 26 Aug 1946; BUSHIPS to Commander Portsmouth Naval Shipyard, 14 Aug 1946, box 1571; BUSHIPS to the Civilian Production Administration, 12 Jul 1946, box 1258, BUSHIPS Confidential CENCORR 1946.

Once the batteries were delivered, another difficulty arose. The building yards did not possess the space to store the batteries and keep them charged until the submarines were ready to receive them. As the office of EB design director McKee reminded the bureau in April 1947, "The contractor appreciates the desire of the battery manufacturer to process the battery in small groups but wishes to stress the fact that no battery shop exists at this plant for battery storage and charging." Thus the bureau and the private sector had to carefully and precisely coordinate each battery delivery with the construction schedule to minimize the demands placed upon EB and the other building yards involved in the program.[35]

Beyond problems of manufacture and supply, the Guppy program posed problems of habitability and fundamental design. Doubling the number of cells required a new battery compartment arrangement, as well as a greater number of dependable switches and more durable circuits. An electrical network of this power within the confines of a submarine also imposed on its designers the need for simplicity to facilitate smooth operation and maintenance. In addition, remaining submerged longer with the benefit of a schnorchel and the possibility of toxic emissions from the batteries required additional air conditioning augmented by improved and expanded ventilation in the engine room and throughout the ship.[36]

Next to increased submerged speed, the schnorchel occupied the most important place in the Guppy program. The bureau wanted to exploit the advantages it offered in submerged diesel propulsion and submarine environmental control. The discoveries of the Naval Technical Mission in Europe and the examination of German schnorchels at Portsmouth and EES in Annapolis provided the initial data on the significance of this device and its implications for undersea warfare. Approximately one month before V–E Day, BUSHIPS authorized the experimental installation of a folding-mast schnorchel in *R 6* (SS 83) and continued experiments with a simulated installation in *Sirago* at Portsmouth the following August.[37]

---

[35] BUSHIPS to Electric Storage Battery Company, 25 Apr 1947; BUSHIPS to SUPSHIPS, Groton, 24 Apr 1947; EB to SUPSHIPS, Groton, 4 Apr 1947, box 908, BUSHIPS Unclassified CENCORR 1947.

[36] SUPSHIPS, Groton, to BUSHIPS, 11 Jun 1948, box 965, BUSHIPS Unclassified CENCORR 1948; National Battery Company to BUSHIPS, 30 Oct 1947; BUSHIPS to National Battery Company, 3 Dec 1947, box 912; McDowell, Portsmouth Naval Shipyard, to BUSHIPS, 28 Feb 1947; BUSHIPS to SUPSHIPS, Groton, 10 Mar 1947; SUPSHIPS, Groton, to BUSHIPS, 21 Feb 1947; McKee to SUPSHIPS, Groton, 19 Feb 1947, box 907, BUSHIPS Unclassified CENCORR 1947. Report of Conference at Portsmouth Naval Shipyard on 23 and 24 Jul 1946, box 1571, BUSHIPS Confidential CENCORR 1946.

[37] CNO Memo for the Commander-in-Chief, U. S. Fleet (Readiness), 8 Apr 1945; BUSHIPS to CNO, 4 Apr 1945; Commander Portsmouth Naval Shipyard to BUSHIPS, 31 Mar 1945; BUSHIPS to CNO, 3 Aug 1945, box 2115, SECNAV–CNO Confidential Correspondence (declassified), RG 19, NA.

Close cooperation between EES, Portsmouth, Electric Boat Company, and the diesel engine manufacturers made possible the development of the best type of schnorchel for the Guppy program. In the spring of 1946 Portsmouth manufactured a schnorchel tube that EES linked to a Fairbanks-Morse submarine engine for testing. Favorable results justified further tests, conducted on the same system, only this time with a General Motors submarine diesel.[38]

While this research proceeded, the preference of the submarine force commanders for a retractable rather than a folding schnorchel mast led the bureau, in May 1946, to draft both Portsmouth and EB into designing such a system. As a consequence, EB engineers were frequent visitors to the schnorchel testing site at EES. The company not only submitted a design for the retractable mast but also worked on an air-operated head valve for the schnorchel. The German float valve proved inadequate to stop the intake of excessive amounts of water. As one of those working on the schnorchel project, EB engineer John S. Leonard recalled, "Ultimately this system . . . evolved and I had a great deal to do with what that system finally looked like. It was a process of trying this . . . [and that] and arriving at the best answer and working with the Experiment Station which built and tested a lot of these things." [39]

When the Navy sent the schnorchel to sea, the bureau discovered a variety of major problems afflicting the system. Portsmouth, EES, and Electric Boat had the retractable schnorchel mast ready by 1 November 1946, roughly two weeks after Commander Submarine Force, Atlantic Fleet selected *Irex* for the first operational installation. It took one month to install the device and additional time for research on tolerances and pressure. The additional investigation ensured the proper operation of the mast and provided a better understanding of the effect of ocean backpressure on the operation of the diesel engines. EES did most of this testing in close cooperation with Electric Boat and Portsmouth.[40]

While putting *Irex* through its standardization and schnorchel trials on 22–23 July 1947, the Board of Inspection and Survey discovered certain potentially debilitating characteristics in the system. The head valve permitted too much seawater to enter the vessel. It appeared as if the

---

[38] BUSHIPS to SUPSHIPS, Groton, 24 May 1946, box 1524, BUSHIPS Confidential CENCORR 1946, RG 19, NA/WNRC.

[39] John S. Leonard, interview with author, 25 Sep 1989, NHC Oral Histories, OA.

[40] BUSHIPS to Commander Portsmouth Naval Shipyard, 13 Nov 1946; Commander Portsmouth Naval Shipyard to BUSHIPS, 14 Oct 1946; BUSHIPS to SUPSHIPS, Groton, 29 Nov 1946; SUPSHIPS, Groton, to BUSHIPS, 1 Nov 1946; EB to SUPSHIPS, Groton, 31 Oct 1946, box 1525; BUSHIPS Confidential CENCORR 1946; SUPSHIPS, Groton, to COMSUBLANT (example of the *Corporal* schnorchel installation—SS 346), 19 Jan 1948, box 994, BUSHIPS Unclassified CENCORR 1948.

relay controlling the valve worked more effectively if the sea struck the schnorchel head-on rather than from the stern. But, more important, the top row of exhaust ports on the schnorchel mast occasionally broached the surface, sending out a geyser that quickly betrayed the location of the submarine. In one series of tests conducted in August on *Amberjack*, the schnorchel emitted 25- to 30-foot streams of fine white spray. The head valve was soon redesigned to control water intake, and in newer schnorchels the exhaust ports appeared approximately six feet lower than before, making geysers far less likely.[41] In September 1948 Lieutenant Commander Edward L. Beach of *Amberjack* expressed his dissatisfaction with the device on his submarine, which still did not open fast enough.[42] However, by the time *Volador* (SS 490) schnorcheled from Pearl Harbor to San Diego on an experimental trip in August 1950, only a single fluctuation in pressure on the first day out caused any physical discomfort or mechanical difficulty.[43]

Battery hazards posed more of a threat to a Guppy's environment than prolonged schnorcheling. When moisture and acid deposits regularly developed in the ventilation system and on the batteries themselves after charging, electrical grounding began to plague the Guppies. According to the commanding officer of *Amberjack*, "since the completion of 'Guppy', or high speed conversion, the principle deficiency experienced has been maintaining the total ground voltage on the main batteries at a low level." A high ground level could incapacitate part of the electrical system. On the average it took thirty-two work-hours per battery group to clear the ground and clean the ventilation system if the ship returned to port. At sea the same procedure required eight more hours per battery group.[44]

Other problems emerged as direct consequences of operating at high speed both on the surface and submerged. In a report filed with BU-SHIPS in June 1948 the commanding officer of *Pomodon*, Commander Guy E. O'Neil, Jr., reported that his crew found it difficult to maintain satisfactory sonar or radar contact during submerged high speed bursts. The same advantage that allowed the submarine to flee rapidly, leaving

---

[41] McDowell, Commander Portsmouth Naval Shipyard to BUSHIPS, 27 Aug 1947; COMSUBLANT to BUSHIPS, 22 Aug 1947; Commanding Officer *Irex* (SS 482), 15 Aug 1947; Board of Inspection and Survey Standardization and Schnorchel Trials, 22–23 Jul 1947; COMSUBLANT to CNO, 25 Jul 1947, box 49, BUSHIPS Confidential CENCORR 1947.

[42] LCDR Edward L. Beach to BUSHIPS, 26 Sep 1948, box 1010, BUSHIPS Unclassified CENCORR 1948.

[43] COMSUBPAC to CNO (report of *Volador* schnorchel cruise), 21 Oct 1950, series 5, file A4(1) Confidential, box 16, Subs/UWD, OA.

[44] CDR William B. Parham to BUSHIPS, 20 Oct 1947, box 49; COMSUBLANT to BUSHIPS, 18 Dec 1947; BUSHIPS to COMSUBLANT, 23 Jan 1948, box 67, BUSHIPS Confidential CENCORR 1947.

wake echoes to confuse pursuing antisubmarine warfare surface vessels, made it impossible to keep track of those vessels and others in the area. O'Neil argued that the Guppies needed increased sonar capability and better equipment, especially in view of improved ASW techniques. Often surface vessels worked in pairs, one tracking and the other attacking. Better tracking of multiple contacts at high submerged speed was necessary to take full advantage of Guppy capability.[45]

In many Guppies high surface speeds produced an odd plunging at the bow, which hampered maneuvering in shallow water and restricted the crew's ability to steer the ship properly. Both BUSHIPS and the David Taylor Model Basin investigated this phenomenon and developed a variety of answers to the riddle. The hydrodynamic action on the ship, the size of the bow wave, and the weight of the water covering the bow at speeds above 12 knots all contributed to the instability of the vessel. Commander William D. Roseborough, assistant head for preliminary and hull design in BUSHIPS's design division, also suggested that the stern shaft-line stabilizers contributed to the instability by having the same effect as a slight downturn on the diving planes.[46] Difficulties of this sort gave many engineers and naval architects a better appreciation of the effect of high speed on a modified fleet submarine hull and fostered research that later furnished alternatives with the *Tang* class and the experimental submarine, *Albacore* (AGSS 569).

The Fourth Revolution

In an article appearing in the September 1986 issue of the U.S. Naval Institute *Proceedings*, the American submarine designer and engineer Captain Harry Jackson has enumerated five revolutions in the history of submarine development.[47] John Holland accomplished the first by inventing the submarine and emphasizing submerged rather than surface performance. The application of diesel propulsion to submarines, allowing greater speed and endurance precipitated the second revolution.

[45] CDR Guy E. O'Neil Jr. to COMSUBPAC, 11 Jun 1948, box 68, BUSHIPS Confidential CENCORR 1948.

[46] BUSHIPS to Commanding Officer and Director, DTMB (see route slip for Roseborough comment), 11 Jun 1951; Commanding Officer and Director, DTMB, to BUSHIPS, 10 Aug 1951; Commanding Officer *Odax* (SS 484) to COMSUBLANT, 31 May 1951, box 1571, BUSHIPS Confidential CENCORR 1946.

[47] The Navy accomplished the fifth revolution with *Skipjack* (SSN 585) by combining the body-of-revolution, or "teardrop," hull design of the experimental submarine *Albacore* (AGSS 569) with a nuclear reactor. This last revolution is discussed in detail in chapter 9. CAPT Harry Jackson, USN (Ret.), CDR William D. Needham, USN, and LT Dale E. Sigman, USN, "ASW: Revolution or Evolution," U.S. Naval Institute *Proceedings* 112 (September 1986): 64–66.

The third revolution, represented by the fleet submarine of World War II, reversed Holland's priorities and emphasized surface performance. For the United States, *Tang* (SS 563) and her sister ships provoked the fourth revolution. According to Jackson, the *Tang* design emulated the German Type XXI and "marked a reemphasis on submerged characteristics at the expense of surface performance." The Guppies probed the limits of adapting a fleet submarine for speed and prolonged submergence in imitation of the advanced German designs discovered in 1945. With the *Tang* class, BUSHIPS and Portsmouth, motivated by concepts and goals that created the Type XXI, designed and built a fast ship with greater submerged endurance.

SOC provided the impetus for building an American variation of the Type XXI U-boat. In November 1945 the General Board proposed a 1600-ton submarine designed as a slightly larger and more capable fleet submarine. Members of SOC argued forcefully against this ship because it incorporated few of the important innovations discovered by the recently decommissioned Naval Technical Mission in Europe. Instead SOC recommended the design and construction of two interim ships built along the lines of the Type XXI.[48]

Over the next year the David Taylor Model Basin, Stevens Institute of Technology (SIT), and the design section of BUSHIPS (Code 400) worked on the problems inherent in high submerged speed. The towing tank at the Stevens Institute worked on the controls for a high speed submarine in conjunction with the Askania Regulator Company. For its part DTMB's research focused on the underwater resistance of a wide variety of current submarine designs, including *Argonaut* (SS 475) of the wartime *Tench* (SS 417) class, the German Type XXI, and *Gato*, the lead vessel of the fleet submarine type.[49]

SIT director Kenneth S. M. Davidson underscored the need for a completely new design, not a variation on the fleet submarine. In a letter to Captain Harold E. Saunders, DTMB's director, Davidson argued that either an effort to improve an existing design or a completely new approach,

> involves, ultimately, the development of: a suitable underwater form, with
> low resistance, adequate stability on course, and easy maneuverability; ap-

---

[48] Minutes of the 6 Nov SOC Meeting, 14 Nov 1945, box 64, BUSHIPS Secret CENCORR 1945, RG 19, NA/WNRC.

[49] Saunders (Director, DTMB) to BUSHIPS Design Division (Code 400), [Aug? 1946], box 1520, BUSHIPS Confidential CENCORR 1946; Isidore Goldman, "The Effective Horsepower of a 261-foot Electric Submarine, Buships Design PD1356, Equipped with Various Appendages, Predicted From Tests of TMB Model 3995" (tests on a type XXI hybrid in the *Tang* research program), n.d. May 1948, BUSHIPS Confidential CENCORR 1948.

propriate propulsive equipment; and a hull structure that will shut the operating needs imposed. By the first method, this would require ceaseless modification and juggling between the various groups, and would probably yield a second rate answer. By the second method we can hope to produce a rational design. This will require concerted action from all groups, and an open-minded point of view with regard to the acceptance of new ideas.[50]

This last strategy, which would leave the fleet submarine behind and pursue true innovation, complemented well the postwar policy of openness, sharing, and mutual support encouraged within the submarine community by the bureau and struck a familiar chord with the yards initiating work on the Guppy Program.

Existing laws and regulations complicated efforts to obtain authorization and funding for the first two vessels of the new class. The Navy Department appropriation act for fiscal year 1947 did not permit the construction of new submarines with funds earmarked for "the increase and replacement of naval vessels." An exemption to that law required congressional action, which did not come until May 1947.

Then the distribution of the contract awards presented difficulties. The Vinson-Trammel Act of 1934 required that the bureau build every second vessel in a naval shipyard. After initially allocating $16 million, later increased to $30 million, for the design and construction of *Tang* (SS 563) and *Trigger* (SS 564), the bureau made Portsmouth responsible for the contract design as well as for the lead ship of the class. Although this was done in part to satisfy the 1934 statute, the Connecticut congressional delegation quickly came to Electric Boat's support in its bid for the second of the two submarines. Representative Horace Seeley-Brown (R–Conn.) and Senator Brien McMahon (D–Conn.) both sent letters to the Navy Department on behalf of Electric Boat.

The Groton yard was the obvious choice, but the bureau could do nothing until Portsmouth completed the contract design. The Navy Department also had to request the approval of the Secretary of the Navy to enter into talks with a private yard on this contract when Philadelphia Naval Shipyard was an available alternative. Unless the Secretary certified that employing EB on this project was "advantageous to the national defense," the Groton firm would not get the contract. Under Vice Admiral Earle W. Mills, BUSHIPS strongly favored EB for the construction of the SS 564 because, "it is decidedly advantageous to the national defense

---

[50] Kenneth S. M. Davidson to Saunders, 26 Jul 1946, box, 1520, BUSHIPS Confidential CENCORR 1946.

to keep one or more private contractors familiar and experienced with the design and construction of submarine type of vessels." Before the summer ended, Electric Boat had the contract for *Trigger*.[51]

The Ships Characteristics Board first disclosed the specific attributes of the high-speed attack-type submarine in March 1947. The vessel would have a streamlined hull, no deck guns or conning tower, retractable masts, and greatly increased battery power. In addition, with their 700-foot operating depth and 1,100-foot collapse depth, the 1,500-ton, 265-foot *Tang*-class submarines broadened considerably the slice of the ocean this submarine might exploit. The *Tangs* also carried enhanced radar and sonar, and at least six tubes dedicated to every submarine-launched weapon currently in use, including the Mark 38 torpedo and the Mark 27 submarine-launched mine.[52]

To achieve high submerged speed and obtain a balanced design, the Ships Characteristics Board determined that the *Tangs* required a "decrease in size and power of the Diesel engines and a reduction in hull length which results in a sacrifice of surface speed." Thus BUSHIPS decided to try the new General Motors model 184 radial "pancake" diesels, which would allow the six vessels of the *Tang* class to match on the surface their top submerged speed of 17 knots while conserving space and weight. These engines possessed less than half the weight of the regular 1,000-brake horsepower opposed piston diesels. Unfortunately, they eventually proved far too difficult to service. One by one during their operational life, these submarines received new propulsion plants in order to avoid extended overhaul periods and the occasional need for a tow back to port for repairs.[53]

In building these revolutionary vessels, the bureau, Portsmouth, and EB encountered some delicate problems. First, BUSHIPS had to apply to Secretary of the Navy John L. Sullivan for permission to negotiate with

---

[51] RADM Charles D. Wheelock (Acting Chief of BUSHIPS) to the Honorable Horace Seeley-Brown, 1 Apr 1947; McMahon to SECNAV, 25 Jul 1947; SECNAV to McMahon, 5 Aug 1945; Seeley-Brown to Navy Liaison Office, 19 Mar 1947, box 659; Wheelock to Commander Philadelphia Naval Shipyard, 2 May 1947; BUSHIPS to CNO, 29 July 1947, box 906; BUSHIPS to Director of the Bureau of the Budget, 16 Jan 1947, box 913, BUSHIPS Unclassified CENCORR 1947; CAPT Ralph E. McShane, BUSHIPS Fiscal Director, to BUORD, 8 Mar 1948, box 961, BUSHIPS Unclassified CENCORR 1948.

[52]Ship Characteristics Board Proposed Characteristics High-Speed Attack Type Submarine, 18 Mar 1947, series 2, file 3, box 8, Subs/UWD, OA; BUSHIPS to BUORD, 22 Dec 1947, box 49, BUSHIPS Confidential CENCORR 1947.

[53] Ship Characteristics Board Proposed Characteristics High-Speed Attack Type Submarine, 18 Mar 1947, series 2, file 3, box 8, Subs/UWD. BUSHIPS to BUORD, 22 Dec 1947, box 49, BUSHIPS Confidential CENCORR 1947. Norman Friedman, *Submarine Design and Development* (Annapolis: Naval Institute Press, 1984), 61. For details on the GM 16–338 Diesel, see LT Robert H. Gautier, USN, *Tang* (SS 563), "The GM 16–338 Diesel Engine." Thesis for Qualification for Command of Submarines, in possession of the author courtesy of retired submariner Richard Boyle.

private component and propulsion manufacturers. Ordering materials and systems for the *Tang* class would make it necessary to reveal highly classified information to private citizens, and bureau chief Admiral Mills felt the need to consult a higher authority. The question of security became all the more important in view of the bureau's policy of developing and training as many private companies as possible to do this type of work. The construction program needed competent vendors in greater numbers to avoid manufacturing and construction defects as well as the possibility of monopoly. The bureau's policy emerged clearly from a December 1947 letter discussing the ships' propulsion plant written to the supervisor of shipbuilding in Groton: "In order to develop more than one source of manufacture for individual components of propulsion and auxiliary machinery, wherever possible the two submarines [viz. *Tang* and *Trigger*] shall be equipped with corresponding machinery of different manufacture." Thus BUSHIPS sought the security of extensive participation by the private sector in support of the close cooperative effort between Portsmouth and Electric Boat.

The collaboration on these two ships between Portsmouth and EB was complete. The former provided the services of a lead yard in supplying the contract design and all of the detail specifications for the class. Portsmouth also ordered materials and components for EB on the company's own purchase orders, speeding delivery direct to Groton.[54]

Electric Boat occasionally found this degree of governmental control disturbing. As *Trigger* began to take shape, EB still labored under the excess profit supervision authorized by the Renegotiation Act of 1942. In November 1948 the amount of Navy Department disallowances for *Trigger* alone was $209,023.45, with another $105,611.42 still under debate. EB's president, O. Pomeroy Robinson, and his corporate accountant, John J. Murphy, traveled to Washington, D.C., in that month to convince BUSHIPS that the company's overhead justified the prices it charged. But they fully expected to have to absorb $160,000 in costs attributable to the *Trigger* project. This type of problem did not disappear until the company became involved in the nuclear submarine program and national priorities led to increased funding and more careful accounting on both sides.[55]

---

[54] Commander Portsmouth Naval Shipyard to BUSANDA (Director of Materials Central, code SP-2/SM-2), 16 Jun 1948; Portsmouth Planning Officer to Portsmouth Supply Officer, 29 Apr 1948; BUSHIPS (code 660—electrical) to Commander Portsmouth Naval Shipyard, 23 Mar 1948, box 71, BUSHIPS Confidential CENCORR 1948; BUSHIPS to SUPSHIPS, Groton, 4 Dec 1947; Commander Portsmouth Naval Shipyard to BUSHIPS, 22 October 1947; BUSHIPS to SECNAV, 4 Dec 1947; Commander Portsmouth Naval Shipyard to BUSHIPS, 7 Nov 1947, box 49, BUSHIPS Confidential CENCORR 1947.

[55] EB Interoffice Memo, O. P. Robinson to J. J. Murphy, 18 Nov 1948, box 003, Contracts File, Historical Records Vault, EB Division, General Dynamics.

As the lead yard for *Tang* and many other projects, Portsmouth was swamped with work during 1948 and 1949. BUSHIPS commissioned the yard's design team to work on the *Tang* class, an Arctic radar picket submarine, submarine rescue chambers and rescue buoys, Guppy conversions, and the more conventional radar picket projects collected under the code names Migraine 1 and 2. These last boats were designed for intelligence collection in support of fleet operations. The yard's work force actually built many of these vehicles and manufactured electrical components as well, obligating virtually every facility at the shipyard. Since the Navy Department placed a high priority on the delivery of the fast attack submarines of the SS 563 class, Portsmouth began to rely very heavily on EB after 1948 for much of the design work on that project.[56] Thus the yard found it impossible to respond positively when Captain Hyman G. Rickover of BUSHIPS Code 390, the nuclear power branch, approached Portsmouth late in 1949 about joining the effort to design and build the first of the Navy's nuclear submarines. The burden of diverse commitments was simply too great.

Observations

As the postwar Navy and submarine industry braced themselves for lean times, the advent of the Guppy and *Tang* programs presented unexpected design and construction challenges. Instead of reducing their output to the lowest levels since the Great War, Electric Boat, Portsmouth, and a handful of other Navy yards found themselves inundated with conversions, turning submarines into high-speed vessels, guided missile platforms, oilers, troop carriers, hunter-killers, and radar pickets.

Concern for the threat posed by the Soviet Union drove much of this construction and conversion. The Germans had initiated a revolution in submarine design and, with it, changed the nature of undersea warfare. Those antisubmarine measures practiced so successfully by the Allies in the recently concluded war would not work again if the Soviets employed a fleet of Type XXI clones. In his report on undersea warfare commissioned by the CNO and issued on 22 April 1950, Admiral Francis Low, former chief of the Tenth Fleet, gave voice to this universal concern within the naval-industrial complex for submarines. The Low Report concluded that if the capable Russian submarine industry built such a fleet within the next five years, American ASW forces could not

---

[56] Commander Portsmouth Naval Shipyard to BUSHIPS, 27 Feb 1948; Commander Portsmouth Naval Shipyard to BUSHIPS, n.d. May 1949, box 43, BUSHIPS Confidential CENCORR 1949, RG 19, NA/WNRC.

contain it. Thus it became imperative both to remain on the cutting edge of submarine design and to acquire an intimacy with the ocean environment that would allow the American submarine force to seek and strike effectively before betraying its presence.[57]

In these circumstances BUSHIPS called upon the navy yards and private contractors to cooperate more closely than ever before. The Soviet menace as described in the Low Report led the Navy to place such a premium on the Guppies and *Tangs* that the traditional competition between EB and Portsmouth in matters of design, by now a time-honored and accepted convention within the Navy, took second place to quick production.

As the bureau and the private sector duplicated and surpassed the advances made by the Germans and the Allies in World War II, the scientific component of the naval-industrial complex led the submarine community toward the next revolution, *Albacore* and nuclear power.

---

[57] Study of Undersea Warfare (The Low Report), 22 Apr 1950, Post 1 Jan 1946 Command File, OA.

Chapter 6

From Harnwell to Albacore, 1946–1953

Victory over Japan did not end the need for research and development directly related to the advancement of submarine capabilities.
Between 1940 and 1945 the Subsurface Warfare Section of the National Defense Research Committee, known as Division 6, section 6.1, coordinated and supported work in Navy laboratories and at major American
universities and centers of learning through a far-reaching contract program. With the breakup of Division 6 in 1945, concerned scientists and officers immediately recognized the need for maintaining a formal scientific
capability in undersea warfare to assist the Navy in its postwar effort to contain the perceived Communist threat manifesting itself in a most frighten-
ing and dramatic way in Korea. Much like the tightly knit submarine design
and engineering community with whom they constantly worked, those in
the submarine scientific specialties took measures to ensure the continuation of essential research, cooperating closely with others in the naval-industrial complex to overcome obstacles to better submarine performance.

Postwar Scientific Support, 1946–1950

In 1946 the Office of Naval Research, the Navy laboratories, and the
National Academy of Sciences (NAS) stepped into the role played by the
OSRD/NDRC organization during the war.[1] They combined institutional authority with individual initiative to advance research into undersea warfare from both the ASW and pro-submarine perspectives.[2]

---

[1] The Office of Research and Inventions, ONR's naval forbearer, was created by Secretary of the
Navy James Forrestal on 19 May 1945. ORI had essentially the same mission as ONR, vis à vis coordinating research activities within the Navy Department, sponsoring naval research in the private sector, and disseminating the results of all naval research within the Navy. ORI absorbed NRL, the special devices division of the BUAER, the Office of the Coordinator of Research and Development,
and the Office of Patents and Inventions. *Administrative History: Office of Research and Inventions, July
31–December 1945*, Navy Department Library, NHC.

[2] For the naval-industrial complex, ASW and prosub were two sides of the same coin. The same research that gave the Navy a better chance to isolate and destroy a submarine provided the means to
enhance the offensive capabilities of American submarines.

Initially working under the direction of Rear Admiral Harold Bowen, ONR continued the contract research program begun by NDRC, but on a more modest scale. Although peacetime contracts were fewer in number, ONR sponsored research at a number of institutions including Woods Hole Oceanographic Institution, Scripps, Massachusetts Institute of Technology, California Institute of Technology, and Bell Telephone Laboratories. In addition, ONR controlled the activities of the Naval Research Laboratory and the Navy's Underwater Sound Reference Laboratory in Orlando, Florida. Both Navy facilities did groundbreaking work in active sonar and underwater sound measurement.

Independent Navy laboratories also pursued basic research in support of submarine design, construction, and operation. The U.S. Navy Underwater Sound Laboratory in New London and the Naval Electronics Laboratory (NEL) in San Diego explored passive and active hull-mounted sonar. David Taylor Model Basin explored hydrodynamics and submarine self-noise along with the Engineering Experiment Station in Annapolis. The latter also became the center for evaluating closed-cycle submarine propulsion. Seven other naval facilities undertook research in areas vital to submarine warfare, including acoustic sensors, mines, sonobuoy systems, and magnetic anomaly detectors.[3]

On the civilian side several influential scientists sought to perpetuate the relationship between the Navy and the scientific community characteristic of NDRC Division 6. Their efforts gave birth to the Committee on Undersea Warfare (CUW). According to James H. Probus, who eventually became executive secretary of CUW, they wanted,

> to keep alive the close contact and mutual understanding that had been established between the Navy and the civilian scientists of Division 6. Their objective was to retain the experience and interest of these scientists, and to interest new scientists in the problems of modern undersea warfare.[4]

In a letter to Admiral Bowen, then chief of Research and Inventions, Dr. Gaylord P. Harnwell, director of the University of California Division of War Research, called for the creation of a committee to "maintain Naval liaison, determine membership, organize and conduct symposia, issue bulletins and summaries of proceedings." In short, this committee

---

[3] Marvin Lasky, "Historical Review of Undersea Warfare Planning and Organization, 1945–1960, with Emphasis on the Role of the Office of Naval Research," *U.S. Navy Journal of Underwater Acoustics* 26 (Apr 1976): 334–36.

[4] J. H. Probus, "History and Activities of the Committee on Undersea Warfare, 1946–1956," Sep 1955, NSBA/NAS. Not all of this document has been declassified, but the proper authorities have declassified those portions used in this chapter.

would facilitate communication within the field of undersea warfare and provide advice to the Navy on the most promising avenues of scientific and technical investigation.

On 16 September 1946 representatives of the Navy and scientific community met to give form to the Harnwell proposal. By this time ONR had succeeded the Office of Research and Inventions and sent its representatives to the meeting, as did the bureaus, the Office of the Chief of Naval Operations, and the Naval Ordnance Laboratory. The National Research Council of NAS and civilian science in general were represented by Detlev W. Bronk (Cornell Medical College), Dr. Harnwell (University of Pennsylvania), John T. Tate (University of Minnesota), Eugene F. DuBois (Cornell Medical College), Walter S. Hunter (Brown University), Philip Morse (MIT), and Columbus Iselin (WHOI).

The conferees decided to approach Admiral Bowen, now chief of ONR, with a proposal for a permanent Committee on Undersea Warfare. It would operate under the auspices of the NAS's National Research Council and seek to fulfill the mission described by Gaylord Harnwell the previous November. Dr. Bronk made the proposal in a letter to Captain Lawrence R. Daspit of ONR, and Bowen's positive response of 23 October 1946 officially established the Committee on Undersea Warfare.[5] A contract between the academy and ONR signed on 20 June 1947 formally defined the broad responsibilities of the committee. John Tate, former head of NDRC Division 6, became the first chairman, with Harnwell serving as vice chairman. Other members included Iselin, DuBois, Morse, Hunter, W. V. Houston (Rice Institute), Frederick V. Hunt (Harvard), and T. E. Shea (Electrical Research Products, Inc.), with John S. Coleman (Pennsylvania State University) filling the role of executive secretary.[6]

Initially conceived only as a consulting body, CUW eventually went as far as participating in the early stages of instrument- and vehicle-prototype development. The committee's duties as defined by the contract with the Navy included:

(a) Reviewing, analyzing, and evaluating the Navy Department's general program of research and development;

(b) Proposing additional fields of investigation within these general fields and additional projects for research and development therein;

(c) Collecting, collating and disseminating scientific and technical information in these fields; and

---

[5] Ibid.
[6] Ibid.

   (d) As determined by mutual agreement, assisting in research and development, including participation in the design and construction of prototype and/or breadboard key components where necessary to predict performance and technical feasibility.[7]

Changes in the nature of undersea warfare and advances in submarine design made it easy to define the major areas of research but no less difficult to master the major problems. What kind of materials would enable submarines to go significantly deeper? How would the designs and hull structures have to change? Which of the available propulsion techniques promised safe, reliable operation at the greatest speed? What sort of sounds would American and Soviet submarines regularly contribute to a deep, subsurface world accustomed only to natural noise? The postwar revolution in undersea warfare generated many questions that the Navy and industry expected science to answer. Those related to underwater sound, hull design, hydrodynamics, and propulsion proved to be the most important.[8]

Understanding how human-made sounds travel underwater, how to detect them, and how to reduce their intensity at the source became a prime occupation of the scientific component of the naval-industrial complex. In spite of the increased speed and submerged endurance of the Guppies and *Tangs*, the limited range of their transducers and hydrophones initially concentrated the research at Navy laboratories and private institutions on extending the capability of equipment available to the submarine force. The submarine bathythermograph pioneered at WHOI was further refined, and oceanographers continued to train submariners in its use.

Environmental factors not exploited by the Germans, such as the refraction of sound in thermal gradient layers, remained an important part of research and instruction. At NRL the physicist Dr. Harvey Hayes and his sound division explored ways of improving the search capability of both submarines and surface vessels by extending the listening range, supplying a better target range, and refining the equipment to permit the location of such small objects as mines and torpedoes. He also wanted to improve the submarine's chances of evasion by providing its crew with visual indication of the bearing and approximate range of attacking vessels.[9]

---

[7] Ibid. Letter (d) in this series of responsibilities was added on 15 June 1951.

[8] Nuclear matters are discussed in the next chapter. Although the work of the scientific community made nuclear propulsion possible, the history of that process is best discussed in the context of the early programs for the development of naval nuclear power at NRL and BUSHIPS.

[9] BUSHIPS to Commanders Portsmouth Naval Shipyard and Mare Island Naval Shipyard, 26 Nov 1946, box 1519; BUSHIPS to Navy Electronics Laboratory (collected telegrams), 9 Jul 1946, box 1574, BUSHIPS Confidential CENCORR 1946; "Report on the Pro-Submarine Program of the Sound Division, NRL," 5 Apr 1945, box 63, BUSHIPS Secret CENCORR 1945, RG 19, NA/WNRC. Lee Hunt (CUW), to Dr. Paul G. Neumann, 18 Sep 1961, NSBA/NAS.

The wartime revolution in submarine warfare and the need to limit the restrictions imposed on the submarine by the ocean environment gave a new significance to the study of underwater sound transmission. In the discovery of the SOFAR (sound fixing and ranging) sound channel by Maurice Ewing and J. Lamar Worzel during the last year of the war, the Navy and private science perceived a fundamental alteration in the common conception of sound behavior in the ocean. Because of the interplay of temperature, pressure, density, and salinity, the sound channel transmitted active sonar signals and submarine noise over vast distances. Experimental explosions at a depth of 4,000 feet detected by Ewing's hydrophones lying on the continental shelf at 700 fathoms demonstrated the feasibility of receiving signals originating nearly 3,000 miles away.

The Navy did not immediately appreciate the significance of this breakthrough in underwater acoustics. Unreceptive in the closing days of the war to applications suggested by the scientists for air-sea rescue and as a distress signal for submarines, it permitted SOFAR research to languish until 1949. At that point ONR realized SOFAR's possibilities and funded construction of a listening station on Eleuthera by Columbia University's Lamont Geological Observatory, now under Ewing's direction. The Lamont team included Worzel and Gordon Hamilton, who would eventually install the first hydrophones and manage the station. When Captain Roy S. Benson, Commander Submarine Development Group Two (SUBDEV-GRU 2) at New London, invited Worzel to a meeting in February of 1949 on methods of detecting submerged enemy submarines, the significance of SOFAR became clear to the operators. The conference participants sought to enhance the acoustic performance of hunter-killer submarines. Worzel offered the startled officers of SUBDEVGRU 2 a way to dramatically extend the two-mile limit on underwater detection imposed by the current understanding of underwater sound transmission. In cooperation with SUBDEVGRU 2, Worzel conducted experiments with two submarines off Bermuda in May 1949. One vessel was a regular fleet type; the other came equipped with a schnorchel. On their first range runs the scientists easily sustained contact with the fleet submarine to extraordinary distances and continued to trace the schnorcheling vessel even further. Once the final report on Worzel's experiments reached the CNO and the submarine desk in the Bureau of Ships, the naval commitment to SOFAR research was never again in doubt.[10]

Building on the wartime SOFAR research, Allyn Vine, William Schevill, and John Brackett Hersey of WHOI further explored the behavior of sound at greater depths. Below the thermocline the speed of any sound

---

[10] Worzel interview, 22 Aug 1990, NHC Oral Histories, OA.

transmission decreases in direct proportion to depth until it reaches a minimum velocity. But Woods Hole research also demonstrated the tendency of sound to both accelerate with the increase in ocean pressure and to bend toward regions of lower speed. Thus a refraction effect took place that turned the sound waves back toward the surface and refocused them at a convergence zone for just a moment before the signal once again plunged to the depths and returned to the surface at another, more distant convergence zone. In this manner the sound made by a submerged submarine or a surface vessel in the Atlantic could be detected in the upper layer of the ocean at 35-mile intervals.

By March 1947 Hersey, Vine, and Schevill had presented their findings to the Navy and contributed significantly to the refinement of sonar technology. Suddenly the restraints were removed, and the submarine's range of detection and attack in shallower waters expanded enormously. Speaking at the Fifth Undersea Symposium in Washington, D.C., Harvard physicist Frederick Hunt commented,

> It is well known to all of you that sounds originating near the axis of the [SOFAR] sound channel can be propagated to almost fabulous distances. But it seems not to be so widely and certainly not so thoroughly understood that the lower side of this channel provides for sounds originating near the surface the same sort of upward refraction that characterizes the return of radiowaves from the ionosphere by so-called "reflection." This phenomenon . . . was described first, I believe, by Dr. Vine and his collaborators at Woods Hole in a memorandum dated March 1947 and I think it remains one of the cardinal discoveries in the field of underwater sound.[11]

The new horizons set by Worzel at Lamont and the discoveries of the Vine group working at WHOI, as well as a desire to go beyond the short-term, problem-solving techniques of NDRC, led CUW to recommend sustained research in areas that would support the submarine force both now and in the future. The committee called for a worldwide survey of ocean sonar conditions. Among other studies, CUW's panel on Underwater Acoustics recommended investigating reverberation, the SOFAR channel, the sea bed, as well as the absorption of sound in seawater and the effect of temperature, bubbles, pressure, and salinity on that process. Such research would offer instrument developers and officers a better idea of the conditions under which sonar systems would have to operate. A survey of this sort would yield a more sophisticated version of

---

[11] Dr. F. V. Hunt, "New Concepts for Acoustic Detection at Very Long Ranges," 15–16 May 1950, NSBA/NAS.

the "Submarine Supplements to Sailing Directions" composed by WHOI, Scripps, and the Naval Hydrographic Office during the war.[12]

Each study served a twofold purpose. Phenomena of vital importance to the submarine community, and therefore to the submarine industry as well, enhanced the Navy's prosubmarine and ASW proficiency. In addition, each project contributed to the understanding of the ocean environment and advanced general scientific knowledge. This was true in spite of the need to classify many of the most recent discoveries related to undersea warfare. Many scientists, like Professor Hunt, wished they would not have to worry "every year lest one of my students discover . . . [convergence zones] for himself and broadcast it outside of the family." [13] In most cases the researchers tied their work directly to the needs of the submariners while drawing conclusions and making recommendations for further research.

A study of echo formation by MIT physicist Lewis Fussel, Jr., offers an excellent example of this dual goal in CUW-sponsored research. His study focused on echo-ranging as a way of identifying objects underwater. In his report Fussel discussed the implications of his conclusions for the design of submarines and the need for sound-absorbent hull coatings. Thus, while augmenting a general understanding of the behavior of sound underwater, this type of research also provided data and conclusions for consideration by designers and engineers.

Fussel did not recommend changing the shape of the submarine hull to gain acoustic advantages, because the sound reflecting off a new hull design could well generate unpredictable echo patterns that might help the enemy ASW effort. His report did, however, encourage the Navy to investigate sound-absorbent coatings. BUSHIPS had already begun studying sound absorption by applying a newly developed compound to the hull of *Salmon* in August 1945. Encouraged by scientists like Fussel, the bureau further pursued this line of investigation by evaluating information on U-boat coatings and application techniques discovered one month later in Germany by the Naval Technical Mission.[14]

Understanding the way sound behaves in the ocean directly affected the Navy's ability to develop detection equipment effective from either

---

[12] "Basic Problems of Underwater Acoustics Research," Report of the Panel on Underwater Acoustics/CUW, Lyman Spitzer, Jr., Chairman, 1 Sep 1948, NSBA/NAS.

[13] Hunt, "New Concepts for Acoustic Detection at Very Long Ranges," 15–16 May 1950.

[14] "Basic Problems of Underwater Acoustics Research," Chap. 8, NSBA/NAS. "Rubber Coatings of German Submarines; Anti-Asdic," Technical Report 352–45, 20 Sep 1945, series 4, box 35, NAVTECHMISEU, OA. BUSHIPS to Dr. R. D. Fay, MIT War Research Project D.I.C. 6187, 11 Aug 1945, box 64, BUSHIPS Secret CENCORR 1945, RG 19, NA/WNRC.

surface ships or other submarines. The ability to detect schnorcheling submarines was one of the highest priorities in the early years of postwar scientific research. The two primary lines of investigation were thermal wake and sound detection.[15]

Early postwar research in sound detection focused on the German Gruppenhorchgerät, or GHG sonar system, discovered by the Naval Technical Mission. The Germans had experimented with precursors of the GHG as far back as 1927, when they developed an experimental hydrophone array particularly sensitive in the 600-to-1200-cycle range. Phasing the hydrophones in the array presented the most difficult problem. What was the best way to coordinate port and starboard hydrophones so the operator could conceive a total picture of the threat outside the hull? For the Germans a special array mounted in a bow blister, called the *Balkon,* solved this problem and became the foundation for postwar American sonars like the AN/BQR–4.[16] By 1948 the investigation into the *Balkon* by the underwater sound laboratory in New London caused BUSHIPS to authorize the removal of the GHG from the captured *U–3008.* The bureau shipped the entire system, including its control console, to Groton-New London, where Electric Boat and USNUSL made a copy and installed it in *Cochino* (SS 345) for operational tests.[17]

Self-noise, an obvious handicap to the effectiveness of any submarine, laid early claim to an important place in the Navy's program of scientific research. Both conventional and nuclear submarines are naturally noisy vehicles. Diesel-electric drive produces detectable cylinder-firing rates and harmonics, as well as the rhythmic rotational sounds of the motors. Using reduction gears in conjunction with the main drive motors produces a constant frequency whine that varies in pitch with the speed of the submarine. Worn bearings further aft often cause a shaft rate "thump." In many cases propellers are the worst culprits, producing cavitation noise, singing, and blade frequency rhythms.[18]

---

[15] The Navy's Radio and Sound Laboratory in San Diego, which later became part of the postwar Naval Electronics Laboratory, pioneered the study of thermal wake detection. Since an exposed schnorchel disturbed the layers of the upper ocean, the Navy scientists at San Diego sought to exploit the effect of the heat and motion produced by the partially submerged vessel to develop a device that would betray the submarine's presence. BUSHIPS to Director, U.S. Naval Radio and Sound Laboratory, San Diego, 21 Mar 1945, BUSHIPS Secret CENCORR 1945.

[16] Lee E. Holt, "The German Use of Sonic Listening," *Journal of the Acoustical Society of America* 19/1, No. 4 (Jul 1947): 678–81.

[17] USNUSL to BUSHIPS (telegram), 29 Jun 1948, box 1008, BUSHIPS Unclassified CENCORR 1948, RG 19, NA/WNRC.

[18] "Block Diagram of Machinery Line-up, and Types of Noise on Diesel Electric Submarines of World War II," n.d., box 6, Marvin Lasky Papers, RC 21–5, Navy Laboratories Archive, David Taylor Research Center (DTRC).

DTRC Archives

David Taylor Model Basin, Carderock, Maryland, where scientists explore hydrodynamics and propulsion, December 1948.

DTRC Archives

The Engineering Experiment Station, which also undertook hydrodynamic research, evaluated the close-cycle submarine propulsion system.

By 1946 BUSHIPS had already taken steps to expand the facilities at EES for the study of self-noise. The shipyards regularly collected data on the amount of ship-generated noise and its various sources when operational submarines put in for overhaul. In July BUSHIPS convened a conference at the New London submarine base, chaired by Captain Armand Morgan of the Portsmouth Naval Shipyard, to discuss the creation of a program to reduce submarine noise. Morgan felt that the Navy's effort to that point had concentrated almost completely on isolating noisy machinery from the hull and, "little effort has been made to reduce noise directly at its sources. The result has been that equipment which did not lend itself to isolation, either had to be replaced or left noisy."

As a direct result BUSHIPS initiated a program in 1946 to reduce sound emissions from submarines. In this effort the bureau, the yards, and the Navy laboratories would accumulate the necessary data, establish criteria for performance as a foundation for new machinery specifications, and cooperate with the other components of the naval-industrial complex to investigate promising methods of reducing or more effectively isolating submarine noise.[19]

The speed of the German Type XXIs made hydrodynamics and its influence on submarine design another critical field of support research for the postwar Navy. The initial postwar evaluation of the advanced German hull forms sent EB and Portsmouth back to work on Guppies and *Tangs* in an effort to arm the United States with vessels capable of high submerged speed.

On 20 July 1948 the Chief of Naval Research requested that CUW create a panel to investigate the hydrodynamics of submerged bodies. Experience with captured U-boats and American Guppy conversions convinced BUSHIPS and ONR to sponsor additional research in submerged resistance, seeking to find the most efficient hull form for the amount of propulsive power available to a conventional submarine. CUW stated it best in its description of the panel's objectives.

> The recent increases in the submerged speed of submarines have indicated a need for basic data pertaining to the hydrodynamic problems associated with the development of such craft. Specifically, it is apparent that there is a lack of information on such fundamental questions as forward

---

[19] BUSHIPS to Commanding Officer, USNUSL, 23 Dec 1946, box 1529; CNO to BUSHIPS, 30 Aug 1946, box 1529; BUSHIPS to Commander Portsmouth Naval Shipyard (conference minutes), 30 Jul 1946, box 1522; COMSUBLANT to BUSHIPS, 9 Sep 1946, box 1554, BUSHIPS Confidential CENCORR 1946, RG 19, NA/WNRC. Wave Mechanics Laboratory (work on vibration isolation), 1948, box 1, Records of EES (1903–63), Marine Engineering Laboratory (1963–67), RC 7–2, Navy Laboratories Archives, DTRC.

motion stability, resistance, depth control, effects of excursions in depth, and surface effects at high speeds.[20]

Before filing an interim report in November 1949, the panel issued two memoranda with specific recommendations. The first memorandum asked for continued support for adequate research on submarine problems, as well as a coordinating group to guide the research. The second strongly suggested that the Navy, in cooperation with private contractors, design and build a high-speed research submarine capable of traveling faster than 20 knots submerged.

With the emphasis in undersea warfare shifting to high-speed and prolonged submergence by the end of World War II, the form of the submarine had already begun to change. The Guppies and *Tang*-class submarines departed significantly from the classic American fleet submarine design. Now the scientific community needed data on the resistance, stability, and control of hull forms better suited to high submerged speed, plus the most efficient and suitable type of propulsion system to power them. Since the available information was scarce at best, the panel suggested that the Navy Department consider an experimental submarine used primarily to generate this basic information.[21]

Defining the Problem: The Low Report and Project Hartwell

In 1950 the findings of the Low Report and the Hartwell Project provided further motivation for expediting the broad spectrum of basic research in undersea warfare. Commissioned by Admirals Louis E. Denfeld and Forrest P. Sherman during their successive terms as CNO, recommendations from both groups caused the U.S. Navy to accelerate long-term scientific inquiry and to determine more precisely the most profitable areas of research. It became increasingly evident that BUSHIPS and private industry could not design and build effective submarines for the future without the continued support of the scientific community. Undersea warfare had come of age. Now, as a matter of course, American scientists, engineers, and naval architects extended the limits of scientific and technical knowledge in support of the submarine fleet.

Between January and April 1950 the committee, chaired by former Tenth Fleet Chief of Staff Vice Admiral Francis Low, undertook a compre-

---

[20] Interim Report of the Panel on the Hydrodynamics of Submerged Bodies, CUW, 7 Nov 1949, NSBA/NAS.

[21] Ibid.

hensive study of undersea warfare as it might be organized and implemented by the postwar Navy. Among those assisting Low in this work were such veterans of the war against the U-boats as Rear Admiral Daniel V. Gallery, who was responsible for the capture of the *U–505*, and Captain Kenneth A. Knowles, head of the Combat Intelligence Division of COMINCH (Commander in Chief U.S. Fleet). These officers identified Soviet advances in submarine design, construction, and deployment as the greatest threat to American sea lanes and the Navy's most formidable problem.[22]

Recognition of the danger posed by Soviet utilization of advanced submarine technology led the Low Committee to recommend the exploration of a wide variety of surface and submerged options. Foremost among the latter was the development of an SSK. The postwar Navy had explored this option as early as 1947. But the formal effort to produce an effective SSK and the strategic and tactical doctrine for its use began with the creation of Project Kayo in 1949.

Kayo received a vote of confidence from the Low committee in addition to suggestions for effective management. Low argued that Submarine Division Eleven and SUBDEVGRU 2 should focus exclusively on training and SSK strategic and tactical development to the Pacific and Atlantic fleets in turn, leaving perfection of deployable instrumentation and systems to the Operational Development Force (OPDEVFOR).[23]

A different type of submarine, the SSK lingered in ambush at slow speed in shallow waters near harbors and at geographic chokepoints through which enemy forces would have to pass. The first of these vessels, commissioned in 1951 and 1952 as the *K 1–3*, each displaced only 765 tons on the surface with a length of 196 feet. The real advantage of these small, cramped, uncomfortable vessels was their large AN/BQR–4 sonar, a direct technical descendant of the GHG hydrophone system.

The necessity to do combat against other submarines as well as surface vessels led the Navy to develop multipurpose attack submarines that could perform the hunter-killer role as part of their regular mission. Rather than continuing with the smaller K series, the Navy spent the balance of the decade fitting seven old *Gato*-class fleet submarines with the more advanced BQR–4 sonar to take over the hunter-killer mission. These ships provided increased speed, better habitability, and the capability of firing pattern-running and acoustic-homing torpedoes like the Mark 37.[24]

In addition to recommending the SSK program, the committee also counseled full development of submarine-guided missiles, acoustic and

---

[22] Study of Undersea Warfare (The Low Report), 22 Apr 1950, Post 1 Jan 1946 Command File, OA.

[23] Ibid.

[24] Friedman, *Submarine Design and Development* (Annapolis: Naval Institute Press, 1984), 67–70; Norman Polmar, *The American Submarine* (Annapolis: Nautical & Aviation Publishing Co. of America, 1981), 85–87.

pattern-running torpedoes, and nuclear and closed-cycle propulsion, as well as research in submerged detection.[25]

Sponsored by MIT and ONR, the Hartwell Project addressed this same threat almost immediately after the Low Report appeared in April 1950, but from a different vantage point. During a concentrated, summer-long brainstorming session at MIT, leading American scientists suggested the best avenues for research and development in undersea warfare. As described by Professor Albert G. Hill of MIT,

> The HARTWELL Project was an attempt to bring to the problems of undersea warfare the combined experience of a number of people who played more or less prominent roles in World War II in the field of atomic warfare, radar, sonar, rockets, fire control, proximity fuses, and so forth. . . . I think all of us started this job with the distinct feeling that this country was very much like a man with an inoperable cancer; that he might linger a while but he was really done. We changed this opinion before finishing, but the change was gradual.

The groups into which the scientists of the Hartwell Project were divided advised the Navy on a wide variety of scientific concepts and technologies for protecting the overseas transport of troops and material from submarine attack in case of war. Recommendations came forth on hunter-killer submarines, radar, enhancement of long-range detection, low-frequency sonar,[26] helicopter-deployed sonar, atomic depth-charges, air-deployed homing torpedoes, and a wide variety of other countermeasures and methods of detection and identification. Indeed the Hartwell Project defined the primary avenues of scientific research in undersea warfare sponsored by the Navy until the 1956 Nobska Conference at WHOI reassessed the progress made by the naval-industrial complex.[27]

---

[25] Study of Undersea Warfare (The Low Report), 22 Apr 1950, Post 1 Jan 1946 Command File; OP 311K to OP 311, "Project KAYO Conference, 10–11 Jan 1950," 18 Jan 1950, series 5, file A 16–3(2), box 20, Subs/UWD, OA. "Report on Project Kayo Conference," 10–11 Jan 1950, box 7, Marvin Lasky Papers, RC 21–5, Navy Laboratories Archives, DTRC. The project seemed to need more determination and direction. The unidentified author of this report commented that he was disappointed in the Kayo conference and was of the opinion that the CUW panels might offer effective direction. In discussion with Vine, Scheville, Worzel, and others it was agreed that a steering committee was needed. The unclassified version of this document at the Naval Studies Board Archive contains National Academy of Sciences programs suggested for USNUSL and DTMB in support of Project Kayo.

[26] Sonar capable of detecting sounds generated in a frequency below 1,000 cycles, but more often than not in the 100–200–cycle range.

[27] Dr. Jerold R. Zacharias, "The Hartwell Project," MIT, 9–10 May 1951, NSBA/NAS. Project Hartwell, MIT: "A Report on Security of Overseas Transport," 21 Sep 1950, Post 1 Jan 1946 Command File, OA. A proximity fuze allowed a torpedo or some other type of ordnance to detonate near a target as a result of magnetic influences on the weapon by the hull or the body of the intended victim.

Some individuals deeply involved in naval research and development during this period recommended a central naval authority or a joint naval-civilian facility that would bring a greater administrative unity to the undersea warfare effort. This recommendation was never implemented because neither partner felt comfortable with so much institutional control. Many scientists, like former OSRD director Bush, wanted to preserve as much freedom as possible for scientists working on naval projects. From his viewpoint controls characteristic of the OSRD/NDRC system guaranteed freedom of inquiry and a better result for the Navy. Thus Harnwell's 1949 proposal for a centralized Undersea Warfare Research Facility received a rather cool reception. On the Navy side Rear Admiral Bowen's efforts to make the new ONR the central authority for all naval research failed as well.

After this rather awkward beginning, ONR soon excelled as the coordinator of naval funding for research and the most generous source of such support in the federal government until the creation of the National Science Foundation (NSF) in 1950. With this patronage, private laboratories and university research projects in support of undersea warfare flourished, as did DTMB, EES, NEL in San Diego, USNUSL, and other naval facilities devoted to scientific investigation.

The positive reception accorded the report of the Hartwell Project exhibited the strength and appeal of the naval-industrial complex as molded by the war. A variation on the extremely successful wartime cooperative effort between the Navy and OSRD/NDRC, it satisfied all concerned better than any alternative.[28]

In any case, centralizing the scientific effort in undersea warfare seemed undesirable and impractical. Commenting in a general memo to CUW on current oceanographic problems in undersea warfare Columbus Iselin, director of WHOI and a member of the committee, pondered the problems involved in managing undersea research. WHOI, Scripps, USNUSL, Columbia University, the Hydrographic Office, and other facilities had research under way on the ocean floor, hydrophones, underwater sound transmission, instrumentation, seasonal variations in detection conditions, and use of detection equipment. He lamented the administrative, budgetary, and scientific problems involved in such a diverse and geographically scattered program, but realized that

[28] Harvey M. Sapolsky, "The Origins of the Office of Naval Research," in *Naval History: The Sixth Symposium of the U.S. Naval Academy*, edited by Daniel M. Masterson, 214–21 (Wilmington, DE: Scholarly Resources Inc., 1987); Sapolsky, *Science and the Navy*; Gaylord Harnwell, "A Research Facility for Undersea Warfare," 17 May 1949, NSBA/NAS. David K. Allison, "U.S. Navy Research and Development Since World War II," in *Military Enterprise and Technological Change*, edited by Merritt Roe Smith, 289–328 (Cambridge, MA: MIT Press, 1985).

the scientific problems are such that for the most part they cannot be effectively solved in the laboratory. They require large scale experiments and careful measurements at sea over extended areas. No one laboratory or operating agency has all the necessary talents or facilities, nor is it probably practical to assemble such an organization.[29]

The Hartwell Project reflected the preferences of science and the Navy. It allowed participating scientists and naval officers maximum freedom to address a broadly defined but critical problem. Called together by the CNO and the conveners at MIT, its members demonstrated their comfort with the forum provided and the inestimable value of the personal professional relationships developed during the war. Naval officers and civilian scientists were accustomed to working together in this manner, all linked inextricably to a defined objective but working in many different places and under a wide variety of preferred conditions and arrangements. Thus the wartime relationship remained productive and continued as part of the fabric of the naval-industrial complex well after V–J Day.

Together, the recommendations of the Low Report and the Hartwell Project motivated the submarine community to promote further scientific investigation. In 1950, ONR demonstrated the Navy's continuing commitment to the field of underwater sound by creating the post of Coordinator of Acoustic Research and an Underwater Sound Advisory Group (USAG). The former determined the work in this area sponsored by ONR. The latter, as the Navy's board of consultants on underwater sound, consisted of eleven scientists from NRL, USNUSL, NEL, and other naval and Defense Department laboratories led by NRL physicist Dr. Harold L. Saxton. Both the coordinator and USAG helped channel available resources to promote research in underwater acoustics.[30]

A memo composed by CUW's Panel on Low Frequency Sonar, issued on 20 October 1950, demonstrated the immediate effect of the Hartwell Project on acoustical research. Composed by six leading American experts in low frequency, underwater sound transmission, detection, and instrumentation, this document discussed not only the best course for continuing research but also ways to ensure funding for the accelerated programs outlined by the Hartwell Project. Columbus Iselin, as chairman of the panel, along with Carl Eckart (University of California), Maurice Ewing (Columbia University), Frederick Hunt (Harvard), Winston Kock (Bell Telephone), and Harold Saxton (NRL) never doubted that moving

---

[29] Iselin, "The Present Status of Long-Range Listening," 15 Jun 1948, NSBA/NAS.
[30] Lasky, "Historical Review of Undersea Warfare Planning and Organization," 337.

DTRC Archives

Turbot (SS 427) rests in a floating lab used to test machinery noise, 1947.

into high gear in acoustic research was possible in the short term. But neither did they underestimate the need to sponsor only well-organized and carefully managed programs. This approach would help justify their plans politically and guarantee the necessary funds and reputation to attract talented people to the field. Obtaining the resources and carrying out the research would be neither cheap nor easy. In the opinion of the panel, "it seems likely that if the low end of the [sound] spectrum is to be exploited fully and with determination it should be planned to spend at least 2 million dollars during the first year and not less than 5 million dollars during the second." [31]

The panel had another major concern. As was the case in Professor Hunt's earlier comparison of America's chances in the Cold War struggle with those of a man afflicted with terminal cancer, this panel also felt strongly that only a crash program addressing the Hartwell recommendations would permit the completion of vital research "before a shooting emergency makes it impractical to conduct controlled experiments at sea." [32] A sense of wartime immediacy did not end with victory in the Pacific.

[31] Memo, Special Panel on Low Frequency Sonar to CUW, 20 Oct 1950, NSBA/NAS.

[32] Ibid.

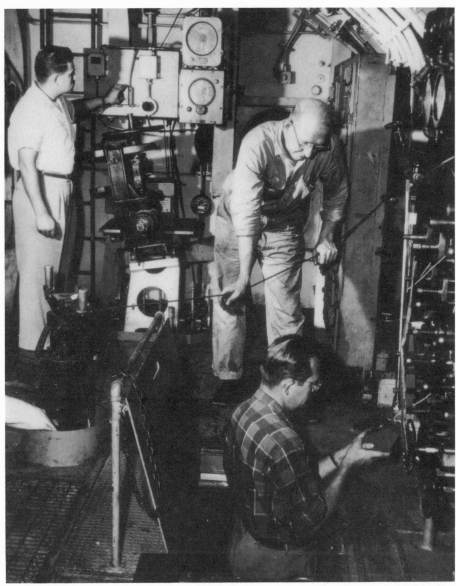

Inside *Turbot*, machinery is set up for noise tests. Underwater hydrophonics placed near the submarine pick up the noise transmitted through the hull into the water.

Albacore

In the spring of 1951 the Navy and the scientific community began pushing back the frontiers of underwater sound behavior and acoustic technology at an amazing rate. SUBDEVGRU 2, working on low-frequency sonar out of New London, first demonstrated the use of acoustic radiation characteristics or signatures to identify different types of submarines. With an experimental 10-kilocycle searchlight sonar installed on board *Guavina* (SS 362), NRL detected the distinct sounds of *Seacat* (SS 399) and the fleet tug *Salinian* (ATF 161) at a distance of between 9 and 10 miles. Standard equipment in the Guppies and *Tang*-class vessels in 1951 could effectively echo-range at only 1.4 miles. NRL also had work under way exploiting bottom reflection and convergence zones in submarine detection, and Captain William L. Pryor of BUSHIPS announced at CUW's Sixth Undersea Symposium in May 1951 that the Navy would test an advanced scanning sonar in the autumn. He also reported that research continued at NRL on variable-depth towed sonar, which would take advantage of the recent improvements in understanding the variation in sound behavior with temperature and depth.[33]

The advent of the high-speed, experimental submarine *Albacore* with its teardrop hull presented a new series of difficulties and possibilities. Portsmouth had built *Albacore* not for quiet operation but for the highest possible speed. In trials this experimental vessel easily surpassed 20 knots submerged, exceeding the best pace of the early Guppies.

The difficult job of quieting this type of submarine fell to the DTMB acoustics branch. As part of a team of physicists working on the acoustical problems of *Albacore* at DTMB, Marvin Lasky explored sources of noise common to all submarines and a few that were more characteristic of the AGSS 569. All of these vessels displayed five major problems: noise over the passive sensors, transmission of vibration through the ship's structure, machinery noise, water flow around the hull, and the noise of the propellers. Of these, water flow was the most important and least understood because no submerged submarine had ever achieved very high sustained speeds.

---

[33] CAPT William L. Pryor, "Detection of Submarines From the Surface and Below," 9–10 May 1951, NSBA/NAS. "From Tripods to SOSUS: Evolution of Sound Surveillance Requirements, Concepts, and Technology, 1917–1952," Appendix A to CAPT Joseph P. Kelly, USN (Ret.), interview by David K. Allison, Oral Histories, RC 6–5, Navy Laboratories Archives, DTRC. An appreciation of the SOFAR sound channel and the recommendation for further research in low-frequency sound made by the Hartwell Project also laid a foundation in the early 1950s for the Sound Surveillance System (SOSUS). The development of this ocean floor-mounted research system began in 1952 with the installation of a Low Frequency Analyzing and Recording (LOFAR) station on Eleuthera Island, about 250 miles east of the southern tip of Florida. Maurice Ewing used this location in 1944 during his groundbreaking research on the SOFAR sound channel. The LOFAR instruments were developed by Bell Laboratories.

Water flow noise at the bow and around the sail presented some interesting problems and conflicts. Lasky worked during the 1950s on a fairing designed to make the JT sonar slide through the water without adding to the submarine's self-noise profile by causing eddies as the boat submerged. The DTMB acoustics team rigged a TV camera on the hull to watch the water flow. A stroboscope provided by Harold Edgerton of MIT facilitated observations. The strobe light also allowed the scientists to take still photos precise to 0.001 of a second, which allowed an accurate view of the bubbles that formed around the JT sonar rig causing the flow noise. Eventually the DTMB physicists decided to build a dome around the structure to prevent bubble formation because the original fairing design proved unsuccessful. A similar dome appeared later on the JT sonar installed on board *Nautilus* (SSN 571), and a comparable video system helped the vessel prevent periscope damage and illuminate the terrain on the underside of the ice field during its transit to the North Pole.[34]

In 1953 *Albacore* received the first glass- and plastic-nose piece to house part of its sonar system. In this section the self-noise group at DTMB created a dead-noise area with acoustical materials, installed directional hydrophones, filled in all of the hull openings to prevent flow-excited vibration, and removed the propeller. When the vessel was towed at 10 knots, the major source of noise proved to be the asymmetry of the sail and the turbulence created by that structure at high submerged speed.[35]

The water flowing past the sail set up a Kármán vortex street, an irregular wake that promptly flowed into the stern control surfaces. Lasky and his associates immediately suggested removing *Albacore's* sail. The submariners argued against this approach because it would entail removing or relocating the periscope. Instead of a sail-mounted periscope, the people at DTMB proposed a towed underwater camera or vidicon of the same type later used on *Nautilus* to view the underside of the ice.

Thomas Gibbons, head of the *Albacore* towing experiments, and his colleague, Sheldon Gay, had worked on towing as part of Project General during the war. Their experiments involved a towed paravane that used explosive tubes to destroy incoming torpedoes. Now, with the towing techniques perfected in Project General, the vidicon became a viable alternative for *Albacore*. But BUSHIPS and a half-century of submarine design and tradition prevented the people at DTMB from removing the sail.[36]

---

[34] Marvin Lasky, interview by David Allison, n.d., Oral Histories, RC 6–5, Navy Laboratories Archives, DTRC.

[35] Ibid.

[36] Ibid. Lasky commented a number of times that in the 1970s and 1980s the Navy was still using technology on towed arrays generated by Project General.

In spite of this disagreement the Navy Department entrusted the civilian scientific community with almost complete control over *Albacore* for research purposes. Lasky explained the Navy's reasons in this way:

> Let me tell you why the civilians were able to control ALBACORE. Because the spillover of scientific effort from World War Two and the respect of the naval officers in charge for civilian expertise in solving naval problems. This has [since] evaporated and [Captain Albert G.] Mumma [Director of DTMB] and his predecessors at the Model Basin gathered together at the Model Basin the best spillover talent that helped win World War Two, that was left over after World War Two. The caliber of people at the Model Basin, I believe was as high then as it ever was. It reached a high water mark. This is validated by the history of where the people went after they left the Model Basin. At that time too, during World War Two, we were thinking of the good of the whole and thinking of systems of warfare rather than research systems which go no place.

Lasky's experiences once again demonstrated the value of the intimate professional relationship between individuals involved in the naval-industrial complex and the trust the relationship inspired. Whether in the industrial sector or in the scientific community, this mutual confidence and understanding facilitated remarkable progress and achievement in a short time.[37]

Hydrodynamics and hull design, always a prime area of interest for the Navy, also assumed a special significance after 1950.[38] The environment created by the Low Report and Hartwell Project led the Navy Department, after some debate, to embrace the idea of a high-speed experimental submarine advanced only a few months earlier by CUW's Panel on the Hydrodynamics of Submerged Bodies. As the noted American submarine designer and engineer Captain Harry Jackson observed years later, the panel

> suggested to the Navy . . . that they build an attack submarine emphasizing submerged characteristics. And they were good engineers and naval architects and they knew that a ship with a single propeller on the axis would be more efficient than twin screw and therefore for the same horsepower you could drive a submarine faster. Their proposal was submitted to the Navy and the Navy turned it down, saying . . . that this was too radical. We don't want to make that kind of move, we are satisfied with the Guppy-type

---

[37] Ibid. This interview is classified confidential. Only the general material from the interview appearing in this book and this one direct quote have been declassified.

[38] Interim Report of the Panel on the Hydrodynamics of Submerged Bodies, CUW, 7 Nov 1949; 20 October 1949 Meeting, The Panel on the Hydrodynamics of Submerged Bodies, CUW, 20 Oct 1949, NSBA/NAS.

submarines and that is the avenue of development that we ought to take . . . Then they [the Navy and CUW] came up with a compromise and said we will make a *research* submarine that can be designed to emphasize submerged operation. I think it's fortunate that that happened, because there were so many things that we did on the *Albacore* that we could not have done on a regular submarine.[39]

When the Panel on the Hydrodynamics of Submerged Bodies began exploring the collective wisdom of the naval and scientific communities on hull forms in 1948, it consulted scientists at various research institutions including DTMB, Brooklyn Polytechnic Institute, Portsmouth Naval Shipyard, and WHOI. The scientists at these and other research centers were investigating the performance and control characteristics of high-speed submarines either independently or under government contracts. In one case, a group at Brooklyn Polytech, working under a contract from ONR, developed a method for determining the precise shape of cylindrical pressure hulls for high-speed submarines and the framing required to build them.[40]

The selection of the best hull form was the critical issue. Reflecting upon his contribution to *Albacore's* design, Dr. Louis Landweber, physicist and head of the Hydrodynamics Division of DTMB, recalled his research into Series 58, a collection of twenty-four different variations on the body-of-revolution submarine hull form. Dr. Landweber remembered that the goal of the model basin's research was to find the body-of-revolution that provided maximum performance "from the point of view, first, of resistance and pressure distribution; and then of stability and control." The best of the series became the hull for *Albacore*.[41]

Although BUSHIPS coordinated the work of several naval and civilian agencies on the *Albacore* project, the staff at DTMB took the lead in conceiving and testing the high-speed submarine design. Landweber's division made particularly important contributions. Georg Weinblum, one of the German Project Paperclip scientists, contributed his expertise on surface-wave effect to determine the influence of surface turbulence on a submerged vessel. Landweber himself concentrated on frictional resis-

---

[39] Harry A. Jackson, interview with author, 24 Sep 1987, NHC Oral Histories, OA. Interim Report of the Panel on the Hydrodynamics of Submerged Bodies, CUW, 7 Nov 1949; 20 October 1949 Meeting, The Panel on the Hydrodynamics of Submerged Bodies, CUW, 20 Oct 1949, NSBA/NAS. Captain Jackson was the head engineer, ship superintendent, and design superintendent at Portsmouth Naval Shipyard during the *Albacore* construction and early trials.

[40] Director, DTMB, to Chief of Naval Research, 18 Oct 1948, box 68, BUSHIPS Confidential CEN-CORR 1948, RG 19, NA/WNRC. Meeting of the Committee on the Hydrodynamics of Submerged Bodies, CUW, 10 Dec 1948, NSBA/NAS.

[41] Dr. Louis Landweber, interview by David K. Allison, 22 Jan 1986, box 1, RC 6–5, DTNSRDC Oral History Collection, Navy Laboratories Archives, DTRC.

tance. Philip Eisenberg and Marshall P. Tulin worked on hydrodynamics. The latter also had a hand in designing the propellers used on *Albacore*. Edgar Hoyt studied dynamic stability and did much of the computer modeling necessary to evaluate the Series 58 hull forms. Both the National Advisory Committee on Aeronautics (NACA) and the California Institute of Technology developed free-running models of *Albacore* to test Hoyt's computer predictions of the vessel's behavior. Caltech performed its own tests, while DTMB put the NACA model through its paces.[42]

Expectations for *Albacore* were high from the beginning. Since the vessel's designers and engineers anticipated a submerged speed greater than any predecessor, this vessel would provide an opportunity to experiment with single-screw propulsion, control surfaces, ship stability at high speed, and hull coatings to reduce frictional resistance. *Albacore*'s double hull and electric drive also promised to make it one of the quietest submarines in the Navy, a fact that interested Marvin Lasky and other DTMB physicists concerned with underwater acoustics.[43]

Albacore was launched on 1 August 1953 and commissioned by December; she completed a year of shakedown and acceptance trials by February 1955. According to Dr. Morton Gertler, who participated in designing *Albacore* and tested the vessel at DTMB's Hydrodynamics Laboratory, this submarine "served the twofold purpose of providing fundamental hydromechanic research data and providing a means for evaluating new and unusual concepts of control, propulsion and quieting."[44]

The tests were divided into four phases determined by alterations made to the submarine's stern control surfaces. These variations included both cruciform and "X" stern planes combined with either *Albacore*'s single screw or a set of contra-rotating screws. In her unmodified form *Albacore* exceeded all expectations with the help of silver-zinc batteries and highly efficient contra-rotating propellers.[45]

This research program provided the Navy with the opportunity to improve the performance of later classes of American submarines significantly. In conjunction with the scientific community, the officers and

[42] CAPT Henry Arnold, USN (Ret.), interview with author, 21 Dec 1987, NHC Oral Histories, OA. Notes on an interview with William Cummins, 2 Aug 1982, box 1, Navy Laboratories Biography Collection, RC–5, series 1, Navy Laboratories Archives, DTRC. CDR J. J. Stilwell, Code 420, BUSHIPS, Presentation on the Hydrodynamics of Submerged Bodies, 30 Dec 1952, NSBA/NAS. For general information on NACA, see James Phinney Baxter III, *Scientists Against Time* (Cambridge MA: MIT Press, 1968).

[43] Minutes of the Meeting of the Panel on Hydrodynamics of Submerged Bodies, CUW, 6 Mar 1952, NSBA/NAS. Note the comments made by J. C. Niedermair, BUSHIPS naval architect.

[44] Dr. Morton Gertler (Head, Stability and Control Section, Hydrodynamics Division, DTMB), "Albacore Research Program," n.d.; Dr. Morton Gertler, "Potentialities of the Albacore-Type Submarine (paper for the ASME)," 12 Nov 1958, box 4, EMB/DTMB 1899–1967 Personnel Subject Files, Navy Laboratories Archives, DTRC.

[45] Ibid.; Friedman, *Submarine Design and Development*, 82.

crew of *Albacore* demonstrated that this type of vessel could produce high submerged speeds and hydrodynamic efficiencies under the control of a single operator. In addition to the stern alterations, *Albacore* also sported two different bow configurations during its useful life and first demonstrated the utility of low-carbon STS, or HY–80, as a structural steel. Concerned about stability and control at high speeds, the Navy and private industry used a new concept in hydraulic systems in *Albacore* to improve the response of the control surfaces as well as single-stick control. The latter, according to Captain Jackson, "has been adopted by every other Navy except us." Further work was done on depth-keeping without the benefit of sail planes or bow planes, arresting snaproll, and placing sonar in the bow of the submarine.[46]

In 1954 BUSHIPS conducted a concept-design competition between EB and Portsmouth to determine the best hull configuration for the next class of diesel-electric submarines. EB would design a twin-screw type, and the bureau asked Portsmouth to compose a single-screw alternative on the *Albacore* model. As design superintendent at Portsmouth, Commander Donald Kern led the effort to develop the single-screw, body-of-revolution design. He prevailed upon Commander Ralph Kissinger, head of BUSHIPS's submarine branch, to recommend diverting funds for the three remaining authorized *Tang*-class vessels to build what became the *Barbel* class.

Kern's concept-design remained as faithful as possible to *Albacore*. The differences reflected the transition from experimental to operational, from a vessel designed to deliver data to one capable of delivering torpedoes. He kept the basic hull form and the single-screw, but

> you had to put a super structure on to cover up schnorchel pipes . . . and it wasn't a pure body-of-revolution. *Albacore* was really a pure body-of-revolution with a little turtle back trailing back to take care of an air-induction pipe. The *Barbel* had to have room to walk on deck and it . . . had to be of a size that it could accommodate the schnorchel refinements for a wartime submarine.

A combat submarine also required more reliable and durable diesel engines and batteries than those that took *Albacore* on her relatively short trial jaunts. But Kern and his colleagues incorporated, unaltered, all of the proven features of the AGSS 569 that would enhance operational performance.

---

[46] Jackson interview, 24 Sep 1987.

Albacore became the trial horse of the submarine community. With this vessel, industry, the Navy, and the scientific community could quickly take ideas to sea and determine their usefulness, permitting the prompt evaluation and adoption of important refinements. From Kern's point of view, "*Albacore*'s value to the Navy, aside from showing that the Series 58 hull form worked, was more in telling us what didn't work. It told us what not to do, far more than it told us what to do."

Without building *Albacore*, the Navy and private industry would have continued to place the stern-control surfaces aft of the propeller on huge, heavy castings. The vessel's remarkable speed might have prompted the addition of dive brakes to ensure recovery in a deep, fast dive before reaching test depth. As it turned out, none of these was necessary to ensure safe submerged control of the submarine at high speed. With a relatively small investment in time and money, the Navy could promptly evaluate either an alternative stern configuration that might stand in the face of traditional building practice or the need for extra protection in a deep dive. With *Albacore*, the naval-industrial complex took their doubts and ideas to sea and came back with firm answers.[47]

Observations

Without the work of its scientific component, the naval-industrial complex would never have made the strides in submarine design, construction, and performance that characterized the first postwar decade. In spite of the dissolution of the OSRD/NDRC in 1945, the Navy and the scientific community sustained the working and personal relationships of that wartime organization well into the postwar era. The response to the priorities set by the Low Report and the nature of the Hartwell Project confirmed the universal preference for a form of close cooperation that allowed scientists working with the Navy a large measure of independence.

Both the scientific community and the Navy Department acknowledged that the professional and personal relationships developed before and during the war were an important asset worthy of postwar preservation. The trust and mutual respect among scientists, naval officers, and industrial leaders, noted by Marvin Lasky and evident in the Harnwell proposals of 1946, created CUW and allowed close ties to live on in naval laboratories across the country as well as within the various panels sponsored by NAS.

[47] CAPT Donald Kern, USN (Ret.), interview with author, 12 Sep 1990, NHC Oral Histories, OA.

In the immediate postwar years the United States moved quickly from the role of student to that of innovator. Initially the naval-industrial complex for submarines simply sought to equal and then surpass the level of technical development achieved by the Germans at the end of the war. The Guppy program and the *Tang* class copied and refined this technology until American scientists and engineers made a series of quantum leaps forward in submarine systems and design. With a few exceptions such progress began in 1946 and was accelerated in 1950 by the recommendations of the Low Report and the work of the scientists involved in the Hartwell Project. The full naval appreciation of the work done in the SOFAR channel by Ewing and Worzel, the discovery of convergence zones by Vine and his colleagues at Woods Hole, as well as the research into the Series 58 hull form at DTMB are the most outstanding examples of these significant advances.

The happy compromise reached between CUW and the Navy Department, which produced the experimental submarine *Albacore*, demonstrated the value of what Professor C. Richard Soderberg of MIT would later refer to as stepping outside the traditional framework of technology.[48] With *Albacore* the Navy, science, and industry regularly stepped outside the traditional framework of American submarine technology and construction habits. The vessel behaved like a submerged aircraft, and her hull, materials, control surfaces, and countless other attributes altered a half-century of American submarine design and construction practice. AGSS 569 became the vehicle through which revolutionary ideas generated by the close relationship between the components of the naval-industrial complex found their way to the operational forces. *Albacore* embodied the essence of the future of undersea warfare perceived a decade earlier by Captain William Ignatius of the Naval Technical Mission, changed forever the character of the world's submarines, and is, in a comprehensive sense, the most significant submarine ever built. She provided a test bed for the future and demonstrated the technical fertility and capability of a naval-industrial complex accustomed to extending, on demand, the frontiers of science and engineering.

[48] C. Richard Soderberg to James Probus, 19 Feb 1960, NSBA/NAS.

Chapter 7

Preparedness, Hopkins, and Gunn's Idea, 1946–1953

While converting Guppies and building *Tangs*, the Navy and private industry took steps to ensure their future through industrial planning and a commitment to basic research and development. These activities led to the postwar industrial reserve program and the advent of nuclear power in the Navy.

The industrial preparedness and nuclear programs succeeded primarily because of the familiarity and easy interaction within the naval-industrial complex. Private industry, accustomed to the demands of mobilization, understood the challenges facing the postwar Navy and had little difficulty adjusting to the readiness programs. Practical experience with the Victory Yard and Kollmorgen Optical Corporation, among others, tempered the Navy's expectations and resulted in a well-organized plan with realizable goals. The revolutionary nature of naval nuclear propulsion demanded a high order of cooperation at all levels in addition to scientific understanding and a deeply experienced organization. All of these assets were available in the American naval-industrial complex after World War II. The system that produced scores of fleet submarines between 1940 and 1945 now drew on experienced officers, engineers, and managers to bring the Navy and industry to the brink of an operational nuclear submarine within a mere seven years after victory against Japan.

The Industrial Reserve Program

The memory of Pearl Harbor and the disintegration of American-Soviet relations in the late 1940s led the Navy Department to create a reserve capacity within the private sector committed to providing essential goods and services in the event of a national emergency. For the submarine community it preserved the capability of a core of key companies to furnish products essential to conversion and construction. In this way the Navy Department tried to prepare for a war that might come without warning.

Although the Navy Department leased or sold a percentage of the naval facilities built to support the war effort between 1941 and 1945, it retained others as insurance against the need to mobilize quickly. The bureaus tied industry to the Navy's future plans through leasing and sale agreements that required the preservation of plant space, equipment, and skills vital to successful mobilization in the shipbuilding industry.

Firms like EB, Bethlehem Steel Company, Fairbanks-Morse and Company, General Electric Company, and Bath Iron Works in San Francisco all continued to operate their wartime facilities, only now under lease in a standby arrangement with the Navy. These agreements gave the companies use of the industrial plants but granted the Navy the option in a crisis to take over the facility and direct its operation for the national defense.

Even when a company sold Navy-financed facilities to third parties, a provision in the transfer agreement entitled the Navy to occupy and run the plant in times of national emergency. For example, in the spring of 1947 Kollmorgen, the Navy's primary periscope manufacturer, sold its Brooklyn facility to the New York State Institute of Applied Arts and Sciences. The property consisted of a four-story brick building with 40,000 square feet of floor space. In a letter of 30 March 1948 to Thomas J. Hargrave, Executive Chairman of the Army-Navy Munitions Board, the War Assets Administration approved the sale but noted:

> One of the conditions of the Transfer [sic] was that during the existence of any emergency declared by the President of the United States, the United States Government should have the right to full unrestricted use of the property conveyed by assuming the entire cost of maintenance of all betterments used, and paying a fair rental for the use of any structures or improvements which were added thereto without Federal aid.

The War Assets Administration also agreed to a Navy request for a provision in the conditions of sale permitting the Secretary of the Navy to anticipate when this action was necessary.[1]

Each company negotiated the particulars of its own arrangement with the Navy Department. In 1947 Secretary of the Navy Forrestal, after discussions with Electric Boat, placed the company's expanded wartime fa-

---

[1] Robert Whittet, Associate Deputy Administrator of the Office of Real Property Disposal, War Assets Administration, to Thomas J. Hargrave, 30 Mar 1948, box 711, BUSHIPS Unclassified CENCORR 1948, RG 19, NA/WNRC. On 6 May 1942 President Franklin Roosevelt commissioned the Army-Navy Munitions Board to set priorities for raw materials, manufacturing, and construction projects. The board had been created in Jun 1922 to coordinate the plans for acquiring munitions and supplies for the Army and Navy. It consisted of the Assistant Secretaries of War and the Navy. Roosevelt's mandate finally ended an open conflict in the early war years between the Munitions Board and OPM over the authority to set standards governing the allocation of war resources. Connery, *The Navy and the Industrial Mobilization*, 35.

cilities in the category of a standby plant. He classified the results of the
Navy's $4,789,000 wartime investment in the yard as Type II and leased
the facilities back to EB on an interim basis.[2]

Only a small portion of the industrial expansion sponsored by the
Navy and the Defense Plant Corporation during the war participated in
this preparedness program. The total investment in wartime industrial
expansion exceeded $2.2 billion and included 1,305 different projects
ranging from new factories to small additions to existing companies.[3] Of
an original investment of $250,747,000 in 364 plants under BUSHIPS's
control, the postwar Navy leased some, transferred others to different
government departments, and sold others.

With the Secretary's approval, the bureau sold $143,280,000 worth of
facilities by 31 July 1947, realizing a return of 30.7 percent on the
amount originally invested in plant expansion and thereafter disposed
of by sale.[4] In only 30 of the 364 plants was the Navy able to tie vital facilities, like those of EB in Groton, to the industrial preparedness program.[5] The case of the Victory Yard and its effect on the Groton-New
London economy demonstrated the difficulties of trying to preserve the
intended mission of these facilities in the postwar world. Closing or
transferring any major industrial facility swiftly transcended the Navy's
immediate interest and became a local or regional political issue, and
pressing economic need naturally overcame the best attempts at long-
range planning.

In spite of such difficulties, by 1948 this bid to prepare for future conflicts became far more comprehensive. In that year President Harry Truman created the National Security Resources Board (NSRB), a civilian
regulatory agency that could, in a crisis, quickly expand to control wages,
prices, and production in the defense industry. Within the military establishment the Army-Navy Munitions Board became NSRB's opposite number in the military establishment for coordinating planning and production for mobilization. These organizations provided administrative
support and central coordination for the direct interaction between the
services, naval bureaus, and the armaments industry. Going beyond issues
of sale, leasing, and retention of facilities by each service, the program

---

[2] Memo, RADM Edward L. Cochrane, Chief of the Navy Department Material Division, to SEC-
NAV, 16 Jan 1947, box 90, Forrestal Records 1940–47, RG 80, NA. Firms falling within the Navy's
Type II industrial classification included all shipbuilding and ship repair industrial facilities.

[3] Memo, John T. Connor to Forrestal Pertaining to the Report "Navy Department: Status of Surplus Property Disposal," prepared by ADM Cotter, 23 Oct 1946, box 127, Forrestal Records 1940–47.

[4] Memo to SECNAV, 31 Jul 1947, box 90, Forrestal Records 1940–47.

[5] Forrestal to Senator Charles Gurney, 25 Feb 1947, box 90, Forrestal Records 1940–47.

now involved many contractors, as well as the three major branches of the Armed Forces, in formal commitments to prepare for mobilization.[6]

The Armed Forces and the companies involved in the program determined in conference the responsibility of each firm for some facet of military or naval supply in the event of war. Following proper procedure, BUSHIPS would apply to the Munitions Board for space allocation at the companies best suited to produce materials and components vital to submarine and surface ship construction. Once the board made its recommendations for each plant, the bureau met with the representatives of these firms to determine the product line each firm would produce as well as a mobilization schedule.[7]

The place of Westinghouse Electric Corporation in the industrial preparedness scheme offers a good illustration of how the system worked. BUSHIPS requested emergency allocations in fourteen Westinghouse divisions scattered all over the country. Perhaps the most important of all for the Navy's purposes was the company's Essington Steam Division in south Philadelphia and the East Pittsburgh Products, Transportation, and Generator Division. The former produced steam turbines for surface ships and reduction gears for surface and submerged operations. In Pittsburgh, Westinghouse manufactured diesel electric propulsion systems and torpedo motors and controls. In case of mobilization, Westinghouse and the armed services agreed that only 10 percent of the Philadelphia plant would remain available for general purpose civilian production. At the Pittsburgh facility 50 percent would continue to serve the civilian economy because of the company's importance to the vital railroad industry. This process was typical, and the bureau negotiated similar agreements with Bethlehem Steel, Fairbanks-Morse and Company, Kollmorgen, GE, and others to ensure smooth mobilization of the submarine production effort in case of war.[8]

Its ambition to sustain the naval-industrial complex for submarines in peacetime also led the Navy Department to investigate further an important wartime innovation in shipbuilding. In 1953, under contract Nobs–3143, BUSHIPS asked Electric Boat to investigate methods of submarine mass

[6] COL Fred W. Kunesh, USA, Chief of Industrial Mobilization Branch, to BUSHIPS, "Chairman Interview—Westinghouse Electric Corporation," 30 Nov 1948, box 733, BUSHIPS Unclassified CENCORR 1948, RG 19, NA/WNRC.

[7] Ibid. For the Army, the Signal Corps took responsibility for these preparations. In the Navy, BUSHIPS played that role for ship construction; the Air Force depended upon its New York procurement office.

[8] Ibid. Naval Inspector of Ordnance, Bethlehem, PA, to Chairman of the Munitions Board, 6 Dec 1948, box 690; Inspector of Materials, Chicago, to Munitions Board, Washington, DC, 30 Aug 1948, box 702; Inspector of Machinery, Schenectady, to BUSHIPS, 4 Nov 1948, box 704, BUSHIPS Unclassified CENCORR 1948. For the BUSHIPS files, the Navy filing manual designator QM holds the key to a good deal of documentation on long-term preparedness planning not only for Westinghouse and Bethlehem Steel, but also for Fairbanks-Morse and Company, Kollmorgen Optical Corporation, General Electric Company, and others.

production. In January Captain Herbert J. Hiemenz of BUSHIPS described the project to the industrial manager of the Eighth Naval District in the following way,

> Broadly speaking, this project centers around the concept of building SS [submarine] type vessels in sub-assembly yards and delivering the sub-assemblies via water transportation to a final assembly site. . . . The triangle—Galveston, Orange [Texas], New Orleans—has been selected as a typical, suitable geographical location for setting up a final assembly site, since deliveries of sub-components could be made via the Mississippi River and the Intracoastal Canal.[9]

No country had employed these mass production techniques since the end of the war. Charles West had utilized sectional construction for EB-type fleet submarines at Manitowoc during the war. The German navy built its Type XXI U-boats in a similar fashion under the guidance of Otto Merker, Director of the Magirus Automobile Works in Ulm and leader of the Central Committee for Shipbuilding. Although the bureau and Electric Boat investigated the industrial potential of the Gulf of Mexico region for submarine construction, the Navy never implemented the plan.[10]

The reason sectionalized submarine construction never caught on had nothing to do with technical problems or difficulties in implementation. Preparing for a potential future conflict and exploiting more efficient construction techniques encountered a more fundamental obstacle. With the postwar American shipbuilding industry on the decline and the Guppy conversion program nearing an end, preserving a strong core of submarine yards in the private sector seemed an almost insoluble political and economic problem.[11] Shipbuilding firms producing both submarines and surface vessels needed new facilities and tools to keep pace with tech-

[9] BUSHIPS to Industrial Manager, Eighth Naval District, 14 Jan 1953; BUSHIPS to EB, 13 Nov 1953, box 56, BUSHIPS Confidential CENCORR 1953, RG 19, NA/WNRC.

[10] Rössler, *Geschichte des Deutschen Ubootbaus,* 297ff. In 1978 Electric Boat Division converted to sectionalized construction methods to build the *Los Angeles*-class attack submarines and the *Trident* SSBNs. The company purchased the site of the old Naval Air Station at Quonset Point, Rhode Island, and built a $120 million, automated, submarine frame- and-cylinder manufacturing facility. Here the company prefabricates hull sections 27 to 42 feet in diameter. The cylinders are manufactured on four sets of machines. The first machine completes the frames, the second fabricates the cylinder shells, the third installs the frames, and the last machine pairs the cylinders. The company has automated the entire assembly, as well as any required welding. Once the sections are complete and filled with as many pipes and components as possible, they are floated down the river on a barge and delivered to the EB Division Land Level Submarine Construction Facility at Groton. Randolph King, ed., *Naval Engineering and American Seapower* (Baltimore: Nautical & Aviation Publishing Co. of America, 1989), 332–39.

[11] Clinton H. Whitehurst, Jr., *The U.S. Shipbuilding Industry: Past, Present, and Future* (Annapolis: Naval Institute Press, 1986). This book gives a clear presentation of the plight of the shipbuilding industry in the United States and the changing roles of the naval shipyards. See chapter 3 in particular for a narrative on the long-term decline of the American shipbuilding industry.

nology and construction methods. Companies like Electric Boat, Kollmorgen, GE, and others required a steady stream of orders from the Navy and the private shipping industry to keep the warship business profitable and a highly skilled work force employed. As the first postwar decade ended, it became increasingly impossible for BUSHIPS to expect sufficient appropriations to meet industrial needs. In a discussion with the Chief of Naval Material in February 1953 about the potential production capacity for mobilization, a BUSHIPS officer pinpointed the problem:

> To remedy this serious deficiency in shipbuilding and ship repair capacity, it is necessary to replace or provide production equipment; to build and rehabilitate piers, ways, buildings, and other facilities, as required to meet the building requirements for the new types of naval vessels. Correction of these deficiencies prior to mobilization will reduce the time required to rehabilitate these facilities under full mobilization conditions. Industry is unwilling to finance conversion or rehabilitation of these facilities at present in view of the current small demand in the shipbuilding industry.[12]

The Navy Department could not guarantee adequate funding, but for private industry, preparing to mobilize was not good business in peacetime. Over the next two decades this conundrum, combined with the certainty that the national defense required industrial preparedness, contributed to a significant, gradual change in the role of private facilities and naval shipyards. The Navy increasingly found itself diverting most of its new shipbuilding work to the private sector at the expense of its own yards. The latter eventually specialized in the overhaul and alteration needs of the surface and subsurface forces, while the Navy sustained vital private firms with contracts for new construction.[13] For the submarine community—especially the work force and design team at Portsmouth—this trend would have serious consequences in the years ahead.[14]

General Dynamics and Gunn's Idea

Dubbed "Hero in War, Orphan in Peace" by one author writing in a popular publication in 1944, Electric Boat also tried to acquire insur-

[12] BUSHIPS to Chief of Naval Material, 11 Feb 1953, box 55, BUSHIPS Confidential CENCORR 1953, RG 19, NA/WNRC.

[13] BUSHIPS to Chief of Naval Material, 3 Mar 1953; BUSHIPS to Chief of Naval Material, 11 Feb 1953, box 55, BUSHIPS Confidential CENCORR 1953; Data Charts for the Industrial Reserve Program, 10 Sep 1954; BUSHIPS Memo from Code 784 to 107, 27 Sep 1954; RADM Wilson D. Leggett Jr., Coordinator of Shipbuilding, Conversion, and Repair, to SECNAV, 9 Apr 1954, box 81, BUSHIPS Confidential CENCORR 1954.

[14] Portsmouth's last submarine, *Sand Lance* (SSN 660), was commissioned in 1971.

ance in an uncertain world. EB's leadership took measures to provide steady business and a secure future.[15] For John Jay Hopkins, selected president of EB in 1947, it meant diversification. Just as the Navy extended its authority in support of its mission in the event of another war, so did Hopkins expand the company's assets with an eye toward penetrating the commercial market while also securing a larger portion of the international defense business.

On 20 January 1947 Hopkins took the first step when Electric Boat purchased Canadair Limited.[16] This Canadian firm, created during World War II, produced a successful line of transports, passenger aircraft, and, two years later, a variation on North American Aviation's F–86 Sabre jet. Canadair, combined with EB's main submarine construction facility in Groton and its Electro-Dynamic Division in Philadelphia, gave Hopkins's organization a much broader base in the aviation and shipbuilding industries. Thus, as the Guppy program began to occupy the Electric Boat facilities in Connecticut, the company also manufactured electric motors and parts in Philadelphia as well as Canadair 4 transports in Cartierville near Montreal. In 1952 Hopkins used EB and its two subsidiaries as the foundation for the new General Dynamics Corporation.[17] The Electric Boat Company became the Electric Boat Division of General Dynamics.

Just as the president of EB expanded the company's industrial base and added to its technical capability, the Naval Research Laboratory and BUSHIPS began making concrete plans to develop a nuclear-propelled submarine for the Navy. In 1939, seven years before Captain Hyman Rickover began his nuclear training at the Clinton National Laboratory in Oak Ridge, Tennessee, Dr. Ross Gunn, one of NRL's senior physicists and technical advisor to the laboratory director, made the first recorded suggestion that nuclear power "would enormously increase the range and military effectiveness of a submarine." [18]

---

[15] "History of the Electric Boat Company" (Unpublished MSS, General Dynamics Corporation, 1949), VI–1.

[16] Ibid., VI–2.

[17] General Dynamics Corporation, *Dynamic America: A History of the General Dynamics Corporation and Its Predecessor Companies* (New York: Doubleday and Co., 1960), 337–47; "History of the Electric Boat Company," VI–2.

[18] Dr. Ross Gunn to Director, NRL (Enclosure 1 to "Notes on Interview with Dr. Ross Gunn," by A. B. Christman, NOTS China Lake, May 1966), 1 Jun 1939, box 3, Naval Weapons Center Oral History Collection, RC 6–2, Navy Laboratories Archives, DTRC. Memo, Dr. Ross Gunn to Director, NRL, "Submarine-Submerged Propulsion—Uranium Power Source—Status as of This Date," 1 Jun 1939, Documents on the Navy's Role in the Development of Atomic Energy, 1939–70, OA. The chain reaction experiments that originally inspired Gunn's 1939 observation were performed by the University of Berlin team of Hahn and Meitner. A Short Summary on the History of the Naval Research Laboratory and Its Work on the Atomic Power Program, 1939–47, 6 Apr 1955, box 17, Papers of Charles A. Lockwood, Manuscript Division, Library of Congress (MD–LC).

With the support of Admiral Harold Bowen, the newly appointed head of NRL, Gunn lost no time in placing the Navy at the forefront of nuclear research. Early in 1941, NRL began experimenting with uranium hexafloride to separate the isotopes U–238 and U–235 for use in fission experiments. The laboratory produced small amounts of this solid form of uranium to support work on isotope separation by Dr. Jesse W. Beams at the University of Virginia and Professor A. O. Nier at the University of Minnesota. At NRL a team led by R. R. Miller and Dr. T. D. O'Brien continued to work on more efficient separation techniques.[19]

In June Gunn brought Dr. Philip H. Abelson from the Carnegie Institution in Washington D.C., to NRL to work on the liquid thermal diffusion method of deriving U–235 from uranium.[20] A tall, energetic man with a long stride and contagious laugh, Abelson had begun his experiments at the Carnegie Institution after completing his doctorate in 1939 under Ernest O. Lawrence at the University of California, Berkeley. In October 1940 he shifted his work to better laboratory facilities at the National Bureau of Standards. Within fourteen months of Gunn's invitation, Abelson's promising research led the Navy to initiate work on a liquid thermal diffusion pilot plant at NRL.[21]

NRL's wartime nuclear program staff rarely had the opportunity to benefit from the data generated by the scientists of the atomic bomb project, known as the Manhattan Engineer District, because a presidential order kept the two ventures completely separate. In spite of this handicap, during 1942 and 1943 Abelson used uranium oxide obtained from the War Production Board to make the uranium hexafloride required for the liquid thermal diffusion experiments held at NRL. By 1943 the project had moved to a new location in Philadelphia to take advantage of the high-pressure steam the navy yard could provide. Although Manhattan Engineering District investigated other methods of separating the U–235 isotope from uranium, the Abelson technique was the first to achieve substantial separations of high quality. On 26 June

---

[19] Ross Gunn, Principal Physicist to Director, NRL, 28 Jan 1941, Documents on the Navy's Role in the Development of Atomic Energy, 1939–70, OA. Uranium hexaflouride is a solid at room temperature.

[20] CAPT J. B. Cochrane to Chief of Research and Inventions, 9 Aug 1945, Documents on the Navy's Role in the Development of Atomic Energy, 1939–70. U–235 represents only 0.7 percent of any sample of mined uranium. U–238 accounts for the other 99.3 percent.

[21] Vincent C. Jones, *Manhattan: The Army and the Atomic Bomb* (Washington: U.S. Army Center of Military History, 1985), 172. Emphasizing the simplicity of the procedure, Jones offers a clear explanation of the liquid thermal diffusion process for the lay person. If a liquid containing isotopes of uranium is placed in the space between two vertical concentric columns, and the inner column is heated and the outer one cooled, thermal diffusion takes place. Heat passing from the hot to the cold wall concentrates the heavier isotopes near the cold wall and the lighter ones near the hot wall. In addition, convection forces the lighter isotopes to the top of the column and the heavier ones to the bottom. Afterward the desired isotopes are extracted from the extreme ends of the column.

1944 Admiral Ernest King, Commander in Chief, U.S. Fleet and CNO, instructed the Naval Research Laboratory to give the Manhattan Engineer District the blueprints for the Abelson process. Three months later General Leslie Groves, director of the effort to produce an atomic bomb, had similar production plants in operation at Oak Ridge. Abelson's method was used as the initial purification treatment before an electromagnetic process refined the isotope to final purity.[22]

Many within NRL and the Navy felt that their long separation from the Manhattan Engineer District wasted valuable time. According to historian Albert Christman, "Dr. Gunn felt that they [Manhattan Engineer District] would have had the bomb six months earlier had they accepted NRL into the partnership." [23] In one of his memoranda Gunn himself asserted that

> reputable officials of the Manhattan Project have stated that the erection of the liquid thermal diffusion plant which was a direct outgrowth of the work at this Laboratory [viz., NRL], shortened the war by at least eight days. This was accomplished by the expenditure of about $20,000,000 for the construction and operation of the plant at Oak Ridge, together with $3,000,000 spent at Philadelphia. This total amount is only about 1% of the total cost of the Manhattan Project.[24]

Although the war and the atomic bomb diverted national attention away from the nuclear submarine, the Navy maintained an interest and expertise in this area. NRL scientists began working on nuclear submarine propulsion in 1939, and sustained a research effort in it throughout the war. Their exploration of the materials and technology related to controlled fission laid the groundwork for solutions that overcame the fundamental obstacles to a practical working atomic pile or reactor suitable for a propulsion system.[25]

The Navy had a program under way at NRL that included projects in three interrelated areas. Isotope separation occupied the attention of one group. Their research focused on deriving isotopes from a variety of

[22] Richard G. Hewlett and Francis Duncan, *Nuclear Navy, 1946–62* (Chicago: University of Chicago Press, 1974), 15–21; CAPT Robert I. Olsen to VADM Charles A. Lockwood, 27 Jan 1964, box 17, Lockwood Papers, MD–LC.

[23] "Notes on an Interview with Dr. Ross Gunn," by A. B. Christman, NOTS China Lake, May 1966; Hewlett and Duncan, *Nuclear Navy*, 15–21; Jones, *Manhattan*, 172–78.

[24] Ross Gunn, Memo for Files—"Early History of Uranium Power for Submarines," 1 May 1946, Documents on the Navy's Role in the Development of Atomic Energy, 1939–70, OA.

[25] Memo to Director (Commodore Henry A. Schade, USN) by Dr. Phillip Abelson (Head, Special Research Section et al.), "Atomic Energy Submarines," 28 Mar 1946, Post 1 Jan 1946 Command File, OA.

metals to achieve a more efficient naval power reactor. Another group concentrated completely on the U–235 isotope, seeking less expensive methods of concentrating it for use in a reactor. The third project undertook a "survey of problems and engineering analysis involved in the design of an atomic-powered submarine." [26] As the newly established Office of Naval Research assumed authority for NRL under the leadership of Admiral Bowen in March 1946, the laboratory staff issued a report on the application of nuclear power to submarines.

This preliminary statement by NRL on the use of nuclear power for submarine propulsion was offered by Abelson, the report's primary author, to gain support for such a proposal and to promote further discussion.[27] As it turned out, his proposals were completely lost in the postwar political debate over civilian control of nuclear power and its possible applications in war and peace. In the years since, historians interested in the naval nuclear propulsion program, and determined to establish cause and effect firmly and clearly, have failed to evaluate properly the elusive influence of the compelling ideas emerging from NRL in the early postwar years. Consequently, the concepts proposed by Abelson often fail to play any significant role in historical analyses of these events.[28]

Bowen fought hard but in vain to make the naval development of nuclear power a mission of ONR. Vice Admiral Earle Mills, a former member of the Tolman Committee for the study of postwar atomic policy and Admiral Edward Cochrane's successor at BUSHIPS in 1947, subsequently undertook this task.[29] BUSHIPS was, after all, the Navy's ship construction and propulsion authority. Unfortunately these major political battles over nuclear power research and the important figures in-

---

[26] Ibid.

[27] The March 1946 report was intended only to prove the feasibility of the nuclear submarine: "Certainly Phil [Abelson]'s boat wouldn't work—it was never intended to—the report was made to prove the feasibility of the system and to get the proper qualified people behind the project to produce an atomic powered submarine. It did just THAT so the report did accomplish what we set out to do." Olsen to Lockwood, 27 Jan 1964, box 17, Lockwood Papers, MD–LC.

[28] The most notable exceptions are Norman Polmar, *Atomic Submarines* (Princeton, NJ: D. Van Nostrand Company, 1963) and Norman Polmar and Thomas B. Allen, *Rickover: Controversy and Genius* (New York: Simon and Schuster, 1984). In *Nuclear Navy* Hewlett and Duncan discuss the report but do not give it the time and exposition it receives in the other two works.

[29] RADM Edward L. Cochrane, wartime head of BUSHIPS, chose Mills and CAPT Thorwald A. Solberg to join the committee, chaired by Richard C. Tolman, a physicist on the staff of General Leslie Groves, Director of the Manhattan Project. Hewlett and Duncan, *Nuclear Navy*, 22. For some involved in the nuclear propulsion project, Mills's speech before the ONR-sponsored symposium on undersea warfare in April 1948, appealing for a national commitment to a nuclear submarine, stood as the most critical event of the early nuclear program. RADM Paul F. Lee, one of the first officers in charge of ONR, believed that this speech generated the kind of support the Navy needed for the project. Statement prepared by RADM Paul F. Lee, USN (Ret.) regarding early discussions and decisions in the Bureau of Ships on nuclear propulsion for naval ships, 8 Sep 1952, box 17, Lockwood Papers.

volved have obscured NRL's role. Without doubt the earliest proposals for a nuclear submarine came from Abelson and Gunn with the approval of NRL's director, Commodore Henry Schade.[30]

Abelson's propositions combined the nuclear expertise at NRL with the findings of the Naval Technical Mission in Europe on the best hull forms for achieving high submerged speed. He suggested that a nuclear-powered submarine with a hull design based on the German Type XXVI U-boat could have indefinite range and reach a submerged speed of 20 knots or better. Perhaps the hull selection was natural, given the Navy's interest in German U-boat technology and Commodore Schade's experience as leader of the technical mission. Abelson also realized that he faced more than the obvious technical challenges. The project would require congressional funding as well as improved relations between the Navy and Manhattan Engineering District. Without support from both any discussion of a nuclear submarine was pointless.[31]

With permission from General Groves, Abelson had spent a few weeks in the spring of 1946 working at the Clinton National Laboratories in Oak Ridge, Tennessee.[32] As the Navy's only representative in power work at Clinton, he became fully aware of the small experimental reactor promoted by the chemist Farrington Daniels to disseminate the basic technology among the Armed Forces, American industry, and the Manhattan Engineering District laboratories. Abelson also familiarized himself with Alvin M. Weinberg's proposal for employing pressurized water as the reactor heat-transfer medium.[33]

Thus the Abelson Report of March 1946 reflected the views of an informed and able scientist who risked proposing a specific design in the early years of the history of nuclear propulsion. The hull configuration of a Type XXVI, Abelson believed, would not require dramatic alteration and could retain much of its machinery, including a diesel engine for emergency alternative propulsion. Since the Germans fashioned the Type XXVI to use the Walter closed-cycle propulsion system, a liquid-metal cooled reactor plant could occupy the spaces beneath the pressure hull originally designed to carry the hydrogen peroxide. The NRL report concluded that

> the principal research and development program needed is in perfecting a suitable pile, and investigating the heat exchange and handling characteristics of certain suitable fluids, including liquid alloys of potassium-sodium. It is proposed that these two programs be initiated immediately.

[30] Hewlett and Duncan, *Nuclear Navy*, 27–28.
[31] Memo to Director (Schade) by Abelson, "Atomic Energy Submarines," 28 Mar 1946.
[32] Clinton Laboratory became the Oak Ridge National Laboratory in 1947.
[33] Richard G. Hewlett and Francis Duncan, *Atomic Shield, 1947–1952* (University Park: Pennsylvania State University Press, 1969), 74; Hewlett and Duncan, *Nuclear Navy*, 29.

> At the proper stage in their advancement, the two could be combined in a shore test installation for endurance and control runs. Simultaneously the rest of the submarine could be entirely fitted and mountings arranged for all of this power plant equipment. Little time would then be consumed in installing the pre-tested power plant and starting operational tests.[34]

Although NRL formulated the first conceptual design of an American nuclear submarine and its power plant, the Navy Department did not permit the laboratory to take the project to its conclusion. Because of a national policy to keep control of nuclear power in civilian hands, the Atomic Energy Commission (AEC) pursued the development of a naval power reactor in conjunction with the Navy's authority on ship propulsion, BUSHIPS. AEC formally replaced Manhattan Project as the nation's central authority in nuclear matters on 1 January 1947. BUSHIPS worked with AEC on reactor development and then supervised the construction of the vessel designed to house the revolutionary propulsion system.[35]

The type of program suggested by Abelson did not differ too dramatically from that formulated by BUSHIPS to develop nuclear propulsion for the Navy. At the end of June 1946 Captain Albert Mumma, veteran of the Alsos and Naval Technical Missions, and acting chief of the bureau's machinery and design division, let the first two contracts for the investigation of methods and materials essential to successful reactor development. The first went to Mine Safety Appliances Company for research on the chemical and physical properties of sodium-potassium alloys. Babcock & Wilcox received the other contract, setting the company to work on the possibility of using liquid metal, in this case sodium potassium, as the heat transfer fluid in a gas turbine generator. Although neither of these companies was aware of it at the time, Mumma had begun the BUSHIPS effort to determine the best types of metals for use in a power reactor.[36]

Many characteristics of the unfolding BUSHIPS nuclear program reflected the groundwork suggested by the Abelson Report. The contracts for basic research authorized by Mills and negotiated by Mumma offer but one early example. The physicists at NRL realized the need to accumulate data on the various metals and materials having properties that might make them useful in a power reactor. The NRL program also proposed concurrent rather than sequential development of hull design and reactor technology to conserve time and produce an operational vessel by the middle of the next decade. This technique would skip the

[34] Memo to Director (Schade) by Abelson, "Atomic Energy Submarines," 28 Mar 1946.

[35] Sapolsky, "The Origins of the Office of Naval Research," 214–21; Richard G. Hewlett and Oscar Anderson, Jr., *The New World, 1939–1946* (University Park: Pennsylvania State University Press, 1962), 620ff.

[36] Hewlett and Duncan, *Nuclear Navy*, 30–31.

usual prototype stage by building a shore-based reactor designed for installation in a suitable submarine hull soon after the completion of preliminary testing. Between 1948 and 1950 BUSHIPS adopted a variation on this approach with the reactor prototypes at Arco, Idaho, and West Milton, New York, in order to meet its goals for the *Nautilus* program. Although the bureau did not intend to install either of these reactors in an operational submarine, both were built to fit within the space limits imposed by the submarine hull design selected for SSN 571.[37]

If the influence of Abelson and Gunn proved significant in the early years of the program, the future belonged to those chosen to direct the development of naval nuclear power. Asked by Admiral Mills and his coordinator of nuclear matters, Captain Armand Morgan, to propose candidates for nuclear training, Captain Mumma nominated many of the officers who would significantly shape the Navy's nuclear program in the coming years.[38] From Mumma's list, Admiral Mills selected Lieutenant Commanders Louis H. Roddis, Jr., Miles A. Libbey, and James M. Dunford for assignment to Clinton National Laboratories at Oak Ridge for nuclear training. All three were graduates of the Naval Academy and MIT. A fourth officer, Lieutenant Raymond H. Dick, a graduate of Ohio State University and an expert in metallurgy, joined them in Tennessee. Over Mumma's opposition, Mills selected Hyman Rickover as Oak Ridge group's senior officer. Rickover's performance as the wartime leader of the electrical section of BUSHIPS led Mills to prefer him over Mumma's choice, Captain Harry Burris. Mills sent Burris, who had directed the Navy's extremely successful destroyer escort program during the war, to Schenectady, New York, as the Navy's representative at GE. Along with another Mumma nominee, Lieutenant Commander Harry Jackson, Burris trained at GE and worked on the sodium-potassium cooled submarine intermediate reactor (SIR) while the company built the Knolls Atomic Power Laboratory (KAPL) as a joint project with AEC.[39]

In the years since Admiral Mills's selection of Rickover for the Oak Ridge team, Admiral Mumma has attributed the choice simply to the captain's availability at the time. If availability was a factor, certainly Rickover's experience as an engineering duty officer, a qualified submariner, and a tested section head also contributed to Mills's decision. Rickover's specialty, as well as his management style, offered the fledgling nuclear program certain distinct advantages. He had years of experience working with

---

[37] Memo to Director (Schade) by Abelson, "Atomic Energy Submarines," 28 Mar 1946; Hewlett and Duncan, *Nuclear Navy*, 164–67.

[38] Hewlett and Duncan, *Nuclear Navy*, 31ff., 43.

[39] Ibid., 31ff. Individual Officer Biographical Files, OA; Jackson interview, 24 Sep 1989; Albert G. Mumma, interview with author, 7 Mar 1988, NHC Oral Histories, OA.

many of the major electrical companies, such as GE and Westinghouse, vital to the atomic energy program. His personal management style led him to choose his section's priorities, select the contractors personally, develop close ties to the responsible executives of a wide variety of companies, and closely monitor the particulars of specifications and contracts.

Although Mills obviously felt that highly centralized leadership in the Rickover style was the essential element needed in this new and vitally important project, Mumma and many others have since regretted the decision. After a career in the Navy that eventually included command of DTMB and BUSHIPS and promotion to flag rank, Mumma still preferred the virtues he found in Burris. He was "a cooperator, he was a developer, he was a leader." [40]

Between 1946 and 1949 the bureau worked simultaneously on several fronts to make the nuclear submarine a reality. The first was the decision to continue sponsoring basic studies that would intimately acquaint the Navy with the materials, technology, and engineering problems characteristic of atomic piles and reactors. This practice also helped determine the private companies best suited to help the Navy overcome the most formidable technical obstacles. Along with the contracts previously let by the bureau through Captain Mumma, the Elliott Company, working with the assistance of Babcock & Wilcox, Foster Wheeler Corporation, and Combustion Engineering, Inc., prepared designs for a "steam condensing turbine plant suitable for propulsion of the submarine on the surface as well as fully submerged." Although this study presumed a closed-cycle system employing a stored oxidant, it addressed many of the problems of space and engineering that might plague a naval nuclear power plant. [41]

GE did the bulk of the early developmental work sponsored by the bureau. Even before AEC assumed control of the national nuclear power program, scientists and executives at GE demonstrated their interest in developing this new source of energy. Cramer W. LaPierre, a member of GE's general engineering and consulting laboratory, proposed to the Navy in May 1946 that his company develop a sodium-potassium reactor for use in a destroyer. In August, as President Truman signed the legislation creating AEC, General Groves approved a BUSHIPS contract requesting a nuclear-destroyer feasibility study from GE. The liquid metal would serve both as coolant and heat-transfer medium. [42] By the end of

[40] Hewlett and Duncan, *Nuclear Navy*, 34; Individual Officer Biographical Files, OA; Mumma interview, 7 Mar 1988.

[41] "The External Combustion Condensing Steam Cycle," n.d. May 1947, prepared by Ronald B. Smith, Elliott Co., BUSHIPS Secret CENCORR 1947, RG 19, NA/WNRC.

[42] Hewlett and Duncan, *Nuclear Navy*, 38–39. VADM Earle W. Mills to Joint Research and Development Board (AEC), 26 Mar 1947; Memo, Alfonso Tammaro, AEC Chicago to BUSHIPS, 30 Dec 1947, BUSHIPS Secret CENCORR 1947.

the year the company also had a contract to run the Hanford Nuclear Plant in the state of Washington as well as a promise from the Atomic Energy Commission to build KAPL in Schenectady. Thus GE established itself early as a leader in liquid-metal power systems.[43]

A full decade after Ross Gunn first perceived the importance of a nuclear submarine, Captain Rickover returned from Oak Ridge, assumed command of BUSHIPS's Nuclear Power Division (Code 390) and initiated his effort to create just such a vessel.[44] In March 1949 the Submarine Officers Conference, under the direction of Rear Admiral Charles B. Momsen, finished a comparative study of the potential advantages of both conventional closed-cycle and nuclear propulsion. SOC gave its complete support to nuclear power in a report issued on 18 May 1949. In less than three months, hard work by Code 390 turned this vote of confidence into a commission from the Chief of Naval Operations, Admiral Louis Denfeld, for a nuclear propulsion system ready for installation in an operational submarine by January 1955.[45]

Initially, Captain Rickover sought to create two partnerships for the production of nuclear submarines. GE, accustomed to supplying Electric Boat with motors, generators, and other components for conventional submarines, would work with this shipbuilder once again. In this case EB was enthusiastic, and Rickover convinced GE to undertake development of SIR.

The captain's effort to form a second partnership, this time between Westinghouse and Portsmouth, met with less success. In conference with Rickover and his associates from Code 390, Portsmouth officers declined to serve as a partner with Westinghouse to produce a vessel propelled by the submarine thermal reactor (STR), a system cooled by pressurized water. Portsmouth was beginning to feel the pressures of multiple post-

---

[43] Hewlett and Duncan, *Nuclear Navy*, 40.

[44] Since this study is not a history of the early development of the Navy's nuclear program but an analysis of naval-industrial relations, refer to Hewlett and Duncan, *Nuclear Navy*, for the broader context and the essential details of Rickover's efforts with AEC and Congress to ensure support for a nuclear submarine.

[45] Hewlett and Duncan, *Nuclear Navy*, 157ff. ADM Louis Denfeld to SECNAV, 3 Aug 1948, box 973, BUSHIPS Unclassified CENCORR 1948, RG 19, NA/WNRC. SOC of 18 May 1949 (Extensive report on the May meeting's discussion and recommendations), series 2, file 5, box 7, Subs/UWD, OA.

The Navy's long-standing interest in closed-cycle propulsion did not immediately end with SOC's recommendation and Denfeld's decision. The staff at the Navy's Engineering Experiment Station in Annapolis continued exploring this alternative for nearly three years. In Project Wolverine they designed a semiclosed-cycle gas turbine employing liquid oxygen as the oxidant to burn diesel fuel. The initial investigation of the original Walter closed-cycle propulsion plant, called Project Hill, was 70 percent complete by October 1946. Its successor, Project Alton, was scheduled to "fire up" a final product by mid-October 1952 when the promise of nuclear propulsion finally ended this line of investigation. "Progress Report of the U.S. Naval Engineering Experiment Station," Apr–Sep 1952, box 3, Records of EES (1903–63), Marine Engineering Laboratory (1963–67), RC 7–2, Navy Laboratories Archives, DTRC. VADM Roscoe F. Good, DCNO (Logistics) to BUSHIPS (Cancellation of Project 67A—Closed Cycle Propulsion), 26 Oct 1953, box 77, BUSHIPS Confidential CENCORR 1953, RG 19, NA/WNRC.

war commitments. The commander of the shipyard, Rear Admiral Ralph E. McShane, did not want to draw design talent and building skills away from the Guppy conversions, *Tang*-class commitments, and the numerous other projects then under way at Portsmouth. He offered to give Westinghouse advice on the project but would not commit himself to the same role EB had assumed for General Electric.[46]

Rickover turned to EB and quickly received assurances of the company's willingness to build both vessels. The nuclear program carried with it the promise of a long-range commitment to submarines and revolutionary technologies that would keep the company in the vanguard of the Navy's future plans for many years to come.

Rickover's offer also appealed to individual engineers and managers at EB who wished to probe the limits of state-of-the-art technology and found the problems posed by research and development stimulating. Frank T. Horan, an engineer and later operations manager of EB Division for *Nautilus*, nearly left the firm for a job in gas turbine research and development with the Elliott Company. Instead the nuclear submarine project seized his interest, and EB sent him to Bettis Laboratory, the Westinghouse nuclear facility 13 miles outside of downtown Pittsburgh. The staff at Westinghouse educated Horan in the particulars of nuclear power and tapped his expertise in submarines and steam-propulsion plant design. The result was the first set of plans for the steam plant that was eventually married to the STR. As Horan later recalled,

> The scientists did the reactor compartment and the engineers did the engine room. A lot of what was in the reactor compartment was also engine room equipment, so we got into it to that extent. . . .Electric Boat eventually got a contract from the Navy to write the specifications . . . for the whole ship, not just the engine room. . . And then we got a contract from the Navy to do the contract plans and we designed the contract plans here [EB]. That was the first U.S. Navy submarine that the specification and contract plans were done by a private contractor rather than by the Navy itself.[47]

Although commonplace before the Great War, private contractors had not assumed the responsibility for generating both specifications and contract plans for nearly thirty years. What was more important for the company and engineers like Frank Horan was the fact that the Navy picked the submarine to lead the way into the nuclear age. The work would be challenging and regular for the foreseeable future. In addi-

[46] Hewlett and Duncan, *Nuclear Navy*, 159–61.
[47] Frank Horan, interview with author, 26 Sep 1989, NHC Oral Histories, OA.

tion, EB agreed to work closely with Bettis Laboratory on STR. In the end Electric Boat built not only the hull sections to house the prototype reactors—STR at Arco, Idaho, and SIR at West Milton, New York—but also laid the keel of *Nautilus* at Groton on 14 June 1952.[48]

In the cooperation between the Navy Department and EB there was much more at work than mutual interest and profit. During the war years a professional intimacy had developed between the naval officers at BUSHIPS and SUPSHIPS responsible for design and construction and their counterparts in private industry. After World War II the company placed many retired EDOs in design, engineering, and management positions. This practice fortified the already flexible and cooperative relationship within the submarine engineering and design community forged by World War II.

Admiral Andrew McKee was one of those who inspired this cooperation among individuals that did so much to advance American submarine technology and design. According to Henry J. Nardone, a former naval officer who worked with McKee when they both moved to EB after the war, "He was one of the last of the breed of engineering duty officers who could sit down and design a submarine almost from scratch." A whole generation of engineering officers on the BUSHIPS submarine desk and their colleagues at EB sought out McKee for professional advice when the admiral worked as director of engineering and design for Electric Boat Division.[49]

When the company accepted Rickover's challenge and found that the nuclear submarine program would require extensive contracting for various specialized services, individuals like McKee fostered constructive communication between the bureau and EB, which removed many obstacles to progress. On the *Nautilus* project, McKee stepped in to ensure that the bureau help Frank Horan over the inevitable bureaucratic obstacles. Horan later recalled that McKee approached the BUSHIPS assistant chief for ships, Rear Admiral Evander W. Sylvester, about improving communication. After mutual and informal agreement, the EB group "could go to him [Sylvester] and tell him what we weren't getting approved and what was still not resolved on the Navy side . . ." and the bureau would promptly address the problem.[50]

In another case EB sought experts in steam engineering to work on the *Nautilus* power plant in support of the group working with Horan.

---

[48] Portsmouth would not begin working on a nuclear submarine until about sixteen months after the commissioning of *Nautilus*. *Swordfish* (SSN 579) of the *Skate* class was the first Portsmouth-built nuclear submarine.

[49] Henry J. Nardone, interview with author, 11 Sep 1990, NHC Oral Histories, OA.

[50] Horan interview, 26 Sep 1989.

This time a conversation between McKee and retired Vice Admiral Edward Cochrane, former BUSHIPS chief and dean of engineering at MIT, produced an effective solution. Cochrane's influence provided Horan with assistance from three sources. One of the best steamship builders in the business, the Central Technical Division of Bethlehem Steel Company, permitted one of its staff to work with Horan at EB. MIT loaned him the services of Curtis Powell, a professor of engineering, and Westinghouse contributed Richard Cunningham, who had an all-important grasp of the design and engineering problems related to the reactor compartment. This level of cooperation between the Navy and industry allowed EB to make progress toward completion at a rate that satisfied the considerable ambitions of the Navy Department and the bureau.[51]

EB's success in staying on schedule and tapping talent from the Navy and other private concerns caused an excitement within the division that benefited both the individual engineers and General Dynamics. Talented people now wanted to enter the nuclear submarine program, diminishing EB's difficulty in recruiting qualified and interested people. As for Horan, his success in pushing the preliminary design and engineering work on *Nautilus* to completion led to his promotion. He became head of production for the Navy's first nuclear submarine and moved to the shipyard floor to direct the construction of the SSN 571. This easy and intimate professional relationship ensured the steady progress of design and engineering work on *Nautilus* and remained one of the most important assets of the naval-industrial submarine community.

Captain Rickover's management style and the nature of his relationship with private contractors added an exciting, yet disturbing, dimension to the character of naval-industrial relations. During the war, Rickover had developed the electrical section into one of the most aggressive and outstanding divisions of BUSHIPS. According to Rear Admiral Robert L. Moore, who was then a junior officer and served as one of Rickover's assistants, his chief was "not the best technician, but he was an excellent administrator. There's no question about that . . . . He had the ability also of getting himself surrounded with nothing but the finest of people. . . . The other technical sections in the bureau couldn't get good people; Rickover could get good people."[52]

Moore served in the electrical section between 1942 and 1946, experiencing firsthand Rickover's determination to get the job done yesterday. Rickover's assistants carried a great deal of independence and responsibility. In return they received Rickover's complete support; they also occasionally felt his displeasure if the task was not done well. Although

---

[51] Ibid.

[52] Robert L. Moore, interview with author, 17 Mar 1988, NHC Oral Histories, OA.

these techniques and the results they achieved contributed significantly to the war effort, Moore felt that the individual paid a high price.

> We did a lot of things we shouldn't do. We disregarded the rules and regulations. If anything held us up so we couldn't get it done here, why, we'd find a way to get it done somewhere else. And nothing ever stopped us from doing it. It [electrical] was one of the most outstanding sections there. This was when I first knew Rick[over] and had come to admire him, although I didn't want to work another tour with him. I'd had four years of that and in order to keep up with that [the relentless pressure and drive] it also makes you a ruthless, domineering person. . . . That's a real fine way to win a war, but it isn't any way to run a peacetime Navy, and it isn't a good . . . habit for anyone to get into. [53]

Whether or not it was a good practice, the captain brought his hard-driving, often ruthless management style with him into Code 390. As a result, the engineers at EB felt the relentless determination and will to succeed that stimulated, drove, and eventually exhausted Moore at BU-SHIPS during the war. Captain Rickover also continued to demonstrate his ability to gather about him the best engineering talent that EB, GE, Westinghouse, and others could attract. He gave them a fascinating challenge, considerable responsibility, and absolute support. In return, he expected results.[54]

Into a naval-industrial complex for submarines already accustomed to close cooperation between the Navy, industry, and science, Rickover introduced extremely close supervision of every contractor. He took no comfort in the responsibilities imposed upon private industry by a contract. Rather, he expected full attention from the contractor to every detail and full value for the government's money. Historians Richard Hewlett and Francis Duncan compared his manner to that of a "suspicious housewife making sure that the butcher kept his thumb off the scale." [55]

In the beginning this vigilance stemmed from his intense desire to get the job done correctly, on budget, and on time. But it did not remain that simple because the technology involved was anything but simple. Harnessing the fundamental forces of the universe in the service of ship propulsion required a degree of professional competence, discipline, and responsibility that surpassed the demands placed upon the electrical section during the war. It also surpassed virtually any challenge heretofore posed to American private industry. Rickover knew how to organize and

---

[53] Ibid.

[54] John S. Leonard, Frank Horan, Henry Nardone, group interview with author, 13 Sep 1988, NHC Oral Histories, OA.

[55] Hewlett and Duncan, *Nuclear Navy*, 100.

administer a large and complex program. But in this case management was not the issue. The potential for major disaster in the nuclear propulsion program caused him to elevate professional competence, discipline, and responsibility to the rank of absolute virtues required of every naval and private participant. The technology itself dictated the conduct its disciples and practitioners must follow. Thus he gradually came to believe that technology had its own rules, which scientists and engineers violated at both their own risk and that of society as a whole.

Unfortunately for a great many people, Rickover's personal and professional manner made the lesson difficult to learn. He allowed those in the Navy and private industry to do their jobs, but under close scrutiny and occasional interference from Code 390. Rickover's drive to impose his discipline of technology on the Navy and each of its contractors resulted in such close scrutiny that "in actual practice . . . the distinction between a suggestion and an order was not very clear." [56] This management style required the naval-industrial complex emerging from the war to adjust quickly both to the demands of the new technology and to Rickover himself.

Shortly after the Mark I pressurized-water reactor was completed at Arco in 1953, Captain Rickover authorized an ambitious trial run that would far exceed the tests originally planned. The Idaho prototype had first gone critical at 11:17 PM on 30 March. On 25 June, in an effort to demonstrate his conviction that the Mark I would perform reliably, Rickover proposed a 100-hour test run simulating a voyage across the Atlantic Ocean. Although the operating staff experienced considerable trouble with the steam plant and mechanical equipment after the sixtieth hour, the reactor performed extremely well and the test became a milestone in American nuclear development. As historians Hewlett and Duncan pointed out many years later, "The test run had been an extraordinary achievement, with a significance extending far beyond the Navy and the United States. The Mark I was the world's first fully-engineered nuclear reactor capable of producing practical amounts of energy on a sustained and reliable basis." [57]

Observations

The conflict with the Axis provided a motive for removing the remaining economic or institutional obstacles to remarkably effective cooperation. These common trials and experiences as well as new challenges,

---

[56] Ibid, 144; Francis Duncan, *Rickover and the Nuclear Navy: The Discipline of Technology* (Annapolis: Naval Institute Press, 1990), 292–94.

[57] Hewlett and Duncan, *Nuclear Navy*, 185–86.

political and technical, helped make the postwar years significantly different from the interwar ordeal.

In the period between the end of the war and the simulated voyage of the STR across the Atlantic Ocean, the naval-industrial complex successfully introduced and managed many revolutionary changes in undersea warfare, from fleet submarine conversions to the advent of nuclear power. These achievements derived from a combination of insightful leadership and professional competence, seasoned by a high degree of collegiality with only minimal significance given to institutional or corporate boundaries.

The industrial preparedness program of the Navy and John Jay Hopkins's creation of General Dynamics demonstrated the wish to provide for the future by learning from the past. No one could be sure that the United States would once again have a grace period of nearly two years before finding itself drawn into another war. Furthermore, the advent of the atomic bomb and the Cold War gave rise to the fear that the next international conflict would bring the possibility of swift attack and the complete destruction of civilization. Preparedness agreements between the Navy and industry ensured that mobilization would be as quick as possible.

But from EB's viewpoint these agreements did not address a more immediate problem. How could the company keep its skilled work force employed and its facilities state of the art? The company's institutional memory had little trouble recalling the desperate conditions of the interwar period. Hopkins decided that the diversity of General Dynamics granted EB a larger portion of the defense market and guaranteed, as far as any measure could, the prosperity of each component of the corporation. In addition, the rapid growth of the nuclear propulsion program promised that private industry would play a significant and profitable role in the future of the submarine force.

The first nuclear-powered submarine, *Nautilus* (SSN 571), at Electric Boat, now a division of General Dynamics Corporation, January 1954.

Chapter 8

Under Way on Nuclear Power, 1953–1956

With the beginning of work on *Nautilus,* the postwar revolution in submarine development and undersea warfare reached its stride. It was an exciting and reassuring time for the naval-industrial complex. Working on nuclear propulsion placed the Navy and the Electric Boat Division on the cutting edge of the most advanced technology of the age and gave the submarine industry a greater guarantee of a stable, work-filled future than ever before in peacetime. As a new member of the company's engineering staff and fresh from over a decade in the Navy, Henry Nardone recalled: "We were really immersed in the nuclear program, and it was exciting because everything was building, everything was growing. We had ships on the waterfront being built. We had ships on the board being designed . . . and it was all concentrated right here." [1]

This contagious excitement had roots that went far deeper than the simple manifestation of growth and prosperity in Groton. The people involved in nuclear propulsion from the Navy, industry, and the scientific community believed that their talent, experience, and history of personal and professional cooperation could overcome all problems, both expected and unexpected. Frank Horan's experience at Bettis Laboratory demonstrated this willingness to share expertise and apply skills and talent without excessive deference to institutional, corporate, or service barriers. Producing the SSN 571 became the most important goal for reasons of national security, mutual profit, and the sheer challenge of harnessing the power of the atom to drive an American warship.

Building *Nautilus* and *Seawolf* tested every person, system, and procedure ever used in building submarines. The three most demanding problems that arose in the course of design and construction represent well the stimulating but taxing conditions under which the naval-industrial complex built the first generation of nuclear attack submarines and the way in which the partners in the naval-industrial complex overcame obstacles.

---

[1] Nardone interview, 11 Sep 1990, NHC Oral Histories, OA.

"A Terrible, Terrible Disaster" [2]

The uncompromising nature of the technology that went into *Nautilus* required adjustment at every level in the submarine industry and a test of every construction procedure used. Under considerable pressure to complete the SSN 571 by 1 January 1955, EB Division had already experienced a Rickover-inspired change in management: in November 1952 John Hopkins replaced O. Pomeroy Robinson, general manager of the division, with Carleton Shugg, former deputy general manager of the Atomic Energy Commission. Under Carleton Shugg and Frank Horan, operations manager for the *Nautilus* project, work went on around the clock to meet the all-important deadline. [3]

A few weeks before scheduled sea trials for *Nautilus,* a mishap occurred that demonstrated the need for improved quality control measures, and revealed the degree of cooperation between EB and the bureau as well as the state of the art in nondestructive testing. In preparation for the launching on 21 January 1954, the EB maintenance department had decided to procure some heating system pipe to steam-heat the portion of the enclosed grandstand from which Mrs. Eisenhower would play the central role in the festivities. This pipe was not of the seamless, stainless-steel variety but rather ordinary pipe manufactured by rolling plate and welding it along a seam. After the ceremony the maintenance crew removed the pipe from the grandstand and returned it to the company storehouse. Upon its receipt, the storehouse staff placed these pipes and others of their kind alongside the seamless, stainless-steel piping ordered for *Nautilus* according to rigorous specification set down by BUSHIPS. [4]

During the night of 16 September 1954, EB ran "hot operations" on *Nautilus* to test the reactor cooling-system. Using shore-side electric power, Horan's technicians ran the cooling pumps at high speed to circulate the water repeatedly through the reactor plant to generate heat. Assisted by an electric heater, the water soon reached a temperature high enough to create steam, permitting them to test the entire system thoroughly before installing the reactor fuel and actually going critical.

According to the investigation held some weeks later, at about 11:25 p.m.,

> use of the starboard standby condenser in the Reactor compartment commenced; a water hammer was heard, and the condenser secured. After a neg-

---

[2] This was Horan's initial reaction when asked to discuss the steam pipe incident of 16 September 1954. Horan interview, 26 Sep 1989, NHC Oral Histories, OA.

[3] Hewlett and Duncan, *Nuclear Navy,* 179ff., 216.

[4] Horan interview, 26 Sep 1989.

ative check for abnormal conditions, the condensate return valve was again opened, where upon the condensate equalizing line ruptured in the vicinity of a bend on the starboard side of the compartment just above the reactor shield and close to and below No. 1 steam drum. This casualty required immediate cessation of the test program and securing of the machinery plant." [5]

Horan's staff managed to get all of the workers out of the vessel with a minimum of injury. Only an EB rigger, Ralph J. Lindquist, working in the immediate vicinity of the rupture, received any burns requiring treatment. After a few days of light duty he returned to the job without suffering any significant long-term effect from the accident.[6]

EB could not immediately appreciate the extent of the problem. Once the vessel's steam plant cooled down, the company staff examined the casualty and discovered that it was caused by welded Bessemer steel pipe, not the type of material required by the specifications governing *Nautilus* construction. Horan immediately initiated an investigation. The company contacted the submarine thermal reactor and submarine intermediate reactor prototype plants in Arco, Idaho, and West Milton, New York; the superintendents at both locations reported similar substandard materials in the reactor steam systems, clearly demonstrating the pervasiveness of the problem. The production scheme used for the SSN 571 permitted the company to trace the origin of every part right down to the nuts and bolts, and Horan ordered his staff to inquire into the history and selection of the pipe in question—only to discover that "it was strictly random, and that there could be a lot of it, and there was nothing that we could do but assume we had it everywhere. We had to find it and we had to get it out of there."[7]

The naval officers at the SUPSHIPS office, like their counterparts at EB, only gradually realized the extent of the problem. As an engineering duty lieutenant on the SUPSHIPS staff in the autumn of 1954, Nardone recalled hearing Commander Ralph Smith, the SUPSHIPS design officer, assure Supervisor of Shipbuilding Captain Robert Moore that the piping problem would be corrected late that same evening. This statement clearly reflected the general consensus at the supervisor's office.

[5] The pipe was No. P–20 EB Div plan number 3678–02. The company could be this specific about the part in question because a newly implemented numerical system accounted for every part installed in the vessel and traced the history of that part back to the contractor who supplied it. Horan interview, 26 Sep 1989. Record of Proceedings of an Investigation Conducted at Groton, Connecticut, by Order of the Bureau of Ships, to Investigate a Casualty in the Boiler and Steam Piping System on Board *Nautilus* (SSN 571) Which Occurred on 16 September 1954, 12 Oct 1954, box 3, BUSHIPS Confidential Research and Development Library Records, RG 19, NA/WNRC (hereafter *Nautilus* investigation).

[6] Ibid.

[7] Horan interview, 26 Sep 1989.

Nobody working on *Nautilus* knew in the early stages the extent of the mistake or its origins. In the end the error cost EB $1.5 million.

Once the company and SUPSHIPS appreciated the magnitude of the predicament, it became essential to find a method for discerning the kind of pipe installed at any and every point in the vessel. Captain Moore assigned Lieutenant Nardone to the task of working with EB to develop a nondestructive test for this purpose without damaging the material or removing it from the ship. As Nardone remembered it, he "worked with Rus Brown [senior engineer in the EB engineering department]. . . and we tried all kinds of things: vibration measurements, conductivity measurements, filings, and we could never really be sure that any of these methods told us exactly every time whether it was or was not [welded steel pipe]." [8]

Brown and Nardone used all of the most reliable methods available at the time to uncover flaws in building materials and welds: radiography, fluid penetrants, the magnetic-particle method, and ultrasound.

Sensitivity and experience were the most critical factors.[9] As of 1943 BUSHIPS required the use of radiography to inspect the reliability of all welds in submarine pressure hulls. But discovering welds or irregularities in construction materials required unusually sensitive equipment and broad experience in interpreting the results. Would radiography prove consistent and reliable when used on pipe already installed in the ship? Nardone and Brown could not be sure.

Fluid penetrants also proved unsuitable for discovering seams or welds under these conditions. Of the fluid methods available, the one most likely to succeed was an acid etching process originally favored by Frank Horan. But the damage a corrosive could do to other parts of the ship and the fumes it might create caused the Navy and EB to set it aside.[10]

Another option, the magnetic-particle technique, required placing metal powder or dust on the pipe surface after providing the pipe with an electrically induced north and south pole. In addition to the impracticality of performing this test on installed pipe, the method proved highly sensitive only to surface defects and not to deeper subsurface flaws.

In 1954 ultrasound lay on the frontiers of testing technology, and BUSHIPS actually had its own special device in development. But this

---

[8] Nardone, Horan, and J. S. Leonard group interview, 13 Sep 1988, NHC Oral Histories, OA.

[9] "The sensitivity of any nondestructive test method may be broadly defined as its ability to detect finite discontinuities or changes in density in a given material or test object." R. J. Krieger, S. A. Wenk, and R. C. McMaster, "The Present Status of Nondestructive Test Methods for Inspection of Welded Joints in Ship Structures (Battelle Memorial Institute)," 5 Oct 1953, box 7, BUSHIPS Unclassified Research and Development Library Records, RG 19, NA/WNRC.

[10] Conference on Various Methods of Determining Difference Between Seamless and Welded Tubing Installed Aboard U.S.S. *Nautilus* (SSN 571), 19 Sep 1954, box 111, BUSHIPS Confidential CENCORR 1954, RG 19, NA/WNRC.

method needed further improvement before the shipbuilders could sanction it as a technique for standard testing. Indeed at this point the major steel companies did not even accept ultrasonic test results as proof of flaws in commercial shipbuilding materials.[11]

Only the proper type of pipe or tubing would guarantee the smooth operation of the reactor and the safety of the submarine, especially while submerged. The pipe materials used on *Nautilus* included carbon steel, corrosion resistant steel (CRES), and copper-based alloys. CRES piping appeared for the most part in the primary reactor loop and other systems related to the nuclear propulsion plant. The copper-based alloys served best in systems carrying salt water and high-pressure air. But, for *Nautilus*, seamless pipe provided that necessary extra margin of safety. In fabricating this material, U.S. Steel Corporation's National Tube Division had to pierce a solid piece of steel rather than roll a flat plate and then close the seam using furnace or electric welding techniques.[12]

The flaw in the production system that allowed the wrong material to find its way into the SSN 571 had little to do with the sophisticated technology characteristic of the vessel. Electric Boat and SUPSHIPS went to unprecedented lengths to ensure complete adherence to specifications. In this case the failure of the most mundane and traditional shipyard procedures to provide the proper materials demonstrated the extent of the technical revolution at hand. Although the company exercised exceptional care during construction, it failed to apply the same attention and discipline in matters of procurement and distribution. As Frank Horan put it, "The method of handling material in the United States [shipbuilding industry] was very, very sloppy."[13]

EB brought over a half-century of experience to procuring pipe and other construction materials for submarines. Its design department prepared piping diagrams acceptable to SUPSHIPS that displayed the system and specified the length and thickness of the pipe needed. One of the next steps was for the material order group of the engineering department to prepare preliminary requisitions. The company's purchasing agent took action based on this paperwork. At the same time the order section of the planning department assigned material, by number, from new purchases or EB stock to every purpose outlined in the requisitions and the rough plans that came with them. Inspectors from the company and SUPSHIPS met all incoming orders at the receiving sec-

[11] Krieger, Wenk, and McMaster, "The Present Status of Nondestructive Test Methods," for Inspection of Welded Joints in Ship Structures (Battelle Memorial Institute)," 5 Oct 1953, 26 Sep 1989. Horan interview, 26 Sep 1989.

[12] *Nautilus* investigation.

[13] Horan interview, 26 Sep 1989.

176 Forged in War

tion of the storehouse, examined them for proper papers as well as for quantity, and gave them a visual surface, dimension, and identity inspection before moving the materials to a storage location.

Segregation of different materials in the storehouse depended largely on visual identification. Chaired by Captain Philip W. Snyder, commander of the Boston Naval Shipyard, the board of inquiry studying the pipe incident found the receiving and inspection records in generally good condition. Indeed the Snyder Board discovered that these records survived a rather complicated transition to an automated Kardex system during 1954 and still served the company well. But the board could not say the same about the pipe-storage procedures. The inability to readily and visually distinguish seamless from welded pipe led to a mingling of sizes and types in the company storage racks. These circumstances led EB pipefitters to draw from the storehouse pipe better suited for keeping the First Lady warm than for building the first nuclear powered submarine.[14]

Other evidence uncovered by the Snyder Board suggested that better internal communication and greater sensitivity to the possibility of error in so ordinary a task as withdrawing material from the storehouse might have averted this disaster. In the summer of 1953, during work on the *Nautilus* steam system, an EB technician rejected a piece of pipe that gave visual indications of a seam or weld. He replaced it with a section of pipe that met specifications. A similar event took place at West Milton, New York, in August that year, illustrating the effect of the Groton procedures on the EB-built STR and SIR reactor prototypes. Unfortunately the discoveries made during the summer of 1953 went no higher in EB management than the foremen pipefitter and the design department liaison people. Thus managers like Shugg and Horan could not take measures to guard against the possibility of a pervasive procurement or storage error. At the same time the company management was seriously considering seven different ways of marking or segregating pipe according to type or purpose. These procedures included using a materials-marking machine, changing the numerical accounting system, and instituting a double-check withdrawal authorization scheme. But the alternatives considered by management for identifying stored materials never made their way down to the storehouse. Thus experiences that, if shared, might have indicated the possibility of a pervasive problem, became general knowledge within the company only after 16 September 1954.[15]

On 12 October the Snyder Board issued its findings. After determining the cause of the pipe rupture, it assigned responsibility.

---

[14] *Nautilus* investigation.
[15] Ibid.

The principal responsibility for the use of welded instead of seamless pipe on NAUTILUS lies with the Electric Boat Division, although secondary, and still important, responsibility for not detecting this substitution at a relatively early stage in NAUTILUS' construction lies with the Office of the Supervisor of Shipbuilding, USN, Groton.[16]

As EB's general manager, Shugg realized more than a week earlier that the company would have to bear the responsibility for the situation. On 30 September, after the search for a practical nondestructive testing method failed, he ordered the removal of every pipe even suspected of not conforming to specifications.[17] BUSHIPS approved this action a few days later, and EB shifted to a seven-day week to accomplish the task and stay on schedule.[18] After a very harrowing experience for BUSHIPS and EB, the SSN 571 was commissioned and under way on nuclear power on 17 January 1955.

Although BUSHIPS took pains to identify those responsible for the *Nautilus* pipe disaster, it did not take any significant disciplinary action.[19] EB Division paid dearly for its mistake. But the problem of identifying, handling, and distributing construction materials remained. As Frank Horan put it,

It wasn't very long before the Navy was acknowledging that this was an industry-wide problem, that it wasn't just here [viz., at EB]. The business of the maintenance department turning back some steel was just how it happened here. Everybody had the same problem one way or another, either in the same material or in other materials.[20]

To make absolutely sure the mistake never reoccurred, the company not only took measures to revise its storehouse procedures [21] but also prohibited the procurement of welded pipe for any reason. After 1954 all pipe ordered by EB, regardless of the project, was of the CRES seamless variety. The results provided EB with absolute assurance against a repetition of the disaster. But sweeping remedial measures often have a humorous side. Many of the company's newest drafting tables subsequently

[16] Ibid.

[17] Shugg to SUPSHIPS, 30 Sep 1954, box 111, BUSHIPS Confidential CENCORR 1954, RG 19, NA/WNRC.

[18] BUSHIPS to SUPSHIPS, Groton, 4 Nov 1954, box 110, BUSHIPS Confidential CENCORR 1954.

[19] Memo, RADM Wilson D. Leggett Jr. (Chief of BUSHIPS) to SECNAV, 25 Jan 1955, box 92, BUSHIPS Confidential CENCORR 1955.

[20] Horan interview, 26 Sep 1989.

[21] BUSHIPS Confidential Memo, Code 300 to Code 200, 26 Dec 1956, box 90, BUSHIPS Confidential CENCORR 1956.

sported legs and cross-braces made of costly seamless pipe, and John Leonard, EB's chief marine engineer on the *Nautilus* project, recalled that "we ended up with the most expensive parking lot railings in the world!" [22]

The Nautilus pipe incident demonstrated the degree of discipline imposed by science and technology on the submarine industry. The kind of care and attention paid to the nuclear propulsion plant and other advanced systems had to apply to every aspect of the job, from the drafting table, through procurement and storage, to the actual construction and operation of the vessel.

The speed with which a diagnosis and correction was made reflected the seasoned maturity of the naval-industrial complex and those working within it. Company employees and naval officers alike realized the importance of *Nautilus* to the country, the Navy, and Electric Boat Division. Smooth personal and professional interaction between Snyder, Shugg, Horan, Brown, Moore, Smith, and Nardone, among others, permitted all those concerned to address a serious unanticipated weakness within the system for building nuclear submarines before the reactor went critical.

"It Endangers the Safety of the Ship."

In 1954 and 1955 all three components of the naval-industrial complex addressed a serious but little-known problem plaguing the SSN 571. At high speeds submarines experienced intense hull vibration, propeller damage, and excessive self-noise.

The symptoms began to manifest themselves in January 1954, soon after *Nautilus* was launched. In the investigation to determine the best type of propeller for the SSN 571, BUSHIPS concluded that whether a three- or five-bladed model was used, the vessel would still experience serious longitudinal vibration. Representatives of the bureau, David Taylor Model Basin, EB, MIT, and the University of Michigan assembled during February at BUSHIPS in Washington, D.C., to address the problem. The experts in attendance, including the ship-vibration specialist Professor Frank M. Lewis of MIT, felt strongly that the difficulty would persist, and the decision to employ one method or another to reduce its effect would suffer from inadequate measuring techniques.[23]

---

[22] Nardone, Horan, and Leonard group interview, 13 Sep 1988.

[23] Professor Lewis was the first scientist to understand the nature of the torsional vibration that plagued American submarine diesel propulsion systems during and after World War I. His paper, "Torsional Vibrations of Irregular Shafts," appeared in volume 31 of the *Journal of the American Society of Naval Engineers* for 1919. Ignorance about this debilitating problem fueled the naval-industrial debates over the Nelseco diesels produced by EB for the S-class submarines between 1916 and 1925. At the time of the article's publication, Professor Lewis was at Webb Academy in New York City.

Lack of experience with this phenomenon on board submarines forced scientists and engineers to concentrate first on methodology and analytical techniques. Lewis and the other experts in attendance recommended further tests to refine analytical methods and to determine the performance of three- and five-bladed propellers in this particular case. They also advised EB to install vibration dampers throughout the propulsion system and urged BUSHIPS to have DTMB investigate some variations on the ship's stern stabilizer configuration to lessen the propeller vibration.

The latter recommendation had the greatest effect. As it turned out, the wake coming off the sail flowed into the twin screws at the stern, exciting the propeller as it turned. Although the problem could not be eliminated, new stern stabilizers did moderate the effect of the wake enough to allow EB to install either a three- or five-bladed propeller without fear of either damage to the propulsion system or a reduction in the ship's stability.[24]

Unfortunately, the longitudinal problem was only the tip of the iceberg. Extraordinary vibrations of uncertain origin continued to afflict *Nautilus*. In another BUSHIPS conference on the subject held on 3 March 1955, Professor Lewis and scientists from DTMB determined that vortex shedding along the sail's trailing edge caused the sail to vibrate.[25] The bureau immediately called for a sharpening of the sail's trailing edge to raise the frequency of the vortex shedding. At 180 cycles per minute the sail vibration frequency came dangerously close to the natural tendency of the hull to flex or vibrate as it passed through the water. If the two frequencies came into harmony, serious structural damage could occur.[26]

In the process of exploring the sail vibration, the bureau uncovered other disturbing data linked with the ship's performance at speeds above 16 knots. E. F. Noonan of BUSHIPS Code 371 observed:

> As a general trend, higher [vibration] amplitudes were noted at the higher speeds and at the lower frequencies. This vibration of submarine hulls, hydrodynamically excited, is typical of such vessels and the amplitude associated with the hydrodynamic excitation of the normal hull modes generally exceed those associated with propeller blade excitation. . . . The magnitude of the amplitudes obtained on the NAUTILUS, however, are considered excessive.[27]

---

[24] Memorandum Report of Conference Held on 26 February 1954, 3 Mar 1954; BUSHIPS to Commanding Officer and Director, DTMB, and Commanding Officer, U.S. Naval Submarine Base, New London, 31 Mar 1954, box 111, BUSHIPS Confidential CENCORR 1954, RG 19, NA/WNRC.

[25] In the flow of fluids past objects, vortex shedding is the eddy or whirlpool motion of a fluid taking place periodically downstream from the restricting object—in this case, the streamlined conning tower or sail.

[26] Confidential Memo for File, E. F. Noonan, BUSHIPS, 11 Mar 1955, box 92, BUSHIPS Confidential CENCORR 1955.

[27] Ibid.

The low frequency of this vibration disturbed the bureau the most. Dangerous resonances from equipment installed on low-frequency sound mounts could pose another structural dilemma, and, given the development of low-frequency sonar, self-noise in the same frequency would create tactical problems. Noonan commented that "it would appear that this problem might well suggest a review of our present efforts at noise reduction on submarines with added emphasis on the low frequency vibration of vessels designed for high speed underwater operation." He suggested reviewing the hydrodynamic studies of the SSN 571 hull and employing the BUSHIPS analog computer to investigate the effect of hydrodynamic excitation on ships.[28]

These recommendations proved valuable indeed, given the results of a three-week-long intensive exercise completed in August. Although the nuclear power plant performed well, *Nautilus*'s commanding officer, Commander Eugene P. Wilkinson, discovered significant flaws in the vessel that needed immediate attention. He reported to the Chief of Naval Operations, Admiral Robert B. Carney:

> Noise generated by hull and superstructure vibration is so great that NAUTILUS sonar capability is practically nil at any speed over 8 knots. This intolerable situation reduces its military effectiveness sufficiently to materially restrict the tactical advantages inherent in nuclear power. Furthermore, it endangers the safety of the ship.[29]

In his communication, Wilkinson submitted several immediate remedial measures to the CNO. EB should remove the marker buoys contained within the forward superstructure, as well as the bow buoyancy tanks. He also advocated shortening the escape trunks to eliminate projections exterior to the pressure hull. For the same reason the commander suggested building the ballast tank main vents inside the hull and reducing any hydrodynamic resistance offered by the vent risers.

Wilkinson's concern stemmed from frustration. He had at his command the most potent submarine in history. *Nautilus* could remain at sea and submerged for a longer period than any submarine before it. If *Nautilus* could reach a speed exceeding 20 knots, even the most formidable naval opponent might find it impossible to subdue the ship. But destructive vibration prevented effective operation beyond 8 knots.

In his endorsement of Wilkinson's report to the CNO, Commander Submarine Force, Atlantic Fleet, Rear Admiral Frank T. Watkins did not

[28] Ibid.
[29] Wilkinson to CNO via COMSUBLANT, 6 Aug 1955, box 91, BUSHIPS Confidential CENCORR 1955.

disguise his determination to solve the problems afflicting the SSN 571. The picture he drew for Admiral Carney offered a stark contrast to the near-perfection with which the nuclear power plant had performed.

> Vibration and superstructure noise prohibit normal conversation in the torpedo room at speeds in excess of 8 knots. It is necessary to shout to be heard in the torpedo room when the ship is in the 15–17 knot speed range. This noise renders worthless all of the installed sonar, active and passive. With the present bow configuration the high performance BQR–4 passive sonar is spare gear. The crude superstructure form is believed partially responsible for the unacceptable hydrodynamic noise generated at maximum speed. It is a serious problem because NAUTILUS realizes its greatest tactical advantages at flank speed where hydrodynamic noise is the maximum.[30]

These conditions required correction at the earliest possible date.

The nature of the problem made a close cooperative effort between the Navy, industry, and the scientific community an absolute necessity. Eventually EB and the bureau would have to implement the solutions. But the analysis of water-flow and self-noise problems afflicting the SSN 571 and guidance in selecting the best remedial measures would have to come from the scientists at the model basin and the academic consultants, like Professor Lewis, intimately acquainted with the natural principles involved.

A telephone conversation of 9 August 1955 between the head of the BUSHIPS submarine branch, Commander Paul K. Taylor, and his predecessor, Commander Ralph Kissinger, who had just assumed the position of chief material officer to Commander Submarine Force, Atlantic Fleet, revealed that *Nautilus* had actually experienced structural damage as a result of destructive vibration.[31] Two weeks after this conversation, Lieutenant Commander Lawrence V. Mowell of BUSHIPS joined a team of inspectors, scientists, and engineers assembled at EB to investigate the problem.

The structural damage occurred at a speed between 12 and 16 knots and affected the outer hull, the vertical floors, and pressure hull frames in the vicinity of main ballast tank number one.[32] The symptoms indicated that the source of difficulty lay in the bow. Covering the flood holes for main ballast tank number one reduced the vibration considerably. Tests on this tank also disclosed a significant variation in pressure with the flood holes open. While vibration and acoustics specialists

---

[30] COMSUBLANT to CNO, (First Endorsement on CO *Nautilus* [SSN 571] conf ltr ser 078 of 6 Aug 1955), 9 Aug 1955, box 91, BUSHIPS Confidential CENCORR 1955.

[31] Memo for File—Telephone Conversation Between CDR Ralph Kissinger and CDR Paul K. Taylor, 9 Aug 1955, box 91, BUSHIPS Confidential CENCORR 1955.

[32] Visit Report, LCDR L. V. Mowell, 6 Sep 1955, box 91, BUSHIPS Confidential CENCORR 1955.

worked to obtain more data, Mowell and EB designers looked at new ideas for streamlined submarine bows employing the body of revolution hull form, clearly demonstrating the value of the experimental work done with *Albacore* at DTMB and Portsmouth. If the fundamental hydrodynamics of the *Nautilus* bow design emerged as the cause of the destructive vibration, the bow might have to be redesigned.[33]

The newly appointed chief of BUSHIPS did not agree. Rear Admiral Albert Mumma argued that all of the information available to the bureau on *Nautilus*'s hull design demonstrated hydrodynamic efficiencies approaching those of Albacore. Mumma concluded a memorandum to the new CNO, Admiral Arleigh A. Burke, by declaring the bureau's determination to ascertain the source of the trouble and solve the problem. But the bureau chief did not agree with some critics who blamed a flawed hull design for the vibration trouble.

> Current indications are that those difficulties may be traceable to a combination of factors such as flood openings, hull shape in way of and abaft the sonar array, and a bow structure not specifically designed to withstand large alternating hydrodynamic pressures. Whatever corrective measures are decided on as a result of the current investigative program will be vigorously carried out on NAUTILUS and other current high-speed designs.[34]

On the basis of a partial analysis by the end of September, Lieutenant Commander Mowell reported to the bureau that the vibration seemed attributable to a Helmholtz resonator effect in the first two main ballast tanks. Caused by the action of seawater on the ballast tank openings, this effect produced vibrations that increased with speed. The size of the tank cavity exacerbated the problem. This situation explained the reduction of destructive vibration when high pressure air was introduced and kept in the tanks during experiments in the summer of 1955.[35] Indeed just a few weeks later tests conducted on *Nautilus* by DTMB scientists confirmed the suspicions of Mowell and others at BUSHIPS. In a report describing the inquiries at New London between 27 and 29 September, the bureau's Lieutenant Commander John M. Martin revealed that

> immediately following the closing of the vents on MBT's No. 1, No. 2, and No. 3 and the introduction of an air bubble into these tanks, a startling change occurred. Vibration and noise ceased. Changes of speed were

---

[33] Ibid.

[34] BUSHIPS to CNO, 16 Sep 1955, box 91, BUSHIPS Confidential CENCORR 1955.

[35] Confidential Memo to File, LCDR Mowell, 26 Sep 1955, box 91, BUSHIPS Confidential CENCORR 1955.

made from 14.6 to 19.2 knots with no noticeable return of the vibration or noise. Remainder of the tests indicated that introduction of air into each tank had an effect in reducing vibration with No. 1 MBT being the major contributor. From the above tests it is concluded that the Helmholtz resonator theory has been substantiated as the primary mechanism causing the vibration.[36]

Contending with *Nautilus*'s self-noise problems gave an entirely new twist to the acoustics program at DTMB. Before these difficulties appeared, most scientists interested in self-noise concentrated on flow phenomena occurring at 10 knots or less. The *Nautilus* case changed the focus of their research. High speed was now the holy grail of the submarine force. Acoustics specialist Marvin Lasky, his colleagues at DTMB, and those scientists working on naval problems in academia shifted their emphasis to speeds well beyond 20 knots, recalling the 30 knots submerged that was first attained by Professor Helmuth Walter's *V 80* in 1933. The capabilities of *Albacore* demonstrated that the best pace attainable in *Nautilus* was only the beginning.[37]

Nautilus continued to provide the naval-industrial complex with a clinic in the acoustical side-effects of sustained submerged high speed. Scientists divided the sounds created by the vessel into two categories. Although it often caused vibration characteristics that hampered efficient performance, self-noise created by operating the vessel did not necessarily radiate for any significant distance. But radiated sounds, like cavitation or propeller rhythm, made the submarine extremely vulnerable to detection and destruction. *Nautilus* provided abundant examples of both. These sounds were characteristic of any submarine. But sustained high speed had now provided an incomparable exciting force. The acoustical problems increased in number and their causes became more subtle and difficult to determine.

Even with its destructive forward hull vibration eliminated, *Nautilus* remained notoriously loud and easily detected. Thus it became a floating operational laboratory for a wide variety of self-noise investigations. In one case, the participants of a meeting held at BUSHIPS on 18 April 1956, which included Rickover, decided to replace *Nautilus*'s propellers to eliminate the "singing" easily recognized at a considerable distance by four SSKs during recent exercises. The switch was scheduled for later that month, and the bureau planned a follow-up exercise with the SSKs shortly thereafter to determine the degree of improvement.[38]

---

[36] Ibid.

[37] Marvin Lasky et al., Preliminary Report of Noise Tests on *Nautilus* (SSN 571), Dec 1955, BUSHIPS Confidential CENCORR 1955.

[38] BUSHIPS Code 371 to Code 300 (1), 19 Apr 1956, box 90, BUSHIPS Confidential CENCORR 1956.

National Archives, RG 19

Head-on view of *Nautilus* under way, 1955.

At a BUSHIPS conference on *Nautilus*'s radiated- and self-noise characteristics held in the spring of 1956, Lasky briefly offered a synopsis of the most demanding problems. New difficulties continued to threaten the SSN 571 with structural damage. Every time the vessel submerged, often to great depths, the ocean applied varying degrees of intense pressure to the ship's main structural elements. This process gradually work-hardened the metal, making it more brittle and causing a variety of discomforting noises and cracks. The conference reported:

> It was observed that NAUTILUS produces sounds of creaks and groans while changing depth and that these sounds are more severe or intense than those observed some six months previously (November 1955). The motion and changes of the ship's hull, stiffeners, and other structural elements are indicated as possible sources of this noise. David Taylor Model Basin personnel regard the ship as "looser" and with more "creaks" than several months ago and the extent of the present phenomena has led the Model Basin personnel, Mr. Lasky particularly, to believe that an immediate inspection of the ship's structural elements should be performed.[39]

In addition, the ship had a number of culprits inducing serious radiated noise. Along with the singing propeller, the gear train and the auxiliary feed pumps serving the reactor plant contributed to the easy long-range detection of *Nautilus*, not only placing the vessel in danger but also further restricting the effectiveness of on-board sonar. Compounding the problem was DTMB research showing that "pure whistles" from hull openings and the sail area could be heard for miles.[40]

By late 1956 the noise and vibration characteristics of the SSN 571 had become a fact of life, and the bureau fully expected *Seawolf* (SSN 575) to suffer from these same difficulties. BUSHIPS immediately applied all of the knowledge derived from the *Nautilus* experience to the SSN 575 and the four-ship *Skate* (SSN 578) class.[41] The latter represented more of a shift in mission than a change in technology. The CNO decreed that, in the design of these submarines, speed should take second place to the capability to wage antisubmarine warfare. Thus, in this case the various acoustic and hydrodynamic problems afflicting the SSN 571 and 575 would decrease slightly along with the demand to sustain high submerged speed. But those within the naval-industrial complex realized that high speed would

---

[39] Preliminary Report of Observations and Tests of the *Nautilus* (SSN 571) in the Key West Area during the Period 2–13 Apr 1956, 23 Apr 1956, box 90, BUSHIPS Confidential CENCORR 1956.

[40] Ibid.

[41] BUSHIPS to SUPSHIPS, Groton (Navy Speedltr), 22 Aug 1956, box 90; BUSHIPS Code 845 to Code 525, box 91, BUSHIPS Confidential CENCORR 1956.

rule the future. With *Albacore* built and undergoing tests, the priorities shifted to a hull form better suited to speed and maneuverability.

Addressing these problems and countless others, the scientific community repeatedly proved itself indispensable to the mission of the naval-industrial complex. In September 1954 the pipe accident at EB clearly demonstrated the extent of the revolution in construction practice demanded by nuclear technology. Similarly, the vibration and noise problems that beset *Nautilus* and *Seawolf* revealed the growing complexity of undersea warfare and the role of naval and private-sector scientists in both defining the problems and suggesting solutions. Without the daily support of physicists, oceanographers, chemists, metallurgists, and other specialists, the interesting and intricate vessel envisioned by Captain Ignatius in 1945 would have remained an enticing fiction.

"I Don't Think Liquid Metal Has Any Place in a Submarine."

Six months after *Nautilus*'s revolutionary maiden voyage in January of 1955, *Seawolf* came down the ways at Electric Boat. This vessel's reactor presented private industry and BUSHIPS with significant and complicated problems in nuclear engineering and naval-industrial relations.

Unlike the water-cooled propulsion system that powered *Nautilus*, the Seawolf plant used liquid sodium as the heat transfer medium. General Electric specialized in this type of technology, having initiated work in the utility of liquid metals in power reactors under the auspices of the Manhattan Engineer District as far back as 1946. Just as Rickover was concluding that a variation on the Abelson-Gunn proposal for a nuclear-powered submarine might be the best possible naval application of this new form of power, so preliminary research by GE determined the feasibility of a liquid-metal-cooled submarine reactor. The company was now willing to discuss replacing the proposed nuclear-powered destroyer with a submarine.

In a meeting with the GE leadership in Schenectady, New York, Rickover and his assistant from BUSHIPS Code 390, Lieutenant Commander Louis Roddis, first took measure of the company's ability and determination to develop this type of power plant.[42] Violating the lines of BUSHIPS command authority, Admiral Mills bypassed his director and assistant director of ship design and nuclear matters, Captains Armand Morgan and Albert Mumma, to give Rickover the opportunity to influence bureau policy on nuclear matters for the first time. In the face of the Atomic Energy Commission's determination in 1947 to develop nu-

---

[42] Hewlett and Duncan, *Nuclear Navy*, 44.

clear power for peaceful, civilian applications, Admiral Mills and Rick-over barely managed to obtain AEC approval for a liquid-metal reactor study at GE. They succeeded only by separating the reactor project from a study of the heat transfer system. The former received token support from AEC, but the Navy funded the latter fully, and the bureau code-named it Project Genie.[43]

In 1949 policy at GE began to shift in favor of Code 390. Up to this point the company's major efforts in nuclear science and engineering were the plutonium production plant at Hanford, Washington, and the breeder project at the Knolls Atomic Power Laboratory in Schenectady, New York. General Electric operated Hanford in support of the Manhattan Engineer District and KAPL, which was built by the federal government under the auspices of the AEC. When the commission decided in March 1950 to postpone the development of a power breeder indefinitely, the bureau sought to turn GE's attention and expertise toward the liquid-metal reactor for ship propulsion. In support of this effort Rickover marshaled considerable backing in Congress led by Senator Brien McMahon (D–Conn.). The young senator's reputation rested on his energetic sponsorship of the Atomic Energy Act of 1946, chairmanship of the Congressional Joint Committee on Atomic Energy, and the interest of his constituency in bringing nuclear submarine construction to Connecticut.

Without the power breeder as an obstacle, Captain Rickover and Rear Admiral David H. Clark, who relieved Mills as bureau chief in March 1949, were able to prevail upon AEC to approve program changes at Knolls. Carroll Wilson and Carleton Shugg, then manager and deputy manager of the AEC staff, agreed respectively on 4 April 1950 to support GE work on the SIR as long as it did not interfere with production at Hanford. At the conclusion of the April meeting Harry A. Winne, GE's vice president for engineering, committed roughly half of the KAPL technical staff to the Hanford project and set the rest to work on the submarine reactor. In agreement with the priorities set for the bureau by Admiral Clark, GE focused on the creation of a land-based, sodium-cooled reactor prototype at West Milton, New York. Construction would begin in 1951 with an eye toward having an operating reactor by 1953.[44]

Although the realignment of GE priorities amounted to a considerable success for Code 390, Rickover could not reform company administrative structure at Knolls the way he had at the Westinghouse Bettis Laboratory. GE was one of the pioneers in nuclear power for both ship propulsion and civilian power applications. The company cooperated with the bureau and the commission, but continued to follow an inde-

---

[43] Ibid., 48.
[44] Ibid., 114ff.

pendent corporate policy. GE's ability to resist pressures from outside the company rested with the absolutely vital functions it performed for the AEC at both KAPL and Hanford. As historians Richard Hewlett and Francis Duncan observed:

> Unlike Bettis, Knolls had vital functions to perform for the commission's production effort and also claimed a role in general research and development on power reactors. These added functions were the responsibility of others in the [AEC] division of reactor development and always appeared to Rickover as a potential source of competition.[45]

Thus in the early stages of developing the SIR, Code 390 had minimal influence over the way GE carried out the research.

In June 1950 the company made the Knolls organization an entity separate from the GE Research Laboratory and appointed the experienced engineer and expert in customer relations, William H. Milton, as director. Milton infused the laboratory with a new vigor and responded quickly to any Navy complaints about weakness in administration of the SIR project. But Rickover still felt uncomfortable because Milton did not control all aspects of the Navy project, and it was not clear that the bureau could hold any one person accountable for the company's performance on the SIR. Furthermore the captain could not find that same single-minded determination to stay on a development schedule at GE that he successfully demanded of other laboratories and contractors. He also complained that too many scientists and not enough engineers worked at KAPL, where the theoretical seemed to dominate the practical. In working with Knolls, some of the engineers at Electric Boat Division got the same impression. Frank Horan recalled that "they were academic people rather than engineering types."[46]

In addressing these concerns, Milton reminded Rickover that GE was in business to make a profit and that the nuclear project was only one component of the company's business. Thus, at least for a time, GE foiled attempts by Code 390 to remake the SIR project at KAPL into the image and likeness of the independent department created by Westinghouse at Bettis Laboratory for developing the water-cooled submarine thermal reactor or STR. Charles H. Weaver, director of Bettis, provided Rickover with a clear line-of-project authority and a person directly responsible for progress. This approach enabled Code 390 to exercise greater influence at Westinghouse than Milton and Winne initially permitted at GE.[47]

---

[45] Ibid., 116–17.

[46] Horan interview, 26 Sep 1989.

[47] Hewlett and Duncan, *Nuclear Navy*, 116–17.

In some fundamental ways the projects unfolding at Bettis and Knolls were not as different as the corporate policies governing them. In a naval nuclear propulsion system, regardless of the coolant used, the reactor core containing enriched uranium in a pressure vessel gives off energy in the form of heat. The primary cooling system absorbs the heat generated by fission in the core and transfers it, via a steam generator, to a turbine for propulsion and auxiliary power generation. The casing for the nuclear fuel is made of a protective metal that becomes the medium for passing heat to the coolant as it makes one or more loops through the core. The coolant also acts as a moderator, slowing down neutron emissions to efficient speeds for the fission process. Control rods, made of a neutron-absorbing metal, are used to control the nuclear reaction and thus the amount of heat generated.

The basic similarities of the system aside, the sodium-cooled SIR Mark A prototype differed significantly from its STR Mark 1 water-cooled counterpart. In naming the SIR, scientists indicated one of the most important differences. Intermediate neutron velocities would be used to promote and sustain fission. These particle speeds exceeded those employed in the STR.

Employing liquid sodium as the heat-transfer medium also made the Mark A distinctive. This metal has superb thermal characteristics. Its extraordinary heat capacity, thermal conductivity, and relatively high specific heat made sodium very promising. At the same time this substance presented problems almost as daunting as its advantages were appealing. The sodium coolant moved through the *Seawolf* reactor plant in a closed-piping system called the primary loop. The bureau had to devise a way of heating the pipes in this loop to a point well above room temperature to keep the sodium in a liquid state. Forced to circulate by special electromagnetic pumps, the sodium drew heat from the fission reaction in the core. This heat was then transferred to water in a steam generator, part of another closed loop called the secondary system.

In the next phase of the process, heat absorbed from the sodium coolant caused the water in the secondary loop to boil, creating steam in the evaporator section of the steam-generating system. Separators then removed water droplets from the steam, producing dry steam that was then raised to an even higher temperature by means of heat derived once again from the sodium. The propulsion system relied on this dry, superheated steam to drive the turbines, electrical generators, and auxiliary equipment. Finally the steam was condensed back to water in the condenser and pumped back to the evaporator for reuse. The system used seawater through an exchanger to draw off any unwanted heat.

Leaks presented an obvious hazard in this delicately balanced system. Sodium reacts violently with water, which could spell doom for a submarine. To avoid any accidents and to detect leaks, a third fluid, an alloy of sodium potassium, separated the sodium and water. It also acted as a leak detector. The sodium potassium was maintained by an inert gas at a pressure higher than both the steam and sodium systems. Any leak into either the sodium or steam loops would cause a reduction in the inert gas pressure, signaling the existence of the leak.

In addition to its volatility, lingering radiation was much more of a problem with the Mark A than with the Mark 1, a factor that finally led many associated with the Mark A and *Seawolf* to question the suitability of liquid metal for use in a submarine. John Leonard, EB's engineer on the *Nautilus* project, commented:

> In starting, I don't think we had any preconceived notions. There were two ways of doing the job and we were all working at getting the boats done. Of course after they [*Nautilus* and *Seawolf*] were done we had some very definite notions about it. . . . I don't think liquid metal has any place in a submarine. It's too hazardous, too hard to work with, too hard to maintain the ship, [and] the radiation is much more severe. Its pretty nasty stuff and I don't think it has any place on a nuclear submarine." [48]

From the beginning the presence of sodium made building *Seawolf* difficult. With help from the Navy EB invested nearly $1.5 million to upgrade and expand its facilities during 1953 to prepare for the construction of nuclear submarines.[49] But installing the *Seawolf* reactor presented countless unanticipated problems.

The excessive radiation retained by the sodium coolant took center stage. In September 1953 BUSHIPS issued a design change that provided for the installation of sodium dump tanks. To allow quicker access to the propulsion system for repairs in case of emergency, *Seawolf's* crew could cease reactor operation and isolate the coolant in tanks outside the reactor compartment. EB decided that the tanks required additional shielding because of the intermediate neutron speeds. Layers of lead and steel were complemented by a hydrogenous layer composed of fuel oil instead of the usual polyethylene. EB's head of research and design, Andrew McKee, insisted that without the hydrogenous layer the Navy risked exposing the crew to a dangerously overheated bulkhead.[50]

[48] Ibid., 134–35. John S. Leonard, interview with author, 25 Sep 1989; Jackson interview, 24 Sep 1989; see also CAPT Ralph Smith's (USN, Ret.), response to the author's written inquiries of 10 Nov 1987, NHC Oral Histories, OA. The author would also like to thank Jonathan Kiel and the staff at the naval Reactors Division of the Naval Sea Systems Command for the information on the operation of the *Seawolf* reactor.

[49] EB to BUSHIPS, 31 Mar 1953, box 77, BUSHIPS Confidential CENCORR 1953, RG 19, NA/WNRC.

[50] EB to SUPSHIPS/Inspector of Ordnance (INSORD), Groton, 6 Nov 1953, box 77, BUSHIPS Confidential CENCORR 1953.

Design changes and alterations of this sort slowed the construction of the vessel considerably. System diagrams and descriptions from EB and KAPL chronically fell behind the preparation and approval schedule. A report on the progress of the SSN 575 written at the end of 1953 enumerated forty-four delinquent plans not yet prepared by EB; three pertained to the reactor compartment.[51] In December many components procured under AEC and BUSHIPS contracts had yet to arrive at Groton, causing the project to fall further behind. In addition, the bureau and EB still had to finalize the design of the dump tank system that, according to the submarine desk at BUSHIPS, "has an important and direct effect on reactor compartment arrangement." [52]

These delays surprised none of the parties involved in building *Seawolf.* As early as January 1953 BUSHIPS, AEC, EB, and the supervisor of shipbuilding at Groton agreed that the company's early estimates of the vessel's completion dates were entirely too optimistic. At a conference hosted by the bureau, they postponed the beginning of trials for three months, from April to July 1953. Actual delivery would take place five months later than expected, on 1 March 1956.[53]

As *Seawolf's* schedule began to slip, both the Navy and the private sector began to feel the pressure. SSN 575 was not the only ship the Navy needed to build, and the desire to get other vessels into the water led EB to request priority for *Seawolf's* materials and systems. In this intense atmosphere the bureau denied EB's application for first priority in steel deliveries. The officers at BUSHIPS knew that EB was trying to protect itself and, under the circumstances, they reacted with caution.

> Code 500 comment—I have already informed code 600, in response to telephone inquiry, that we will *not* give SSN575 an over-riding priority for steel as requested by EB Co. We must keep an eye on EB since they are already endeavoring to maneuver us into a possible embarrassing situation with respect to SSN575. Had we complied with EB request it would have been at the expense of CVA60 [*Saratoga*].[54]

At one point the Bureau of the Budget suggested that a navy yard might build the SSN 575 more cheaply. Rear Admiral Evander Sylvester, assistant bureau chief for ships, put a quick end to that suggestion by arguing that the Groton submarine-builder had the best-trained personnel and the most

---

[51] SUPSHIPS/INSORD, Groton, to BUSHIPS, 28 Dec 1953, box 77, BUSHIPS Confidential CENCORR 1953.

[52] BUSHIPS Memo, SSN 575 Conference on the Progress of the Construction of, 22 Dec 1953, box 77, BUSHIPS Confidential CENCORR 1953.

[53] BUSHIPS Memo for File, SSN 575 Scheduling Conference, 21 Jan 1953, box 77, BUSHIPS Confidential CENCORR 1953.

[54] Ibid., Route Slip for.

National Archives, RG 19

Subjected to numerous building delays caused by the sodium coolant in the reactor, *Seawolf* (SSN 575) was finally launched at Electric Boat in 1955.

experience in the field. He knew that the additional expense of expansion, the struggle to stay on schedule, and the anxiety over the amount of time it took to complete the vessels were the consequences of applying new discoveries in science and technology to submarine design and construction.[55]

During 1954 design problems continued to prevent EB from keeping up with scheduled construction on SSN 575. Some of the delays resulted from difficulty with sonar technology and the same type of hull vibration that plagued *Nautilus*. But the sodium cooling-system and dump-tank design changes posed the most continuous dilemma. In March the latter problem actually prompted the bureau to lengthen the ship by eight feet to permit easier and quicker access to the reactor compartment for repair. In October the supervisor of shipbuilding at Groton, Captain Moore, anticipated a further delay of two to three months beyond the scheduled delivery date of 1 March 1956 because of late and frequently complex design changes.[56]

---

[55] BUSHIPS Code 400 to Code 101, 22 Apr 1953, box 77, BUSHIPS Confidential CENCORR 1953.

[56] BUSHIPS to CNO, *Seawolf* (SSN 575) Delay in Completion of Construction, 19 Oct 1954; BUSHIPS to CNO, 31 Mar 1954, box 112, BUSHIPS Confidential CENCORR 1954; Commanding Officer and Director of the U.S. Naval Shipbuilding Activity to BUSHIPS and SUPSHIPS/NAVINSORD, Groton, 6 Sep 1955, box 90; SUPSHIPS/NAVINSORD to BUSHIPS, 16 Dec 1955, box 92, BUSHIPS Confidential CENCORR 1955.

Rickover and his staff, now known collectively as BUSHIPS Code 1500, gradually came to realize that *Seawolf*'s reactor displayed disturbing characteristics that might outweigh the advantages of using liquid sodium as a coolant and heat-transfer medium. Sodium's terribly corrosive effect damaged steam generators and superheater piping and required extraordinary measures to ensure safe operation of the reactor.[57] In September 1956 leaks in the superheaters and the starboard steam generator during propulsion plant trials prevented the ship from going to sea until EB made difficult repairs.

Barely two months later Admiral Rickover decided to discontinue the liquid sodium plant as an alternative to the STR for ship propulsion. Difficult experiences with *Seawolf* finally outweighed the attractive attributes that initially led the bureau to explore this method of harnessing nuclear power. A Code 1500 study authorized by Rickover in 1956 determined that

> in addition to the leakage of the heat transfer units, and associated problems, it now becomes evident that the inherent characteristics of sodium reactors make the SEAWOLF propulsion plant expensive to build, complex to operate, susceptible to prolonged shutdown as a result of even minor malfunctions, and difficult and time consuming to repair. . . . These facts clearly demonstrate that sodium is less desirable for naval reactors than pressurized water.[58]

Although Rickover assumed complete responsibility for the unfavorable outcome of the SIR project, two factors reduced the impact of his decision. The unequivocal success of the pressurized water reactor in *Nautilus* diminished the need to explore the sodium-cooled type further. Rickover no longer felt compelled to accept the limitations imposed by the hazards of liquid metal. Second, the problems plaguing the *Seawolf* power plant had effectively reduced the ship's maximum submerged speed to an unacceptably low 20 knots.[59]

Although designed as warships fully capable of working with the fleet, *Nautilus* and *Seawolf* served as test beds for the Navy's pioneering efforts in nuclear ship propulsion. If the SIR failed from an operational standpoint, its development proved vital for a wide variety of other reasons. During the course of the SIR project, the naval-industrial complex generated an entire library on the properties of metals and materials suitable for liquid-metal reactors, considerably advancing knowledge in the

[57] Code 390 was changed to Code 590 in Jul 1954 and then to Code 1500 in Jul 1955.
[58] Rickover to Chief BUSHIPS, 2 Nov 1956, box 91, BUSHIPS Confidential CENCORR 1956.
[59] Ibid.

field. Radioactive sodium's toxic properties also gave those working on the project a heightened appreciation for ship and crew safety that went beyond measures taken in relation to the STR. The use of the hydrogenous layer bulkheads is but one example.

Rickover's decision to halt further development of the *Seawolf* reactor also speaks volumes about his principles and tactics. The sodium cooling system, like other technologies, dictated its own discipline to those who would tame it for propulsion purposes. If the hazards of this system outweighed the benefits, the naval-industrial complex had to appreciate its own limits and the demands of the technology. In the end sodium presented risks against which the naval-industrial complex could provide no defense. Besides, with the success of the *Nautilus* power plant, the political climate was right for making such critical decisions. The pressurized water reactor would provide the political cover for the Navy's withdrawal from SIR research.

Rickover took complete responsibility for the cancellation of the program. It was the kind of accountability he sought in his relationships within the Navy and with private industry. He had successfully reorganized Bettis to achieve this end and strove for the same kind of singular responsibility at Knolls against a strong and independent GE.

Observations

Building *Nautilus* and *Seawolf,* as well as the *Skate* class that followed them, wrought fundamental changes in the naval-industrial complex and the way the Navy and private industry built American submarines. The pipe incident of 16 September 1954 demonstrated that the same vigilance governing the design of the vessel and the development of the new power plant had to apply to the most mundane aspects of the project. The naval-industrial complex risked a nuclear disaster of unequalled proportions. Both EB and the Navy made this discovery the hard way.

They also realized the necessity of promoting better internal communication between the shop floor and company management. The Snyder Board Report took special note of those times when workers discovered a section of inadequate pipe that had found its way into the submarine. But these experiences did not result in early and effective remedial measures. Both management and the shop supervisory force had their own proposals for improved handling of construction materials, but poor communication turned these ideas into lost opportunities.

The ability of the naval-industrial complex to compensate quickly for the loss of time and wasted effort demonstrated its flexibility and the importance of its three components to the submarine design and construction effort. The Navy and Electric Boat Division actually replaced the substandard material installed in SSN 571 and other facilities, but the scientific community played a valuable consulting role and addressed anew the problem of nondestructive testing and the ultrasound technique.

The vital role played by science became even more evident with the hull-vibration problems haunting *Nautilus*. The nature of these difficulties made them the peculiar property of the scientific community. Without the hydrodynamic expertise at the David Taylor Model Basin, Admiral Watkins might have prevailed over BUSHIPS and Rear Admiral Mumma in demanding a redesigned bow section for the SSN 571. Hydrodynamic testing indicated that such drastic measures were not required. The peculiar nature of self-noise and radiated noise also led to a surge of scientific interest in very low frequency sound transmission through seawater, pioneered during the 1940s by such physicists as Maurice Ewing and J. Lamar Worzel. The ease with which *Nautilus* was detected turned the sources of its radiated sounds and how to dampen them into a major national and scientific priority.

Nuclear power also demonstrated the limits of American science and engineering. Although the properties of liquid sodium made it appealing for use in nuclear reactors, the intense, sustained radiation and corrosive attributes of the metal made its use in submarines unwise. Research and development programs like SIR often perform a valuable service when they demonstrate what is possible as well as what is not.

All through this period the influence of Admiral Rickover represented in the extreme the exercise of the Navy's dominance in the naval-industrial complex since its birth during World War II. The admiral took the Navy beyond science, engineering, and design. In the postwar era he demonstrated the power of the Navy to go beyond merely drafting shipyards like Manitowoc into the submarine business. In 1940, BUSHIPS had insisted that EB supply Manitowoc with designs, training, supervision, and complete cooperation. In the early years of the nuclear program Rickover went one step further, forcing companies to restructure and exerting considerable influence on corporate policy by virtue of the profits promised by the submarine program. This policy, and the manner in which it was implemented, initiated major, and not always welcome, adjustments in the relationship between the Navy, industry, and the scientific community.

A submarine model is attached to the towing carriage for a test run down the
David Taylor Model Basin, November 1959.

Chapter 9

Nobska and the Nuclear Debate, 1956–1961

S ome contemporary historians suggest that by 1953 the U.S. Navy began to discard its strategy of forward projection of forces adopted during the first postwar decade. Admiral Forrest Sherman helped fashion this early approach to the Soviet threat during his tenure as Chief of Naval Operations from November 1949 to July 1951. It called for American naval retaliation against the Soviet heartland from European and Asian coastal waters. Later in the decade, forward projection of forces appeared inadequate or, perhaps, an unwise provocation. The people molding American strategy began to demonstrate a preference for the defensive, engendered by technological advances like the sound surveillance system and the growing Soviet nuclear threat. As the latter made forward projection a terrible risk, the American offensive perspective slowly gave way to defense by massive retaliation.[1]

These influences helped shift the emphasis of American undersea warfare to antisubmarine warfare. Armed with a deterrent mission, submarines constituted the Navy's first line of defense against the growing Soviet fleet. In response, the naval-industrial complex had to sustain a high order of technical and design creativity at the beginning of the second postwar decade.

The naval-industrial complex answered the Navy's needs in two stages. In the first stage developments extending back to both the beginning of the nuclear propulsion program and the experiments with *Albacore* culminated in the creation of *Skipjack*. With this submarine the naval-industrial complex produced the fastest and most maneuverable underwater craft in history.

The second stage began in 1956 even before EB workmen finished assembling *Skipjack* on the ways in Groton. Admiral Arleigh Burke, who had assumed the position of CNO the previous summer, asked the Committee on Undersea Warfare of the National Academy of Sciences to study the effect of advanced technology on undersea warfare. The result

---

[1] For the best statement on the development of American strategy in the first postwar decade, see Palmer, *Origins of the Maritime Strategy*.

was Project Nobska. WHOI hosted this summer-long intensive study of submarine warfare and ASW patterned after Project Hartwell at Massachusetts Institute of Technology six years before. By summer's end the Nobska scientists and engineers had focused the attention of the naval-industrial complex on the need for deeper-diving, ultraquiet submarines armed with long-range sonar. In the process they helped the Navy and private industry lay the foundation for *Tullibee* and *Thresher*, two vessels that made quiet operation and underwater acoustics the forté of the American submarine force and provided the Navy with a leading edge in undersea warfare for the next two decades.

The Road to *Skipjack*

To a certain extent the Navy Department had already determined the nature of its response to the Soviet challenge and ASW. The *Skate* class of smaller nuclear submarines emphasized ASW and arctic operations. It is not surprising that EB built the lead ship of the class, and Code 1500 designed and supervised the installation of a new reactor. The company laid the keel plate for *Skate* on 21 July 1955, just moments after the yard launched *Seawolf.* To ease EB's heavy burden of new and ongoing projects, Rear Admiral Albert Mumma, Chief of BUSHIPS, assigned two of the *Skate*-class submarines, *Swordfish* (SSN 579) and *Seadragon* (SSN 584), to Portsmouth. He became concerned that EB could not simultaneously build two vessels of the *Skate*-class, design and build *Skipjack*, and work with Knolls on yet another reactor type for a radar picket submarine.

BUSHIPS's assistant chief for nuclear propulsion worried about the safety of allowing Portsmouth to build nuclear submarines. It would take study, training, and months of hard work to bring Portsmouth to a state of expertise comparable to EB's. Although he did not foil Mumma on the construction assignments, Rear Admiral Hyman Rickover successfully fought the admiral's inclination to shift the design responsibilities for the entire *Skate* class to Portsmouth.[2] Code 1500 saw the decision delaying the completion of the class and placing additional burdens upon naval reactors and Bettis Laboratory, who would have to prepare Portsmouth as a lead yard in the same way they had EB.

This debate ran deeper than just a series of contested decisions. Mumma and Rickover frequently clashed over the extent and independence of the latter's authority. The BUSHIPS chief resisted the growing

---

[2] *Swordfish*, a *Skate*-class vessel designed by Portsmouth, was the only nuclear submarine of that class built by Portsmouth.

influence of Code 1500 and restricted the scope of Rickover's sway whenever possible. Mumma first took this approach when he limited Rickover's influence on the Polaris submarine program, which began in 1955.[3] As historians Richard Hewlett and Francis Duncan observed,

> Mumma might well have seen assigning the *Swordfish* design to Portsmouth as a way of breaking the hold of Electric Boat on this activity. His action could also have been a part of an effort to bring nuclear propulsion back into the bureau's fold. Implicit in Rickover's opposition was his determination that he would be the one who would decide when a yard was ready to build a nuclear ship.[4]

Through the end of Mumma's tenure as Chief of BUSHIPS in 1959, he and Rickover remained contentious over where the ultimate authority for building nuclear ships lay.

In one of their rare agreements Mumma's own judgment coincided with Rickover's advice, and the bureau brought Ingalls Shipbuilding Company of Pascagoula, Mississippi, and Newport News Shipbuilding and Drydock Company into the submarine business. In September 1954 William E. Blewett, president of Newport News, offered to begin building submarines in Virginia after training his people in nuclear construction at no cost to the government. Eight months later, Monro B. Lanier, president of Ingalls, made the same offer.

Under Mumma's leadership both yards began building nuclear submarines with the *Skipjack* class. Ingalls built *Sculpin* (SSN 590) and *Snook* (SSN 592); Newport News signed a contract for *Shark* (SSN 591) on 5 February 1957. One year later Mumma estimated to a House standing committee on shipbuilding and conversion that, in an emergency, EB, Portsmouth, Mare Island, Newport News, and Ingalls could produce forty-eight attack and missile submarines per year at the rate of four per month after a 27-month work-up period.[5]

Skipjack and her sister ships brought to fruition scientific and technical ideas made possible by cooperation within the naval-industrial complex earlier in the decade. The SSN 585 represented the consummation of a marriage between nuclear power and the *Albacore* hull. At 3,075 tons *Skipjack* displaced approximately 500 tons more than *Skate*. The SSN 585's

---

[3] Mumma interview, 7 Mar 1988, NHC Oral Histories, OA.

[4] Hewlett and Duncan, *Nuclear Navy*, 300–301.

[5] Ibid., 305–7; William L. Tazewell, *Newport News Shipbuilding: The First Century* (Newport News, VA: Newport News Shipbuilding and Dry Dock Company, 1986), 210; Mumma interview by Paul Stilwell, USNI Oral History Collection; BUSHIPS to Chairman of the House Standing Committee on Shipbuilding and Conversion, 27 Feb 1958, box 58, BUSHIPS Confidential CENCORR 1958, RG 19, NA/WNRC.

A topside view of *Skate* (SSN 578), the first in a line of smaller nuclear submarines designed for ASW missions and the arctic environment, 1957.

Skate sponsors' party *(left to right)*: Retired Vice Admiral Charles B. Momsen, Captain A. Chester Smith, Frank Pace, Jr., Mrs. Pace, and Lewis L. Strauss in Groton, 16 May 1957.

hull configuration made her shorter than *Skate*, but her beam, at 31 feet 6 inches, was nearly seven feet greater. After easily exceeding all expectations for submerged speed during sea trials in March 1959, *Skipjack*'s commanding officer, Commander William W. Behrens Jr., commented that if someone would give the vessel a simonize job, he would buy her! [6]

The origin of the *Skipjack* design demonstrated the sensitivity of the Navy, industry, and science to the evolution of submarine design and the most profitable course for the future. Original concept designs that formed the basis for the preliminary plans composed by BUSHIPS emerged simultaneously from both the bureau and EB. In late spring 1955 the BUSHIPS preliminary design branch, under the command of Captain John H. McQuilkin, began to explore ways of increasing submerged speed and maneuverability.

In *Skate* the bureau designed a twin screw nuclear submarine exhibiting most of the Guppy characteristics, but with a few important innovations. The vessel demonstrated better underwater handling and slightly higher speed in a shorter hull and only modestly increased displacement.

In their investigation of future design possibilities, Captain McQuilkin and his assistant, Commander Edward S. Arentzen, reviewed four alternatives for future submarine designs. The first would change *Nautilus* to

---

[6] Duncan, *Rickover and the Nuclear Navy*, 17–18.

single screw propulsion. Another suggested modifying the SSN 571 hull to a body of revolution with a single screw. Two other options were based on *Skate.* The first option suggested altering this submarine to a single screw configuration and increasing the power of the nuclear plant. The second option used a similar approach, but kept the twin screws of the original *Skate* design.

Both the Navy and private industry explored the potential of these alternatives. Engineers at EB preferred to examine the last two options, BUSHIPS considered all four. Most bureau engineers and architects preferred to keep the shorter length of *Skate* but not its hull configuration. BUSHIPS first successfully adapted the series 58 hull shape for a warship in the *Barbel* (SS 580) design. The promise of *Barbel* and the performance of *Albacore* made the new hull design the way of the future. Like *Nautilus, Barbel* had three internal levels and a diameter measuring 22 feet 8 inches to ensure sufficient volume and buoyancy.

After making preliminary weight and volume calculations for the SSN 585, McQuilkin and Arentzen decided upon an *Albacore*-like hull with four levels and a diameter of at least thirty feet. Arentzen calculated that 31 feet 6 inches would permit the most efficient use of the available internal volume while guaranteeing general stability. On 3 August 1955, using the results of the Navy's series 58 hull experiments, Arentzen sketched a concept design for *Skipjack* based roughly upon David Taylor Model Basin's submarine model number 4176.[7]

EB did not mark time while McQuilkin's preliminary design branch composed its initial sketches of *Skipjack.* EB nuclear engineer John Leonard recalled that none of the alternative designs considered by the company in 1955 seemed to offer anything new.

> We were working with the advanced submarine fleet reactor program, and we looked at five or six or seven designs and they were all twin screw and none of them seemed to be an improvement. And we just said, well, we knew about the work on the *Albacore . . .* and said well maybe somebody wants to go fast!

In August 1955, Leonard began working with two of his EB colleagues on a new option. Together with marine engineer Russell Brown and naval architect, Harlan Turner, Leonard composed a concept design for a single screw submarine with a series 58 hull that might well exceed all expectations for underwater speed. Leonard said:

---

[7] CAPT Edward S. Arentzen, Request for designation as EDO, qualified in submarines, 5 Jul 1958, box 60, BUSHIPS Confidential CENCORR 1958, RG 19, NA/WNRC.

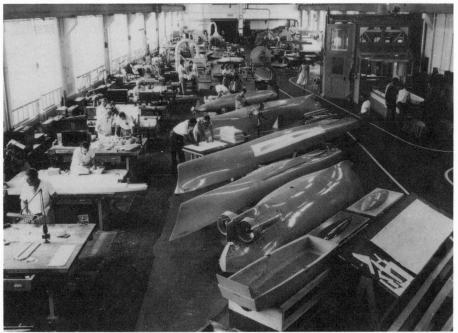

A *Skipjack* model is last in a line of hull models in the woodworking shop, David Taylor Model Basin, September 1957.

With our own money, we sat down and designed a ship which was the forerunner of the 585 and we sold it to Rickover's project officer. On August 5, 1955, we sat down and had a go around with Rickover. We presented all of the plans. We had a complete ship design, with all of the machinery designed and fitted in . . . and that's the only time Rickover came in and said you people have done a tremendous job for the United States Navy.[8]

All of the *Skipjack* advantages, including an internal volume greater than *Nautilus* and remarkable submerged speed, depended on the bureau's approval of HY–80 steel for pressure hulls. *Skipjack*'s diameter made using the new material necessary. High tensile steel (HTS), the accepted material for pressure hulls, proved unsuitable for the new configuration and size of the SSN 585. Experience had demonstrated that the desirable physical properties of HTS rapidly degraded in thicknesses greater than two inches. For deep-diving submarines of a restricted displacement, therefore, the maximum possible HTS hull diameter was approximately 28 feet. Only HY–80 could provide the size required for *Skipjack*.

---

[8] J. S. Leonard interview, 25 Sep 1989, NHC Oral Histories, OA.

Blueshark (SS 587), a *Skipjack*-class submarine built at Ingalls Shipbuilding Corporation, Pascagoula, Mississippi, October 1959.

Rear Admiral Armand Morgan, assistant chief of BUSHIPS for ship design and research, initiated an evaluation of HY–80 in late August 1955. From the beginning Morgan admitted that this steel would significantly increase the cost of building submarines, but he valued HY–80's more uniform physical properties. Although the bureau certainly needed to develop more effective manual and automatic welding techniques sensitive to the steel's characteristics, Morgan expected that these techniques would evolve as the naval-industrial complex became more familiar with the metal. Thus he approved HY–80 for fabricating pressure hulls in early September 1955.[9]

HY–80 proved more difficult to work with than first expected. It presented persistent cracking problems for *Skipjack* throughout this period. Fissures opened up in piping systems and along some welded seams in July 1959. For the most part, these flaws occurred because of hydrostatic

[9] Arentzen, Request for designation as EDO, 5 Jul 1958. Weldability proved far more difficult than first imagined. In addition, the chemistry of HY–80 changed slightly according to thickness, which further complicated the welding process. Captain E. S. Arentzen and Philip Mandel, "Naval Architectural Aspects of Submarine Design," *SNAME Transactions* 68 (1960): 656–57.

Hull sections of *Shark* (SSN 591), a *Skipjack*-class submarine, under construction in the fabrication shop of Newport News Shipbuilding and Dry Dock Company, August 1958.

pressure, explosion, and cyclic fatigue. HY–80 can withstand hydrostatic pressure in a range from 55,000 pounds per square inch to 80,000 per square inch. The latter represents the limits of the material's endurance, exhausting the design safety factor of approximately 1.5. The shock of explosions occasionally generated cracks at the intersection of frames and the submarine's outer shell. Liquid or air trapped in tanks and lines also generated pressure that might cause a fracture.

In other cases work-hardening due to repeated dives also presented a reason for concern. The bureau certified that a hull fabricated from HY–80 could endure only 10,000 individual dives or cycles from less than 200 to more than 500 feet before the likelihood of failure due to steel fatigue became critical. As the speed of American submarines increased, so did the need to dive deeper and more frequently. High-speed maneuvering required a larger slice of the ocean to allow the submarine a safe margin for recovery from high-speed dives and turns. More than ever before, material fatigue placed definite limits on a submarine's service life.[10]

---

[10] Memo on *Skipjack*; HY–80, prepared by SUPSHIPS, Groton, 1 Jul 1959, box 61; Memo for File, BUSHIPS Code 440, box 59, BUSHIPS Confidential CENCORR 1959; COMSUBLANT to CNO via CINCLANT, 25 Jan 1960, box 39, BUSHIPS Confidential CENCORR 1960, RG 19, NA/WNRC.

Shark's hull section is being tilted into place at Newport News, summer 1958.

As the submarine moved faster, self-noise also posed a greater problem for both sonar operation and the general effort to make American
submarines quieter. *Skipjack* carried the active AN/SQS–4 and passive
AN/BQR–2 sonars. To derive maximum speed and keep hydrodynamic
flow noises to a minimum, the bureau designed the ship to hold its
sonar internally rather than in arms or domes protruding from the hull.
Commander Arentzen designed the torpedo tubes in a unique manner.
Instead of three tubes each to the right and left of the submarine's centerline, the new design moved a set of three tubes above and below the
centerline to permit more room for the sonar. In addition, the bureau
took the suggestion of EB architect Harlan Turner and moved the bow
planes to a permanently extended position on the sail. In this location

Starboard view of *Shark*, Newport News, summer 1958.

they would provide excellent lift at a lower speed but not fill the bow hydrophones with additional machinery and flow noises.[11]

After a presentation by Arentzen on 6 September 1955, the Ships Characteristics Board chose the general scheme for the SSN 585 suggested by the bureau's preliminary design branch. The vessel best suited to fill the Navy's needs had a series 58 shape, a new high-power pressurized-water nuclear propulsion plant, a single screw, and a 31.5-foot hull diameter. With the SSN 585 the Navy took its first step into a future dominated by this type of submarine. According to a memo prepared by Captain McQuilkin in March 1956, "SSN585 SCB Project 154 is now designated as the mobilization prototype nuclear powered attack submarine." His preliminary design branch announced in early April the bureau's intention to build *Skipjack* with HY–80 tee-frames and hull plating.

Although BUSHIPS did not expect to complete the contract plans until mid-June 1956, EB laid the keel of the SSN 585 on 29 May and launched

---

[11] Arentzen, Request for Designation as EDO, 5 Jul 1958; J. S. Leonard interview, 25 Sep 1989.

the vessel almost exactly two years later.[12] EB officially turned *Skipjack* over to the Navy for trials on 22 September 1958.[13] When the submarine went through preliminary trials between 6 and 14 April 1959, the Board of Inspection and Survey noted that only extensive operational experience would reveal the suitability of HY–80 and the welding techniques used as well as the noise radiation levels, which seemed to exceed the acceptable for certain components.[14] Indeed *Skipjack*'s many new attributes made her an important developmental platform for the submarine force.

Monitoring *Albacore*'s other swift and deep-diving progeny occasionally produced important results applicable to *Skipjack*. The stress of operation revealed flaws in the detail design and workmanship of *Barbel*'s hydraulic system causing two failures of the stern plane system. Other casualties included a lost antenna, failure of a high-pressure air line, and water leaks into storage battery areas. The problems came in such rapid succession before they were solved that Rear Admiral Frederick B. Warder, Commander Submarine Force, Atlantic Fleet, commented: "Although overall performance of BARBEL as a high speed diesel electric submarine has been outstanding, the number of casualties to vital systems is of grave concern to COMSUBLANT and forces the conclusion that currently BARBEL's operational readiness and reliability are marginal, at best."[15]

In *Skipjack*'s final acceptance trials, the Board of Inspection and Survey did not discover difficulties similar to those plaguing *Barbel*. The SSN 585's hydraulic system performed well. But the same could not be said of the periscopes and the schnorchel. The latter occasionally jammed; number two periscope flooded, while number one suffered from misalignment. The HY–80 cracking discovered in July did not reoccur, but regular inspection remained the rule in an effort to accumulate as much knowledge about the material as possible.[16]

If *Skipjack* represented the future of American submarine, so did her propulsion plant. As BUSHIPS Code 1500 and the Westinghouse Bettis Laboratory designed the reactor during 1956 and 1957, it soon became apparent that the task of multiple production would present almost as

---

[12] BUSHIPS to Commanding Officer, Norfolk Naval Shipyard, 10 Apr 1956; BUSHIPS to Commanding Officer, Naval Ordnance Laboratory, 22 Mar 1956, box 89, BUSHIPS Confidential CENCORR 1956, RG 19, NA/WNRC. Launching and Technical Information on the *Skipjack*, 1958–present, SSN–585 Binder, Individual Submarine Historical Files, Submarine Force Library and Museum, Groton, CT.

[13] SUPSHIPS, Groton, to CNO, 22 Sep 1958, box 60, BUSHIPS Confidential CENCORR 1958.

[14] Board of Inspection and Survey, Preliminary Acceptance Trials of the *Skipjack*, 6–14 Apr 1959, box 61, BUSHIPS Confidential CENCORR 1959.

[15] BUSHIPS to COMSUBLANT, 2 Dec 1959; COMSUBLANT to BUSHIPS, 22 Oct 1959; BUSHIPS to CNO, 13 Nov 1959, box 58, BUSHIPS Confidential CENCORR 1959.

[16] Board of Inspection and Survey, Final Acceptance Trials of the *Skipjack*, 21–23 Mar 1960, box 39, BUSHIPS Confidential CENCORR 1960.

many obstacles as the process of development. By the time the *Skipjack* class took shape on the drafting boards of BUSHIPS and EB, the Polaris program presented its requirements for a fleet ballistic missile submarine. BUSHIPS and Rear Admiral William F. Raborn's Special Projects Office intended to adapt the last vessel of the SSN 585 class as the first ballistic missile submarine, *George Washington* (SSBN 598). With this decision the *Skipjack* reactor suddenly became the workhorse of every attack and missile submarine, projected or under construction.

Convinced that the Navy procurement bureaucracy could not handle the job, Rickover quickly took measures to assist Bettis in procurement and production. As seen from the perspective of AEC historians Hewlett and Duncan,

> Rickover had no intention of letting these tasks fall to the Navy. He was convinced he could not meet his commitments if he had to move at the ponderous pace which resulted from following regular procedures. He was equally convinced that the Navy's methods of contract administration would never produce equipment of the quality required for a nuclear propulsion plant.[17]

Consequently, the admiral approached Westinghouse. Together with Charles Weaver of Bettis, Rickover set up a new procurement division within the Westinghouse organization in 1956 to cope with the production of their new propulsion plants. The new division, called the Plant Apparatus Department (PAD), would assume responsibility for procuring all plant components once Bettis perfected the first of each type. In this way Rickover kept the process under his control and moving at the pace he set, independent of AEC or any opposition within the Navy. PAD, under the direction of lawyer and Rickover political ally William L. Borden, built up an impressive organization for procuring components and recruiting experienced engineers. Code 1500 did not want to diminish the engineering expertise of Bettis in staffing PAD, so new engineering talent ensured the presence of vital technical competence at both the laboratory and the new division. Furthermore, subcontractors often needed instruction in the standards of quality demanded by nuclear technology. This too was PAD's function. By the end of 1958, PAD managed millions of dollars worth of Navy contracts with 400 vendors. The following year, Rickover induced General Electric to create a similar nuclear procurement division, with an equally cryptic name. Dubbed the machinery apparatus operation, the GE nuclear procurement division became known as MAO.[18]

---

[17] Hewlett and Duncan, *Nuclear Navy*, 283.
[18] Ibid., 284–87.

The only responsibility for nuclear acquisition not vested in PAD was reactor-core procurement. Here the technology required particular care in contractor selection, and Code 1500 worked with only the most experienced companies available. Firms involved in fabricating the cores for *Nautilus* and *Seawolf,* as well as the reactor cores for the *Skate* class, formed the basis of Rickover's industrial support for these components. The companies included the atomic fuel departments of Westinghouse, Combustion Engineering, Inc., and the Lynchburg, Virginia, plant of Babcock & Wilcox Company. When production accelerated on the *Skipjack* reactor, Rickover added Metals and Controls Corporation as well as the Olin-Mathieson Chemical Corporation to his list of core fabricators. The former had worked on fuel elements for both the experiments at Bettis and the GE sodium-cooled propulsion plant installed in *Seawolf.* Olin-Mathieson also supported Bettis and had experience with the submarine advanced reactor. In conjunction with Bettis these five contractors produced 110 cores for *Skipjack* reactors between 1955 and 1966.[19]

Project Nobska

During the first Eisenhower administration the strategic emphasis for the submarine community shifted away from offense and forward projection of forces to defense and ASW. The challenges facing the naval-industrial complex changed accordingly. On 18 October 1955 Admiral Arleigh Burke, who has assumed the position of CNO two months earlier, wrote to the Chief of Naval Research, Rear Admiral Frederick R. Furth, requesting through ONR that the NAS's Committee on Undersea Warfare undertake an antisubmarine warfare weapons study. His concern rose from the advent of nuclear submarines. *Nautilus* was at sea and *Seawolf* would soon follow, along with the entire *Skate* class. The Navy also looked forward to the unmatched speed and maneuverability expected from the *Skipjack* design, then less than seven months away from construction at Electric Boat. These vessels had no equal. But Admiral Burke realized that the Navy could not expect to sustain its technological edge over the Soviets without aggressive planning for the future. He needed an appraisal of the effect an enemy nuclear submarine fleet might have on American security plus advice on the type of research and development that would help preserve the American technical advantage.

CUW proposed a summer study following the pattern established by Project Hartwell. Columbus Iselin, director of the Woods Hole Oceano-

[19] Ibid., 293–95.

graphic Institution and a member of the committee, accepted responsibility as project director, and the committee scheduled the study to take place at Woods Hole in the summer of 1956. Of the sixty participants, one-third came from the officers and civilian personnel assigned to naval staffs and laboratories. Industry and academe supplied the balance of the group. Their study, entitled "The Implications of Advanced Design on Undersea Warfare," became known as Project Nobska, named for the old Nobsque, or Nobska, lighthouse that marked the Massachusetts coast at Woods Hole.[20]

NH 95852–KN

Oil portrait of Admiral Arleigh Burke by Cedric Egeli, 1968.

The Nobska Project covered the entire range of subjects critical to the success of American ASW and undersea warfare. Under Iselin's guidance scientists formed groups to study detection, classification and countermeasures, navigation, communication, weapons, propulsion, ships for undersea warfare, strategic use of the undersea, containment of submarines and defense of the continental United States, protection of ships at sea, and the role of overseas transport vehicles. Each of these areas had a group assigned to it consisting of at least ten policymakers, scientists, and engineers.

Before the groups began their studies, Iselin established a set of formidable assumptions regarding enemy capabilities. Nobska participants had to assume that the Soviets possessed ten to twenty submarines "combining the best features of ALBACORE and NAUTILUS." Each would merge quiet operation with extraordinary submerged speed. Missile submarines with surface launch capabilities and a range of 150 miles also formed part of this projected enemy fleet, which had adequate submarine bases in both the Atlantic and Pacific. Iselin set the passive sonar detection range of both sides at 50 miles and gave the Soviets an effective

---

[20] Project Nobska: The Implications of Advanced Design on Undersea Warfare, Final Report, Volume 1: Assumptions, Conclusions, and Recommendations, 1 Dec 1956, box 17, Records of the Immediate Office of the Chief of Naval Operations, OA. This study is still classified secret. But the version of volume 1 used as a source in this chapter and currently in the possession of the author was sanitized by ONR in January 1991.

torpedo range of 30,000 yards against American surface ships more easily detectable than the submarines hunting them.[21]

The participants appointed to Nobska's committee on ships for undersea warfare included Martin A. Abkowitz of MIT as group leader, Manley St. Denis of DTMB, Philip Mandel from the BUSHIPS preliminary design division, Harlan Turner of MIT, Robert McCandliss and Lyndon Crawford from EB, and Allyn Vine of WHOI. Although there were thirteen other groups studying various aspects of undersea warfare, these seven men had an extraordinary influence on the types of submarines the naval-industrial complex would design and build.[22]

In their conclusions this group wholeheartedly suggested adopting, as a regular practice, the process that had created the high-speed conventional submarine *Barbel* and nuclear *Skipjack*. Both were under construction at Portsmouth and EB while the summer study progressed at Woods Hole. In designing these vessels, the naval-industrial complex combined the best features of a preprototype submarine and an experimental submarine, *Nautilus* and *Albacore*, respectively. As a preprototype, the SSN 571 actually worked as a unit of the fleet with one of its operational characteristics—nuclear propulsion—emphasized over characteristics not tied to the submarine's primary mission. In the experimental *Albacore* all aspects of the revolutionary design were tested without any effort to equip the vessel for battle. The experience gained in both cases permitted the Navy and EB to build two classes of highly effective submarines. Thus in their conclusions the ships for undersea warfare group argued that "the principle of building pre-prototype and experimental ships on a continuing basis must have acceptance in order to fully exploit militarily what a rapidly unfolding technology has to offer and permit ship design and construction to keep abreast of the advances in other elements of undersea warfare systems."[23]

This process gave those working within the naval-industrial complex a chance to adjust to the unconventional in submarine design and construction. The new aspects of *Albacore* and *Nautilus* proved themselves through this mechanism of preprototype and experimental construction and testing. Comparing the approach to that used in aircraft design, the Nobska group commented,

> No aircraft designer would dare to incorporate new and untried features in an aircraft which had to be acceptable for service immediately upon completion. However, the new features having been proven through the

---

[21] Iselin, "Project Nobska: A Preliminary Assessment," May 1956, NSBA/NAS.

[22] Harlan Turner would succeed Robert McCandliss as chief naval architect of the Electric Boat Division, General Dynamics. Project Nobska, vol. 1, 1 Dec 1956; "A Word about the National Academy of Sciences and the Origin of Project Nobska," 29 May 1956, NSBA/NSA.

[23] Project Nobska, vol. 1, 1 Dec 1956.

testing of rather speculative designs, can then be incorporated in operational craft. This philosophy is certainly not new to the Navy. Submarine design concepts which were considered extremely radical before the construction and testing of ALBACORE are now being incorporated in vessels designed for combat.[24]

Abkowitz and his colleagues chose to emphasize specific submarine attributes in their recommendations to the Navy for the future. Because ASW took priority in the Navy's strategic thinking, the group singled out silent operation, optimum sonar range, and increased depth as the most desirable characteristics. They insisted that the Navy should first build a preprototype in which quietness was made the primary consideration ahead of the size, equipment, and passive sonar capability of an advanced hunter-killer submarine.

The Nobska ships group then recommended a deep-diving submarine capable of sustained operations at the axis of the SOFAR, or deep sound channel, as the Navy's primary experimental project. Here a submarine might hide from weapons launched by surface vessels or actually sit on the bottom in many parts of the world. In addition, the extraordinary sound transmission and detection properties of the channel would increase the effectiveness of both active and passive sonar.

Although the group studying ships for undersea warfare hailed the value of nuclear propulsion, they viewed the size and expense of nuclear submarines as major liabilities. Going against the current design trends in the naval-industrial complex, Abkowitz's group suggested a reduction in reactor size and smaller special-purpose submarines over the ever-larger multipurpose types. Aircraft reactors, like the reflector-moderated Fireball, were "highly attractive power sources for relatively small ASW surface vessels and for submarines as small as 500 tons." So they suggested modifying some of the proposed aircraft reactors for submarines and using alternate structural materials and hull designs to increase operating depth without adding prohibitive amounts of weight. In addition, the naval-industrial complex had to make a determined effort to quiet nuclear propulsion systems.[25]

The Nobska propulsion group, led by Everitt P. Blizard of the Oak Ridge National Laboratory, made an even stronger argument for pursuing new avenues in nuclear propulsion. After all, the reality of the nuclear submarine had given birth to Project Nobska. This type of power

---

[24] Project Nobska: The Implications of Advanced Design on Undersea Warfare, Final Report, Volume 2: Technical and Systems Studies, 1 Mar 1957, 243, box 17, Records of the Immediate Office of the Chief of Naval Operations. The paragraph cited here is unclassified, but the remainder of the report is classified secret.

[25] Project Nobska, vol. 1, 1 Dec 1956.

had to assume a central place in their deliberations. Preserving and advancing the early American advantage in nuclear power certainly qualified as a national defense priority and demanded Nobska's attention. The propulsion group's scientists and engineers, including Gaylord Harnwell, Harlan Turner, and Harvey Brooks, Dean of Harvard's School of Engineering and Applied Physics, earnestly believed that Code 1500's pressurized water reactors had reached a plateau with the amount of additional weight now required to increase a nuclear submarine's shaft-horsepower. In quieter nuclear plants of reduced weight, they believed, the Navy would find the perfect ASW vessel. But gaining disciples for these ideas within the Navy was difficult, especially in face of the success and the determination of the Rickover group to keep reactor development within the latter's sphere of influence. In the opening remarks of the propulsion group's final report, members noted: "The improvements in performance of both submarines and surface ships that can be gained through a large reduction in the weight of the power plant seemed not to be generally recognized in the Navy." [26]

The propulsion group was not without suggestions for further developments in the field. For the short run they recommended looking into reducing shield weight, and thus the displacement of the entire submarine, by isolating the reactor in an external blister or in the lower section of a double hull configuration. The latter resembled the concept design for the first nuclear submarine suggested in 1946 by Philip Abelson of NRL.[27]

Nonnuclear options also offered interesting alternatives. Nobska's propulsion group suggested continuing experiments with closed-cycle, hydrogen-peroxide propulsion in small submarines like the X–1. The Fairchild Engine Division of Fairchild Engine and Aircraft Corporation built X–1 in 1955. Designed for harbor penetration in imitation of the British X-craft of World War II, an open-cycle oxygen diesel reciprocating engine served X–1 as main propulsion. The breakdown of concentrated hydrogen peroxide provided a submerged oxygen source. Aware of the dangers in handling high-test hydrogen peroxide, the Nobska propulsion group still considered the system feasible and, as such, an alternative worthy of exploration.[28]

At Nobska anticipating the future was far more important than evaluating the present or past. Although clearly impressed with the accomplishments of Code 1500 and *Nautilus,* the propulsion group called for research and development that reached beyond the pressurized water

[26] Ibid.

[27] Memo to Director (Schade), by Abelson, "Atomic Energy Submarines," 28 Mar 1946, Post 1 Jan 1946 Command File, OA.

[28] Richard Boyle, "X–1 Power Plant, 1956–57," *Naval Engineers Journal* 84 (Apr 1972): 42–50.

reactor. Few doubted that Rickover and his team would work to perfect and exploit current nuclear technology to overcome the rigors of performance at sea. Rickover would also insist that those involved in building and operating nuclear propulsion plants acquire the discipline necessary to measure up to the demands of the technology and safety. But what of the future? Which lines of research would provide the best opportunities to reduce propulsion plant weight and noise?

For the Nobska propulsion group the 1960s offered some concrete research options in both nuclear and alternative methods of propulsion for submarines. They felt the Navy should explore a variation on the reflector-moderated aircraft reactor studied by the Air Force. An airborne system would have to be light, and "considerable improvement in the reliability and lifetime of such reactors can be achieved by reducing operating temperatures and fluid flow rates well below those required for aircraft operation, while retaining temperatures as high as can be profitably used for ship propulsion." [29]

Although it would not provide the submerged speed of a *Skipjack*-type propulsion plant, a primary battery system characterized by the continuous feed of electrochemical reactants also offered some promise. This quiet mode of electrical propulsion could provide speeds similar to those attained by the Guppy conversions in the early postwar years. In addition, Nobska recommended investigating the combination of a nuclear reactor as a heat source with a continuous feed battery in a closed-cycle system. The two major components could provide virtually unlimited endurance and the quiet necessary for stealthy offensive operations and ASW.

Scientists and engineers at Nobska argued that limiting nuclear research to variations on present submarine technology would retard long-term development. Nuclear propulsion for ships had to advance in step with other marine technologies and engineering techniques. If the state of engineering, systems, or materials did not make a promising nuclear technology viable in 1956 or 1960, research planned for the long-term became even more important. Those at Project Nobska felt strongly that a broad spectrum of technical and scientific progress would provide a future context within which a particular technology might fulfill its potential for the Navy.

The Nobska Post Mortem and the Debate Over Nuclear Research

In August 1957, a few months after Project Nobska, twenty of the participants met to review their findings. The Naval War College in Newport,

---

[29] Project Nobska, vol. 1, 1 Dec 1956.

Nobska Conference participants at Woods Hole, Massachusetts, with WHOI Director and conference organizer Columbus Iselin *(top row, center, with dark jacket)* and Admiral Arleigh Burke *(second to the left of Iselin)*, summer 1956.

Rhode Island, hosted this follow-up meeting at which each technical group made its recommendations even more specific in certain categories.

Martin Abkowitz's group studying ships for undersea warfare once again emphasized the need for an ultraquiet submarine. Such a vessel would make an ideal passive sonar platform and permit full exploitation of new sonar technologies as they emerged from the research and development programs. Through preprototypes, scientists and engineers could explore combinations of new and old techniques to help achieve the lowest levels of radiated noise possible in a submarine. The committee applauded the advances in the strength and resiliency of hull steel. This achievement made greater test depths possible and complemented perfectly their request for more acoustically capable submarines. Greater depths would eventually give sonar operators an opportunity to use the propagation characteristics of the deep sound channel and developments in convergence-zone sonar against potential enemies.[30]

---

[30] Review of Project Nobska, 5–9 Aug 1957, Defense Technical Information Center (DTIC) Reports, OA. The document cited here was sanitized by ONR in March 1991. The original version and portions of the sanitized document remain classified secret.

On the heels of these great expectations the group on detection, classification, and countermeasures warned of an impending crisis. They had recommended not only further research into long-range passive sonar, but also pointed out the need to provide the submarine community with more effective active systems. In both cases the submarine community would need sufficient redundancy so that an adversary, having outwitted one system, might fall prey to another. Unfortunately Navy priorities now threatened to limit the availability of ships and aircraft for assisting the underwater sound laboratories in their work. For the Nobska participants, this posture demonstrated shortsightedness and a failure to appreciate the importance of long-term research: "To have satisfactory antisubmarine capabilities in the 1965–70 period, adequate supporting submarine, ship and aircraft service must be available to the laboratories working on research and development." Without sufficient cooperation from the operating forces, the work at these facilities could slow to the point where they would lose valuable staff members not easily replaceable. Even dramatically increased funds would not remedy such a tragedy.[31]

The propulsion group continued to exert pressure on BUSHIPS to seriously investigate nuclear and conventional alternatives to pressurized water plants for submarines. They urged long-term research into smaller, lighter, and more efficient reactors for naval propulsion. Frequently using the aircraft nuclear propulsion (ANP) project as a starting point, the group contended that monitoring the ANP and other promising reactor types did not fulfill the Navy's responsibility to itself or the nation. The success or failure of the ANP was not the point. Keeping abreast of the technology could not compare with a broad, determined effort to develop alternatives for the future. In the report issued at the end of the Newport meeting, the propulsion group concluded:

> We would therefore encourage a vigorous search for feasible new reactor propulsion systems which promise major improvements in size and space over present systems. It is essential that this search, particularly in the exploratory stage, include wide participation by those working in the nuclear engineering field. . . . If, subsequent to promising feasibility-practicability studies, the decision is made to develop a new propulsion system, undoubtedly calculated risks will be involved and will have to be accepted. However, new developments in nuclear propulsion are of such importance to both ships and submarines that studies must go forward without delay.[32]

In the years after Nobska a rift began to develop in the naval-industrial complex between Rickover and many scientists and engineers over

---

[31] Ibid.
[32] Ibid.

the issue of long-term research and the development of alternatives to the pressurized water reactor. Code 1500 had the authority and obligation to remind others within the naval-industrial complex that reactors, like the ANP and others, might not meet the standards necessary for ship propulsion. In the transition from aircraft to submarine, the system could well become heavier and more costly. Rickover was justified in demanding a safe, easily operated, and maintainable propulsion plant for American nuclear submarines. But, given the current technology, Rickover admitted that "to achieve long life trouble-free machinery operation at continuous high power level, [one] must employ heavy machinery. Naval reactor plants are going to become heavier rather than lighter in weight."[33] Since this situation flew in the face of the Nobska recommendations, many within the naval-industrial complex questioned whether this trend was necessary. Could not well-planned, long-term research projects in physics, metallurgy, chemistry, and the development of new engineering techniques provide other viable choices?

In presenting their suggestions in the early sixties, the various NAS committees working on naval vessels and things nuclear encountered obstacles to any open discussion on the direction of scientific and technical developments. The precise impediment appeared to be BUSHIPS Code 1500. Although applauding Rickover's many accomplishments, exacting standards, remarkable foresight, effective organization, and willingness to examine advanced nuclear power systems, James H. Probus, the CUW's executive secretary, still found one important element missing. The Naval Reactors Branch, while under tremendous pressure to meet short-term goals vital to the national security, was in no position to undertake essential development projects of a five- or ten-year duration to ensure the future of naval nuclear propulsion. Programs designed to realize a radically new kind of reactor could hardly be greeted with enthusiasm by Code 1500 unless the need were manifestly an urgent one.[34]

Indeed Nobska had called for research and development programs that would anticipate broad future scientific progress in many fields. While serving on Nobska's weapons effects and limitations group in 1956, Edward Teller of the Radiation Laboratory at the University of California, Berkeley, encouraged this kind of thinking and, in doing so, provided a key element in the success of the Polaris program.[35] Addressing submarine design from a new perspective in June 1961, the CUW panel on naval vehicles called for cooperation between the naval architect, the

[33] "Vice Admiral Rickover's Presentation of 24 March 1960 on Naval Reactors," 24 Mar 1960, #85–R–532, NSBA/NAS.
[34] James H. Probus, "A Survey of the Naval Reactors Program," 28 Apr 1961, NSBA/NAS.
[35] See chapter 12.

power and propulsion engineer, the electronics engineer, and those concerned with the human factor. Assuming progress in each area of expertise, the panel foresaw the possibility of a modest reduction in size and cost for a deeper-diving nuclear submarine.[36]

Nobska's naval vehicles panel called attention to those propulsion alternatives already available for evaluation. A submarine study, sponsored by ONR in 1958 and not immediately made available to the panel, discussed an intermediate to fast reactor with a new generation of fuel elements, as well as liquid-metal and pressurized water reactors supporting a closed-cycle gas or steam-turbine propulsion plant. General Dynamics Corporation's General Atomic Division explored a helium-cooled reactor, and from the aerospace industry came two other alternatives, General Electric's ANP and the Lockheed/Pratt and Whitney Empire Project. Furthermore, in November 1962 the panel actually proposed a five-phase, ten-year program for the development of new shipboard nuclear power plants.[37]

Rickover's people evaluated alternatives to pressurized water in the context of current technology and feasibility for the near future. Arguing that prices would rise along with size and risk, Code 1500 expressed a sincere concern for the effectiveness of the submarines and the safety of their crews.[38] But in exercising strong political and technical control over the Navy in nuclear matters, Rickover and his organization made some scientists and engineers wonder if the admiral paid for today's success by neglecting tomorrow. Important research went without funding to support immediate needs. Richard L. Mela, an engineer affiliated with Dynatech Corporation in Cambridge, Massachusetts, and a member of the panel on naval vehicles, found himself constantly frustrated by this aspect of working with Code 1500. In a letter to James Probus in June 1961, he vented some of his disappointment: "I think that over the years, as they [Code 1500] have come closer to grips with an increasing number of practical problems their scope of vision has narrowed, and now most of them are unable to translate what they have learned to new frames of reference."[39]

[36] CUW Report: Summary of Principle Observations and Conclusions of the Panel on Naval Vehicles, 1 Jun 1961, series 1: Nuclear Propulsion Background, 1957–64, box 1, Records of Assistant SECNAV (RE&S) James H. Probus, RC 24, Navy Laboratories Archives, DTRC (hereafter Probus Records).

[37] Summary Report of the Panel on Naval Vehicles, January 1962; C. Richard Soderberg, Chairman, Panel on Naval Vehicles, to Professor Harvey Brooks, Chairman, CUW, 28 May 1962; Nuclear Power Plants—Propulsion Task Group of the Panel on Naval Vehicles, Jun 1962, series 1: Nuclear Propulsion Background, 1957–64, box 1, Probus Records.

[38] "Naval Nuclear Propulsion Plant Development," Report on Conference Held by the CNO, ADM George W. Anderson, Jr., 3 Feb 1962, series 1: Nuclear Propulsion Background, 1957–64, box 1, Probus Records.

[39] Richard L. Mela to Probus, 29 Jun 1961, series 1: Nuclear Propulsion Background, 1957–64, box 15, Probus Records; Richard L. Mela to C. Soderberg, MIT, 4 Dec 1961, NSBA/NAS. Note especially the link Mela makes with these ideas on long-term research and the Nobska Project.

In the summer of 1962 Professor C. Richard Soderberg of MIT made similar comments in a note to Harvey Brooks. The Code 1500 perspective on safety, reliability, and suitability for naval propulsion did not admit any change in the methods of technology. He found the admiral's gospel of safety, responsibility, and technical conservatism in nuclear matters absolutely vital, but held that even a virtue can do damage if taken to an extreme. Throughout history innovators made significant progress "in spite of this comfortable doctrine of legislated reliability." Rickover's program itself was the best example.[40]

Harvey Brooks summed up the debate in November 1962 with a persistent call for continued research into promising nuclear and conventional alternatives to the reactors employed by the Navy. An essential consideration, besides Rickover's objections to the alternatives currently available, was the Navy's need to build new submarines within the next eight years in order to avoid block obsolescence. Although the lighter nuclear plants were still between ten and twelve years away, Brooks held that these new reactor designs should also play a major part in the Navy's research and development plans. BUSHIPS needed to project new programs well into the 1970s, rather than through the next five years. This task was certainly no more difficult than that facing the Rickover group in 1946. Brooks emphasized, however, that an authority other than Code 1500 should do the long-term planning and execution. Immediate problems and technical matters consumed Rickover's people, and a new organization could assume responsibility for anticipating the most profitable course for the next ten or fifteen years. Although he fully concurred with Rickover's concern for safety, reliability, and suitability for naval application, Brooks cautioned against taking technical conservatism too far:

> I would be inclined to agree with Rickover that the low-cost-per-ton argument for compact nuclear power is insufficient to justify the development. On the other hand, I likewise feel that in a period as far off as ten years, one cannot afford to be too specific as to precise operational requirements and not undertake a new development merely because it is difficult to blueprint its precise operational use. This must be regarded as an evolving program with several benchmarks of soul-searching review and re-evaluation.[41]

Clearly, Brooks spoke as one accustomed to the cooperation and professional intimacy characteristic of the naval-industrial complex since World War II. An effective soul-searching review and reevaluation re-

---

[40] Soderberg (MIT) to Brooks (Harvard School of Engineering and Applied Physics), 7 Jun 1962, series 1: Nuclear Propulsion Background, 1957–64, box 1, Probus Records.

[41] Brooks to Assistant SECNAV James H. Wakelin Jr., 29 Nov 1962, series 1: Nuclear Propulsion Background, 1957–64, box 1, Probus Records.

quired an easy interaction between the Navy, industry, and the scientific community. However, Code 1500's reaction to the Nobska recommendations and the debate over the Navy's commitment to long-term research into nuclear alternatives demonstrated that the foundation of cooperation upon which the naval industrial complex rested had begun to erode.

The Quiet Strategy

The first American submarines to embody the shift in American naval strategy and the recommendations of Project Nobska were *Tullibee* and *Thresher*. In designing both vessels the bureau emphasized quiet operation and ASW.

With *Tullibee* (SSN 597) in 1960, the Navy, EB, and the scientific community enhanced the effectiveness of the SSK. *Tullibee* introduced three major innovations in submarine warfare. At the point on the submarine furthest away from propulsion noise, *Tullibee* sported the first bow-mounted spherical sonar array. With the bow otherwise occupied, BU-SHIPS moved the torpedo tubes amidships, mounted at an outward angle. Both of these innovations found their way into the *Thresher* class and later attack submarines. At the other end of the vessel, a quiet turboelectric power plant built around a new reactor, developed by Code 1500 and Combustion Engineering, Inc., powered the vessel's relatively small 2460-ton submerged displacement. *Skipjack* had a greater displacement, beam, and draft, but *Tullibee* was longer. Since this propulsion system made the SSN 597 the most silent submarine in the fleet, BUSHIPS, with help from Code 1500, employed this type of propulsion once again in *Glenard P. Lipscomb* (SSN 685) in a bid to reduce drastically the noise generated by pressurized water nuclear propulsion plants.[42]

Early in 1958 BUSHIPS, under Admiral Mumma, assigned *Thresher* (SSN 593) to the Portsmouth Naval Shipyard. This vessel led a new class and exploited a variety of innovations in materials, sound detection, and quieting to make it a supremely effective ASW ship. Portsmouth had responsibility, not only for construction but also for the contract and detail designs.[43]

Thresher made three fundamental contributions to undersea warfare. The Portsmouth design significantly reduced radiated noise by further

---

[42] The same motive gave birth to *Narwhal* (SSN 671), laid down by Electric Boat Division in January 1966. With this vessel the Navy tried to combat noise generated by the coolant pumps with a natural circulation reactor (S5G). In this case, convection, rather than a noisy mechanical pumping system, would ensure the proper flow of the reactor coolant at slow speeds. Duncan, *Rickover and the Nuclear Navy*, 23–24.

[43] CAPT William Roseborough, USN (Ret.), 5 Oct 1988, interview with author, NHC Oral Histories, OA.

streamlining the hull, cutting the size of the sail by over half, and quieting the *Skipjack*-type propulsion plant. This method led to a 50 percent reduction in the noise generated by the vessel's propulsion plant. With this submarine the bureau also substantially increased the test depth. According to Commander William Roseborough, who then served as the material officer for Commander Submarine Force, Atlantic Fleet,

> the test depth had not been significantly increased since the days of the *Nautilus* and yet here we had made fantastic advances in both speed and maneuverability and the operational characteristics of the ship were considerably restricted by not having safe maneuverability in the third dimension, namely depth. So, in essence, that gave twice as much ocean to operate safely in.

Greater active sonar capability constituted the third contribution, supplemented by the 16-foot passive sonar sphere mounted in the submarine's bow.[44]

Other new systems and engineering advances made their debut in the SSN 593. The Navy explored the effectiveness of flexible pipe joints and, in fabricating the pressure hull and frames for deeper diving, demonstrated the advances made in working with HY–80. Without the advantages of this new steel, the Ships Characteristics Board asserted that Portsmouth would have to build a submarine 75 feet longer, 900 tons heavier, 4 knots slower, and much less resistant to shock. In addition, the new ship had the capability to deploy and retrieve towed array sonar. Once he detected a foe, the commander of this vessel could dispatch the adversary with torpedoes or the newly deployed SUBROC missile. After a torpedo tube launch this ballistic missile emerged from the sea to kill an enemy submarine operating 30 miles away.[45]

Approximately six months after Portsmouth laid *Thresher*'s keel in May 1958, Admiral Burke asked Rear Admiral Denys W. Knoll, chairman of the Ships Characteristics Board, to convene a meeting of those people within the naval-industrial complex most familiar with the *Thresher* program. Burke wanted the group to address questions of safety and suitability raised with regard to new materials and systems employed in the submarine's design and specifications. The Navy's next four Polaris and eight attack submarines depended upon the operational success of many of these innovations. Admiral Knoll recorded that "these items, in general, were associated with the use of low carbon high alloy steel [viz.

---

[44] Ibid.; Memo, RADM Denys W. Knoll, Ships Characteristics Board (SCB) to ADM Burke, 13 Jan 1959, Post 1 Jan 1946 Command File, OA.

[45] Duncan, *Rickover and the Nuclear Navy*, chaps. 2 and 3; Friedman, *Submarine Design and Development* (see applicable sections of chaps. 8, 9, and 10); Memo, Knoll (SCB) to Burke, 13 Jan 1959.

HY–80] in the hull, the modification of equipment for greater depth, and the elimination of self-noise."[46]

One of the officers in attendance did not feel comfortable with the proceedings. Captain Eugene Wilkinson, *Nautilus*'s first commanding officer, expressed his concern that all of the developmental aspects of the *Thresher* design would hold up the production of submarines badly needed in the fleet. Any unexpected delays in the development of certain systems could throw off the production schedule for months.[47]

Construction schedules and the difficulties with HY–80 took center stage. Most of those at the meeting met Captain Wilkinson's expression of doubt with comments on their own experiences with the sequence and timing of construction as mandated by Congress and permitted by budget appropriations. Those responding to Wilkinson included Knoll, Admiral Morgan, assistant chief of BUSHIPS for ship design and research, and Rear Admiral Robert Moore, commander of the Portsmouth Naval Shipyard. They also sought to assuage Wilkinson's doubts with exhaustive technical tests and assurances from BUSHIPS, DTMB, and the yards.[48]

Although Wilkinson's concerns lay primarily with delays in construction, he made an excellent observation regarding what he called the philosophy of the *Thresher* project. As far as he was concerned, he said,

> I don't think we have the right fundamental question. The question is not the THRESHER. I think those things are wonderful. The presentation today make them sound encouraging as can be but the problem is that in subsequent shipbuilding programs we have 12 follow ships . . . which are now predicated on the 593 design improvements that really aren't yet solved because that ship hasn't been built and tested. If you want to try something take the flexible steam lines. . . . How are you going to test that steam line? Is that going to be at sea? . . . However, I don't want to talk about individual items, but the philosophy. We have compounded development with production.[49]

He admitted that development—by definition, the implementation of innovations that lie well within the confines of current technology—always took place in the process of regular construction programs. Admiral Morgan cited his experiences with the fleet submarines of World War II, and Wilkinson readily agreed. But the contemporary process of imple-

[46] Knoll to Fleet Commanders in Chief et al., 2 Mar 1959, Post 1 Jan 1946 Command File, OA.

[47] Transcript of a Special Meeting of the SCB, Fleet and Submarine Force Commanders, and Representatives of the Shipbuilding Industry to Review the Building Program of *Thresher* (SSN 593), 27 Jan 1959, Post 1 Jan 1946 Command File.

[48] Ibid.

[49] Ibid.

menting highly sophisticated changes in materials and systems in greater numbers than ever before led him to wonder if the production stage was the best time. Had these technologies, materials, and systems really come of age? If not, introducing them simultaneously or prematurely could lead to production delays that would leave the fleet wanting.

The captain's observations had implications beyond the statements made in that meeting room at the Pentagon in January 1959. Wilkinson's immediate concerns, and his persistence in spite of the views of experienced colleagues, raised an implicit question. In an increasingly complex and difficult process, was it possible or wise to introduce several newly developed innovations in a relatively short time frame during the production of a single submarine? Was the naval-industrial complex seriously overextending itself? From his perspective as a submarine operator, Wilkinson was not sure but certainly worried. After thanking everyone at the table for the opportunity to voice his concerns, he left the meeting unsatisfied.[50]

Observations

In the late 1950s the naval-industrial complex reached a turning point. *Skipjack* and Project Nobska demonstrated the sustained creativity and effective personal relationships that matured within the naval-industrial complex and served the Navy over the course of more than a decade. However, pressures, old and new, began to test the naval industrial complex as never before.

The country could not look forward to any relief from the Cold War between America and the Soviet Union. During this period the Soviet navy introduced its first nuclear attack submarines and by 1961 had deployed a modest version of the Polaris, complete with submerged launch capability. The advances within the Soviet submarine fleet pushed American planners and designers to preserve the edge represented by *Skipjack*.

As the materials and technology became more sophisticated and difficult to work with, the pressure to maintain the advantage took its toll. In spite of recommendations by the Nobska ships group calling for the regular use of preprototypes and experimental vessels, BUSHIPS and the shipyards did a remarkable amount of innovation and development during production. The Navy's responsibility to respond to international threats and the inevitable domestic political pressures made even the shortest design and development cycle seem like forever. These circumstances and the rapidity of technical change gave rise to Wilkinson's feel-

---

[50] Ibid.

ing of urgency and deep concern and Rickover's uncompromising attitude toward building and operating seagoing nuclear power plants.

The most important factor lay with the technology. One example, and perhaps the most critical, was HY–80. Given the frequency of cracking, how could the bureau and the yards determine absolutely the strength and permanence of a weld? At the time Rickover placed great faith neither in the procedures established to examine the quality of the welding on nuclear submarines nor in the personnel assigned by the yards to do the job. At one point he expressed satisfaction with the procedures and personnel at Mare Island, but not with those at EB or Portsmouth! [51] Plans for the *Thresher* class multiplied greatly the number of developmental factors integrated into production. The dependence of at least twelve other submarines on the success of the *Thresher* developments increased the pressure on the naval-industrial complex to succeed as it had so many times in the past.

Finally, the strong stand taken by the scientific community on long-range nuclear research came into direct conflict with Rickover's definition of a power plant suitable for use in naval ships. Rarely since the conclusion of World War II had a major activity within BUSHIPS rejected so completely the recommendations of the scientific component of the naval-industrial complex. The absolute authority over nuclear matters gradually acquired by Code 1500 began to disrupt the relationships and understandings upon which the naval-industrial complex rested.

---

[51] Duncan, *Rickover and the Nuclear Navy*, chaps. 2 and 3.

Chapter 10

Adapting to Missile Technology, 1946–1958

During the 1920s and 1930s basic missile technology was the common property of many nations around the world. Missiles captured the imagination of civilians as well as the military. This technology inspired a popular culture preoccupied with speed and space travel while tempting professional warriors with new weapons possessing revolutionary potential.[1]

Although the naval-industrial complex was certainly involved in the development of the Navy's submarine-launched missiles, from Loon to Polaris, the central issue for this study remains the submarine. The naval-industrial complex had to develop a launching system that would ensure the safety of the submarine and its crew. Could designers and engineers adapt the fleet submarines then in service to accommodate missiles and missile support and guidance gear? Indeed, which submarine design offered the most suitable platforms for missiles? The two avenues of development pursued by the Navy, the Regulus and Polaris systems, offer different approaches to the problem of mating missiles and submarines as well as insights into the naval-industrial complex during some of the most important construction and design work since World War II.

The critical period for the postwar development of American missile submarines occurred between 1953 and 1956. From the end of the war through 1953 the Navy's first submarine-launched, guided missiles, Loon and Regulus I, drew on wartime experiments with remote control targets and pilotless aircraft conducted by the Bureau of Aeronautics at the Naval Aircraft Factory (NAF), Philadelphia, later the Naval Air Material Center (NAMC). German submarine and missile technology captured during World War II and the state of the art in international jet aircraft development also proved critical.

In the process of searching for new roles and missions in the postwar world, the Navy Department sought the best formula for combining the

---

[1] For example, see Michael J. Neufeld, "Weimar Culture and Futuristic Technology: The Rocketry and Spaceflight Fad in Germany, 1923–1933," *Technology and Culture* 31 (Oct 1990): 725–52.

range of the missile with the submarine's speed, endurance, and stealth. Fleet submarines converted for this purpose, like *Tunny* (SSG 282), gave the silent service a completely new strategic mission. Submarines armed with missiles would have the capability to strike deep into enemy territory with a minimum chance of early detection. But, what was more significant was the the technology's potential to present the Navy with a second nuclear-weapons delivery system after the carrier.

Background

When flight testing began on the Loon after World War II, the Navy's experimental version of the German V–1, the naval aviation community already had a great deal of experience with guided missiles. Although BUAER developed none of these weapons for submarine launching, the Naval Aircraft Factory in Philadelphia had begun working on assault drones in October 1941 as a direct result of a directive from Admiral Harold R. Stark, then Chief of Naval Operations. In carrying out Stark's order, the NAF drew on research into television guidance systems for aerial torpedoes, an effort begun nearly three years before under the code name Project Fox. In 1942 the drone development team, led by Commander Delmar S. Fahrney, created the TG–2 assault drone, which carried out the first successful pilotless torpedo attack ever conducted. During the experiment, a dummy torpedo from a TG–2 passed amidships under *Aaron Ward* (DD 483) as the destroyer made 15 knots. After the NAF became a part of NAMC in 1943, BUAER also developed the Glomb, or radio-controlled bomb, as well as the Gorgon missile. For use against ships or aircraft, the turbojet-powered Gorgon weighed 760 pounds and could attain a speed of 475 to 510 miles per hour. For BUAER the V–1, Loon, and Regulus began a new phase in an old and interesting field.[2]

The German Bequest

Like so many other technologies developed by the naval-industrial complex after World War II, modern American submarines armed with guided or ballistic missiles also found their technical ancestry in Hitler's navy. The latter turned to missile technology in an attempt to foil both the Allied bombing campaign and antisubmarine warfare efforts against Admiral Karl Dönitz's U-boats.

---

[2] William Trimble, *Wings for the Navy: A History of the Naval Aircraft Factory* (Annapolis: Naval Institute Press, 1991), 258–87.

The earliest German efforts at marrying submarines to missile technology came in 1938. In that year the prewar Kriegsmarine altered the *U–38*, a Type–IXA U-boat just completed at Deschimag Shipyard in Bremen, to accommodate short-range rockets. The U-boat launched these weapons, while submerged, at convoy escorts by manual control from inside the vessel from a range of only a little more than 200 yards. The launcher had an elevation range of from zero to 70 degrees and a lateral scope of 360 degrees. The sound-ranging system was effective between 15 and 70 degrees elevation within the transverse limits of the launcher, save for a blind spot caused by the conning tower.

Alterations to the U-boat consisted of a crate-like launcher mounted in a well carved out of the deck forward of the conning tower. Although the Germans briefly abandoned the idea, the naval high command authorized renewal of the work after three years of war. When the Allied victory suddenly stopped the German war effort in May 1945, the Type 10 rocket was ready for operational use and production in quantity. Only defeat prevented its deployment in greater numbers and the installation of the launcher in more U-boats. Two Kiel-based firms built the system. Electro-Acoustic Company made the rockets and Deutsche Werke designed and produced the launcher.[3]

In another effort to adapt rockets to undersea warfare, Dr. E. A. W. Steinhoff, Germany's chief of development in guided missiles at Peenemunde, initiated a project in 1941 to investigate the feasibility of firing large rockets under water. The weapons weighed from 400 to 500 pounds, with a 100-pound warhead effective at a range of about 7.5 miles. In the course of the research the Germans increased the range to 30 miles, and planned to install ten racks of twenty-four rockets each on a U-boat. At a depth of 50 feet the Germans had some success in launching single rockets and salvos at a 45-degree angle of elevation. Deeper launches, some down to 150 feet, caused the missile to behave erratically, and the Germans decided to discontinue the program.

This action did not discourage scientists who wanted to investigate other systems that might successfully marry missiles and submarines. The Peenemunde group investigated the possibility of adapting the antiaircraft Wasserfall rockets for use in submarines. They recommended converting these weapons into horizontal, low-altitude, beam-riders with a 20-mile range and jet-assisted take-off (JATO). The Kriegsmarine also considered the submarine deployment of cruise missiles and the much larger V–2 ballistic missile, which the Germans called the A–4. The adaptation of the V–2 model for underwater launch demonstrated imagination, determination, and creative

---

[3] Technical Report No. 500–45, Oct 1945, series IV, box 43, NAVTECHMISEU, OA.

engineering. The missile would be carried in a converted food, fuel, and ammunition container designed for towing behind a submerged submarine. Originally used to supply German bases in Norway, these containers were 120 feet long and 19 feet in diameter. Pumping and flooding controlled the attitude of the container while under tow and in preparation for launch.[4] The success of the German missile program naturally drew the attention of the postwar U.S. Navy as it searched for new roles and missions.

Exploring the Possibilities

Adapting submarines to launch either ballistic or guided missiles appeared on a list of recommendations for discussion within the Navy composed by the Submarine Officers Conference in November 1945. By the following March the commanders of the Atlantic and Pacific submarine forces, as well as the General Board, joined Secretary of the Navy James Forrestal in approving the development of two guided-missile and one ballistic-missile conversion.[5]

Seven months later the weapons and countermeasures group of SOC addressed the future significance of submarine-launched guided missiles in response to a memorandum generated in July by the Deputy CNO for Operations. The group studied the disadvantages as well as the promise of the new weapon from the submariner's standpoint and concluded that the ship-to-shore bombardment role seemed the most profitable course of development. In this manner the submarine would help extend the Navy's inland reach while supplementing weapons already in the arsenal designed for surface and subsurface targets. With the services debating the best way to use the power of the atom and each seeking the leading role in military applications, SOC also wanted to strengthen the Navy's position by developing submarines capable of raining nuclear destruction on land targets. In October 1945 the Navy's Operations Research Group (ORG) had suggested the feasibility of producing submarine-launched missiles with nuclear warheads.[6]

---

[4] Report of Conference with German Scientists at Fort Bliss, 1 Apr 1947, series 2, file 2, box 7, Subs/UWD, OA.

[5] Berend D. Bruins, "Navy Cruise Missile Programs to 1960: Examination of Weapons Innovation Hypothesis" (Ph.D. diss., Columbia University, 1980), 4:7.

[6] ORG founded in 1944, grew out of the wartime ASWORG, created in 1942, which had pioneered operations analysis for the Navy under the direction of Philip Morse of MIT. The group was reestablished as the Operations Evaluation Group (OEG) in 1945 and affiliated with MIT as a semi-official Navy activity equipped to evaluate "the operational deployment of existing [naval] systems." Keith R. Tidman, *The Operations Evaluation Group* (Annapolis: Naval Institute Press, 1984); Bruins, "Navy Cruise Missile Programs to 1960," 4:8.

The Bureaus of Ships, Ordnance, Yards and Docks, and Aeronautics received authorization from the CNO, Fleet Admiral Nimitz, and Secretary Forrestal on 5 March 1946 to initiate a coordinated guided-missile program. BUSHIPS had responsibility for the submarine conversion and the design of a launcher that BUAER would first inspect at its own facility. Yards and Docks would build and install the launcher at a location determined by the BUAER. The CNO instructed BUAER to test-launch the experimental Loon missile and control the procurement of additional missiles and parts.[7]

Commenting on the efforts made in this direction by BUSHIPS, the weapons and countermeasures group of the SOC noted the significance of the Navy's effort to increase submerged speed and the importance of German research and development. The heavy load of design and conversion work in support of both the infant Guppy program and the early planning for the *Tang* class completely consumed the full-time efforts of Portsmouth Naval Yard, Electric Boat, David Taylor Model Basin, and other naval and private facilities. Although these programs took priority over missile conversions, they certainly contributed to the formula for an effective guided-missile submarine (SSG). Furthermore, the increasing size of guided missiles under development suggested to SOC that both larger submarines and towed barges or canisters on the German model might lay ahead for the submarine Navy. SOC urged the Secretary and the CNO to grant the bureaus the widest possible discretion in guided-missile research and development and suggested a study by the Operations Evaluation Group (OEG), based at Massachusetts Institute of Technology, on the best land targets for submarine-launched guided missiles.[8]

In one major way the course taken by the Navy with these missiles reflected American preferences and differed significantly from Germany's pioneering effort with the V–1 "buzz bomb." The German weapon was not a guided missile capable of receiving in-flight course adjustments. Instead it carried a small magnetic compass that provided guidance for a preset system. The Loon had a direct radio-command link capable of course changes in five-degree increments provided by a submarine radar plot. A briefing given at a SOC meeting on 8 December 1948 noted that the "Loon carries a beacon operating on the submarine radar frequency to fa-

[7] RADM Delmar S. Fahrney, "BUAER History of Pilotless Aircraft and Guided Missiles," [1958?], 547–49, boxes 401–2, WW II Command File (Shore Establishments), OA. As a lieutenant commander in 1936, Fahrney directed the Navy's first remote control target aircraft project. Trimble, *Wings for the Navy*, 188ff.

[8] Minutes of the Sixth Meeting of the Weapons and Countermeasures Group of the SOC, 22 Oct 1946, series 2, file 4, box 8, Subs/UWD; Fahrney, "BUAER History of Pilotless Aircraft and Guided Missiles," 1157–58.

cilitate tracking out to a maximum line-of-sight range," which translated into 80 miles at 5,000 feet. If guidance was shared by two submarines passing control from the launching vessel to another farther away, the missile's range could be extended to 130 miles. As the Loon approached its target, destructor units blew off the wings, and the missile dropped like a bomb, also a departure from German practice. When the veeder root counter stopped its engine, the German V–1 followed a glide path to its target.[9]

The Loon gave SOC and the bureaus valuable experience with submarine-launched missiles. In November and December 1946 the Naval Air Missile Test Center (NAMTC) at Point Magu, California, conducted launch tests with the missile. Since the Army Air Force had experienced ignition-explosions with the T10E1 launch rocket chosen as a booster for the Loon, the Bureau of Ordnance and BUAER requested the Naval Ordnance Test Station (NOTS), Inyokern, California, to conduct a special investigation. The bureaus involved in the project needed to know the effect an explosion might have on a submarine hull. Writing about these events many years later, Rear Admiral Delmar S. Fahrney, a pioneer with pilotless aircraft and guided missiles, discovered a NOTS dispatch to BUAER on 2 February 1947 reporting that "in ten tests the rocket was exploded 18 inches from ⅞-inch STS and ½-inch MS plates and that there was no damage to the plates. The BUAER took further precautions by procuring 2AS11000 rockets from the Aerojet Company which had a record of higher stability that the T10E1." [10]

On 18 February 1947 the Navy launched its first Loon from a modified fleet submarine of the *Balao* class, *Cusk* (SSG 348). Unfortunately, an autopilot, or flight-control, system failure caused the missile to crash 6,000 yards from the submarine. The Loon gave a much more successful performance on 7 March. According to the commanding officer of *Cusk*, Commander Paul E. Summers, "At the instant of release the Cusk had a one degree port angle. The Loon successfully gained its flying altitude and answered both right and left turn signals given by the ship as directed by NAMTC shore plot. Cusk lost the target at nine miles, due to poor radar reception." [11] When the P–80 pursuit airplane proved unable to shoot the missile down, an internal, preset signal programmed before launch placed the Loon into a 30-degree dive, sending it into the Pacific from an altitude of 2,700 feet. If this short, flawed flight only demonstrated the excellent behavior of the missile at launch and in short-range responsiveness, the nearly perfect test of Loon number six on 17 March proved far more satis-

---

[9] SOC, 8 Dec 1948, series 2, file 3, box 7, Subs/UWD, OA.

[10] Fahrney, "BUAER History of Pilotless Aircraft and Guided Missiles," 551–52. MS stood for medium steel and STS for special treatment steel.

[11] Ibid., 555.

fying. *Cusk* successfully controlled the missile for 75 miles, when NAMTC took over guidance for the final 20 miles of the flight.[12]

Mare Island Naval Shipyard converted both *Cusk* and *Carbonero* (SS 337) into SSGs to serve the missile program initiated by the Loon experiments.[13] With the Guppy and *Tang* programs occupying most of the available talent and yard space at EB and Portsmouth, Mare Island took the lead in their conversion and construction. Initially only *Cusk* had a launch ramp installed on the after portion of the deck and received the missile guidance and control equipment. *Carbonero* received its launch ramp later, after spending time as a control and guidance ship.

The limited range of the Loon, and later the Regulus, I made additional guidance ships necessary. The launch vessel would pass control of the missile to another submarine closer to the target, extending the range and increasing the missile's precision. Mare Island fitted each vessel with a watertight hangar aft of the sail that was large enough to accommodate two missiles. Initially the volume of the hangar presented a stability problem. If it accidentally flooded, the submarine would have a difficult time returning to the surface. Thus BUSHIPS and Mare Island took great care both to reduce atmospheric moisture in the hangar and ensure its watertight integrity.[14]

Although the weapon was never intended for operational use, experiments with the Loon demonstrated the feasibility of the submarine launching system. Before the Navy turned its attention from the experimental Loon to the operational Regulus I, the crew of *Cusk* could surface, rig, and launch the Loon in a mere six minutes.[15] At the behest of the CNO, Loon launchings continued through 1949 to refine guidance techniques and investigate the tactical applications of submarine-launched guided missiles.[16]

Regulus

In 1949 the bureaus applied all of this experience to the design and production of Regulus. A product of the cooperative effort between BUAER, BUSHIPS, and BUORD, the Regulus I roughly resembled the German V–1 on the exterior. But there the similarity ended. Regulus cruised at speeds up to mach 0.95, demonstrating a much

---

[12] Ibid., 555–57.

[13] *Carbonero* never officially received the SSG designation.

[14] Fahrney, "BUAER History of Pilotless Aircraft and Guided Missiles," 550; Alden, *The Fleet Submarine*, 161.

[15] SOC, 8 Dec 1948.

[16] Fahrney, "BUAER History of Pilotless Aircraft and Guided Missiles," 561.

National Archives, RG 19

A launcher-shop test at Mare Island Naval Shipyard, January 1953. These launchers, installed on *Cusk* and *Carbonero,* allowed the submarines to launch the Regulus guided missile.

greater velocity on launch and descent. The missile could reach at least 35,000 feet and carry a 3,000-pound warhead to a target 500 nautical miles distant. This payload capacity was more than enough to accommodate the atomic Mk–5 implosion bomb and gave the Navy its second nuclear delivery system.

The Navy Department awarded Chance-Vought Aircraft, Inc., of Dallas, Texas, the primary responsibility for Regulus construction under a BUAER contract, supported by the Naval Electronics Laboratory, Stavid Engineering, Inc., Reeves Instrument Corporation, Ultrasonic Corporation, and West Coast Electronics Company. The Allis-Chalmers Company provided the propulsion system for the Regulus I and the Bendix Company fashioned some of the guidance components.

The Trounce I guidance system made deep penetration to enemy land targets possible for submarine-guided missiles. The crew of the vessel could preset the initial flight path or employ an on-board computer to achieve the same end. Once airborne, control of the missile passed to one or two radar picket (SSR), or guidance, submarines, which would govern the final approach and select the moment Regulus began its descent toward the target.[17]

The Navy began flight tests with the Regulus I in February 1950, some six months after the Navy deployed its first nuclear capable carrier in the Mediterranean Sea. To keep the costs of the program down, the Regulus team performed most of the initial tests on a recoverable flight test vehicle (FTV). Early land-based testing was conducted at Edwards Air Force Base in California using an FTV equipped with aircraft landing gear. When the test program shifted to NAMTC in 1952, the FTVs went aloft from a launch rail with the help of two jet-assisted take-off boosters, thus better simulating the expected launch conditions on board a submarine. The flight course took the missile over a 54-mile distance to San Nicholas Island, where the FTV touched down on an airstrip.[18]

As these tests proceeded, BUSHIPS called the moth-balled *Tunny* (SS 282) into commission for the third time, only this time the bureau sent this distinguished battle veteran of World War II to Mare Island for conversion to an SSG. After considerable delay *Tunny* received the Trounce guidance system and all of the external features necessary to carry and launch the Regulus I.[19] These additions included a launch rail fabricated at Mare Island and a water-tight hangar, similar to that installed on board *Cusk*, which held two missiles. Mare Island mounted the hangar on the deck just aft of the conning tower, which was modified into a sail similar to those sported by the fleet schnorchel conversions. Although it seemed to recall the German towed canister, the Regulus hangar remained in a fixed position and had more modest dimensions. Its 16-foot diameter came close to the German design, but *Tunny*'s hangar was only 31.5 feet long, as opposed to the German canister, which was 120 feet.[20]

After the first Regulus I submarine launch from the deck of *Tunny* in July 1953, the SSG program became interrelated with the SSRs. Along with *Carbonero* many of these vessels were designed to serve as the downrange guidance submarines for the Regulus missile. In 1954 the Ships Characteristics Board issued the preliminary characteristics for the most capable of the picket submarines, the twin-reactor *Triton* (SSRN 586). The board made missile guidance an essential part of the submarine's primary

---

[17] SOC, 18 May 1949, series 2, file 7, box 7, Subs/UWD, OA; Chance-Vought Engineering Department, "Regulus: Trounce System of Radar Guidance," 15 Nov 1952, box 83, BUSHIPS Confidential CENCORR 1954, RG 19, NA/WNRC.

[18] Annual Progress Report, U.S. Naval Air Missile Test Center, 1–31 Dec 1953, Post 1 Jan 1946 Command File, OA; Chance-Vought Aircraft, Regulus I Progress Report Number 10, 1 Dec 1954, box 9, BUSHIPS Research and Development Library Records, RG 19, NA/WNRC.

[19] Commanding Officer, Mare Island Naval Shipyard, 12 Sep 1952, box 93, BUSHIPS Confidential CENCORR 1952, RG 19, NA/WNRC.

[20] SOC, 18 May 1949.

A Chance-Vought Regulus I guided missile is launched on board *Barbero* (SSG 317).

mission: "To extend the force radar and air control range while remaining on station undetected, and provide radar command of missiles."[21]

The next year, BUSHIPS began converting and building more SSGs to carry the Regulus I and its faster successor, Regulus II. Mare Island completed alterations to *Barbero* (SSG 317) in 1956. *Barbero* and *Tunny* served as the Navy's only Regulus platforms until the next postwar generation of submarines and the more advanced missile superseded them.[22]

In the Regulus II, Chance-Vought improved significantly upon the performance of the first generation of these missiles. The fuselage of this monoplane-guided missile exhibited a greater length and improved aerodynamic characteristics. Its 19,063-pound takeoff weight included a 3,000 pound warhead. From nose to tail the missile measured 56.5 feet and boasted a 20-foot foldable wingspan. As opposed to the speed of the Regulus I, the new model could accelerate to 0.9 mach after JATO on its way to an altitude of from

---

[21] Ships Characteristics Board Memo No. 205–54: First Preliminary Characteristics SSR (Nuclear), Shipbuilding Project No. 132, 22 Oct., 1954, box 113, BUSHIPS Confidential CENCORR 1954.

[22] Alden, *The Fleet Submarine in the U.S. Navy*, 161.

25,000 to 35,000 feet. At that point the Regulus II could accelerate to mach 2 while climbing to 50,000 feet to cruise for a minimum of 350 miles to the target. The new missile's maximum range was 1,000 miles.[23]

Not five months after *Tunny* made the first successful Regulus I launch from a submarine in July 1953, BUSHIPS began to build a generation of postwar submarines designed specifically to carry both generations of Regulus guided missiles. As it had done with the fleet submarine conversions, Mare Island took the lead in building the first of these new SSGs, *Grayback*. This vessel had a submerged displacement of 3,638 tons and could make 15 knots on the surface and, after diving, 12 knots on electric power. The SSG 574 and the only other ship of its kind, the Portsmouth-built *Growler* (SSG 577), did not have the can-like hangar characteristic of the fleet submarine conversions. In the new SSGs two parallel hangars were faired into the forward hull, and each accommodated either one Regulus II or two Regulus I missiles. On 16 September 1958, *Grayback* became the first and only submarine to successfully launch a Regulus II.[24]

Hurdles

Over the course of the Regulus program advanced technologies presented the bureaus and private industry with significant obstacles. The joint effort between the BUAER, BUORD, and BUSHIPS in the Regulus program occasionally spawned some jurisdictional disputes and technical disagreements. In the case of the hangar and launcher design for *Grayback* and *Growler*, BUAER argued forcefully for a twin-launcher arrangement as opposed to the single arrangement advocated by BUSHIPS. As the design agent for BUSHIPS, Mare Island pointed out that the engineering criteria for these vessels would not permit the additional weight of a second launcher. Clearly not pleased by Mare Island's position but reluctant to delay the project, BUAER bowed to BUSHIPS's authority over the actual design of the ship.

> The Bureau of Aeronautics, although of the firm belief that the dual launcher concept provides a basically simpler and more reliable system, nevertheless recognizes that the weight and moment restrictions legislates against such a concept for the subject vessels. Therefore the installation of the single launcher system on SSG 574 and SSG 577 is acceptable to this bureau.[25]

---

[23] Chance-Vought Aircraft, Regulus II Progress Report Number 7, 15 Mar 1954, box 9, BUSHIPS Technical Library Records, RG 19, NA/WNRC; Polmar, *The American Submarine*, 105.

[24] Polmar, 105.

[25] BUAER to BUSHIPS, 8 Feb 1957, box 76, BUSHIPS Confidential CENCORR 1957, RG 19, NA/WNRC.

Missile guidance presented one of the more important problems. The Bendix Bipolar navigation and the BUSHIPS radar-based Trounce midcourse system for the Loon and Regulus I presented problems of reliability and durability. In September 1954 Commander James B. Osborn, commanding officer of *Tunny*, at that time the Navy's only active SSG, set an unusually blunt letter to the chiefs of BUAER and BUSHIPS, as well as to CNO, seeking respite from scores of difficulties with missile guidance.[26]

These problems did not quickly subside. By the summer of 1956 Stavid Engineering could not keep up with the anticipated construction schedule for *Growler* at Portsmouth. If Stavid sent the developmental models of its AN/BPQ–2 guidance radar for testing in the submarine, the company feared that research would be interrupted and it would fail to meet the contractual goals on final production models. To avoid a delay of up to four months in component delivery from Stavid, the bureau decided to retrofit the new SSGs with the late guidance equipment as it became available. The final production run of the perfected guidance system components would not begin until the autumn of 1958.[27]

Predicaments of this sort led Chief of BUSHIPS Admiral Mumma to suggest a different course to CNO Admiral Burke. Mumma urged the use of developmental models in operational testing in spite of the reservations expressed by some private firms. This approach would ensure the readiness and availability of radars like the AN/BPQ–2 when construction schedules at Portsmouth, EB, or Mare Island required delivery. New submarines would then receive fully tested components suited for fleet operations. In Mumma's opinion this use of concurrent rather than sequential development for the guidance system "appears to provide this essential lead-time without delaying the availability of the subject submarines with 'full' Regulus I/Regulus II capability for the scheduled Regulus II evaluation program." Once adopted, this practice anticipated some aspects of the management style characteristic of the PERT (Program-Evaluation-Research-Task) system employed on the Polaris project.[28]

If guidance presented difficult challenges to the missile program, Nuclear propulsion seemed to present grand opportunities. With Rick-

[26] Bruins, "Navy Cruise Missile Programs to 1960," 5: 32.

[27] BUSHIPS Code 800 to Code 500(2), 10 Jul 1956, box 88, BUSHIPS Confidential CENCORR 1956, RG 19, NA/WNRC.

[28] BUSHIPS to CNO, 1 Oct 1958, box 88; COMOPDEVFOR to CNO, 30 Oct 1957; BUAER to BUSHIPS et al., 30 Aug 1957, box 76, BUSHIPS Confidential CENCORR 1956. The latter source also discusses the late delivery of the SINS and RINS navigation systems for *Grayback*. The major issue here was the coordination of component delivery and the evaluation of the Regulus II by OPDEVFOR. There was a need to extend the time of the scheduled tests performed on the submarine and the missile after delivery. The 30 August letter to BUSHIPS et al. is a commentary on the BUAER negotiations with the missile contractors and possible delivery dates.

over's transatlantic "voyage" of the Mark I reactor prototype in June 1953, this technology promised to enhance submarine capabilities and make extended offshore patrols near important land targets a possibility. At a briefing on the Navy's guided missile program in September 1953, Assistant Secretary of the Navy for Air James H. Smith became one of the first to suggest exploring the possibility of a nuclear-propelled SSG. But he did not desire simply to add one more capability to the traditional role of the submarine. Smith viewed nuclear SSG as a submarine with an entirely new mission, signaling a significant departure from the traditional role of employing torpedoes and mines against the enemy.[29]

Due primarily to postwar interservice rivalry over nuclear roles and missions, the advent of *Nautilus* and *Seawolf*, and the initiation of the *Skate* class, the Navy Department waited until the spring of 1956 to pursue the construction of a nuclear-powered SSG. The original design of *Halibut* (SSGN 587) had called for a diesel-electric submarine of approximately 8,100 shaft horsepower (shp). Apparently their concurrent work on nuclear submarines gave the bureau designers other ideas as well. In a communication to the BUSHIPS chief, Rear Admiral Martin J. Lawrence, the commander of Mare Island, noted that the need for missile capability in the fleet initially led the bureau to discard a nuclear-propelled design some engineers found attractive.

> The BuShips SSG587 Preliminary Design History turned over to this shipyard indicates that considerable interest was shown in her having a nuclear rather than a diesel electric propulsion plant. One BuShips preliminary design study shows her as a rather large (7500 tons) nuclear boat. It is understood that the urgency of her delivery militated against designing her for a large or new nuclear plant and dictated her being a diesel boat with excellent surfaced sea-going characteristics and compromised submerged speed and endurance.[30]

In January 1956 Admiral Lawrence advised BUSHIPS that a timely decision to adopt nuclear power after all might bring operational advantages as well as substantial economies. "Recent studies made at this shipyard indicate that delivery date might actually be advanced by as much as two months if a prompt decision were made at this point to change the design to a composite of the 6,600-shp SSN578 [*Skate*] and the missile features of SSG587."[31] The bureau might also realize a significant reduction in cost. With *Sargo* (SSN 583) also under construction at Mare Is-

---

[29] Bruins, "Navy Cruise Missile Programs to 1960," 4:92.

[30] Commander Mare Island to BUSHIPS, 27 Jan 1956, box 89, BUSHIPS Confidential CENCORR 1956, RG 19, NA/WNRC.

[31] The SSN 578 was *Skate*, first of its class, built between 1955 and 1957 by EB in Groton.

land, the bureau might reduce expenditures if it could obtain another set of 6,600-shp propulsion machinery and keep the delivery of other components no more than four months behind those ordered for *Sargo*.[32]

Admiral Lawrence saw the economies possible on a nuclear *Halibut* deriving from two sources. Using the S3W reactor from the *Skate* class would allow Mare Island to benefit from propulsion plant designs and practices already in place for that class. Coupled with the experience gained at EB and Portsmouth while building *Skate* and *Swordfish*, Mare Island would benefit from a tried and tested nuclear propulsion system. Since the yard had not yet qualified for nuclear power installation, the opportunity to draw on previous experience, firm designs, and tried engineering solutions would prove critical. In addition, with *Sargo* under construction Mare Island would have a *Skate*-class submarine on the ways alongside *Halibut*. According to Admiral Lawrence, "Significant production advantages would result from building two boats essentially alike; simultaneously-shared lofting, templates, tooling, mockup, and mechanic orientation costs could easily total one million dollars [in savings]."

These advantages would also allow the yard considerable lead time in ordering construction materials for the nuclear SSG. Indeed Lawrence asserted that his purchasing department could order 30 percent of the steel for the submarine within eight hours of the decision to go nuclear.[33]

In April 1956 Admiral Burke approved the change from diesel electric to nuclear power and ordered a study by the Ships Characteristics Board to determine the final configuration of the SSGN 587.[34] The preliminary characteristics composed by the board determined that the twin-screw *Halibut* should have the capability to carry not only the Regulus II missile, but also the Regulus I and the new Triton missile, not yet cancelled and still under development. The vessel would measure 346 feet in length, have a 29-foot beam, and displace 5,000 tons submerged. The board requested special care in preparing the submarine to avoid the entanglements and dangers of nets and mines in enemy waters. In addition to the missile carrying-and-launch capability, the board provided *Halibut* with four 21-inch torpedo tubes in the bow and two in the stern for a normal load of twelve torpedoes. An auxiliary diesel-electric plant, complete with 126 Sargo II battery cells, complemented the main propulsion system

---

[32] Commander Mare Island to BUSHIPS, 27 Jan 1956.

[33] Ibid. For further information regarding the extension of personnel and expertise from BUSHIPS Code 1500 to Portsmouth and Mare Island, see Hewlett and Duncan, *Nuclear Navy*, 301–3. Rickover's nuclear power superintendents were CDRs Marshall E. Turnbaugh and John J. Hinchley at Portsmouth and CDRs Edwin E. Kintner and David T. Leighton at Mare Island.

[34] CNO to BUSHIPS, 4 Apr 1956, box 89, BUSHIPS Confidential CENCORR 1956.

built around the S3W reactor. Fully loaded the ship could carry ninety days of provision for a crew of ten officers and eighty-five enlisted men.[35]

Advent of Polaris

As BUSHIPS proceeded to apply nuclear propulsion to an SSG, a specter loomed on the horizon for Regulus. Decisions made in 1955 and 1956 had also initiated the Polaris program to create a sea-based ballistic missile with a range of 1,500 miles. In both the Navy and in Congress the Navy's plans now posed a conflict. Were Regulus and Polaris complements or competitors? In public and in private BUSHIPS and BUAER strongly espoused the complementary nature of the two systems.

Admiral Lawrence demonstrated that in matters of technology and design, one system could certainly benefit from the insights applied to the other. In January 1958 he suggested that the submarine missile compartment designed for Polaris might also prove suitable for Regulus. Lawrence contended that BUSHIPS should shift the on-board missile facilities destined for *Halibut*'s bow into a centrally placed missile section in imitation of the Polaris installation. This would grant BUSHIPS the freedom, even during construction, to employ either missile in a standard submarine design simply by installing the appropriate weapons section amidships. With this approach, BUSHIPS could "change during construction of specific hulls to either REGULUS or POLARIS capability . . . and post construction conversion of one configuration to the other could be considered if developments and operational requirements so dictate."[36]

This proposition spoke volumes about the Navy's missile programs. Taking this line of development, the bureau might reduce labor hours and design and construction costs while providing the country with greater tactical and strategic flexibility in a quickly unfolding war. The promise of meaningful economies of cost and time would certainly appeal to a Congress. It also exposed a feeling within the construction community that the projects did not compete with one another.

By the end of 1958, however, the Navy Department could not escape the consequences of the growing opinion within the Navy and on Capitol Hill that the two missile systems were competing for the same role and that Polaris had already overshadowed Regulus. Although Admiral Mumma of BUSHIPS and Admiral Burke from his position as CNO both

---

[35] Ships Characteristics Board Memo #91–56, 24 Apr 1956, box 88, BUSHIPS Confidential CENCORR 1956.

[36] Commander Mare Island to BUSHIPS, 29 Jan 1958, box 59, BUSHIPS Confidential CENCORR 1958.

repeatedly cast the two missiles as complementary and necessary weapons, the Bureau of the Budget commented in September 1958 that "the relative emphasis to be placed on the Regulus submarine in view of the sharp acceleration of the competitive POLARIS program should be resolved before the Navy initiates the construction of the one SSG(N) REGULUS in the 1959 program." Three months after the first Regulus II launch from *Grayback*, the Navy discontinued Regulus production and diverted all of its resources to guarantee an early deployment of Polaris.[37]

Observations

The perception of conflict with the Polaris missile drove the Navy's submarine-launched, guided missile project into hibernation after 1958. But Loon and Regulus demonstrated the ability of the naval-industrial complex to tap foreign wartime developments and link them with domestic efforts to produce a versatile weapon.

Regulus was caught in a time of transition as the Navy Department sought the best possible way of combining missiles and submarines without sacrificing stealth and submerged speed, now considered the two most valuable assets in undersea warfare. Admiral Lawrence's proposal for a standardized missile submarine, which gave the Navy the option of a Regulus or Polaris midsection, illustrated the desire within the submarine community to exploit the advantages of both systems without creating a slower or noisier vessel. However only Polaris survived the debate over competing and complementary systems. It presented a practical configuration combining speed, stealth, submerged launching, nuclear power, and long range with strategic advantages. Developing the Navy's seven guided-missile submarines helped bridge the gap between the German V-weapons and Polaris while laying a foundation for those submarine-launched guided missiles, like Harpoon, developed in later years.

---

[37] BUSHIPS to Comptroller of the Navy, 1 Oct 1958; CNO to Comptroller of the Navy, 15 Oct 1958; Memo, W. J. McNeill to Assistant SECNAV, 18 Sep 1958, box 58, BUSHIPS Confidential CENCORR 1958. Polmar, *The American Submarine*, 105.

Chapter 11

Brickbat 01, 1955–1960

The accomplishments of the postwar naval-industrial complex reached a zenith with the Polaris project. With a sense of urgency characteristic of those years after Pearl Harbor, the Navy, industry, and the scientific community drew on its technical competence and professional intimacy to produce a submarine-based, fleet ballistic-missile system in record time. This was the naval-industrial complex that produced Andrew McKee; stimulated Allyn Vine, John Leonard, Harry Jackson, Albert Mumma, and Henry Nardone; and would cause Marvin Lasky to lament its passing.

Is a Submarine-Launched Ballistic Missile Possible?

Drawing on the flexibility and adaptability characteristic of the postwar naval-industrial complex, the Office of Naval Research asked General Dynamics Corporation and Convair Pomona in early 1955 to study the broad range of possibilities for a practical submarine ballistic-missile system. The report, "Strike Submarine Missile Weapons Systems Study," was one of the first examples of systems analysis. It emphasized not only the engineering feasibility of a missile submarine fleet but also the necessity for developing better solid-rocket propellants and more sophisticated inertial-navigation systems.[1]

As private industry submitted its report to ONR, the Eisenhower administration was exploring the best way to combine the submarine's stealth with a long-range missile. In early 1955 the National Security Council published a report emphasizing the deterrent value of an intercontinental ballistic missile, and President Dwight Eisenhower asked the Killian Committee, chaired by the president of the Massachusetts Institute of Technology, Dr. James R. Killian, to make recommendations on the most promising avenues of missile development. This committee recommended the development of land- and sea-based ballistic missiles that could reach Moscow with a range of at least 1,500 miles.[2]

---

[1] CAPT Dominic A. Paolucci, USN (Ret.), "The Development of Navy Strategic Offensive and Defensive Systems," U.S. Naval Institute *Proceedings* 96 (May 1970): 213–14.

[2] Ibid.; R. A. Fuhrman, "Fleet Ballistic Missile System: Polaris to Trident," *AIAA von Kármán Lecture* (1978): 1, Special Projects Office (SPO) Technical Library/Archives.

Captain Robert F. Freitag, a driving force behind the unsuccessful attempt in 1952 to get naval commitment for a Viking missile with a 500-nautical-mile range, took the lead in persuading the committee to consider a new sea-based system. As the director of the Guided Missile Division of the Bureau of Aeronautics, Freitag and his ally, Abraham Hyatt, chief scientist for the bureau's Research Division, successfully funnelled their research studies through Commander E. Peter Aurand, one of the Killian Committee's naval members.

At first, the Freitag-Hyatt alliance faced formidable opposition. Many within the Navy felt that a ballistic-missile program would either draw money away from more valuable projects or endanger the development of other promising technologies. Admiral Robert Carney, Chief of Naval Operations, and Admiral John H. Sides, director of the CNO's Guided Missile Division, for example, supported air-breathing guided missiles like Regulus II, which would have to compete with ballistic missiles for appropriations and priority. Their position did not deter Captain Freitag. He presented a 1955 survey of twenty-two private firms to Professor Killian and his colleagues on the state of the art in solid propellants, guidance systems, fire control, and navigation. The findings demonstrated the economic and technical feasibility of the sea-launched ballistic missile to the satisfaction of the committee.

Two important allies helped the captain's cause. James H. Smith, Assistant Secretary of the Navy for Air, lobbied Secretary Charles S. Thomas and many important members of Congress. Freitag's other ally was the vigorous new CNO, Admiral Burke. The admiral adopted the new missile proposal early and championed the program during a time of intense competition with the Army and Air Force. Although the political clash between the services during the debate on defense unification reached a climax in 1949, the distribution of roles and missions was still a sensitive issue into the early 1960s. The Air Force viewed naval control over a strategic missile system as a violation of its prerogative and mission.[3]

Perhaps Burke's most effective contribution to the development of the fleet ballistic-missile system came on 5 December 1955, the day he appointed Rear Admiral William Raborn as chief of the Special Projects (SP) Office of the Bureau of Ordnance. Secretary Thomas had created this organization less than a month before to manage the Navy's portion of the joint effort with the Army to perfect the Jupiter missile system. After the joint Jupiter project dissolved in 1956, the Bureau of Ships and SP each went their own way and discovered the four keys to deploying a more compact, sea-based, nuclear ballistic missile.[4]

[3] Vincent Davis, *The Politics of Innovation: Patterns in Navy Cases* (Denver: University of Denver Press, 1967), 32–39.

[4] VADM William F. Raborn, USN (Ret.), interview by John T. Mason, 15 Sep 1972, 18–19, USNI Oral History Collection, OA.

SPO Naval Sea Systems Command

A Polaris test missile leaps from the launch pad at Cape Canaveral, Florida. The Polaris fleet ballistic-missile weapons system became operational on 15 November 1960.

The Four Keys to Success

The Navy already possessed the first key. Nuclear-powered submarines made prolonged submergence and extended deployments possible. The idea of combining nuclear power in a submarine with missiles preceded *Nautilus*. Assistant Secretary Smith had proposed such a combination for the Regulus missile in 1953. The Navy had designed the nuclear-powered *Halibut* for the Regulus II in 1956 and laid her keel in April 1957. It showed that the endurance, stealth, and mobility of a nuclear submarine would provide a perfect ballistic-missile platform if the Navy and Westinghouse could complement the *Skipjack* reactor with a reliable underwater launch technique.

Finding a more efficient solid-rocket propellant was the second key. In 1955 it seemed doubtful that solid-fuel missiles could provide the power necessary to achieve the 1,500-mile range expected of Polaris. Neither the submarine community nor SP ever viewed the liquid-fuel Jupiter as a safe choice for a submarine-launched ballistic missile. With its highly volatile propellant, the Jupiter presented far too many risks.

The Navy had considerable experience with specialized aircraft as well as solid propellants in smaller rockets and was aware of their limits. In this case ONR's habit of supporting a broad spectrum of basic research into many naval-related sciences came to the rescue. Working under an ONR contract, Atlantic Research Corporation made what Admiral Raborn later called "some rather startling advances in the specific impulse that you could get from solid propellants." Charles B. Henderson and his colleagues achieved a more powerful specific impulse by changing the chemistry of the solid-propellant mixture. This made possible the 1,200- to 1,500-nautical-mile ranges the Navy desired.[5]

The third key was the need for a compact inertial navigation system that would guide the missile to its target without increasing the size and weight of the projectile. In this case, Dr. Charles Stark Draper and his colleagues at the Instrumentation Laboratory at the Massachusetts Institute of Technology provided the answer. The final product grew out of Draper's work on ship navigation. He invented a package for Polaris only one-sixth the size of the system designed earlier for the Jupiter. General Electric's Pittsfield division supported MIT's effort, and SP retained a corp of subcontractors, including Hughes Aircraft Company and Honeywell Corporation, to ensure that private industry could manufacture the device in a satisfactory manner. SP kept the project on sched-

---

[5] Ibid., 19–20. "Brief History of Navy Solid Propellant Fuel Experience," [1960?], SPO Technical Library/Archives.

ule by allowing extra lead time and retaining more companies than it expected to need in the long run. According to Admiral Raborn,

> We generated our own competition in industry after we got started. For instance, the guidance platform was a very difficult thing to do. As a matter of fact, the gyros and accelerometers that went on the platform were very, very difficult to manufacture, and we had five major companies trying to build them and there were only about two that wound up being able to do it.[6]

SP had full authority from the Secretary of the Navy to select the contractors best suited to design and build the submarine and the missile system. Lockheed Missile and Space Company, Inc., built the Polaris, Westinghouse Corporation managed the submerged launching system, and Aerojet General Corporation took responsibility for the solid-fuel rocket motors. An executive order from President Eisenhower set aside the provision of the 1934 Vinson-Trammell Act governing the involvement of naval shipyards in every submarine program and authorized BUSHIPS to award the SSBN 598 contract to Electric Boat Division.[7]

Imitating standard BUSHIPS practice, SP placed a team of its own inspectors at each contractor facility to maintain close supervision. But Admiral Raborn permitted private industry and naval facilities to do their own work with a minimum of interference. In the case of EB, Special Projects left the ultimate responsibility for construction matters at the Groton shipyard to BUSHIPS. After some initial friction over supervisory responsibility for building the submarine and the allocation of funds, the BUSHIPS's chief, Admiral Mumma, appointed Rear Admiral James M. Farrin, Jr., as his liaison with SP to enhance communication and understanding. It worked like a charm. Raborn and Mumma strongly believed that the Polaris project should use existing chains of command and corporate responsibility. Years later Raborn still insisted that BUSHIPS

> knew the people, they knew how to do it, they knew it all far better than we did. And that was the same thing as we did in industry. We utilized their management and their management people to do the job, rather than going in and trying to tell them how to do the job, as is so much the case these days. That was a very happy arrangement.[8]

SP found the fourth and last key to the success of the Polaris project in Woods Hole. In its final report filed with the CNO in September

[6] Raborn interview, 51–52; Fuhrman, "Fleet Ballistic Missile System: Polaris to Trident," 1.

[7] Raborn interview, 30–34; Eisenhower to SECDEF Neil H. McElroy, 23 Dec 1958, box 58, BUSHIPS Confidential CENCORR 1959, RG 19, NA/WNRC.

[8] Raborn interview, 52–55.

1956, the participants in Project Nobska argued forcefully for anticipating the future achievements of scientific research, suggesting that the Navy would not serve its own best interests by planning only for the near future. Given the rate of progress in many scientific and technical areas related to undersea warfare, anticipating the state of the art a decade down the road did not seem foolish or excessively optimistic. In this vein, Edward Teller asserted during the Nobska conferences that by 1963 the Navy could expect a significant reduction in the size of nuclear warheads. According to the project's report,

> it is therefore reasonable to expect that warhead weights, for a given yield, will be decreased significantly during the next seven years. Missile designers should ask for new warheads to meet their design requirements instead of designing new missiles around existing warheads, which would be obsolete by the time of missile production.[9]

It was the first indication from any source that the Atomic Energy Commission might provide a nuclear device small enough for a compact missile like the Polaris A–1.

About one year after the Nobska group communicated its results to Admiral Burke, twenty members of the original group met at the Naval War College in Newport, Rhode Island, to review and clarify the findings of the Nobska report. Those attending included, among others, Columbus Iselin and Allyn Vine of Woods Hole Oceanographic Institution, Frederick Hunt of Harvard University, Thomas Dunn of Electric Boat, and Manley St. Denis of David Taylor Model Basin. This review committee strongly supported the statements by the Nobska Project Group on Weapon's Effects and Limitations, of which Edward Teller was a part. The members were confident that the AEC would produce more compact warheads in the near future. Indeed, they felt that the 1956 report seemed too conservative, given the progress in this area over the past year. They insisted that by 1965 the Navy could either arm a newer, lighter submarine-launched ballistic missile with a much smaller nuclear warhead or extend the range and destructive power of the existing Polaris Type A–1. In an interesting observation they voiced their concern about the high cost of nuclear submarines, not by insisting on a smaller missile system but by asking for a much smaller propulsion system. The latter seemed to be driving up the size and cost of the vessel.[10]

---

[9] Project Nobska, vol. 2, 1 Mar 1957, 260, box 17, Records of the Immediate Office of the CNO, OA. Admiral Burke received the Nobska results in September 1956. The report was published and distributed to concerned activities within the Navy in two volumes. Volume one appeared on 1 December 1956, volume two on 1 March 1957.

[10] Review of Project Nobska, 5–9 Aug 1957, DTIC Reports, OA.

Design and Conversion: "The Error Is Anybody's Guess."

Along with nuclear submarines, the advances in solid propellants, inertial navigation, and the expectation of reduced warhead size made Polaris possible. Immediately after Nobska, SP formulated plans for a missile that would weigh approximately 30,000 pounds, establishing the final parameters for the missile in 1956, about six months after the termination of the joint Jupiter project with the Army in November. The Navy Department expected a Polaris surface-ship capability by January 1960 and a ballistic-missile submarine by January 1965.[11]

Special Projects, in conjunction with EB and BUSHIPS, had responsibility for designing the first fleet ballistic-missile submarine. SP's Steering Task Group (STG) supplied its estimate of the best Polaris submarine system to Admiral Raborn and then to BUSHIPS. STG coordinated the preliminary design discussions, determined the Navy's expectations of the various subsystems, and furnished advice on the technical progress of the venture. Meeting bimonthly under the direction of Captain Levering Smith, head of SP's Technical Division, STG's composition reflected a cross-section of the naval-industrial complex. Members included Lockheed, Aerojet, GE, Westinghouse, Sperry Rand Corporation, MIT, AEC, BUSHIPS, the CNO, and the Naval Ordnance Laboratory.[12]

The philosophy governing the design of the SSBN 598 reflected the urgency of Cold War politics and a rapidly changing technical environment. Early proposals for the missile section had included both vertical tube-launch and bow-launch schemes. Two options were considered for the tube launch. According to one suggestion elevators would bring the missiles to launch tubes located in the sail. An alternative plan provided individual tubes for each missile with an air-ejection system for submerged launch. In the bow-launching plan an elevator system would feed the missiles into tubes inclined at an angle and pointing out through the hull forward of the sail. Although the individual tube method emerged as the favorite, it quickly became evident that these designs, regardless of which appeared most feasible, rested on a great many unproved assumptions. Indeed, was air ejection of the missile for submerged launch actually possible? [13]

Preliminary designs generated by a BUSHIPS team under the supervision of Commander Harry Jackson, BUSHIPS project design officer for

---

[11] Stuart S. Murray, "An Historical Review of the Polaris Fleet Ballistic Missile Program," RPJ–TR–0162–001, Final Report, Jan 1977; Fuhrman, "Fleet Ballistic Missile System: Polaris to Trident," 1, SPO Technical Library/Archives.

[12] "Incomplete History of SP (Special Projects)," n.d., SPO Technical Library/Archives.

[13] Proceedings of the SPO/STG, Task 1 (Submarine Envelope), 2d Meeting, 24–25 Jan 1957, SPO Technical Library/Archives.

Polaris, called for adding a segment 141 feet, 1 inch in length containing sixteen Polaris missile tubes to the midsection of a barely completed, nuclear-attack submarine hull.[14] The Bureau of Ships reordered this *Skipjack*-class submarine, already under construction as *Scorpion* (SSN 589), as *George Washington* and planned to take advantage of the long lead time in procurement and design afforded by using a vessel currently under construction.

Both BUSHIPS and EB appreciated the risks and engineering challenges involved in converting *Scorpion* into *George Washington*. At an STG meeting in July 1957 Commander Jackson reported on the progress of the SSBN 598 with both pleasure and caution. The bureau and EB had made excellent headway. Locating three, newly developed inertial navigation sets forward on the upper level of the submarine would segregate the missiles in their own compartment and greatly simplify the construction of the vessel. But Jackson knew that the swift design of *George Washington* presumed, in the spirit of Project Nobska, that scientists and engineers could provide timely solutions to many unsolved problems. On that warm summer day he reminded STG:

> As I have said throughout, the design is based on certain assumptions. If these assumptions turn out to be good, then we are in fine shape. If they turn out to be bad, then we will have to do some additional work and there will be some delay in our design. The amount of this delay will be proportional to the error in our assumptions. At this moment, the error is anybody's guess.[15]

To allow Admiral Raborn's activity to deal with as many of these uncertainties as possible while measuring the progress of the project, a team consisting of SP, Lockheed, and the consulting firm of Booz, Allen, and Hamilton designed the PERT management system. SP implemented PERT to keep track of essential aims, changes in established plans for accomplishing program goals, and the effect of these changes on SP's general plans while STG continued to set program objectives. Thus PERT would provide managers with "a periodic summary evaluation report across the top of the entire project backed by sub-summaries of the more detailed project areas. Where problems appear, alternate courses of action will be presented for consideration." Although SP never ap-

---

[14] The section was installed in a space between 7 inches forward of frame 37 and 7 inches forward of frame 42. SSGN (FBM)—Polaris: Summary of Preliminary Design, 13 Jan 1958, box 58, BUSHIPS Confidential CENCORR 1958, RG 19, NA/WNRC.

[15] Proceedings of the SPO/STG, Task 2 (Monitor and Sponsor FBM Development Program), 1st Meeting, 25–26 Jul 1957, SPO Technical Library/Archives.

plied PERT completely during the Polaris project, industry and the informed public later came to identify it with the success of this program, and the technique quickly spread beyond the Navy to private industry.[16]

Effective management permitted Electric Boat Division and BUSHIPS to collaborate more closely than ever before on the preliminary and contract designs for the SSBN 598. Henry Nardone, one of EB's design managers on the Polaris submarine project, led a group of fifteen engineers dispatched to Washington by the company to collaborate with BUSHIPS in preparing the contract designs. As they produced plans in cooperation with their naval colleagues, Nardone's people kept in contact with Groton so the detail design work at EB would remain in step with the progress made at the bureau. This approach permitted the quick transition of *Scorpion*'s partially completed hull into *George Washington*. Indeed the entire process reflected the customary flexibility and responsiveness of the naval-industrial complex to a national commitment. Many years later, Nardone recalled,

> I can remember talking [from Washington] with our engineering people who were ready to submit to the government for approval procurement documents for certain components that we were putting into the contract design. I would call the supervisor [of shipbuilding]'s office and say this is what is in the plan. This is what is in the contract requirements . . . and the contractor, the Electric Boat people, will be coming with a procurement document that needs your approval and I am telling you that that document is consistent with what we are doing, and it is OK to approve that. And the circuit closed and the document would be approved even though we were [still] in the process of doing the formal documentation. . . . This was all in the effort to expedite things.[17]

BUSHIPS finished the preliminary design for the SSBN 598 on 31 December 1957. Bureau engineers and Nardone's group developed their contract designs, completed the following April, from these preliminary plans.

Although converting an attack submarine to carry missiles saved a considerable amount of time, it also imposed many restrictions on the naval-industrial design team. Since the submarine grew significantly as a result of the conversion, BUSHIPS had to rethink the operation of *Scorpion*'s control surfaces and adapt the linkages operating the planes and

---

[16] SPO (BUORD), PERT Summary Report Phase 1, July 1958, Post 1 Jan 1946 Command File, OA; Harvey Sapolsky, *The Polaris System Development* (Cambridge, MA: Harvard University Press, 1972), see especially 110–30.

[17] Nardone interview, 11 Sep 1990; Nardone, Horan and J. S. Leonard, group interview, 13 Sep 1988, NHC Oral Histories, OA.

rudders to apply and withstand much greater force.[18] When EB began converting *Scorpion,* the forward section became the bow of the new SSBN 598 and yard work force placed the machinery spaces in the stern. Since the relative diameters of the severed hull and the new missile compartment were different, BUSHIPS designed conical sections to connect the new with the old, and EB changed the ballast tankage to ensure the stability of the new configuration. The company also worked with the bureau in anticipating the next class of SSBNs in the *George Washington* design by building the midsection to the tougher specifications formulated for the future *Ethan Allen* (SSBN 608) class. In this way SP and BUSHIPS completed the first generation of Polaris submarines ahead of schedule, all the while planning for the deeper-diving type to follow.[19]

In spite of some arguments to the contrary, including those of Admiral Rickover and Code 1500, the chief of BUSHIPS, Admiral Mumma, successfully made a case to the CNO for retaining single screw propulsion and the elongated series 58 hull form adapted from the original *Scorpion* design. Imitating *Albacore* and *Skipjack,* the latter having come down the ways just as the cooperative effort on the contract design concluded, the SSBN 598 would take advantage of the greater propulsive efficiencies that came with using a single propeller. Mumma felt that the bureau might also find it easier to quiet a single screw submarine.[20]

Although SP and its contractors moved quickly toward an operational missile submarine, other events overtook them and forced an acceleration of the program. After the Soviet Union launched Sputnik into Earth orbit on 4 October 1957, the threat of foreign superiority in missile technology led to a national commitment to deploy the Polaris much earlier than originally planned. Secretary of Defense Charles E. Wilson authorized the acceleration and on 8 December his successor, Neil H. McElroy, called for the construc-

[18] Jackson interview, 24 Sep 1987, NHC Oral Histories, OA.

[19] BUSHIPS Submarine Design Subcommittee to Chair, STG, 10 Jan 1958, box 58, BUSHIPS Confidential CENCORR 1958, RG 19, NA/WNRC. Rodger P. Johnson, "An Executive Summary of the Polaris FBM Program History," Jan 1977; Proceedings of the SPO/STG, Task 2 (Monitor and Sponsor FBM Development Program), 4th Meeting, 23–24 Jan 1958; 5th Meeting, 27–28 Mar 1958, SPO Technical Library/Archives.

[20] Mumma advocated this viewpoint for all submarine types except those expected to operate under the ice. In that case he preferred a twin-screw, double reactor design for vastly increased reliability. Rickover suggested the *Triton*-type plant. Chairman, Submarine Design Subcommittee, to Chairman, Steering Committee, STG, 6 Nov 1957; Raborn to Westinghouse, 14 Jun 1957; BUSHIPS to BUORD (SP), 16 Aug 1957; BUSHIPS to CNO (SCB), 7 Jun 1957; BUSHIPS Code 1500 to Code 100, 23 Dec 1957, box 77, BUSHIPS Confidential CENCORR 1957; BUSHIPS to CNO, 12 Mar 1958, box 58, BUSHIPS Confidential CENCORR 1958, RG 19, NA/WNRC.

At its launching one year later, *George Washington* displaced 5500 tons in the light condition. With the missile compartment installed amidships holding sixteen tubes arranged in pairs, the 373-foot-long submarine had a beam of 33 feet.

tion of three fleet ballistic-missile submarines. The first two would go to sea in October and December 1960, with a third following in March 1961.[21]

During the Steering Task Group meetings of 21 and 22 November 1957 Commander Roy G. Anderson, SP planning officer, reported that the AEC would deliver the best and lightest warhead possible on an emergency schedule. Lockheed committed itself to deliver the missile prototype by December 1959, and SP expected EB to work around the clock to deliver the first three Polaris submarines roughly ten months ahead of schedule.[22]

The Department of Defense assigned the Brickbat 01 emergency designator to the Polaris project in January 1958, while Henry Nardone's people worked in Washington on the contract designs. SP then received the bureau's DX certification for controlled materials, giving Polaris priority over all other naval activities in procurement. To keep up with the accelerated pace of construction, BUSHIPS also increased the size of the SUPSHIPS naval inspection team at EB. The supervisor's office consisted of 19 officers, 10 of whom were engineering duty officers. Of the 135 civilian employees, 35 served as engineers, 34 as inspectors, and the rest were in support roles. Responding to the demands of the Polaris project, SUPSHIPS assigned his best EDO to wear two hats, serving as both submarine project officer in Groton and SP's on-site ordnance officer. He was supported by two EDOs at the rank of lieutenant, one of whom underwent training at SP in management and technical matters directly pertaining to the submarine.[23]

The bureau suspended the usual administrative and technical obstacles to quick construction and granted SUPSHIPS the authority to approve necessary overtime in advance. A meeting between the Office of Naval Material, BUSHIPS, and the supervisor's office in Groton also addressed the problem of procurement and the need to streamline acquisition procedures. As a result, SUPSHIPS was given the authority to issue change orders to speed up the process in the event of procurement bottlenecks, with the bureau heeding SUPSHIPS's preference for fixed-price contracts, which were easier to manage in a complex, accelerated program.[24]

---

[21] Wyndham D. Miles, "The Polaris," in *The History of Rocket Technology*, edited by Eugene M. Emme, 167–68 (Detroit: Wayne State University Press, 1964). For a social reconstruction perspective on the rapidity of Polaris guidance development, see Donald Mackenzie, *Inventing Accuracy: A Historical Sociology of Nuclear Missile Guidance* (Cambridge, MA: MIT Press, 1990); and Murray, "An Historical Review of the Polaris Fleet Ballistic Missile Program," RPJ–TR–0162–001, Final Report, Jan 1977, SPO Technical Library/Archives.

[22] Proceedings of the SPO/STG, Task 2 (Monitor and Sponsor FBM Development Program), 3d Meeting, 21–22 Nov 1957, SPO Technical Library/Archives.

[23] SUPSHIPS–INSORD, Groton, to BUORD Strategic Special Projects (SSP), 7 Jan 1958, box 58, BUSHIPS Confidential CENCORR 1958, RG 19, NA/WNRC.

[24] BUSHIPS to SUPSHIPS–INSORD, Groton, 26 Feb 1958, box 58, BUSHIPS Confidential CENCORR 1958.

In a manner similar to the arrangement between Manitowoc Shipbuilding Company and EB during World War II, EB cooperated with BUSHIPS in creating a joint procurement program for the fleet ballistic submarines. Without taking ultimate responsibility for the price or the timeliness of delivery, EB acted as a central clearing house for purchase of all components and materials not supplied by the Navy for the Polaris submarines. This procurement responsibility both accelerated purchase and delivery, and paved the way for other submarines of the *George Washington* class scheduled for construction at yards other than EB Division.[25]

From the vantage point of SUPSHIPS Groton, only the phenomenal level of cooperation between EB and BUSHIPS made the accomplishment of the Polaris schedule likely. In a letter to Admiral Mumma on 12 February 1958, the supervisor, Captain Arthur C. Smith, commented:

> The progress of the SSG(N)598 Class submarine construction program is considered excellent. The detailed coordination necessary to get this important program started within the Bureau has been accomplished by the Bureau of Ships, Code 525, with the full cooperation of Bureau Design and Technical Branches and the Special Projects Office. The Electric Boat Division has responded to this new challenge with remarkable zeal. The wholehearted cooperation of Electric Boat Division personnel has made possible the present advanced state of the SSG(N)598 design and extremely satisfactory state of Contractor Furnished Material procurement.[26]

Smith knew the value of the cooperation and dedication exhibited by the EB employees, and shipyard responsibilities were some of the most critical in the entire program. EB had to supervise all of SP's on-site contractor representatives—over 100 men from twenty companies at the peak of the program. All of these people needed office space, supervision, and direction. EB also had to deliver the submarine ahead of schedule, balancing Polaris with competing construction projects, as well as building and testing the entire ship and all of its systems.[27] To help organize this last task, SP designed a program for the yard called the Weapons System Installation and Test Program. These procedures

---

[25] L. A. Fowler (EB Div. Purchasing Division Agent) to BUSHIPS, 7 Jan 1958, box 58, BUSHIPS Confidential CENCORR 1958.

[26] SUPSHIPS, Groton, to BUSHIPS, 12 Feb 1958, box 58, BUSHIPS Confidential CENCORR 1958. At first the ballistic missile submarines used the SSGN designator employed for the *Halibut* nuclear guided-missile submarine. By 1959 a unique designator was adopted for the Polaris submarines—SSBN.

[27] Rear Admiral Mumma authorized unlimited overtime to put many of the projects delayed by Polaris priority back on schedule. BUSHIPS to CNO, 13 Jan 1958, box 61, BUSHIPS Confidential CENCORR 1958.

permitted testing systems as they were installed to avoid having to pursue problems later in the complex maze of a completed submarine.

SP also provided additional training. To deepen the expertise of those involved with Polaris, it established schools at the facilities of major contractors. Technical representatives from SP also worked with the contractors to implement suggestions for better management made by SP.[28]

By mid-1958 BUSHIPS anticipated completing the submarine by 31 December of the following year. With fully tested missiles on board by 30 April, the Navy Department expected to deploy the fully operational SSBN 598 on 1 October 1960. In the race to call the first fleet ballistic-missile submarine an accomplished fact, Admiral Burke noted that he might waive the vessel's final trials. Sputnik and the Cold War made these usually mandatory measures expendable.[29]

Overcoming the Obstacles

Every project has its conflicts, and Polaris was no exception. But seeking out potential problems and searching for solutions reflected the nature of the management system governing SP. One good illustration of this approach is the way SP and Lockheed discovered and addressed some potentially debilitating problems in their joint effort to build and test the Polaris A–1 missile that would go to sea in *George Washington.*

In a communication to Admiral Raborn on 9 December 1957, the general manager of Lockheed Missile Systems Division suggested that significant problems existed affecting their association. Captain Levering Smith, chief of SP's Technical Division, asked the Navy management office in January 1958 to study the situation and to recommend ways to improve the vital relationship between SP and Lockheed.[30]

The management office discovered a curious and interesting collection of grievances in the Lockheed letter. Initially the company wanted to implement a series of organizational reforms that, on the surface, did not seem extraordinary in nature. These reforms included effectively making the company the weapons program manager for Polaris by vesting Lockheed with responsibility for the launcher and the missile system. The contractor believed that central authority of this sort would not only make the project more efficient but also streamline the SP organization.

---

[28] "Incomplete History of SP (Special Projects)."

[29] CNO to BUSHIPS, 23 Sep 1958, box 62, BUSHIPS Confidential CENCORR 1959; BUSHIPS to CNO via BUORD (SP) and the President of Bd I/S, 20 Jun 1958, box 59, BUSHIPS Confidential CENCORR 1958.

[30] The Navy management office was a division of the executive office of the Secretary of the Navy directed by E. D. Dwyer in early 1958.

The firm also wanted a more precise definition of the responsibility assigned to the inspector of naval ordnance at Lockheed's facility in Sunnyvale, California. Giving this naval officer genuine on-site authority would make both relations with the Navy easier and company decisions more informed and effective.

Beyond these matters of relative responsibility and organizational structure, Lockheed questioned the excessive use of committees. Committees worked well when they allowed an exchange of information or provided a forum for the frank and constructive discussion of problems. But many within Lockheed felt that committees had no business making decisions.

> They should recommend to a line official who has responsibility for making decisions. Responsibility for making decisions and taking actions should be clearly fixed in line officials. Committees should not be used so as to spread responsibility or to permit line officials to escape responsibility.

As a result of this investigation, the report composed by the Navy management office noted that existing abuses of the committee method reflected an undesirable and counterproductive situation. Company officials needed to know the decisions made and those who took responsibility for them.

The company also drew attention to friction between Lockheed engineers and their counterparts at SP's Technical Division. Of all the issues raised, this one was the most important to private industry. Lockheed took the excessive supervision of company employees by naval officials most seriously. Engineers attached to the SP Technical Division demanded fundamental engineering information from their Lockheed colleagues and detailed justification for decisions reached and alternatives discarded. The contractor did not have difficulty providing the information, but the firm resented the implied lack of trust in private-sector engineers.

> The objection is to the fact that such detailed information will be used by Technical Division engineers for the purpose of checking and questioning all of the basic work done by Lockheed professional engineering staff. In interviews with the Lockheed staff there was frequent reference to their belief that they didn't need supervision from "civil service" engineers.

The management office report reminded SP of the value of trust and the difference between engineering administration and engineering supervision. The former was identified as definitely within the authority of SP. The latter properly belonged to Lockheed. The authors of the report concluded their comments on this problem by arguing that SP needed to trust its own judgment: "It is inconceivable that Navy would hire a contractor if there was reason to believe that the contractor did not have a competent engineering staff." [31]

SP responded positively to most of Lockheed's grievances, but the company did not obtain complete satisfaction. Although the issues of unproductive committees, stifling supervision, and technical competence were successfully addressed by SP, the history of the project conspired against the management authority Lockheed wanted. Polaris had accomplished too much and come too far without a weapons management contractor for the missile system. SP was satisfied with the quality and the rate of progress and did not care to alter the system in midstream.[32]

Tested management and competent engineering were absolutely necessary and probably the most valuable assets on the Polaris project. Nowhere did this become more evident than in the management of excess weight. Some bureau and SP engineers warned that *George Washington*'s *Skipjack*-type reactor had its limits. Even though this model pushed the SSN 585 well past 20 knots, it could not meet expectations on a larger ship in the face of significant weight overruns.

Unfortunately SP encountered unexpected weight increases with the launching system, the missile, the heavy sound-isolation mountings, and the turboelectric drive suggested as a main drive unit early in the program.[33] By September 1957 the excess weight situation became critical. Just before the month ended, Commander Jackson presented a long list of dimension and weight inquiries at an STG meeting. To complete the ship design, his committee needed to have this data. Would the growing weight of the missile equipment exhaust the capabilities of the planned propulsion system?

> Progress on the FBM submarine preliminary design is progressing on schedule. However, there is a large unknown in the area of launching equipment. The weight of this machinery continues to grow. Unless there is a drastic reduction in the weight of this equipment, the submarine will have to be enlarged. The weight of this equipment is now estimated about 225 tons compared to 53½ tons in the original estimates.[34]

Weight remained a persistent headache in the planning of the entire first generation of Polaris submarines. In June 1959 Commander Donald

[31] Technical Division, SPO, "Study of Navy-Contractor Relationships," 17 Mar 1958, SPO Technical Library/Archives.

[32] Sapolsky, *The Polaris System Development*, see especially 80–81ff.

[33] Proceedings of the SPO/STG, Task 1 (Submarine Envelope), 3d Meeting, 13–15 Feb 1957, SPO Technical Library/Archives.

[34] Proceedings of the SPO/STG, Task 2 (Monitor and Sponsor FBM Development Program), 2d Meeting, 26–27 Sep 1957.

H. Kern, Jackson's relief as the BUSHIPS Polaris project officer, reported to STG on the growth of weight attributable to the missile system. The bureau considered the steady increase unacceptable. The original margin allowed for overruns in the contract designs was 220 tons. By the time of Kern's report, with 90 percent of the figures considered firm, the weight margin had fallen to 44 tons for the SSBN 598 and *Theodore Roosevelt* (SSBN 600), and 39 tons for *Patrick Henry* (SSBN 599), *Robert E. Lee* (SSBN 601), and *Abraham Lincoln* (SSBN 602). Their design could not support the weight of the missile complex if growth continued at this rate. Kern asked the ship subcontractors to submit to EB all weight figures on their components, both present and projected, so the company and the bureau could head off any unacceptable total.[35]

Although weight overruns persisted, SP and the bureau finished *George Washington* with a few tons to spare. Four months after Commander Kern's report to the STG, the weight margin fell to 28 tons. But careful management allowed SP, the bureau, and EB to finish the submarine with a total of 40 tons of growth weight left. They achieved similar results with *Theodore Roosevelt*. These cases proved the exception rather than the rule. The weight margin for the SSBN 601 and 602 was completely spent by March 1960. Only the severe tonnage restrictions placed on the submarine contractors permitted the bureau to control the displacement of *Robert E. Lee* and *Abraham Lincoln*.[36]

Exact determination of a submarine's displacement and the best distribution of that weight contributed to precise control while under way. Successful Polaris missile launches would depend entirely on such deft ship-handling at unusually slow speeds. The submarine would have to hover and compensate for the effect of currents and wave motion. In the spring of 1957 Commander Harry Jackson visited *Raton* (SS 270) in an effort to gain preliminary data on ship motion to assist in designing the launch equipment.[37] Requiring a submarine to hover at less than 3 knots, 90 feet below the surface, posed questions about ship handling and the effect of waves and current never before addressed.[38] But this problem did not confine itself to engineering. While Jackson and his colleagues defined

---

[35] CDR Donald H. Kern (BUSHIPS), Submarine Design Committee Report, Proceedings of the SPO/STG, Task 2, 12th Meeting, 8–10 Jun 1959.

[36] LCDR C. R. Bryan, Submarine Design Committee Report, Proceedings of the SPO/STG, Task 2, 15th Meeting, 22–23 Oct 1959; 17th Meeting, 24–25 Mar 1960.

[37] Jackson to BUSHIPS, 10 May 1957, box 77, BUSHIPS Confidential CENCORR 1957, RG 19, NA/WNRC.

[38] The specifications for the hovering system were governed by the conditions required for launch. The submarine had to hover submerged at 90 feet (plus or minus 10 feet) in a state five sea. Travel Report, Ernest E. Zarnick (BUSHIPS Code 442), 30 Dec 1959, box 62, BUSHIPS Confidential CENCORR 1959.

Work progresses on *Abraham Lincoln* (SSBN 602) at the Portsmouth Naval Shipyard, November 1960.

Robert E. Lee (SSBN 601), a *George Washington*-class Polaris fleet ballistic-missile submarine built at Portsmouth.

the problem and tried to devise engineering solutions, scientists at the David Taylor Model Basin explored the hydrodynamics of wave motion, making an interesting discovery quite by accident.

"How can you get the effects of waves on the submarine?" A naval officer asking this question of William E. Cummins did not immediately receive an answer. A naval architect and marine engineer specializing in hydrodynamics at the DTMB, Cummins did not know the answer. But the problem interested him enough to set the process of inquiry in motion.

Cummins belonged to an innovative circle of DTMB scientists gathered about physicist Louis Landweber, chief of the Hydrodynamics Division. In addition to Cummins the group originally included Philip Eisenberg, later head of the mathematics branch at ONR; John P. Craven, who became chief scientist at SP; and Georg Weinblum, the German expert on surface wave effect. Some years earlier Landweber, Eisenberg, and Weinblum helped develop the series 58 hull design that determined the shape of *Albacore*. Now this inquiry drew the group into the problem of hovering, wave-effect on a submarine and submerged missile launching.

Cummins extended the Legally theorem used to find the forces and moments acting on a ship in a steady flow. His variation on this theorem provided a way of determining those same forces in a changing flow that would affect a submarine passing under a wave. With this information Cummins calculated the forces acting on a body of revolution in this environment. In her computations an assistant mathematician working for Cummins on this problem discovered a second-order motion, or oscillation, affecting ships encountering waves. A more experienced mathematician might easily have dismissed this second-order effect. But in model tank research data gathered by a DTMB colleague, Paul Golovato, Cummins discovered a secondary oscillation that contributed to a change in the direction or position of the ship scale model that conformed exactly with his assistant's mathematical results. As it turned out, this nearly discarded second-order effect explained why hovering submarines tended to rise to the surface in a rough sea. As Cummins recalled:

> A little bit later we had a full scale trial . . . on the NAUTILUS. They wanted to get some information on the way submarines behave at very low speeds, because they were concerned with the [Polaris] launch . . . because their controls won't work at low speed. One of our people ran the trial on the submarine and came back and said it seemed to be a bit odd. The officers felt . . . as if something was trying to draw them to the surface. We remembered this result that we dug up. . . . It turned out to be the critical thing in developing the control system for the Polaris submarine in carrying out the launch.[39]

[39] William E. Cummins, interview by David K. Allison, 2 and 12 Aug and 14 Oct 1982, Oral Histories, Navy Laboratories Archives, DTRC.

Cummins incorporated this discovery in DTMB report C–910. Scientists could now predict wave effects on the hull design of *George Washington* with greater precision. Thus, he concluded that the crew would have little difficulty launching all sixteen Polaris missiles in rapid succession while keeping the submarine submerged and stable. When R. D. Rung, an engineer for Westinghouse, one of the submerged launch-system contractors, visited DTMB on 12 February 1958, J. W. Church of the Stability and Controls Division familiarized him with the contents of C–910, giving the Navy and industry the ability to transform the problem into engineering and construction tasks. These were no less formidable but, with the submerged launching of

Dr. John P. Craven, chief scientist on the Polaris project, holds a Polaris model on the testing carriage in the circulating water channel at David Taylor Model Basin, April 1959.

Polaris missiles, it was no longer a question of "if" but "when." [40]

In July 1957 welding difficulties emerged as a most formidable scientific and engineering problem in the construction of modern submarines and systems. In this case questions of welding and metallurgy caused a slowdown in the production of the Polaris missile housing and the rocket motors. An NRL report on the incident blamed the failure of materials in both cases on flawed welds and poor welding procedures.

The laboratory suggested reducing the number of welded joints and improving welding techniques and inspection methods. Without properly welded and inspected joints the missile would never perform properly.[41] Such a failure would send a submarine to the bottom of the ocean, costing the lives of the entire crew. After BUSHIPS introduced low-carbon, high-strength structural steel, also known as HY–80, into

[40] Travel Report, R. D. Rung, 25 Feb 1958, box 59, BUSHIPS Confidential CENCORR 1958, RG 19, NA/WNRC. The hovering system designed for the SSBN 598 presented a great many technical problems to the bureau and EB all the way through sea trials. Travel Report, LCDR C. R. Bryan, 30 Nov 1959; Travel Report, Ernest E. Zarnick (BUSHIPS Code 442), 30 Dec 1959, box 62, BUSHIPS Confidential CENCORR 1959.

[41] Record of Visit to Lockheed Missile Systems Division, Sunnyvale, and Aerojet General Corporation, Sacramento, California, 14–18 Jul 1958, NRL TM–27 c.1, SPO Technical Library/Archives.

submarine construction, precision welding became absolutely critical. First used in *Albacore* and *Barbel* to enable American submarines to dive deeper, HY–80 could sustain ocean pressures of 80,000 pounds per square inch. But unless an experienced welder followed a set of rigorous procedures to the letter, HY–80 tended to crack.

At a meeting of STG's submarine design committee in March 1960, Lieutenant Commander Clarence R. Bryan announced that Admiral Burke had approved the use of HY–80 for use in SSBN construction.[42] Finding a safe and dependable way of welding HY–80 was one of the bureau's most perplexing trials. Cracking problems were universal, and many facilities had neither the nondestructive testing skills nor the capability to guarantee that every HY–80 weld was secure. As Francis Duncan recently observed in his analysis of the *Thresher* (SSN 593) disaster of 1963, "Although there was debate over the significance of the cracks, one fact was certain: welds that had passed inspection had cracked days and even months later. . . . Repairs were difficult, costly, and time consuming. Some welds had to be reworked six times before they were satisfactory."

Unless data and experience demonstrated the unreliability of HY–80, the strategic and tactical importance of deeper diving for high-speed submarines made this material a critical component of the submarine program. Despite the sensitivity of the material and the difficulty of working with it, nobody suggested abandoning HY–80 as a structural steel. It was so new and experimental that the bureau had little data on the effects of heat, fatigue, or work-hardening after repeated dives. Rear Admiral Ralph K. James, Chief of BUSHIPS, created a special committee to examine the problem. Responding to the report submitted by the committee on 5 January 1960, he issued more comprehensive and precise regulations and procedures to govern work with HY–80.[43]

On 1 September 1959 the supervisor of shipbuilding provisionally accepted the SSBN 598 from EB on behalf of the Commandant Third Naval District. EB and many of the contractors still had to install some of the ship's systems before delivery on 31 December 1959, including some sonar components, the underwater IFF system, navigation equipment, and the retractable maneuvering and emergency propulsion motor.[44]

The submarine went through a demanding trial schedule and all of the nuclear systems operated flawlessly. It traveled 415 miles in 34 hours,

[42] LCDR Clarence R. Bryan, Submarine Design Committee Report, Proceedings of the SPO/STG, Task 2 (Monitor and Sponsor FBM Development Program), 17th Meeting, 24–25 Mar 1960, SPO Technical Library/Archives.

[43] Duncan, *Rickover and the Nuclear Navy*, 55–57.

[44] SUPSHIPS, Groton, to CNO, 1 Sep 1959, box 58; BUSHIPS to CNO, 16 Oct 1959, box 62, BUSHIPS Confidential CENCORR 1959, RG 19, NA/WNRC. IFF is an acronymn referring to "identification friend or foe."

approaching 20 knots on the surface, and moving even faster when submerged. Admiral Rickover complemented the crew of *George Washington*, under the command of Commander James B. Osborn, for exceptional performance during the initial sea trials.[45]

At 0800 on 20 July 1960, *George Washington* launched its first Polaris missile. Among the 122 special passengers on board that morning were Dr. Charles Draper from MIT; Dr. George B. Kistiakowski, President Eisenhower's science advisor; Admirals Burke and Rayborn; Captain Levering Smith; a seven-man team from the Johns Hopkins Applied Physics Laboratory; and assorted representatives from the project's major contractors. An attempt two days earlier had miscarried for two reasons. A battery in the missile malfunctioned, and an umbilical failed to detach from the missile. But everything functioned well on the twentieth, and Lieutenant Donald Johnson became the first officer to launch a ballistic missile from a submerged submarine.[46]

After the SSBN 598 successfully launched its first few missiles at sea, the emphasis shifted to the submarine's behavior and performance characteristics. At an STG meeting in late March 1960, Captain Henry Arnold, Polaris program assistant for BUSHIPS and assistant for shipbuilding in SP, reported excessive noise during sound trials. From the operating community's vantage point, radiated noise and the capability of *George Washington*'s active and passive sonar took priority after the missile system. Months earlier John Craven had urged every contractor to make its components as quiet as possible before delivery to the yard. He had hoped that his exhortations would minimize the acoustical problems the bureau would have to solve after the submarine went to sea.

The three components of the naval-industrial complex already addressed some of the acoustic weaknesses of *George Washington*. Noise radiation declined after EB treated the hull with a sound-absorbing material. SP and BUSHIPS also initiated studies to determine the acoustical signature of the SSBN 598 and the chance of its detection.[47] Until the Navy knew more about the personality of its newest warship, still-classified naval and industrial research programs provided a small, temporary margin of safety.[48]

---

[45] RADM Hyman G. Rickover to CNO via BUSHIPS, 17 Nov 1959, box 62, BUSHIPS Confidential CENCORR 1959.

[46] Recollection of the first Polaris launch as recorded by Robert E. Kemelhor, part of the APL (Johns Hopkins) launch team, 20 Jul 1960, SSBN–598 Binder, Individual Submarine Historical Files, Submarine Force Library and Museum, Groton, CT.

[47] Dr. John P. Craven, Systems Appraisal Report, Proceedings of the SPO/STG, Task 2, 15th Meeting, 22–23 Oct 1959, SPO Technical Library/Archives.

[48] Submarine Design Committee Report, Proceedings of the SPO/STG, Task 2, 21st Meeting, 29–30 Sep 1960.

George Washington (SSBN 598) test fires the first Polaris missile from beneath the surface on 20 July 1960.

Observations

Polaris was the product of clearly defined goals, effective leadership, a well-integrated naval-industrial complex, and remarkably consistent advances in the postwar science of undersea warfare. The national commitment to the project made the work both important and exciting to the nation's naval and political leaders, as well as to those interested in its more technical and scientific aspects. But as William Cummins later observed, once SP guided Polaris through the first phase, "things were never really the same. Money was harder to get. Things were much tighter and things were being done differently. A lot of the excitement had gone." [49] Subsequently Rickover's power and authority over parts of the naval-industrial complex began to adversely affect professional relationships that could be traced back to World War II. With the election of President John F.

---

[49] Cummins interview, 2 and 12 Aug and 14 Oct 1982.

Kennedy in 1960 and the arrival of Robert S. McNamara at the Defense Department in 1961, a completely new management system swept over the naval-industrial complex. The productive informality and professional intimacy that sustained the complex for fifteen years began to wither in an atmosphere of systems analysis and close budgetary scrutiny.

Carleton Shugg, EB Division's general manager, realized the significance of the unaffected relationships and mutual trust within the naval-industrial complex during these years. During a 1973 interview concerning the construction of *George Washington*, America's first Polaris submarine, he recalled,

> My man responsible [for ordering steel] came over to my house on Christmas Day with all of the mill orders for steel, which were based on an estimate of what we would need, and we got the steel on order before ever seeing a piece of paper [i.e. a contract]. And we made other heavy commitments, and that was the way the relationship was between EB and the Bureau . . . it's the way business should be done more often. I mean we each knew the other.[50]

Polaris, SP, and the PERT management system thrived in an environment of motivation, commitment, and professional freedom. The fleet ballistic-missile system was placed high on the list of naval and national priorities. SP had the complete support of the Administration and Congress, which guaranteed the necessary funds. All of those participating in the program had the freedom to take advantage of the close professional relationships between scientists, engineers, and managers within the Navy and the private sector. These relationships were already in place when Polaris got under way and rested on a combination of long-standing familiarity, respect, and trust that permitted Admiral Raborn to depend heavily upon judgment and expertise outside of the Navy.

When asked if this kind of close, productive cooperation is possible today, Henry Nardone, now the Trident program manager for EB Division, replied in the negative. Much as they did in the early days of the development of a naval-industrial complex for submarines after the Great War, the Navy and the private sector are now busy overseeing each other and protecting their own interests. Nardone's observations on the absurdity of the contemporary situation are both familiar and revealing.

> We can't even have a naval officer up here on business and give him a lunch. We sit there and have a working lunch and tell him you owe me $5.45 for that sandwich that you just had and, oh, by the way, the soda is a dollar a can. I think that mentality would absolutely prevent us from going

[50] Carleton Shugg, interview by John T. Mason, 16 Nov 1973, 7, USNI Oral History Collection, OA.

down and working in the Navy Department as a part of the Navy and I think some horrible thing would develop if you picked up the phone and called the supervisor [of shipbuilding] and said: hey, the contractor's coming over with something and its OK to approve it, when you're part of the contractor's organization. I don't think you can do that nowadays . . ., and consequently I don't think you could get a submarine designed in the time that we did in those days—and get it to sea. . . . I think it's just that the rules that are now placed on all of us make it impossible. The bean counters have inherited the earth.[51]

---

[51] Nardone interview, 11 Sep 1990, NHC Oral Histories.

Chapter 12

Conclusion: The End of an Era

Institutions have a life of their own. Like the people who create them, they come into being and mature, developing relationships along the way that sustain them. When we come of age after adolescence, the personal freedom is exhilarating; we accept no limits and recognize few obstacles. Only when society imposes its requirements and restraints do these circumstances change in, it is hoped, a constructive manner.

In much the same way the mature interwar command technology of 1940 was transformed by the war into the naval-industrial complex for submarines. During the next twenty years of hot and cold war below the surface of the world's ocean, this energetic, remarkably informal institution accepted and conquered a seemingly endless procession of complex challenges with youthful vigor and determination.

In 1940 the submarine command technology was ripe for transition. During the interwar years the submarine community had struggled with the technical impediments characteristic of submarine development and for years anguished over the best strategy for submarines. But as the engineers worked and the debates raged, the Navy Department and the Bureau of Ships made some wise decisions regarding the industrial base for submarines. As a result, BUSHIPS could respond quickly to the threat of war.

With money scarce and the Navy's commitment to the submarine occasionally tenuous, BUSHIPS decided to pour all of its assets into the naval shipyards. Consequently, while Portsmouth Navy Yard and its follow-yard, Mare Island Naval Yard, received the few available interwar contracts for new construction, the private sector went begging. The Lake Torpedo Boat Company went bankrupt in 1924. Electric Boat Division's diversity just barely ensured its survival until the construction dry spell ended with the contract for *Cuttlefish* (SS 171) in 1931. In spite of the distressing loss of private facilities and skilled labor, BUSHIPS turned Portsmouth into a state-of-the-art submarine design and construction yard. Combined with its traditional authority over ship design and construction, this accomplishment gave the bureau primacy in its relationship with private-sector submarine contractors. When construction resumed in earnest after the congressional authorizations of 1934 and 1938, BUSHIPS could effectively direct the command technology for submarines. By using the experience, capability, and potential of both Portsmouth and Electric Boat, the Navy Department could rapidly expand its industrial base for submarines from three to five yards before the end of 1940.

War provided the ultimate motivation. BUSHIPS moved fast to increase its industrial capacity by building on the expertise at Portsmouth, EB, and Mare Island. When the memory of America's brief involvement in the Great War and the interwar fate of the private sector made many companies reluctant to commit their own assets for additional plant capacity, the Navy resorted to defense plant contracts, committing federal funds to cover the cost of building new facilities. This decision drew contractors into the submarine business in sufficient numbers to satisfy the demands of war. Bringing Manitowoc Shipbuilding Company and Cramp Shipbuilding Company into the picture allowed the Navy to accommodate construction projects that far surpassed anything since 1918.

As submarines and antisubmarine warfare became more sophisticated, the participation of the scientific community became absolutely essential. The creation of the National Defense Research Committee in 1940 and the Office of Scientific Research and Development the following year provided the ideal opportunity for scientists to develop a productive relationship with those who built and served in American submarines. Many scholars have described the relationship between civilian science and the Navy as the debate between Rear Admiral Harold Bowen and Dr. Vannevar Bush over the control of scientific research writ large. Research for this book has shown that, in practice, the nature of the interaction between science and the Navy was much more complex, certainly more varied, and largely positive and constructive. Some within the Navy, notably the Naval Research Laboratory's director, Admiral Bowen, fought to keep applied scientific research under tight naval control. However, with President Roosevelt's approval, Vannevar Bush's Office of Scientific Research and Development largely preserved the independence of the individual scientist and research institution while successfully applying skills and facilities to war work. Consequently a strong professional relationship between equals emerged, tying many of the nation's best scientists to submarine research as full-time specialists or consultants.

The cancellation of many contracts and the general contraction in the industry immediately after the war made it impossible to keep all five prime submarine yards constantly occupied. Manitowoc and Cramp quickly withdrew from the scene, and the industrial base for submarine construction fell once again to the two primary yards of the interwar years, EB and Portsmouth, with Mare Island supporting the latter.

Although the industry expected a postwar contraction, the market for submarines did not take the severe downturn many predicted. The Cold

War and the discoveries of the Naval Technical Mission in Europe sustained the naval-industrial complex into the postwar era. Although contracts were fewer in number, the threat of a clash with the Soviet Union made exploiting and extending innovations in German U-boat technology absolutely vital. Captain Ignatius's "intricate and interesting vessel" now had to go faster, deeper, and more quietly for longer periods of time.

This revolution in undersea warfare changed the rules of the conflict and forced both the Americans and the Russians to come to terms with the significance of the German contribution. Once the Navy combined German innovation with American engineering and design in numerous Guppies and the *Tangs*, BUSHIPS looked to the naval shipyards to expand American construction capacity. Experience with the Victory Yard taught the postwar Navy the difficulty of reconstituting private facilities without the benefit of a clear national emergency. Bringing Cramp and Manitowoc back into the picture, or keeping shipyards built during the war inactive against the day when they would once again produce submarines to defend against America's enemies, proved politically and fiscally impractical. Americans wanted peace, economic stability, jobs, and a chance to prosper. Placing shipyards in mothballs for the future simply meant unemployment and lost local property taxes. Furthermore, the Navy would find reconstituting a skilled labor force a slow and difficult process.

Political pressure and economic need forced the Navy Department to sell facilities like the Victory Yard to companies able to provide jobs for local residents. Under these circumstances BUSHIPS resorted to using the naval shipyards as alternative prime contractors. These facilities provided the advantages of using naval resources as opposed to private resources. On the subcontractor level the Navy sought to preserve a mobilization base by permanently tying many major submarine vendors to the Navy's future emergency needs through the industrial reserve program.

As the OSRD/NDRC organization demobilized, the National Research Council of the National Academy of Sciences, the Office of Naval Research, and other Navy laboratories stepped into its place. At the invitation of those in the profession interested in preserving wartime relationship, the academy sponsored the creation of the Committee on Undersea Warfare; in so doing it confirmed and perpetuated the link between the submarine community and civilian science. When Admiral Bowen failed to capture authority over naval nuclear propulsion, ONR was recast as the best and only source of federal funds for basic research until the National Science Foundation received adequate appropriations after the Sputnik launch in 1957.

When the Navy laboratories participated with ONR and the CUW in Project Hartwell in 1950 to probe the dangers facing overseas transport in the event of war, they confirmed the appeal, continuity, and utility of their wartime relationship. From this association came advances in nuclear propulsion, quieting, active and passive sonar, navigation, hydrodynamics, and materials, and a deeper understanding of undersea sound transmission and the usefulness of experimental submarines for future developments.

The experimental submarine suggested by CUW in 1948 eventually took shape with *Albacore*. The many experiments performed with this vessel made possible the swiftness of *Skipjack* and her progeny as well as the stealthy submarines of the *Thresher* class. *Albacore* also served as a test platform for basic ideas in speed, control, and hydrodynamics suggested and pursued by all three components of the naval-industrial complex.

Albacore also provided truly unique and important opportunities. For twenty-five years during the interwar period the submarine community made only slow and painful progress in engineering and design with the S-class. The bureaus and industry frequently found themselves at odds about solutions to the many problems exhibited by these fifty submarines. The obligations of the S-class vessels to an operating fleet made finding answers to their many problems much more awkward and difficult. The concerns voiced by Captain Eugene Wilkinson in 1959 about the potentially expensive consequences of mixing development with production during the *Thresher* program sprang from a preference for truly confident and gradual steps forward based on the careful testing characteristic of both the nuclear program and the preliminary experiments performed with the AGSS 569.

With *Albacore* the naval-industrial complex tested countless changes and variations in submarine design and ship-construction practice with great success and at minimal cost. Indeed in 1956 the scientists and engineers of Project Nobska insisted that employing an experimental ship to determine the characteristics of the next two or three generations of submarines was a fundamentally sound practice; it would exhibit technical and fiscal responsibility. *Albacore* provided sufficient historical precedent for any future project of the same type. Today, however, introducing innovation during production, with its attendant technical difficulties and increased costs, is common practice.

Although *Albacore* certainly influenced the outward characteristics of all future American submarines, nuclear power revolutionized propulsion and ended the age of the submersible. After *Nautilus* American submarines had virtually unlimited submerged endurance and the ability to conduct extended patrols in a hostile environment. Admiral Hyman Rickover and his team can take credit for the practical success of the nuclear program, but neither the first nuclear-submarine design nor the idea to apply nuclear power to a submarine originated with the controversial head of BUSHIPS Code 1500. Credit for these ideas must go to Philip Abelson and Ross Gunn of NRL. Gunn perceived the applications of nuclear power as early as 1939, and both he and Abelson worked at NRL as part of Admiral Bowen's early effort to develop this type of energy as the primary mission of ONR.

The advent of nuclear power for ship propulsion had a profound effect on every aspect of the naval-industrial complex. Since the technology was completely new, Rickover had to provide the EB staff with a broad education in physics, nuclear engineering, and steam systems suited for submarine propulsion. The admiral also knew that the technology would, in its own way, teach both the Navy and EB. *Nautilus* forced the naval-industrial complex to learn more about quieting, highly toxic liquid metals, vibration as a consequence of sustained high speed, and the necessity of carefully managing construction materials. Frank Horan and his colleagues at EB learned the most fundamental lessons of all; even the most minor oversight or failure to respond to the demands of the technology could cost the life of a crew. The lessons thus ran from the most complex to those that seemed ordinary and routine.

At Project Nobska, Admiral Arleigh Burke called together representatives from the Navy, industry, and science to assess the effect of the nuclear-powered submarine on American national security. As with Project Hartwell six years earlier, this meeting demonstrated the professional intimacy characteristic of the naval-industrial complex between 1940 and 1961. Representatives from forty-one different commands, laboratories, universities, companies, and research institutions attended and exhibited the cooperation and motivation characteristic of World War II, in which many had participated.

Links forged during that conflict from a sense of duty, professionalism, patriotism, ambition, profit, and necessity still bound both institutions and individuals. Marvin Lasky cherished a mutual trust between scientists and naval officers at the David Taylor Model Basin, which he felt contributed significantly to a productive work environment. Allyn Vine built oceanographic instruments and taught submariners the basics of oceanography, all the while expressing a fascination with the way his students applied their lessons. Andrew McKee used his contacts within the Navy to help Frank Horan get the *Nautilus* project properly staffed with highly specialized engineers.

At Nobska this same kind of interaction between industry, science, and the Navy produced some of the most important decisions in the history of the American submarine program. Edward Teller assured those working on ballistic missiles that a nuclear warhead small enough to suit the Polaris A–1 was possible. Other committee members recommended intensive work on sonar; quieter, deeper-diving submarines; use of experimental and preprototypes in design and development; and commitment to long-range research.

This last suggestion proved unacceptable to Code 1500. Preoccupied with developing the *Skipjack* reactor and making provisions for producing in quantity, Admiral Rickover found all of the possible alternatives to pressurized water unsuitable for naval applications. Faith in scientific progress along a broad front motivated those participating in Nobska to believe in the future viability of some nuclear alternatives, and some scientists privately wondered if the BUSHIPS naval-reactors staff could break out of old, comfortable frames of reference. Out of this concern came the Nobska suggestion, made by Harvey Brooks of Harvard University's School of Engineering and Applied Physics, that a new naval activity should take responsibility for long-range naval nuclear research. Admiral Rickover's political influence and his strength within the Navy and Atomic Energy Commission, however, ensured that the Nobska recommendations on nuclear power would have little effect. Rarely in the history of the young naval-industrial complex had a BUSHIPS code so completely rejected informed scientific advice. Thus although the Navy's pressurized water reactors certainly became safer, more efficient, and increasingly sophisticated, they also grew much larger and more expensive in a perpetual quest for the extra power and knots needed to drive American submarines in the 1960s.

The postwar naval-industrial complex reached its zenith with the design and construction of the guided- and ballistic-missile submarines. As with other submarine developments the bureaus drew on both World War II German innovation and American progress in the field. Derived from the German V–1, Loon and Regulus I and II benefited from the wartime work conducted at the Naval Air Material Center on drone targets, television guidance, and pilotless aircraft. Only the greater compatibility of the Polaris ballistic system with submarines, made possible by submerged launch, placed guided missiles on hold. This limbo lasted for over twenty years, until the Tomahawk became a potent weapon for the *Los Angeles*-class attack submarine in the 1980s.

Each component of the naval-industrial complex contributed a key element to making the system a reality and gave substance to Carleton Shugg's assertion that "we each knew the other." Discussions at Nobska set the Navy on the road to a light nuclear warhead. BUSHIPS and EB provided the nuclear submarine to carry the weapon on silent, extended patrols. The Massachusetts Institute of Technology provided the guidance system, and private industry found the recipe for a more powerful solid rocket propellant. Polaris demonstrated the performance of the naval-industrial complex at its best.

In its first twenty-one years the naval-industrial complex built on its interwar heritage and developed a unique character peculiar to its time. It grew organically, responding to the demands of World War II and the Cold War, and it was shaped by the Navy's aims, the committed but fiercely independent scientific community, and the able and ambitious industrial establishment.

Close cooperation among the members of the naval-industrial complex still takes place, but today the fundamental nature of the relationship is different. One legacy of World War II was a foundation of familiarity and established ties that produced a distinctive way of doing things and infused the naval-industrial complex with the urgency of mobilization. In many cases personal acquaintances and lasting friendships enhanced the situation. Only in this climate could Henry Nardone and his party of EB engineers work within BUSHIPS, handing out instructions to both the contract people at EB and the Navy's supervisor of shipbuilding.

These relationships, developing in an evolutionary manner, sustained the naval-industrial complex from World War II through the Polaris project, but started to wither in the early 1960s. Different perspectives on the relationship between the Navy, industry, and science began to change the naval-industrial complex in a fundamental way. Rickover's growing influence over every aspect of submarine design and construction and the systems analysis brought to the Department of Defense by Secretary Robert McNamara played a significant role in precipitating these changes. New views on both the best management techniques and the most efficient methods for setting priorities certainly stemmed from good intentions, including the desire to save the nation unnecessary expenditures and enhance technical excellence and individual responsibility. But the new systems of management and political and personal imperatives imposed on the naval-industrial complex gradually displaced the creative professional intimacy and the sense of immediacy that, for twenty-one years, drove and nourished the activities of the Navy, industry, and science. Clearly by 1961 the postwar era had ended for the naval-industrial complex and a new one was about to begin.

Abbreviations

AEC	Atomic Energy Commission
AGSS	auxiliary research submarine
ANP	aircraft nuclear propulsion
ASW	antisubmarine warfare
ATF	fleet ocean tug
Bd I/S	Board of Inspection and Survey
bhp	brake horsepower
BUAER	Bureau of Aeronautics
BUC&R	Bureau of Construction and Repair
BUENG	Bureau of Engineering
BUORD	Bureau of Ordnance
BUSANDA	Bureau of Supplies and Accounts
BUSHIPS	Bureau of Ships
BT	bathythermograph
CENCORR	Central Correspondence
COMINCH/CNO	Commander in Chief, U.S. Fleet/ Chief of Naval Operations
COMSUBDIV	Commander Submarine Division
COMSUBLANT	Commander Submarine Force, Atlantic Fleet
COMSUBRON	Commander Submarine Force, Pacific Fleet
COMSUBRON	Commander Submarine Squadron
CRES	corrosion resistant steel
CUDWR	Columbia University Division of War Research
CUW	Committee on Undersea Warfare
DTIC	Defense Technical Information Center
DTMB	David Taylor Model Basin
DTRC	David Taylor Research Center
EB	Electric Boat Company; Electric Boat Division, General Dynamics Corporation
EDO	engineering duty officer
EES	Engineering Experiment Station
FTV	flight test vehicle

GE	General Electric Company
GENCORR	General Correspondence
GHG	Gruppenhorchgerät
GM	General Motors Corporation
HOR	Hooven, Owens, Rentschler Company
HTS	high tensile steel
INSORD	Inspector of Ordnance
JAG	Judge Advocate General
JATO	jet-assisted take-off
KAPL	Knolls Atomic Power Laboratory
LOFAR	Low Frequency Analyzing and Recording
LUT	Lage unabhängiger Torpedo (position independent torpedo)
MAN	Maschinenfabrik Augsburg-Nürnberg
MAO	machinery apparatus operation
MIT	Massachusetts Institute of Technology
MSC	Manitowac Shipbuilding Company
NACA	National Advisory Committee on Aeronautics
NAMC	Naval Air Material Center
NAMTC	Naval Air Missile Test Center
NA	National Archives
NAS	National Academy of Sciences
NAVTECHMISEU	Naval Technical Mission in Europe
NDRC	National Defense Research Committee
NEL	National Electronics Laboratory
Nelseco	New London Ship and Engine Company
NHC	Naval Historical Center
NOTS	Naval Ordnance Test Site
NRL	Naval Research Laboratory
NSBA	Naval Studies Board Archive, National Academy of Sciences
NSF	National Science Foundation
NSRB	National Security Resources Board
OA	Operational Archives, Naval Historical Center
OEG	Operations Evaluation Group
ONR	Office of Naval Research

OPDEVFOR	Operational Development Force
OPM	Office of Procurement and Materials
OPNAV	Office of the Chief of Naval Operations
ORI	Office of Research and Inventions
OSRD	Office of Scientific Research and Development
OWMR	Office of War Mobilization and Reconversion
PAD	Plant Apparatus Department
PERT	Program-Evaluation-Research Task
ppsi	pressure per square inch
RFC	Reconstruction Finance Corporation
RG	Record Group
SBT	submarine bathythermograph
SECDEF	Secretary of Defense
SECNAV	Secretary of the Navy
SIR	submarine intermediate reactor
SIT	Stevens Institute of Technology
SOC	Submarine Officers Conference
SOFAR	Sound Fixing and Ranging
SOSUS	Sound Surveillance System
SPO	Special Projects Office
SSBN	nuclear-powered fleet ballistic-missile submarine
SSG	guided-missile submarine
SSGN	nuclear-powered guided-missile submarine
SSN	nuclear-powered attack submarine
SSK	hunter-killer submarine
SSO	Submarine Supply Office
SSRN	nuclear-powered radar picket submarine
STG	Steering Task Group
STR	submarine thermal reactor
SUBDEVGRU	Submarine Development Group
SUPSHIPS	Supervisor of Shipbuilding
UCDWR	University of California, Division of War Research
USAG	Underwater Sound Advisory Group
USNI	United States Naval Institute
USNUSL	U.S. Navy Underwater Sound Laboratory
WHOI	Woods Hole Oceanographic Institution
WNRC	Washington National Records Center
WPB	War Production Board

Bibliography

Although the insights and information offered in this history depend primarily on a wide variety of neglected archival sources, considerable stimulation and knowledge came from William McNeill's *Pursuit of Power* and other studies in the corpus of classic and current secondary literature in the field. Professor McNeill's concept of command technology provided both a central idea and familiar terminology upon which to build. Work by Dean C. Allard and Benjamin Franklin Cooling on the American iron and steel industry supplied much-needed context and background to the American naval-industrial relationship. Their analyses of the various conflicts between the Navy, industry, and Congress at the turn of the century provide an excellent perspective on the educational role such confrontations can play in the development of a productive relationship.[1]

While working on *Building American Submarines, 1914–1940* and *Forged in War,* the two books I have written on the history of U.S. submarine construction, I discovered the truth of historian I. B. Holley's assertion that no technology matures completely without a strategic doctrine to provide foundation and motivation. The protracted interwar debate over submarine strategy and the effective design adopted and built as a result demonstrate the validity of his thesis, first offered almost forty years ago in *Ideas and Weapons,* now a modern classic. Initially restrained by the political legacy of unrestricted U-boat warfare, the fleet submarine certainly demonstrated after Pearl Harbor the productivity of the freewheeling *guerre de course* that gave it form. In the same way, the advent of the Cold War on the world's ocean, as well as the ensuing heated confrontations in Berlin and Korea, provided both the motivation and strategic formulas that sustained undersea warfare research into the postwar era. This research effort was soon rewarded with *Albacore*'s speed, *Nautilus*'s prolonged submergence capability, and the combination of these characteristics in *Skipjack.*

A desire to penetrate the complexity and diversity of the relationship between the Navy, science, and industry has prompted many other historians to improve our understanding of the naval-industrial complex by adding

---

[1] For another example of such an analysis, see Gary E. Weir, "The Navy, Industry, and Conflicting Expectations: Fried. Krupp of Essen and the Electric Boat Company," in William R. Roberts and Jack Sweetman, eds., *New Interpretations in Naval History: Selected Papers from the Ninth Naval History Symposium* (Annapolis: Naval Institute Press, 1991), 350–68

their particular piece to the puzzle. John Alden's *Fleet Submarine in the U.S. Navy* proved essential for an understanding of the engineering and design concepts used during and after World War II. *Forged in War* also benefited from the insights provided by Paul Koistinen's *The Military Industrial Complex: A Historical Perspective* and the fine collection of essays entitled *War, Business, and American Society*, edited by Benjamin Franklin Cooling.

In addition to these works, our current perception of the nature of the naval-industrial relationship from the beginning of mobilization in 1940 through nuclear power also depends in large part upon the insights and research of historians Robert Connery, James W. Fesler, Francis Duncan, and Richard Hewlett. On the scientific side, James Phinney Baxter's *Scientists Against Time* was an essential guide to the undersea warfare effort against the Axis, as was Willem Hackmann's *Seek and Strike*. The latter focuses on the Royal Navy but its careful treatment of developments in the United States from the Great War through the nuclear era makes it important to any study of the American naval-industrial complex.

In recent years some of the best scholarship in the history of technology, increasingly the product of cooperation between history and the social sciences, has reaffirmed the need to master the bewildering variety of influences contributing to innovation and the formation of technical systems and processes. Elting Morison certainly led the way in this effort and contributed to the composition of the present study with *Men, Machines, and Modern Times*. Although the terminology of historians and social scientists like Thomas P. Hughes, Donald MacKenzie, and John Law may occasionally prove awkward, historians must applaud the validity of the multicausal approach they use in studying the "social construction" of innovation, invention, systems, and relationships.

Works like Hughes's *Networks of Power*, MacKenzie's *Inventing Accuracy*, and essays by John Law on the Portuguese maritime expansion of five centuries ago also provide essential intellectual support for another viewpoint central to this study. To accomplish their purpose and make the naval-industrial-scientific relationship work, engineers like the Navy's Captain Harry Jackson and Electric Boat's Henry Nardone, as well as scientists like Allyn Vine of Woods Hole, applied their professional skills not only to the ocean and submarines but also, in another sense, to admirals, industrial leaders, and colleagues. Sociologists Law and MacKenzie have christened this process "heterogeneous engineering," a concept essential to an effective analysis of the human relationships that gave coherence to the naval-industrial complex for submarines between 1940 and 1961.

Primary Sources

Archival and Special Collections

Hagley Museum Archives, Wilmington, DE.
  Elmer Sperry Papers.
  Records of E. I. du Pont de Nemours & Company.
  Sperry Company Records.

Historisches Museum, MAN AG, Augsburg, Germany.
  von Lassberg, Dietrich Freiherr. *Augsburger M.A.N. Dieselmotoren.*

Library of Congress, Manuscript Division, Washington, DC.
  Papers of Charles A. Lockwood.

National Archives and Records Administration, Washington, DC.
  RG 19:   Bureau of Construction and Repair, Repair and Design Data for
              U.S. Naval Vessels, 1914–27.
              Bureau of Construction and Repair Research Data, 1913–37.
              General Correspondence of the Bureau of Construction and Repair,
              1925–40.
              Confidential Correspondence Regarding Research and Design of
              Radio and other Communications Apparatus (BUENG).

  RG 38:   Board of Inspection and Survey (Reports of the Material Inspection
              of Naval Vessels).

  RG 45:   General Board Miscellaneous Subject Files, 1919–50.
              General Board Studies, 1949–50.
              General Board Subject Files, 1900–47.

  RG 80:   Assistant Secretary of the Navy Alpha File.
              Compensation Board.
              General Correspondence of the Secretary of the Navy, 1926–40 and
              1940–42.
              Records of the Secretary of the Navy James Forrestal, 1940–47.
              Secretary of the Navy–Chief of Naval Operations Correspondence,
              1940–41.
              Secretary of the Navy Confidential Correspondence, 1927–39.

  RG 298: Office of Naval Research–General Correspondence of the Coordi-
              nator of Research and Development.

National Archives, Washington National Records Center, Suitland, MD.
  RG 19:   Bureau of Engineering General Correspondence, 1910–40.
              Bureau of Ships Confidential Research and Development Library
              Records.

Bureau of Ships General Correspondence, 1940–45.

Bureau of Ships Secret and Confidential Central Correspondence, 1945–62.

Bureau of Ships Unclassified Central Correspondence, 1946–50.

Naval Ocean Systems Center Library, San Diego, CA.

"Completion Report Made to the Chief of the Bureau of Ships Covering the Operations of the University of California Division of War Research at the U.S. Navy Electronics Laboratory, San Diego, CA."

Naval Studies Board Archive, National Academy of Sciences, Washington, DC.

"Basic Problems of Underwater Acoustics Research." Report of the Panel on Underwater Acoustics/Committee on Undersea Warfare, Lyman Spitzer, Jr., Chairman. 1 September 1948.

Harnwell, Gaylord. "A Research Facility for Undersea Warfare." 17 May 1949.

Herrick, John. *Subsurface Warfare: The History of Division 6, National Defense Research Committee.*

Hunt, Frederick V. "New Concepts for Acoustic Detection at Very Long Ranges." 15–16 May 1950.

Hunt, Lee (Committee on Undersea Warfare), to Dr. Paul G. Neumann. 18 September 1961.

Interim Report of the Panel on the Hydrodynamics of Submerged Bodies, Committee on Undersea Warfare. 7 November 1949; 20 October 1949 Meeting, The Panel on the Hydrodynamics of Submerged Bodies, Committee on Undersea Warfare. 20 October 1949.

Iselin, Columbus O'D. "The Present Status of Long-Range Listening." 15 June 1948.

———. "Project Nobska: A Preliminary Assessment." May 1956.

Meeting of the Committee on the Hydrodynamics of Submerged Bodies, Committee on Undersea Warfare. 10 December 1948.

Mela, Richard L., to C. Richard Soderberg, MIT. 4 December 1961.

Memo, Special Panel on Low Frequency Sonar, to the Committee on Undersea Warfare. 20 October 1950.

Minutes of the Meeting of the Panel on Hydrodynamics of Submerged Bodies, Committee on Undersea Warfare. 6 March 1952.

Probus, James H. "History and Activities of the Committee on Undersea Warfare, 1946–1956." September 1955.

———. "A Survey of the Naval Reactor Program." 28 April 1961.

Pryor, CAPT William L. "Detection of Submarines From the Surface and Below." 9–10 May 1951.

"Report of the Subcommittee on the Submarine Problem" (Colpitts Report).

Soderberg, C. Richard, to James Probus. 19 February 1960.

"Vice Admiral Rickover's Presentation of 24 March 1960 on Naval Reactors." #85–R–532. 24 March 1960.

"A Word about the National Academy of Sciences and the Origin of Project Nobska." 29 May 1956.

Navy Department Library, Naval Historical Center, Washington, DC.

Administrative History: Office of Research and Inventions, July 31–December 1945.

Office of the CNO. "U.S. Naval Technical Mission to Europe." No. 25, *United States Naval Administration in World War II.*

Navy Laboratories Archives, David Taylor Research Center, Carderock, MD.

EMB/DTMB 1899–1967 Personnel Subject Files.

Marvin Lasky Papers.

Naval Weapons Center Oral History Collection.

Navy Laboratories Biography Collection.

Oral Histories

Cummins, William E. Interview by David K. Allison, 2 and 12 August and 14 October 1982.

Kelly, CAPT Joseph P., USN (Ret.). "From Tripods to SOSUS: Evolution of Sound Surveillance Requirements, Concepts, and Technology, 1917–1952," Appendix A, interview by David K. Allison.

Landweber, Louis. Interview by David K. Allison. 22 January 1986.

Lasky, Marvin. Interview by David K. Allison. N.d.

Records of Assistant Secretary of the Navy James H. Probus.

Records of the Engineering Experiment Station, 1903–63, and Marine Engineering Laboratory, 1963–67.

Operational Archives, Naval Historical Center, Washington, DC.

Bemis, Samuel Flagg. "Submarine Warfare in the Strategy of American Defense and Diplomacy, 1915–1945." Unpublished MSS.

Biographical Files of Naval Officers.

Documents on the Navy's Role in the Development of Atomic Energy, 1939–70.

Defense Technical Information Center Reports.

Hearings of the General Board of the Navy (Microfilm).

Naval Technical Mission in Europe.

Oral Histories *(All are NHC interviews unless otherwise indicated.)*

Arnold, CAPT Henry. Interview with author. 27 October 1987.

Bethea, CAPT James. Interview with author. 4 March 1991.

Hersey, John Brackett. Interview with author. 4, 11, and 23 October 1991.

Horan, Frank. Interview with author. 13 September 1988 and 26 September 1989.

Jackson, Harry. Interview with author. 24 September 1989.

Kern, CAPT Donald. Interview with author. 12 September 1990.

Land, Emory. Interview by John T. Mason, Jr. 30 January 1963. Columbia University Oral History Project, New York, NY.

Leonard, John S. Interview with author. 13 September 1988 and 25 September 1989.

Leonard, John V. Interview with author. 13 September 1990.

Moore, RADM Robert L. Interview with author. 17 March 1988.

Mumma, RADM Albert G. Interviews by Paul Stillwell. 3 October 1986 and 2 April 1987. U.S. Naval Institute Oral History Collection, Annapolis, MD.

Mumma, RADM Albert G. Interview with author. 7 March 1988.

Nardone, Henry. Interview with author. 13 September 1988 and 11 September 1990.

Raborn, VADM William F., USN (Ret.). Interview by John T. Mason. 15 September 1972. U.S. Naval Institute Oral History Collection, Annapolis, MD.

Roseborough, CAPT William M. Interview with author. 5 October 1988.

Schevill, William. Interview with author. 16 October 1991.

Shugg, Carleton. Interview by John T. Mason. 16 November 1973. U.S. Naval Institute Oral History Collection, Annapolis, MD.

Smith, CAPT Ralph. Interview with author by correspondence. 10 November 1987.

Vine, Allyn. Interview with author. 27 April and 23 September 1989.

Worzel, J. Lamar. Interview with author. 22 August 1990.

Post 1 January 1946 Command File.

Records of the Immediate Office of the Chief of Naval Operations.

Strategic Planning Division Records.

Submarines–Undersea Warfare Division Records.

World War II Command File.

Submarine Force Library and Museum, Groton, CT.

Electric Boat Collection (Individual Submarine Historical Files).

Technical Library and Records Vault, Electric Boat Division, General Dynamics Corporation, Groton, CT.

American Enterprise Association. "Analysis of H.R. 9246, to Provide for the Renegotiation of Contracts and for Other Purposes," 10 August 1950. Box 003.

EB Interoffice Memo, O. P. Robinson to J. J. Murphy. 18 November 1948. Box 003, Contracts file.

"History of the Electric Boat Company." Unpublished MSS.

Orr to Spear, 10 November 1942. Box (marked) 1328, 1328–1, 1328–2.

Spear, L. Y. (President of EB). "Statement on Renegotiation." Made to the House Committee on Naval Affairs, 28 June 1943. Box (marked) 1328–2, 1328–21.

Spear to Bridges. 21 October 1943. Box (marked) 1328(9), 1328(10), 1328(11), 1000(V–1).

U.S. Navy Strategic Special Projects Office Technical Library/Archives, Arlington, VA.

"Brief History of Navy Solid Propellant Fuel Experience." [1960?].

Fuhrman, R. A. "Fleet Ballistic Missile System: Polaris to Trident." AIAA von Kármán Lecture. 1978.

"Incomplete History of SP (Special Projects)." N.d.

Murray, Stuart S. "An Historical Review of the Polaris Fleet Ballistic Missile Program (U)." RPJ–TR–0162–001, Final Report. Jan 1977.

Record of Visit to Lockheed Missile Systems Division, Sunnyvale, and Aerojet General Corporation, Sacramento, California, 14–18 July 1958. NRL TM–27 c.1.

Records of the Special Projects Office Steering Task Group.

Technical Division, Special Projects Office. "Study of Navy-Contractor Relationships." 17 March 1958.

Woods Hole Oceanographic Institution, Woods Hole, MA.

McLean Laboratory, Woods Hole Oceanographic Institution Data Library and Archives.

"Compilations of Reports, etc., for SSs in WW II."

Iselin, Columbus O'D. "WHOI History During the War Years, 1941–1950." [1960?].

McCurdy, R. J. "Report on Discussions With Captain Baker and Commander Todd Concerning Some Oceanographic Aspects of Anti-Submarine Warfare, August 1, 1942."

"Use of Submarine Bathythermograph Observations as an Aid in Diving Operations." Joint publication of WHOI, BUSHIPS, and NDRC. March 1944. Courtesy of Allyn Vine.

"USS *Herring* (SS 233), 11–17 June 1943." Book 2, Submarine Patrol Reports, Hawkbill to Whale, 1942–1944.

WHOI Yearly Reports for the Years 1943–1945.

Smith Laboratory, Woods Hole Oceanographic Institution Records Vault.

Knudson, V. O., R. S. Alford, and J. W. Emling. "Survey of Underwater Sound—Report No. 3: Ambient Noise." NDRC (Office of Scientific Research and Development) Division 6, Section 6.1. 26 September 1944.

"Survey of Underwater Sound, Report No. 2: Sounds From Submarines." NDRC Division 6, Section 6.1. 31 December 1943.

Published Primary Sources

Annual Report of the Navy Department. Washington: 1940–47.

Bowen, Harold G. *Ships, Machinery, and Mossbacks.* Princeton, NJ: Princeton University Press, 1954.

Lockwood, Charles A. *Down to the Sea in Subs.* New York: W. W. Norton & Co., 1967.

Secondary Sources

Books

Alden, John D. *The Fleet Submarine in the U.S. Navy: A Design and Construction History.* Annapolis: Naval Institute Press, 1979.

Allen, E. P. *Policies Governing Private Financing of Emergency Facilities, May 1940 to June 1942.* Special Study Number 12. Washington: U.S. Civilian Production Administration, 1946.

Allison, David K. "U.S. Navy Research and Development Since World War II." In *Military Enterprise and Technological Change,* edited by Merritt Roe Smith, 289–328. Cambridge, MA: MIT Press, 1985.

Baruch, Bernard M., and John M. Hancock. *War and Postwar Adjustment Policies.* Washington: American Council on Public Affairs, 1944.

Baxter, James Phinney, III. *Scientists Against Time.* Cambridge, MA: MIT Press, 1968.

Bijker, Wiebe E., et. al. *The Social Construction of Technological Systems: New Directions in the Sociology and History of Technology.* Cambridge, MA: MIT Press, 1987.

Brown, David T. *A History of the Sulzer Low-Speed Marine Diesel Engine.* Winterthur, Switzerland: Sulzer Brothers, 1984.

Carey, Omar L., ed. *The Military Industrial Complex and U.S. Foreign Policy.* Pullman, WA: Washington State University Press, 1969.

Cocker, M. P. *Observer's Directory of Royal Naval Submarines.* Annapolis: Naval Institute Press, 1982.

Connery, Robert H. *The Navy and the Industrial Mobilization in World War II.* Princeton, NJ: Princeton University Press, 1951.

Cooling, Benjamin Franklin. *Gray Steel and Blue Water Navy.* Hamden, CT: Archon Books, 1979.

Cooling, Benjamin Franklin, ed. *War, Business, and American Society.* Port Washington, NY: Kennikat Press, 1977.

Davis, George T. *A Navy Second to None.* New York: Harcourt, Brace, and Co., 1940.

Davis, Vincent. *The Politics of Innovation: Patterns in Navy Cases.* Denver: University of Denver Press, 1967.

Duncan, Francis. *Rickover and the Nuclear Navy: The Discipline of Technology.* Annapolis: Naval Institute Press, 1990.

Fesler, James W. *Industrial Mobilization for War: History of the War Production Board and Predecessor Agencies.* Washington: Civilian Production Administration, 1947.

Friedman, Norman. *Submarine Design and Development*. Annapolis: Naval Institute Press, 1984.

Furer, Julius Augustus. *Administration of the Navy Department in World War II*. Washington: GPO, 1959.

Gebhard, Louis A. *Evolution of Radio-Electronics and Contributions of the Naval Research Laboratory*. Washington: Naval Research Laboratory, 1979.

General Dynamics Corporation. *Dynamic America: A History of the General Dynamics Corporation and Its Predecessor Companies*. New York: Doubleday and Co., 1960.

Gröner, Erich. *Die Deutschen Kriegschiffe, 1815–1945*. Munich: J. F. Lehmanns Verlag, 1966.

Hackmann, Willem. *Seek and Strike: Sonar, Anti-Submarine Warfare and the Royal Navy, 1914–54*. London: HMSO, 1984.

Harrington, Roy L., ed. *Marine Engineering*. New York: Society of Naval Architects and Marine Engineers, 1971.

Henry, David. "British Submarine Policy, 1918–1939." In *Technical Change and British Naval Policy, 1860–1939*, edited by Bryan Ranft, 80–107. London: Hodder and Stoughton, 1977.

Hewlett, Richard G., and Oscar Anderson, Jr. *The New World, 1939–1946*. University Park: Pennsylvania State University Press, 1962.

Hewlett, Richard G., and Francis Duncan. *Atomic Shield, 1947–1952*. University Park: Pennsylvania State University Press, 1969.

———. *Nuclear Navy, 1946–1962*. Chicago: University of Chicago Press, 1974.

Holley, I. B., Jr. *Buying Aircraft: Materiel Procurement for the Army Air Forces*. Washington: Office of the Chief of Military History, 1964.

———. *Ideas and Weapons*. Washington: Office of Air Force History, 1983.

Hoover, Robert A. *Arms Control: The Interwar Naval Limitation Agreements*. Denver: Graduate School of International Studies, 1980.

Hughes, Thomas P. *Networks of Power*. Baltimore: Johns Hopkins University Press, 1983.

Huntington, Samuel P. "The Defense Establishment: Vested Interests and the Public Interest." In *The Military Industrial Complex and U.S. Foreign Policy*, edited by Omer L. Carey, 562–84. Pullman, WA: Washington State University Press, 1969.

Jolie, E. W. *A Brief History of U.S. Navy Torpedo Development*. Newport, RI: Naval Underwater Systems Center, 1978.

Jones, Vincent C. *Manhattan: The Army and the Atomic Bomb*. Washington: Center of Military History, 1985.

King, Randolph, ed. *Naval Engineering and American Seapower*. Baltimore: Nautical & Aviation Publishing Co. of America, 1989.

Koistinen, Paul. *The Military-Industrial Complex: A Historical Perspective*. New York: Praeger, 1980.

Kollmorgen Corporation. *The Submarine Periscope, 1916–1966*. Northhampton, MA: Kollmorgen Corp., 1966.

Law, John. "Technology and Heterogeneous Engineering: The Case of Portuguese Expansion." In *The Social Construction of Technological Systems: New Directions in the Sociology and History of Technology*, edited by Wiebe E. Bijker, Thomas P. Hughes, and Trevor J. Pinch. Cambridge, MA: MIT Press, 1987.

Leutze, James. *A Different Kind of Victory: A Biography of Admiral Thomas C. Hart*. Annapolis: Naval Institute Press, 1981.

Lipscomb, F. W. *The British Submarine*. Greenwich, CT: Conway Maritime Press, 1975.

Lott, Arnold S. *A Long Line of Ships: Mare Island's Century of Naval Activity in California*. Annapolis: Naval Institute Press, 1954.

MacKenzie, Donald. *Inventing Accuracy: A Historical Sociology of Nuclear Missile Guidance*. Cambridge, MA: MIT Press, 1990.

McNeill, William H. *The Pursuit of Power*. Chicago: University of Chicago Press, 1982.

Manchester, William. *The Arms of Krupp*. Boston: Little, Brown and Company, 1968.

Miles, Wyndham D. "The Polaris." In *The History of Rocket Technology*, edited by Eugene M. Emme, 162–75. Detroit: Wayne State University Press, 1964.

Morison, Elting E. *Men, Machines, and Modern Times*. Cambridge, MA: MIT Press, 1966.

Naval History Division. *Dictionary of American Naval Fighting Ships*. 8 vols. Washington: GPO, 1959–1992.

Nelson, William T. *Fresh Water Submarines: The Manitowoc Story*. Manitowoc, WI: Hoeffner Printing, 1986.

O'Connor, Raymond G. *Perilous Equilibrium: The United States and the London Naval Conference of 1930*. Lawrence: University of Kansas Press, 1962.

Palmer, Michael A. *Origins of the Maritime Strategy: American Naval Strategy in the First Postwar Decade*. Washington: Naval Historical Center, 1988.

Polmar, Norman. *The American Submarine*. Annapolis: Nautical & Aviation Publishing Co. of America, 1981.

Polmar, Norman, and Thomas B. Allen. *Rickover: Controversy and Genius*. New York: Simon and Schuster, 1984.

Raitt, Helen, and Beatrice Moulton. *Scripps Institution of Oceanography: First Fifty Years.* La Jolla, CA: Ward Ritchie Press, 1967.

Ranft, Bryan, ed. *Technical Change and British Naval Policy, 1860–1939.* London: Hodder and Stoughton, 1977.

Rössler, E. *Geschichte des deutschen Ubootbaus.* Munich: J. F. Lehmanns Verlag, 1975.

Sapolsky, Harvey M. "The Origins of the Office of Naval Research." In *Naval History: The Sixth Symposium of the U.S. Naval Academy,* edited by Daniel M. Masterson, 214–21. Wilmington, DE: Scholarly Resources, 1987.

———. *The Polaris System Development.* Cambridge, MA: Harvard University Press, 1972.

———. *Science and the Navy: The History of the Office of Naval Research.* Princeton, NJ: Princeton University Press, 1990.

Schlee, Susan. *On the Edge of an Unfamiliar World.* Boston: E. P. Dutton, 1973.

Sitterson, J. Carlyle. *Development of the Reconversion Policies of the War Production Board, April 1943 to January 1945.* Washington: Civilian Production Administration, 1945.

Stewart, Irvin. *Organizing Scientific Research for War: The Administrative History of the Office for Scientific Research and Development.* Boston: Little, Brown and Co., 1948

Sumida, Jon Tetsuro. *In Defense of Naval Supremacy, Finance, Technology, and British Naval Policy, 1889–1914.* Boston: Unwin Hyman, 1989.

Tazewell, William L. *Newport News Shipbuilding: The First Century.* Newport News, VA: Newport News Shipbuilding and Dry Dock Company, 1986.

Tidman, Keith R. *The Operations Evaluation Group.* Annapolis: Naval Institute Press, 1984.

Trimble, William. *Wings for the Navy: A History of the Naval Aircraft Factory.* Annapolis: Naval Institute Press, 1991.

Walker, Bruce H. *Periscopes, People, and Progress.* North Adams, MA: Excelsior Printing, 1984.

Wechsler, Laskar. "Medium and High-Speed Diesel Engines." In *Marine Engineering,* edited by Roy L. Harrington, 246–79. New York: SNAME, 1971.

Weir, Gary E. *Building American Submarines, 1914–1940.* Washington: Naval Historical Center, 1991.

———. *Building the Kaiser's Navy: The Imperial Naval Office and German Industry in the Tirpitz Era, 1890–1919.* Annapolis: Naval Institute Press, 1992.

Whitehurst, Clinton H., Jr. *The U.S. Shipbuilding Industry: Past, Present, and Future.* Annapolis: Naval Institute Press, 1986.

Winslow, Robert E., III. *Portsmouth-Built: Submarines of the Portsmouth Naval Shipyard.* Portsmouth, NH: Portsmouth Marine Society, 1985.

Yurso, Joseph F. "Decline of the Seventies." In *Naval Engineering and American Seapower*, edited by Randolph W. King, 334–36. Baltimore: Nautical & Aviation Publishing Co. of America, 1989.

Articles

Alden, John D. "Development of the High-Speed Diesel Engine for United States Submarines." *Naval Engineers Journal* 91 (August 1979): 43–49.

Arentzen, Edward S., and Philip Mandel. "Naval Architectural Aspects of Submarine Design." *SNAME Transactions* 68 (1960): 622–92.

Boyle, Richard. "USS X–1 Power Plant, 1956–57." *Naval Engineers Journal* 84 (April 1972): 42–50.

Jackson, Harry, William D. Needham, and Dale E. Sigman. "ASW: Revolution or Evolution." U.S. Naval Institute *Proceedings* 112 (September 1986): 64–71.

Lasky, Marvin. "A Historical Review of Underwater Acoustic Technology 1916–1939, With Emphasis on Undersea Warfare." *U.S. Navy Journal of Underwater Acoustics* 24, no. 4 (October 1974): 597–624.

———. "Historical Review of Undersea Warfare Planning and Organization, 1945–1960, With Emphasis on the Role of the Office of Naval Research." *U.S. Navy Journal of Underwater Acoustics* 29, no. 2 (April 1976): 327–57.

Lewis, F. M. "Torsional Vibrations in the Diesel Engine." *SNAME Transactions* 33 (1925): 109–45.

Neufeld, Michael J. "Weimar Culture and Futuristic Technology: The Rocketry and Spaceflight Fad in Germany, 1923–1933." *Technology and Culture* 31 (October 1990): 725–52.

Paolucci, Dominic A. "The Development of Navy Strategic Offensive and Defensive Systems." U.S. Naval Institute *Proceedings* 96, no. 5/807 (May 1970): 204–23.

Schade, Henry A. "German Wartime Technical Developments." *Transactions of the Society of Naval Architects and Marine Engineers* 54 (1946): 83–111.

"Special Research in the Navy." *Journal of Applied Physics* 15, no. 3 (March 1944): 241–42.

Talbott, James E. "Weapons Development, War Planning and Policy: The U.S. Navy and the Submarine, 1917–1941." *Naval War College Review* 37 (May–June 1984): 53–71.

Weir, Gary E. "The Navy, Industry, and Diesel Propulsion for American Submarines, 1914–1940." *Naval Engineers Journal* (May 1989): 207–19.

———. "The Search for an American Submarine Strategy and Design, 1916–1936." *Naval War College Review* 44 (Winter 1991): 34–48.

Papers

Allard, Dean C. "The Influence of the United States Navy Upon the American Steel Industry, 1880–1900." M.A., Georgetown University, 1959.

Bruins, Berend D. "Navy Cruise Missile Programs to 1960: Examination of Weapons Innovation Hypothesis." Ph.D. Diss., Columbia University, 1980.

West, Michael A. "Laying the Legislative Foundation: The House Naval Affairs Committee and the Construction of the Treaty Navy, 1926–1934." Ph.D. Diss., Ohio State University, 1980.

Index

☆ U.S. GOVERNMENT PRINTING OFFICE: 1993   336–530